Praise for *Strung Up*

"*Strung Up* is an argumentative masterpiece whose civilizational reproach beggars scholastic punctiliousness. Chapter eight—'Pediatric Experiments, Birth Records, and the War on Southern Black Midwives'—shows federal law transmogrified by clinicians and birth-record bureaucrats into a white supremacist century. To quote Patton: 'Doctors and bureaucrats traded ropes for scalpels, torches for birth certificates, and refined white supremacy into a clinical [American] project.' *Strung Up*, a necessary but terrible read."

—DAVID LEVERING LEWIS, author of the two-volume
Pulitzer Prize–winning *W. E. B. Du Bois*

"*Strung Up* is an unflinching and visionary work that recovers the central role of children in the making of racial violence. With depth and urgency, Stacey Patton shows how terror reached into the most intimate spaces—family, childhood, and even birth—to sustain white supremacy across generations. This is not just history—it is a powerful reckoning with forces that still shape American life."

—MICHELLE ALEXANDER, author of *The New Jim Crow*

"*Strung Up* is one of the boldest, most searingly honest examinations of racial terror and trauma ever put to paper. Herein, Stacey Patton has provided us with a history largely unspoken until now but broadly embedded in the cell memory of the nation, passed down as a haunting inheritance of cruelty and its consequences—sadism not as deviation from an otherwise caring and compassionate norm but as the norm itself. It is not an easy read, but it is a necessary one. As our so-called leaders move to censor history, erase memory, and purge conscience from America, it will take courageous truth tellers like Patton to redeem what is left of our nation's soul. Here's hoping we are worthy of being redeemed."

—TIM WISE, author of White Like Me: *Reflections on Race
from a Privileged Son* and *Dispatches from the Race War*

"Penned by one of America's most important and necessary scholars, this is not just a book about history, lynching, or even Black children. In *Strung Up*, Dr. Stacey Patton skillfully examines how America defines violence, which lives our society values, and why others are expendable."

—MICHAEL HARRIOT, *New York Times*
best-selling author of *Black AF History*

"*Strung Up* is a marvel of a book. Stacey Patton succeeds in blending history, psychology, and sociology into a brilliant excavation of systemic violence. The brutality that Black children have historically suffered continues in myriad forms to this day. *Strung Up* is precisely the kind of study needed to uproot the deeply embedded systems in American society that make this violence possible, one reader at a time."

—KIMBERLÉ CRENSHAW, executive director, African American Policy Forum, and professor of law at Columbia University and UCLA

"*Strung Up* is a monumental text. With stunning intellectual, political, and moral clarity, Stacey Patton has provided the first full-fledged examination of Black child lynching in the United States. Anchored in history but in deep conversation with a dazzling array of disciplines and traditions, the book spotlights the wide range of forces that have normalized America's long-standing and unyielding war on Black children and Black childhood. This book is beautifully written, persuasively argued, and desperately needed."

—MARC LAMONT HILL, Presidential Professor of Urban Education and Black, Race, and Ethnic Studies, City University of New York Graduate Center

"Stacey Patton lays bare—with searing text and haunting images—the unspoken script behind 'the talk' Black parents give their children about surviving a world where driving or walking while Black still carries danger. She traces how European child-rearing traditions helped create the very cultural logic that made the abuse of Black children seem permissible, even justified. As Patton shows, white parents once believed harsh discipline protected their own children from evil; that same belief system ultimately helped fuel the racism, exploitation, and terror inflicted on Black children and their families. This book is essential reading—an unflinching examination of the roots of racialized harm and the urgent need to confront it."

—MARY FRANCES BERRY, author of *History Teaches Us to Resist: How Progressive Movements Have Succeeded in Challenging Times*

"*Strung Up* is a heart-wrenching but necessary examination of how children have been and are used as vehicles for indoctrination into this country's long-standing tradition of white supremacy. Do not turn away—bearing unflinching witness to the violence that disciplines us into submission, and the why behind it, can be the key to ending this, once and for all."

—ALICIA GARZA, cofounder, Black Lives Matter Global Network

"In powerful and unforgettable prose, *Strung Up* forces a reckoning with one of the most devastating truths in American history: Racial violence has never been about punishment but rather it was and is a weapon of domination, an object lesson on power and submission, especially for the young. By centering the experiences of Black children as victims of lynching and white children as its witnesses, Stacey Patton shows that violence has been a civic project meant to reproduce white supremacy one generation to the next."

—KHALIL GIBRAN MUHAMMAD, professor of African American studies and public affairs, Princeton University

"This book is essential reading—an unflinching examination of the roots of racialized harm and the urgent need to confront it."

—MARY FRANCES BERRY, author of *History Teaches Us to Resist*

"Strung Up is a heart-wrenching but necessary examination of how children have been and are used as vehicles for indoctrination into this country's long-standing tradition of white supremacy."

—ALICIA GARZA, cofounder, Black Lives Matter Global Network

"Stacey Patton shows that violence has been a civic project meant to reproduce white supremacy one generation to the next."

—KHALIL GIBRAN MUHAMMAD, professor of African American studies and public affairs, Princeton University

STRUNG UP

STRUNG UP

How White America Learned to Lynch Black Children

STACEY PATTON

BEACON PRESS, BOSTON

BEACON PRESS
24 Farnsworth Street
Boston, Massachusetts
www.beacon.org

Beacon Press books
are published under the auspices of
the Unitarian Universalist Association of Congregations.

Printed in the United States of America

1st Printing

This book is printed on acid-free paper that meets the uncoated paper
ANSI/NISO specifications for permanence as revised in 1992.

Text design and composition by Kim Arney

*Library of Congress Cataloguing-in-Publication
Data is available for this title.*
Hardcover ISBN: 978-0-8070-1620-6
E-book ISBN: 978-0-8070-1621-3
Audiobook: 978-0-8070-2285-6

The authorized representative in the EU for product safety and
compliance is Easy Access System Europe 16879218, Mustamäe tee 50,
10621 Tallinn, Estonia: https://beacon.org/eu-contact.

To the mentors who guided me in thinking and writing like a historian: David Levering-Lewis, Ginny Yans, Jackson Lears, and the late Rudy Bell. And to Toby Rollo, who held my hand and walked with me through this chamber of horrors.

I love y'all.

History, despite its wrenching pain,
cannot be unlived,
but if faced with courage,
need not be lived again.

—MAYA ANGELOU

CONTENTS

You are about to see something terrible.
But it is something America refuses to look at.
Now, take a deep breath and turn the page.

INTRODUCTION

"Ought Children Be Born to Us?"

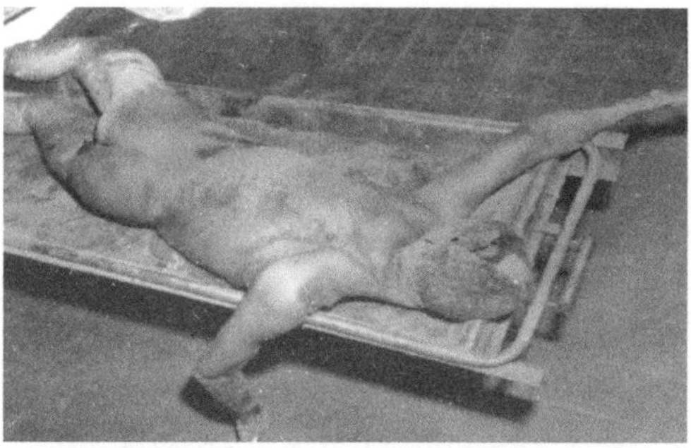

The body of Robert G. Harris Jr. inside the Hudson County morgue in Jersey City, New Jersey, March 29, 1969. Photo courtesy of the Kearny Police Department.

The body on the gurney is my grandfather, Robert "Bobby" G. Harris Jr. He was forty-nine, dapper, and had money. He was a well-known Black "numbers" kingpin and associate with the Genovese crime family in New Jersey. He was born in Ruckersville, Virginia, in 1919 and escaped north after he and his brothers were "run out of the South."

When Black folks say somebody was "run out of the South," it's never just about leaving town. It's shorthand for a thousand unspeakable things. Maybe there was bootlegging. Maybe there was trouble with the law, or the wrong white sheriff. Maybe somebody got too successful. Or too mouthy. Or too close to a white woman. Or maybe, like in so many stories, the real reason was whispered only at funerals and behind closed doors. Being "run out" meant danger. Shame. Survival. It meant you were lucky to get out alive.

In this photo, my grandfather is naked, face down, limbs splayed unnaturally. His flesh is bloated, mottled, half-eaten. One hand hangs limp off the metal tray, fingers curled toward the floor. His skull is caved in. His abdomen is hollowed by bullets and scavengers.

There's a second photograph of him that I saw in the police file. He's still wrapped in the quilted piano blanket they dumped him in. There was no dignity in its use here. It was cinched tight with a length of clothesline, like packaging. Underneath it, his body was hogtied. A cord looped viciously around his neck, snaked behind his back, and yanked his wrists toward his ankles. The ligature forced his body into a grotesque arch and the posture of prey or punishment. The rope didn't just restrain; it silenced. It erased. It turned a man into cargo.

A boy on a bike found him in the winter of 1969 after the snow began to melt. Had the cold temperatures lasted a few more days, we may never have known what those white men did to him. His body lay crumpled in a swamp behind a defunct gas station in Kearny, New Jersey, about twenty minutes from where I'd be placed in foster care as a baby a decade later. The weeds loomed around him like witnesses.

They discarded him like refuse in an industrial dumping ground known to be used often by Italian crime families. His killers took his money, his watch, and whatever humanity he still carried. Michael "Mickey Cigars" Coppola and the late Tino Fiumara, a relative of former New Jersey governor Chris Christie, were named as suspects in his torture and murder. My grandfather's race was initially listed as "unknown." His face was so destroyed the coroner couldn't tell if he was Black or white. They had to cut off his hand to identify him, then drive it to the police station, where they rolled his decomposing fingers in ink and matched the prints to an old gambling charge.

Newspapers ran headlines about his grisly murder, about the swamp, the hogtie, the missing money, the mafia, the ongoing investigation, his burial and grieving family. But they also printed a photo. The grainy black-and-white image shows his high hairline, steady eyes, and a mouth that seems to be holding back a private joke. Even under the smudges of newsprint, you can see the dignity. The quiet confidence. The cool defiance. He's not just a body dumped in a swamp. He's a man who mattered.

And when I look at that photo, I see myself.

The slope of his brow. The deep-set eyes. The soft fullness around the mouth. The way he's looking just off-camera, like he's watching a world he already knows too well. I see that expression in my own reflection sometimes, especially when I'm writing. When I'm listening. When I'm remembering.

In life, my grandfather owned a bar and grill and other businesses in Paterson. He purchased groceries and provided burial funds for struggling families. He financially supported the NAACP, Democratic campaigns, and Black churches. He took care of Black children when the state wouldn't. That photo, for all its faded ink, restores what the racial violence tried to erase. It gives him back a name. A face. A legacy. He wasn't just a headline.

I was just a teenager in boarding school when I learned what they did to him. Too young to understand the words "organized crime" or "white supremacy" or "state violence." Too young to name what I was looking at. But not too young to feel its echoes. To carry it. That's the thing about white supremacy—it doesn't just go after the men and women it kills. It goes after the children left behind. It does so through grief, through silence, through the stories families cannot safely tell, and through the developmental environments that shape how children come to understand danger, memory, and survival. It embeds itself in the silence, in the photos that haunt your sleep. It lodges in the questions grown-ups won't answer, in the aching blanks of a family story half-erased. It burrows into the silences, into the photos that rattle loose in drawers.

ROBERT HARRIS

Police mugshot of Robert G. Harris, Jr. December 1957.

And the loss leaves you with the cruelest inheritance of all: *the what-ifs*. What if they hadn't died? What if they'd raised you? What if they'd lived long enough to protect you from what was coming? The hardest part isn't just the loss. It's knowing nothing will ever be done. There will be no trial.

No arrest. No reckoning. Just a permanent hole where justice should have been.

The goal of lynching wasn't just to destroy the Black body. It was to break the child who survived it. But it didn't always break them. And that's why whiteness tries to catch us young. Because if it can rupture a Black child, it can dismantle the entire community.

But I survived. And I remember. Now I'm an adult writing about lynching, naming its roots, dragging its ghosts into the light. I've looked at the photographs. I've read the autopsy reports. I've gone into the archives and traced the rope back centuries. I was supposed to look away. Or forget. Or implode. Instead, I write. I remember. I indict. White supremacy didn't break me. It built the witness who's coming for its memory.

To some readers, the photo I shared might seem too graphic. But it is real. And it is no more graphic than the violence this country has already absorbed, and too often ignored, when it's happening to Black bodies. Jesse Washington. Emmett Till. James Byrd Jr. Michael Brown Jr. George Floyd. The photo of my grandfather is not just a private family trauma; it's part of a national archive of unresolved, unpunished, and racialized brutality.

That said, context matters. These images need narrative armor. Not shock for shock's sake, but a clear framework: *This is not spectacle.* This is testimony. This is what erasure looks like until we show the racial terror. This is what so many Black families in America live with: the echo of grief unanswered and justice denied. I'm showing what it looks like when a Black man becomes unrecognizable not just because of what they did to his face, but because the country didn't think he mattered enough to remember.

On August 31, 1982, thirteen years after my grandfather's murder, my biological mother would allegedly hang herself from a heating pipe in a house in Montclair, New Jersey. Her rope, like her father's cords, tied her body to silence.

But even that silence has cracks.

Over the years, people I've interviewed have questioned whether it was truly suicide. There were whispers. Stories. That she had been asking too many questions. That she was still investigating her father's murder. That what happened to him wasn't just mafia business; it was sanctioned by the corrupt and racist former Paterson mayor Frank Graves Jr. and his police department.

My mother died with questions. Years later, I set myself to asking those questions, picking up where she left off. I gathered news archives. Filed FOIA requests for police records and FBI cold files. All of them kept getting denied. I even sat in a federal courtroom in Brooklyn during the RICO trial of one of his alleged killers. I listened to the evidence. I watched the faces. I studied the silences.

When Michael Coppola was found guilty and sentenced to a long stretch in federal prison for his RICO charges, I thought maybe, *finally*, there would be momentum. Maybe the door would crack open. So, I stood outside that courtroom and asked an FBI agent assigned to my grandfather's case, "Will the Bureau continue to investigate his murder?"

He didn't give me a straight answer. I never heard from them again. And that's what justice feels like for so many Black families like mine: a long hallway of closed doors. You knock. You wait. You hope. And eventually, you realize no one is coming. The system isn't broken. It's functioning exactly as it was designed, to let Black death rot in silence while the paper trail fades.

This wasn't the kind of lynching most people are taught to picture. He wasn't hogtied in some field in the South. There was no tree, no massive crowd, no postcard. But it was still a rope. Still a message. Lynching, as I use the term throughout this book, is not confined to the spectacle of a crowd beneath a tree but includes acts of racialized killing that functioned to discipline, terrorize, and send a public or private message about the boundaries of Black life. Still a Black body rendered disposable by systems that punish Black defiance and erase Black grief.

This was the era when Black underworld figures in North Jersey started to vanish. Some were found shot in marshes or slumped in alleyways. Others "committed suicide" in the Passaic County Jail. These were men who entered with cuffs and left in body bags, hanging from windows, bunk rails, or radiator pipes.

My mother was part of that underworld lineage, but she was also a daughter with a grief that wouldn't quit. Her autopsy report is missing and the social security number on her death certificate is fake. Maybe she tied that rope herself. Or maybe someone else tightened the knot.

Either way, the result was the same: another unresolved death, another generation silenced, another ghost added to my inheritance.

I was eventually adopted by a Black Christian couple in central Jersey. And in my adoptive family, my grandfather would still cry as he told the story of the Ku Klux Klan wrapping his father in a white sheet and leaving him for dead on the porch in front of his crying mother and brothers in Mississippi sometime in the 1920s.

Two men. One woman. Three generations. Three traumas. One nation that never called it what it was. What happened to my family was not exceptional. It was patterned, legible, and repeated across time and place, and part of a broader architecture of racial violence that extended far beyond any single life. This book begins with the Black bodies. With the swamp. With the silence. With what no one in my family has been allowed to call the wounds of lynching.

But I name them now—because I study lynching not as a historian chasing footnotes, but as a Black child who inherited the aftermath. A child born into the echoes. Into the scream. Into the silence. Into the long tail of violence braided through both sides of my lineage. Before I ever opened an archival box, I already knew what it meant to be *strung up*.

So, why begin a book about the lynching of Black children with the deaths of adults? Because lynching never only targeted men, and it never only happened at the end of a rope. What happened to my grandfather, to my mother, to my adoptive family's patriarch was not a series of isolated tragedies. They were part of a larger system. A long, intergenerational rehearsal of cruelty that did not spare the youngest among us. Black children have always lived within range of that rope.

Childhood is about surviving adults. And, so, *Strung Up* is about children. About the ones who died, and the ones who watched. About the ones who were made into warnings, and the ones who inherited the silence. This book is about the terror carved into the bones of Black America. It is about the names America was supposed to forget, the unhealed trauma, and the unrelenting grief that calcified in the DNA of Black families and communities for generations.

We think of lynching not only as a uniquely American, Southern phenomenon but as something that happened specifically to Black men. But white supremacy never waited for adulthood. It came for the cradle. It came for the classroom. It came for the child. It even came for the unborn.

This book argues that the Black child has always been central to America's racial order, not just as collateral damage but as a deliberate target. Lynchings were not just public executions. They were rituals of instruction. For white children, they were lessons in power. For Black children, they were lessons in terror. And both were shaped by it. Neurologically. Spiritually. Culturally.

Many believe racism is passed down like a bedtime story, taught through words, absorbed like osmosis. But that's not how white supremacy works. White supremacy destroys all children. Not in identical ways, and not with identical consequences, but through a system that deforms the emotional, moral, and social development of every child it touches. It grooms white children through cruelty to their own bodies so they can destroy others. It wounds Black children through terror and grief. It demands obedience through pain. It is not just inherited. It is performed. Practiced and burned into the nervous system.

Strung Up follows the rope. From the noose to the nursery. From the town square to the kitchen table. From the Black child whose body swung, to the white child who was told to watch and not flinch. Because the target was never just the man in the tree. It was the child beneath it. It was the family that had to keep living afterward. It was the generations who weren't supposed to remember.

"THAT'S THE NIGGER THAT DID THE DEED"

Take another deep breath and look at this next photograph.

It captures the opposite end of that continuum: a teenager, still unfinished, still wide-eyed, burned alive in a Texas town square while white children look on without flinching. My grandfather was born ten years after this boy's lynching. Though they didn't share space in this world, they were both claimed by the same machinery of white supremacy.

Different bodies. Same fire.

It's July 28, 1908. Greenville, Texas. A crowd of 2,500 white adults and children stand shoulder to shoulder in the sun. Shirtsleeves rolled up. Straw hats tilted. Some with arms crossed in smug satisfaction. Others with hands on hips or shoved in pockets. The scene is casual, almost businesslike.

A crowd of white men and boys in Greenville, Texas, on July 28, 1908, watch the burning of eighteen-year-old Ted Smith, who was accused of raping a young white woman. She later recanted.

At the front of the circle, closest to the fire, are white boys. To be clear, participation did not always require physical action. Presence, attention, and emotional alignment were themselves forms of involvement in a ritual designed to instruct. At least four of them are clearly visible. Not tucked behind parents. Not shielded from the sight. One, maybe twelve years old, struts through the inner ring, studying the flames with the detached interest he might give a campfire or hog roast. Their postures are relaxed. Their expressions curious. As if they've seen this before. And will see it again. While photographs cannot give us direct access to interior thought, they do capture posture, proximity, and expression. These are clues that, when read alongside historical context, help us understand the social meaning of these moments.

This wasn't just memory-making. It was indoctrination. A baptism by fire in the church of white supremacy. I use the term "ritual" deliberately to describe not just repetition but structured acts with shared meaning, predictable roles, and an audience conditioned to understand their significance. The children weren't bystanders. They were acolytes. Not because they chose freely but because they were being shaped and socialized into roles, emotions, and responses that made participation in racial violence feel normal, even necessary. Because in Jim Crow

America, this is how white children became white adults, by watching Black children die.

In the center of the frame is what's left of eighteen-year-old Ted Smith. His bones are charred black. Flesh melted. Legs crumpled inward like collapsed scaffolding. His body smolders atop an impromptu pyre, scraps of wood, kerosene canisters, scorched cloth. Flames lick the twisted metal. The stench of burning human remains cuts through the heat, mixing with the acrid tang of iron and smoke. You can almost taste it in the back of your throat.

Ted Smith was accused of raping the daughter of R. H. Delancey, the white farmer his family worked for. The teens had been secretly involved with each other. When her parents discovered them, she accused him. The sheriff brought Smith before her. "That's the nigger that did the deed," she said, leaving him in shock. The sheriff expressed doubts about the allegation. She later recanted. But the truth didn't matter.

This is what I mean when I say: Childhood is about surviving adults. Ted Smith didn't survive them. And neither did the white boys in that photograph—*not fully*. Because white supremacy destroys all children. It kills Black children outright. And it hollows out white children from within. It teaches them to cheer at death. To call violence tradition. To mistake silence for safety. It trains them to inherit power without empathy, and to wield that power without question.

When I look at this old photo of Ted Smith smoldering on a pile of kerosene-soaked timber, I can't help but think of the photograph of my grandfather. The settings are different—one public, one hidden. One body staged in a civic ritual, the other discarded like trash. But the message is the same: This is what happens when Black men trespass the boundaries of white power. That's what ties these two images together. The swamp and the square are just coordinates. The logic of the violence is the same.

Somewhere nearby, Ted's mother and father, if they weren't already dead inside, were crying and screaming into silence. Maybe they had to explain to other children in the family why Ted would never come home. Somewhere in the crowd, a white parent was squeezing their child's shoulder and saying, *Watch carefully. This is how we keep niggers in their place.* Whether or not those exact words were spoken, the lesson was unmistakable and repeatedly documented in the historical record.

Some of those children in the large crowd likely went home that night, ate dinner, and slept soundly. This coexistence of care and cruelty reflects a social world in which violence was woven into everyday life rather than set apart from it. Some likely remembered the smell of burning hair and the sound of skin blistering. Maybe years later some of them brought their own children to such an event. Because this is how whiteness reproduces itself: not through blood alone, but through ritual and numbing children to Black suffering.

In July 2023, 115 years after Ted Smith's murder, eight of his family members gathered at a memorial service in the same courthouse where justice had been denied. His first and second cousins came to honor a relative whose death had haunted their family for more than a century.

"A lot of family didn't want to come because they didn't want to rehash this horrific thing that happened to him," said Audry Ashford Rester, whose mother is Smith's first cousin. "When I did research, I cried. When I talked to my mother, she cried. She cried today."[1] The grief, still fresh. The wound, still open.

Imagine the weight of living in chronic fear, where a glance, a word, being in the wrong place at the wrong time could unleash horror: a shooting, a mutilation, a burning, a hanging. Imagine raising your child in a country where one misstep, or doing nothing wrong at all, can get them shot down, hanged, or burned in the street while other people's children watch and learn.

Imagine the soul-wrecking agony of having your child snatched from the future, and their murder not only unpunished but mocked in newspapers, printed on postcards, etched into local lore.

Imagine watching your child's killers go on about their lives, promoted to sheriff, elected to office, celebrated as pillars of the community, tucking their own children into bed at night, untouched by consequence or conscience.

Imagine trying to explain to your child that their innocence is invisible. That the world sees them as a threat before they've even learned how to tie their shoes. That their very breath is a provocation. Imagine having to say: *Be small. Be silent. Come home alive.* And knowing, deep in your bones, that even that might not be enough.

Ted Smith's parents may have said those things to him. May have prayed them. May have begged the sky to make their son invisible to the racist gaze. And yet his charred remains lay in the town square while white children giggled in the sun.

Black parents will feel this truth deep in the marrow of their bones. In their breath. In the quiet dread that settles into the body every time a child walks out the door. That truth rarely makes it into words. But it lives in the trembling breath of goodbye. In the whispered prayers. In the breath held until the front door reopens. It lives in the impossible task of teaching children how to survive adults. How do you promise them safety when history has shown, time and again, that Black parents can't always protect their own lives?

Some of you will wince and cry as you turn these pages. Some will nod in bitter recognition and validation. Some of you will get angry at me for making you look. And I get that. I hate that I must write this book. I hate that it exists. That there's *enough* blood, *enough* bodies, *enough* names to fill its pages.

But this book *must* exist. Because the horror didn't end in 1908. The grief isn't over. It's ancient now, fossilized in the cells of Black families. It moves through our blood like memory. It lives in our parenting. It lives in our whispers and our silence. It's so old it feels like inheritance.

It haunts.

It festers.

When I describe this inheritance as living in the body or in the DNA, I am naming both metaphor and mechanism and drawing on research in trauma, stress physiology, and epigenetics, while also acknowledging the cultural and social transmission that binds memory to the body across generations.

It still hurts in places where language can't reach.

Strung Up is not trauma porn. You won't find page after page of mutilated Black bodies for shock value. Yes, there are horrors we must look at. But not to gawk. Not to wallow in the spectacle, nor revel in it like those white children in Greenville. Many histories of lynching linger on the scenes of Black dehumanization while rarely interrogating the perpetrators, the culture that raised them, and the systems that protected them. This book reverses the gaze. It is not about Black death. It is about white pathology. By pathology, I mean a historically produced system of beliefs, practices, and emotional conditioning, not an inherent or immutable trait but one that was learned, enforced, and reproduced.

This book is not a eulogy for Black childhood. It's an autopsy of whiteness. A dissection of how racial violence became ritual and how white people were socialized into cruelty and learned to perfect the art of killing children.

The pathology I am exposing is this: White identity has been built emotionally, spiritually, politically on the dehumanization of Black children. On their disposability. On their pain. On the stories we were never meant to tell. Child murder became a form of communal bonding. Joy and familial love were built beside burning bodies. Black death became a civic celebration.

And that legacy didn't die with Jim Crow.

It still breathes in parenting, in policy, in schools, in law, in the daily rituals that shape white identity and normalize Black suffering. This book is not about the past. It's about the inheritance.

Greenville wasn't a one-off. This is the dangerous inheritance white families refuse to exorcise from their institutions, their ideologies, and even their own bodies.

The names may have changed. The tools may be more discreet. But the target remains the same. The Black child is still marked for surveillance, control, and obliteration. The war on Black futures is still being waged.

"A SNEERING, CRUEL WORLD"

Racial violence against Black youth often ignites outrage, trending for a moment in the churn of social media and the twenty-four-hour news cycle. But it is not new. It belongs to an unbroken lineage of generational terror that stretches back to Jim Crow, when the brutal ritual of lynching made Black childhood a public target.

Scholars agree: After Reconstruction, white supremacists understood that maintaining the racial order required terrorizing Black communities through brutality not just against adults but also against children.[2] Black adults were seen as an immediate threat to white supremacy, but Black children represented something even more dangerous—*the future*. And the future of whiteness was even more precarious because it held the possibility of Black freedom, permanence, and power.

Black adults could be surveilled, controlled, locked away. But Black children carried the potential to *outgrow* subjugation. To become literate, organized, rebellious. To inherit the struggle and sharpen it. To dream beyond the plantation, the chain gang, the schoolhouse, and the ghetto, and make those dreams tangible.

Black children represented endurance. Continuity. The idea that despite everything, Black life would not only survive but multiply. That terrified the hell out of white supremacists. Because if the children lived, if they thrived, then the future of white dominance was not guaranteed. A Black future was dangerous because it couldn't be negotiated. It had to be stopped.

So, white terror turned its gaze downward. Toward the smallest bodies. Children were easier to reach because they were smaller, less protected, often beyond the reach of law or community defense. Killing them wasn't random cruelty. It was strategy. It sent a message to Black people: *No one is safe. Not your babies. Not your lineage. Not your future.* It was a psychological warfare designed to break Black hope at its root before it could grow into resistance.

That war on Black children never ended. It continues today in classrooms, courtrooms, policing, and policy. Consider the state execution of fourteen-year-old George Stinney in 1944. The lynching of fourteen-year-old Emmett Till in 1955. The arrests of six-year-olds like Salecia Johnson in 2012 and Kaia Rolle in 2020. How the vigilante murder of seventeen-year-old Trayvon Martin in 2012 triggered adults to argue whether unarmed youth deserved to die. Think about the state-sanctioned deaths of eighteen-year-old Michael Brown Jr. in 2014, twelve-year-old Tamir Rice that same year, and countless others. These are not isolated tragedies. They are echoes of the same message: Black children are disposable.

W. E. B. Du Bois understood this. He clearly saw the gauntlet through which Black children were forced to run beginning at birth. In 1920, he wrote bitterly, "There is no place for Black children in this world." His hyperbolic use of "this world" conveys the mean-spiritedness of mainstream life for Black children coming of age in a racist society where opportunities were attitudinally and institutionally foreclosed. His anguish was cosmic. Du Bois even questioned whether it was ethical to continue giving birth to Black children: "Is it worthwhile? Ought children be born to us? Have we a right to make human souls face what we face today?"[3]

Sit with this Black father's words for a moment. Not just as history, but as a haunting question that Black parents still wrestle with today. Imagine the agony of birthing a child into a world built to break them at every developmental milestone. Imagine loving them so fiercely that you wonder if not giving them life would have been the kinder act. That wasn't philosophical musing. That was grief. And it was personal.

Du Bois and his wife, Nina, lost their infant son, Burghardt, in 1899. The baby died of diphtheria because no white doctors in Atlanta would treat a Black child. The desperate father frantically searched for help, but by the time he returned home with a Black physician, it was too late. The couple arranged for Burghardt's tiny coffin to be sent north for burial. At the funeral, as Du Bois and his wife followed behind in mourning, white bystanders jeered and called them "niggers."

What kind of people can watch two grieving parents walking behind their baby's coffin and choose that moment to hurl slurs? What lives inside souls so hollow, so corroded, that they reach for cruelty in the presence of death? Who stands at the edge of another's sorrow and spits venom, just to remind them they are hated even in their mourning? That is the kind of moral rot that makes child lynching not just possible but inevitable.

Years later, Du Bois reflected on his son's death with unspeakable sorrow and a grim relief. He was "awfully glad" Burghardt had escaped the color line. "No bitter meanness shall sicken his baby heart. No taunt shall madden his happy boyhood." Death had spared his son from growing up "choked and deformed," but not his daughter.[4]

There's this genteel image of Du Bois as the bow-tied scholar with a walking stick and a library of classical references. But in September 1906, when his daughter Yolande was six years old, Du Bois found himself sitting on the front steps of his Atlanta University campus home with a double-barreled shotgun and two dozen rounds of shells filled with buckshot as thousands of angry whites took to the streets for four days burning Black people's homes, businesses, and schools. Venting their frustrations over successful and politically assertive Black folks stepping out of place, the mobs assaulted hundreds and massacred scores of Black victims.

They did not spare the children.

A crippled boy was badly beaten. A small child was used for target practice.[5] The underlying causes of the riot were lingering tensions from Reconstruction, job competition, resentment over newly gained Black voting rights and efforts to secure civil rights, growing Black wealth, and sensational news stories about Black men allegedly assaulting white women.

"If a white mob had stepped on the campus where I lived, I would without hesitation have sprayed their guts over the grass," Du Bois recalled decades later in his autobiography.[6]

That wasn't just a threat. It was a war cry and a liturgy at the altar of his child's right to live. Behind the tweed suits and lectures stood a Black father ready to turn his front porch into a front line. In a world hell-bent on destroying Black children, Du Bois's words cut through the terror: *My child will not be your casualty*. His willingness to meet racist violence with deadly force was a radical act of love, a refusal to let Black childhood remain undefended. He reminded us that Black people have always been willing to fight, even to kill, for the right of our children to live.

Du Bois's grief, questions, and rage were not just the musings of a public intellectual. They were the raw, lived realities of a Black parent trying to protect his children from a world designed to destroy them. His story is a window into the deeper, systemic truth: that the violence inflicted on Black children is *foundational*. It is the blood tax this nation has extracted to build and preserve its illusions of racial superiority and democracy.

That inheritance, however, stretches beyond American borders and even predates them.

A TRANSATLANTIC INHERITANCE

The lynching of Black children did not begin in the American South. It was not born in cotton fields or Jim Crow courtrooms. It is the bastard child of empire, raised in the shadows of European cathedrals, whipping posts, and wooden stocks.

Before American mobs gathered to hang and burn alive Black youth like Ted Smith, European children were being dragged into public squares, beaten in classrooms, and marched to executions for the moral instruction of the community. These were not acts of care but rituals and lessons in dominance disguised as discipline. And when Europeans crossed the Atlantic, they carried with them that violence, folded into their Bibles, stitched into their parenting philosophies, and encoded in their laws.

What they left behind in Europe was not violence itself—every culture has that—but a specific worldview: that children are property. Their vulnerability is suspicious. Their discipline requires pain, and their domination is love.

Lynching didn't sprout from American soil fully formed. It finds its roots far earlier in the nascent stages of Western civilization where the cultural logic of brutalizing, humiliating, and killing the most vulnerable, especially children, was normalized and institutionalized. The cultural and legal groundwork for spectacle violence was established in western Europe, long before it crossed the Atlantic and evolved into the extrajudicial terror targeting Black people.[7] We can't understand the targeting of Black children without tracing it back to Europe's own child-hating, patriarchal, punitive culture and its global machinery of domination. The political and economic structures that made lynching possible—plantation economies, racialized legal codes, the culture of public punishment—were extensions of the European imperial system.

In medieval and early modern Europe, white children were beaten publicly, watched people hang and get their heads chopped off as a form of moral instruction, and were taught obedience through terror. The church preached that children were born sinful, their bodies bent toward evil, and that their wills had to be broken to save their souls. These cultural norms in Europe and child-rearing philosophies rooted in religious doctrines set a long-standing pattern of brutality that primed generations of people to accept and perpetuate systemic violence. Parenting ideologies, laws, and religious doctrine shaped how European societies treated the concept of vulnerability and personhood, and were part of the larger European worldview that treated violence as a tool of moral and social control.

These "cultural technologies" of punishment—parenting systems, theological justifications, the moralization of pain—formed a foundational logic carried into the Americas. These practices didn't vanish when Europeans colonized North America. They *evolved*. America *adapted* them, *racialized* them, and *scaled* them up. And it *institutionalized* them into social violence and the modern state. First, through the brutal discipline of indentured adults and child laborers and African slaves. Then, through the spectacle of racialized public executions. And ultimately, through the lynching of Black children. To fully understand this violence, we must see lynching as the culmination of centuries of normalized European child abuse, social control, and state terror.

No, Europe didn't invent violence. But Europe institutionalized and normalized certain forms of ritualistic violence, especially family-based and state-sanctioned punishment that shaped how colonizers and their descendants treated Black bodies and children in America. The specific form of racialized spectacle violence that became lynching in the US, with its community participation, body mutilation, burnings, photo souvenirs, and generational terror, *was not a global phenomenon*. They echo medieval European punishment practices, like drawing and quartering, hanging, and gibbetting, as well as dissecting the corpses of the executed. The *targets* of lynching in America were mostly Black bodies, but the *methods* were European.

I am not claiming that European parenting norms *singlehandedly* caused lynching. But they did prime white people to see domination, humiliation, and pain as legitimate tools for controlling those deemed "inferior." European cultures exported that mindset to America, where it fused with anti-Blackness, capitalism, and settler colonialism to form a *unique* racial caste system. In other words, parenting norms aren't the sole cause of lynching, but they're a *foundational* piece of the cultural toolkit that made it possible.

This transatlantic inheritance of untreated intergenerational trauma metastasized into a culture of white-supremacist terror.

By centering Black children, disaggregating their experiences from adult victims, and documenting their unique experiences and stories, I seek to honor the lives and struggles of a group whose experiences have been obscured in the broad strokes of history. Naming and locating Black child victims is a reclamation and a humanizing step in that process. My aim is to ensure that their memories are upheld in service of ending violence against racialized children and youth today.

But remembering is not enough. To honor these children is also to confront the forces that destroyed them and to understand how those forces persist. If we are to combat racial violence, we must trace its lineage. We must ask not just *what* happened to these children, but *why*, *how*, and *through whom*. That means facing the full, intergenerational architecture of terror—cultural, psychological, and historical—that made their deaths possible.

Strung Up departs from conventional scholarship by rejecting the quiet assumption that violence against Black youth is merely a junior version of violence against Black adults, and that it can be understood according to the same logics, patterns, and motivations as violence against their elders. No. This book, following an intersectional approach, asserts that Black children are often targeted for specific reasons and have experiences that are often distinct from adults. Black children are often targeted for racial violence not because they are expedited into perceived maturity, but *precisely because they are children.*[8]

Methodologically, this book draws from critical childhood studies to expose how systems of power isolate, target, and erase Black youth. Just as Black feminism taught us how race, gender, and class interact in specific ways, critical childhood studies reveals how age and developmental status structure the violence inflicted on Black children. Their pain isn't just an echo of adult suffering; it is its own category of harm.

BLACK FREEDOM, WHITE TERROR

Strung Up asks a difficult question: What does the intergenerational transmission of trauma, what we now call "adverse childhood experiences," or ACEs, have to do with Black child lynching in the United States? The answer is a lot. And it also asks us to stretch our historical imagination. As I discussed earlier, the timeline of lynching doesn't start in the postbellum South. It begins long before, in the punitive traditions of precolonial Europe, and it evolved and sharpened into a uniquely American expression of white terror.

But let's begin with the four million enslaved Black people emancipated after the Civil War. Let's not forget that half of them were children, young souls who had witnessed things no child should ever see. Whipped and branded flesh. Mothers and sisters raped. Fathers sold. Babies pried from loving arms. They endured sexual violence, starvation, backbreaking labor, and abandonment. Their childhoods weren't just stolen; they were crushed under the boot of a system that called itself Christian.[9]

Emancipation meant those children and their parents could finally possess their own bodies. They moved. They married. They named their children. They searched for loved ones. They learned to read. They saved coins. They built schools and churches. They tested the boundaries of their new rights in the courts and at the ballot box. They imagined something that had been forbidden for centuries: *a free future.*

The passage of federal civil rights laws and the adoption of the Thirteenth Amendment (1865), the Fourteenth Amendment (1868), and the Fifteenth Amendment (1870) to the Constitution guaranteed certain protections to the freedpeople even as they continued to face fierce opposition and abuses like those that they had experienced under slavery. Black men were granted the right to vote. Blacks served on juries as well as ran for, and won, political office from the local level all the way up to the United States Senate. Republican-controlled legislatures enacted laws granting Black people equal access to transportation and other public accommodations. The birth of Black politics and activism produced Equal Rights Leagues and protest conventions against racist Black Codes that severely restricted Black people's educational opportunities, access to courts, and ability to own property, seek employment, conduct business, and move freely.

But for white society in post-emancipation America, the free children and grandchildren of former slaves, who now enjoyed the rights of full citizenship, presented a serious problem. These young people, unshackled from the physical and psychological bondage of plantation life, represented an unpredictable future. No longer property, they could not be bought or sold. No longer chattel, they could not be disciplined with impunity. And perhaps most terrifying of all to white supremacists, they could now be educated, control their own labor, aspire to wealth, and pass on freedom to future generations. Without recourse to a regime of daily cruelties and the confining discipline of slavery serving the function of subduing Black bodies and suppressing their potential, how else could the future of white-dominated society and the perpetuation of white supremacy be guaranteed?

This upheaval went beyond economics. The vision of enslaved Black children growing into free adults sent tremors through the established social hierarchies. The former slave owners' worst fears materialized: These free Black children could potentially vote, hold office, and assert their rights, directly challenging white supremacy.[10]

And it didn't stop there.

There was an underlying dread of a rising, confident Black culture that would assert its own history, traditions, and rights, a cultural shift that threatened to dismantle the narrative of white dominance and rewrite the story of the South. For those who once wielded power, this wasn't just about losing control; it was about the terror of a confident, empowered, and unyielding Black future.[11]

Former slave owners were also haunted by a deeper, more visceral fear: that this new generation of Black children, unschooled by slavery and proper racial etiquette of the past, might seek revenge for the centuries of brutality and oppression. The thought of retribution loomed large, a dark shadow over their attempts to reestablish racial dominance. This anxiety was not unfounded; they had witnessed the brutalities of the system they upheld, and they feared that the anger and trauma passed down through generations of Black families would ignite a desire for vengeance.

CHILDHOOD AS AN ANTI-BLACK WEAPON

The fastest way to tear a Black community apart was to kill its children. Not just kill them, but do it publicly, slowly, cruelly, ceremonially, so that Black parents within the vicinity and beyond would hear the screams, smell the smoke, and understand that their love could not protect what they had brought into the world. But while Black families mourned and braced for more loss, white families staged a different kind of ritual. They handed their children over to the spectacle of Black death, not just as witnesses, but as students, apprentices, and junior executioners.

White children were deliberately ushered into these blood-soaked gatherings, running, skipping, jumping, clutching their mother's skirts, or perched on their father's shoulders as human beings were tortured and murdered. They cheered and laughed. They scratched, kicked, spit, and carved off body parts for souvenirs. They posed for photographs beside mutilated bodies, some still smoking. The message was clear: This is what white power looks like. This is what happens when Black people forget their place. And this is your inheritance.

Through these barbaric rituals, white children were taught to see violence not as a violation but as a virtue. They learned that Black suffering was not only acceptable but a necessary sacrifice to maintain their place in the racial order. Over time, their hearts hardened. Their empathy withered. Many grew into adults who were incapable of compassion, emotionally calcified, addicted to control, and spiritually hollowed out by the legacy of the violence they had once clapped for.

This was not passive absorption. It was active indoctrination. Racial violence became a family heirloom, passed from generation to generation like a treasured photograph or grandfather's watch, as something to hold, polish, and protect. White supremacy required this grooming, because its survival depended not only on the destruction of Black life but on the moral mutilation of white children who must be conditioned to carry it forward.

This socialization process was most effective during young people's most sensitive period of neurological development. During children's formative years, their brains are highly plastic and impressionable, making them particularly susceptible to the values and beliefs imparted by their caregivers and community. From a young age, children absorb the attitudes, behaviors, and prejudices of the adults around them. Through direct instruction and more subtle cues, they learn to internalize and normalize racial hierarchies and violence—including, in post-emancipation America, sadistic lynching. Parents, educators, and community leaders play crucial roles in shaping a child's worldview, using everything from storytelling and cultural rituals to punishments and rewards to instill these beliefs. The reinforcement of racial superiority/inferiority becomes embedded in a child's psyche, forming the bedrock of their identity and moral framework.

This process is further reinforced by the surrounding environment. Educational systems, media representations, and peer interactions all contribute to a child's understanding of racial dynamics. As young minds take shape, the normalization of racial violence becomes ingrained, perpetuating a cycle of intergenerational transmission. The socialization of racial violence extends beyond mere attitudes; it shapes emotional responses and behaviors. Children learn to respond to perceived threats to hierarchy with fear, anger, or aggression, mirroring the reactions they observe in adults. This emotional emulation and conditioning ensures that racial violence remains a reflexive, deeply embedded response to social challenges. Thus, the cycle of racial violence continues, passed down and finding deep roots in the psychic and emotional fabric of each new generation. This is how racism became biology for generations of white children socialized to become racists and perpetrators of lynching.

At the center of this historical autopsy is the white family and its reliance on fear, punishment, and control. Coercive discipline was more than a parenting strategy; it was a template for society. In these homes, children were taught that obedience was maintained through pain, and that disobedience must be crushed. Those same children then grew into adults who carried that logic with them into every arena of life, from schoolyards and courtrooms to politics and policing. They didn't just witness lynchings. They were raised to understand them.

Western culture, especially in its most performative Christian forms, soaked its children in blood. They were beaten in the name of love. They were dragged to executions for moral instruction. They were taught that their suffering was redemption through punishment, order through pain. Over time, this didn't just shape the mind. It shaped the nervous system. It embedded itself in breath, reflex, gaze. And when those children became parents, they passed it on, not just as belief but as *embodied* knowledge.

My analysis demonstrates how, over successive generations, the transmission of these violent norms within white families contributed to the entrenchment of a culture of violence, particularly during periods of intense racial conflict, such as the era of Jim Crow. Understanding how familial practices of coercion and violence were passed down and institutionalized helps explain how communities could come to see lynching as a justified and even necessary means of maintaining the racial order. Lynching, in this context, was not merely an act of individual brutality but part of a broader cultural pattern linked to domestic discipline.

The conventional assumption is that racism is perpetuated by introducing children to racist ideas, at which point the job is done. But racism is more complex and insidious than this. White supremacy is not just a set of ideas but also one of emotions that gets tuned to those ideas' racist frequencies. Our deepest emotional and psychological dynamics are conditioned not only, or even primarily, through exposure to ideas but also from exposure to patterns of parental aggression and affection, and our habituation to rituals and community practices that impress upon us as children a racist worldview, below the level of consciousness. These emotional calibrations happen in the spaces between punishment and praise, inside the rituals of mealtime prayers, public admonishment, Sunday sermons, and—in the case of lynching—family photographs beside mutilated corpses. The child may not remember the moment they internalized the logic of white supremacy, but their body does.

The ingrained attitudes and conditioned responses alter white children's neurological development and stress responses to difference, embedding "othering" behaviors and violent tendencies into their very biology. This deep-seated conditioning is passed on to each successive generation and operates at a subconscious level, functioning as an epigenetic tick. The changes in stress response and behavior patterns are both taught and inherited, ensuring that the legacy of racial violence and prejudice continue to influence individuals long after childhood.[12]

Neuroscience has shown that repeated exposure to violence changes the way the brain processes fear and empathy.[13] This is why white children who were forced to witness lynchings or who were subjected to violent discipline at home grew into adults whose physiological and neurological responses to Black people were steeped in aggression, dehumanization, and dominance. Epigenetics tells us that trauma is not just remembered, it is *embedded* in the body, influencing the development of future generations. This means that the violent socialization of white children in the past has left biological and psychological imprints on generations to come, contributing to the enduring persistence of white-supremacist violence today.

My exploration into child lynchings during the Jim Crow era reveals in ways not previously understood how the Black child's body has served as the foundational nexus of white-supremacist dogma and ground zero for racial projection and punishment inflected by sexualized projection. Children were not simply victims of racism—*they were central to its reproduction*, because racism cannot persist through time without inducting every new generation into a racist order through dehumanizing coercion. What I want to show you is that the story is yet more complicated. My hope is that you will walk away from this journey understanding that white supremacy, at its core, is an anti-child system that requires the sacrifice of young people.

No child is spared.

Previous scholars of lynching have focused primarily on adult perpetrators, legal structures, and sociopolitical contexts but have failed to center the child as both victim and witness, target and transmitter. Nor have they incorporated insights from developmental psychology, neuroscience, or epigenetics, or scholarship on ACEs. As a result, they have missed how lynching was not just a tool of terror but also a method of socialization. A ritualized process that biologically groomed white children into cruelty and disfigured Black children through terror.

This omission has left us with an incomplete understanding of how racial violence is sustained. Without accounting for how white children are conditioned and how Black children are dehumanized, we cannot grasp the full reach of white supremacy. Lynching was both an act of domination and a lesson: a performance of power designed to indoctrinate children into racial hierarchy through the dual trauma of participation and exposure. By examining the intersection of these fields, we can see how lynching was used to indoctrinate white children into a legacy of violence and control, ensuring the perpetuation of racial hierarchies through both psychological conditioning and biological inheritance.

This cycle of manipulation and emotional abuse set the stage for the oppression and legal and social segregation that entrenched itself as Reconstruction's moment of interracial democracy ended in the closing decades of the nineteenth century. It primed white children to inherit *Plessy v. Ferguson* without question. To accept poll taxes, literacy tests, grandfather clauses, and the convict leasing system not as cruelty but as common sense. It normalized the destruction of Black families as the maintenance of civic order.

While white children were increasingly seen as quasi-adults and future citizens, the promise of whiteness, Black children were positioned as threats. As proto-citizens or quasi-adults, white children were viewed as young people stumbling toward adult responsibility and on the trajectory toward full humanity, a process that must not be inhibited. It is this linkage with adulthood, not childhood, that white youth have long benefited from. Black children, by contrast, were denied both innocence and futurity and cast not as budding citizens but as dangers to be controlled.

BLACK CHILDREN AS ENEMY COMBATANTS

At the height of these crimes, Du Bois used his editorship of *The Crisis*, which was the official communications hub of the NAACP, to bring national attention to these horrific acts and to document the other daily indignities Black youth endured. The NAACP eventually formed a Children's Department, based in Washington, DC, to investigate crimes against Black children.[14] Child victims of lynching who were featured in *The Crisis*, and in the NAACP's investigative files, included young people from various regions of the country—teenagers, adolescents, infants, and yes, even the unborn.

As we shall see further in this book, collectively sharing the brutal murder of a Black person—some directly involved, others taking part vicariously—was a cathartic process that enabled whites to relive family tensions and cleanse themselves of old untreated family and ancestral victimhood. Many Southern parents were survivors of corporal punishment and neglect mixed with religiosity and righteous sadomasochism that produced what one scholar has called a "residue of rage." All that

A crowd of fifteen thousand witness the lynching of seventeen-year-old Henry Smith in Paris, Texas, on February 1, 1893. Courtesy of the Library of Congress.

untreated trauma "resulting from the abuse of southern children fueled the fires that engulfed blacks in the blood sport of lynching."[15]

The Jim Crow era's Black children grew up as potentially free citizens and free laborers with the dangerous potential to disrupt the white-supremacist order. And so, a new ideology of repression emerged to contain them, to cast doubt upon their capacity for citizenship and intellect, and to demean the value of their labor. Absent the racialization of Black children, without white-supremacist control over their minds and their bodies, they would have grown to be full and equal citizens with the potential to disrupt the dominant system.

With emancipation, the categories of master and slave could no longer apply, so the binary of authoritative adult and subordinate child took over to define citizenship rights. Abolition threw into question the idea that citizenship was exclusive to white people, that only they could be viewed as fully adult, fully human, and therefore deserving of rights. Now, according to the law, Black people too could achieve adulthood and full citizenship. Racial logic demanded that some differentiation be made if whiteness was to be preserved in the construction of America as a white nation. At the same time, the hordes of impoverished, criminal white kids running around picking pockets and getting into trouble were now joined by newly freed Black youth.

So, extralegal steps were taken to reaffirm the depiction of Black people as inherently lawless children. The definition of childhood as a state of primitive ignorance and moral shortcomings did not change, but the categorization of white youth as children had to change to place them beyond childhood. Black youth, by contrast, would be permanently entrenched Black youth in that category. What were known as the "child-saving movements" of the eighteenth and nineteenth centuries began with the purpose of improving the education, health care, and safety of white youth and accelerating their growth into citizens.

Only when white youth became full citizens could white supremacy be effectively perpetuated. Black youth, on the other hand, remained children—truant, juvenile offenders and sexually unrestrained thugs who could be targeted by vigilante justice with impunity. In a white-supremacist society, there can be no mature adult Black people. They are always children. And so, Black youth are considered the "children of children," doubly doomed by their categorization as biological children as well as offspring of an inferior race existing in a permanent condition of cultural infancy, of lawlessness and criminality, for whom coercive discipline and death are white society's only recourse.

Consider this observation that abolitionist Frederick Douglass made in *My Bondage and My Freedom*, published in 1855. Juxtaposing his own adolescence with the maturation of Tommy, his childhood companion and master, Douglass said: "He could grow and become a Man; I could grow, though I could not become a man; but must remain, all my life, a minor—a mere boy."[16] Here Douglass articulated the deep logic of white supremacy: the dehumanization and enslavement of Black people through their permanent designation as children. As Black children, especially Black males, grow into physical maturity, they are viewed as overgrown children, as a monstrous combination of irrationality and strength.[17] It's essential to frame this violence within the lens of how Black individuals were portrayed as "childish" or impudent, juvenile, puerile, or infantile. Underneath these anxieties lay white society's deep-seated fears of lawless behavior from Black people, who were seen as lawless children of adult size and strength disrupting the mature order of America.

Beyond all the rhetoric of racial superiority, scientific validations for white domination, cultural or religious explanations, legal and political definitions, beyond all these constructs, white supremacy at its purest focuses its aggression on Black children because white supremacy requires the destruction of actual children to perpetuate itself. Because Blackness is inherently equated with a state of childhood, the children of Black people are the primary targets of white-supremacist ideology and violence. To perpetuate white supremacy, for a white future without end, all childhoods must be destroyed, albeit in different ways. White children must be made into instruments for the enforcement of inhumanity in their Black peers, which occurs through white children's exposure to racialized communal violence.

In this book, I am not going to rehearse the exhaustive history of childhood in America or Europe, nor will I be going down the conceptual rabbit hole of discussing the myriad definitions of childhood. Nor am I concerned with legal definitions of childhood, because these change over time. I am concerned with attacks on the young, people who are excluded from politics and power and not considered full citizens. Up until 1971, anyone under age twenty-one was not considered a full political agent—an adult. What matters to me is what Black and white youth became during the century following the Civil War.

Today many Americans, disturbed by the brutality of lynchings, assume that these crimes were perpetuated by a minority of white people—rednecks, drunks, or mobs of lawless fringe elements. But the truth is that these thoroughly planned murders were often done with the full cooperation and active participation of police, sheriffs, militias, district attorneys, judges and juries, local newspapers, educators, and churchgoing defenders of the American way of life. "All the white folks are invited to the party," a local paper announced as it detailed plans for the 1934 lynching of Claude Neal, who was made to eat his own penis and testicles before he was killed. Children reportedly plunged his corpse with sticks and knives before it was placed on the steps of a jail for hundreds of spectators.[18]

More than four thousand human souls were lynched in America between 1882 and 1968, and doubtless there were many more victims whose names have been lost to history.[19] Most of these crimes—80 percent—took place in the South, and the overwhelming number of documented victims were Black males. But it is difficult to get accurate data on the age of victims. For the most part, news coverage of lynchings often did not include age, because those kind of details about Black lives did not matter. When the coverage did include age, there were often errors. People generally did not carry identification, like drivers' licenses, until at least the 1920s; for poor Black folks, it was much later than that. Significant age-based milestones had yet to be established by the spread of compulsory education and the enactment of laws on alcohol consumption. The identification of one's specific age, as commonly established in sources other than death certificates, is a relatively modern development that did not become commonplace until right before World War II.

In a 2015 study that sought to rescue lynch victims from anonymity, researchers were able to determine the ages of 913 Black and mixed-race male victims. It found that most of those victims were teenagers or young adults, with Black children and teens making up 21 percent of the victims, compared with 5 percent of white male youths. The authors also reported that it was relatively uncommon for victims to be younger than sixteen years of age.[20] But since their study focused on only ten states and a sampling of fewer than a thousand victims with a recorded age, we cannot say with certainty that lynching young children was "uncommon." As one scholar has noted, "Those missing altogether from the record are inaccessible to historical inquiry. Many lynching victims belong to a secret and irrecoverable past."[21]

What should be highlighted here is that 21 percent of Black youths were lynching victims, a much larger segment than what one might expect. To put it into perspective, imagine if 21 percent of police-related fatalities involved Black children today! This raises the important question: Why were Black youths targeted then (and even now)? Ultimately, however, whether child lynching was common or uncommon is irrelevant to the observation that white vigilante justice targeted children.

Child lynchings have been obscured in the historical records (crime statistics, newspaper reports, legal cases). The cover-up went on for decades with the collusion of local governments and federal agencies. Though we must accept that a definitive count of lynching victims is impossible to know, including the percentage of victims aged nineteen and under, this book will introduce you to many of these young people to redress their omission from the historical record. In my research, I have uncovered the names of scores of child victims in local newspapers that have now been digitized. Many of these names have not been previously recorded in the three main lynching-victim inventories: those of the Tuskegee Institute, the NAACP, and the *Chicago Defender*.

CENTERING BLACK CHILDREN

Despite the plethora of scholarly articles and books, I have yet to see a project centered primarily on the lynching of Black children and how these murders impacted families like mine and their communities. As Helen McLure noted in her 2009 doctoral dissertation on America's culture of collective violence, children have been filtered out of studies as victims, participants, and perpetrators of lynchings. The archives reveal that children across race, ethnicity, and region attended and participated in lynchings in America as far back as the eighteenth century. So, the capacity to engage in collective murder transcended age.[22]

I have been wondering why more scholars have not given robust attention to child lynching beyond occasional mentions in grim histories.

Why have they not placed children at the center of their analyses, or traced the developmental origins of lynching to the transgenerational mistreatment of white children in the Old South, and centuries earlier in the traumatogenic environments of European cultures? Or acknowledged that white child-rearing sustained the South's flourishing culture of sadistic racist violence? Or considered how racism is a function of childhood experiences? Is it too uncomfortable to confront racist violence against children? Are we in collective denial about white America's long-standing pathological hatred of Black children? Black children were not simply bystanders who were swept up in racial violence and lynchings. They were the pivotal axis on which the story of American race turns, and Black children are the convergence point of white racial sadism.

Throughout this book, I will show you how the brutalities of slavery, of Jim Crow lynchings, and of police violence against Black youth exist on a continuum. I am writing about these killings from decades not long after a pandemic and the racial unrest following the murder of George Floyd by a Minneapolis police officer, and the fatal police shootings of Daunte Wright, age twenty, Adam Toledo, thirteen, Anthony J. Thompson Jr., seventeen, and Ma'Khia Bryant, sixteen. In the chapters that follow, I explain how and why the ghastly murders of Black children happened and explore the generational echoes of that trauma on Black families and communities, particularly how anti-Black violence shaped Black parenting practices. I want to know why deeply religious and ostensibly civilized people accepted and participated in such sadistic behavior. What were white supremacists' motivations, and what did they hope to achieve by publicly and privately lynching Black children? What did it mean to rip the root out of a Black family tree and burn a member of the next generation? What combination of forces acted upon the participants and fed their frenzy? What messages did those who murdered children intend to send Black parents and communities?

These questions and the related historical gaps led me to turn my attention to the neglected study of racialized child murder. This is not a history of Black childhood per se, and it is not only about the sadistic lynching of young people. It is an exploration of how Black childhood in America was constructed to normalize the dehumanization process. I will show how the socialization of white children and the racialization of the Black child—and all its insidious consequences, past and present, in high and low culture—helped structure the post-emancipation racial hierarchy. I will explore the social function that lynching fulfills and how these horrible crimes morphed into the less ghoulish forms of Black child devaluation and terror that were useful to a racist society. Dear reader, the child is the centerpiece and the foundational explanation for how racism is reproduced intergenerationally.

EXPANDING THE CIRCLE OF MORAL RESPONSIBILITY

This book exposes the foundational site of white-supremacist reproduction so that we—*especially Black Americans*—can effectively challenge today's persecution of Black youth. Just as during slavery, Black fathers and mothers were forced to internalize the powerlessness and terror of racial violence and the fear of losing their children into harsh parenting practices, such as whuppings, to keep their children alive. Black families are constantly on guard against the potential loss of their children and preparing them to live in a world where their bodies are constantly under threat. Generations of Black children have been brought up according to a master narrative that they must be whupped "for their own good" and to protect them from racial harm. The beatings and deep disruptions in Black children's early relationships with their parents have ultimately shaped their brains, their self-worth and -image, and their perception of their bodies in the social world. As colonized and formerly enslaved people, African Americans have internalized the Western view of childhood itself as a state of naturalized violence in the service of peaceful assimilation into a racial order.

We need to decolonize Black parenting and purge our culture of the poisonous ideas about the nature and character of children, including the notion that their bodies must be processed through harsh punishment to keep them safe from the police, racist vigilantes, the criminal justice system, and a culture of people still haunted by ancestral demons from another place and time. We do not realize the masterful job that white supremacy has done to get generations of Black parents to reproduce trauma on our own children. Understanding child lynchings as an instrument for white supremacy will provide insight into the more recent killings of Black youth.

As you journey with me through this terrible saga, I am going to show you how lynchings are connected to cultural systems and institutions, consumer products, and professional policies and practices—all meant to support, justify, rationalize, and popularize the main project of whiteness—destroying childhood at each of its developmental milestones: the perinatal period, infancy, puberty, and adolescence. The fact that child lynchings occurred during the Progressive Era, which heavily overlapped with Jim Crow, is not a coincidence. It is also not a coincidence that white people discovered that white youth needed protection immediately after emancipation. Many scholars look back on the child-saving era with celebratory eyes, and readers are seduced by the era's promises to protect children and nurture them into healthy citizens. But child lynchings challenge the idea that child-saving campaigns were merely an imperfect and ongoing project of recognizing childhood innocence and creating a universally equitable path toward adulthood.

Child-saving campaigns during the Progressive Era primarily targeted European immigrant youth as part of the Americanization process and the broader project of preserving whiteness. Reformers and child experts, shaped by white-supremacist ideology, recognized the political and economic significance of Black childhood and systematically excluded Black children from protections extended to white youth. These efforts were not about valuing childhood itself but about shielding white youth from the degraded category of childhood—one increasingly linked with racialized savagery. The so-called Age of the Child was a rhetorical facade. It elevated white youth not as vulnerable children but as developing citizens who required insulation from the consequences of their mistakes. Meanwhile, Black children were criminalized, sexualized, and subjected to violence with scientific and cultural justifications rooted in racist ideologies. Pediatrics, white pseudoscience, and the progressive child study movement all participated in a broader ecosystem that treated Black childhood as disposable. This violence against Black children was not an anomaly but a continuation of Western traditions of child-targeted brutality, extending from European communal practices to the anti-Black terror of the post-Reconstruction United States.

When possible, I try to expand the story beyond victimization, toward hope, possibility, and progress. I will tell you about how African

American parents, leaders like Ida B. Wells-Barnett and W. E. B. Du Bois, along with Black journalists, attorneys, and ordinary folk, prevented a few lynchings and created a counternarrative to defend and protect their young. Countless parents, grandparents, aunties and uncles, and siblings hid their youthful relatives from pursuing mobs and sent them north under the cover of night. Some relatives endured brutal torture and death in their efforts not to disclose the whereabouts of an accused young person.

While some parents were too afraid to retrieve the remains of their children after a lynching, there were others who picked up severed and charred body parts, brought them back home, and honored their dead. There were others who attended lynchings. Some brought their own children to teach them about the cruelty of white people and to warn them not to step out of line. It is likely that some Blacks who attended large lynchings where thousands were in attendance may have shown up to assure the victim that he was not dying alone. Mothers like Mamie Till-Mobley and Emma Dowdy used the power of photography and the press to show in graphic detail what racist killers in Mississippi did to the bodies of their fourteen-year-old sons. You will read about how the parents of sixteen-year-old Louisiana native Freddie Moore turned to the courts to win simple justice in the form of convictions and lawsuits against their son's killers.

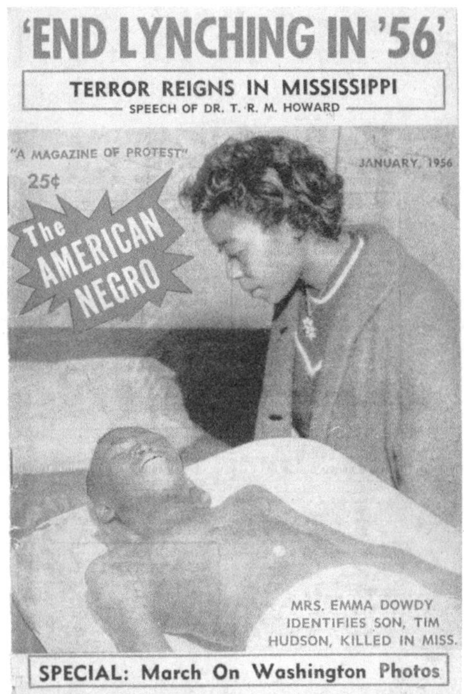

Emma Dowdy looks over the slain body of her son, Tim Hudson, who was killed in Mississippi in 1956. This photo appeared in the January edition of The American Negro *magazine.*

It is important to acknowledge that any success in the courts to prosecute child lynching was part of an elite-driven shift in white nation-building away from terror and toward indoctrination. A similar shift occurred in Europe with respect to public executions. Elites gradually convinced themselves that public executions were so barbaric that they fostered uncivilized behavior in the people, which was not good for the future of European (white) civilization. So, what many people identify as a victory of liberal morality over the immorality of conservatives was really an in-house disagreement over how best to secure white privilege.

Black people's love for their children embodies a powerful, often overlooked form of resistance. This quiet fortitude has sustained Black families and communities through generations, revealing the profound strength found in simply surviving and nurturing the next generation amid relentless adversity.

Lastly, this book serves as a cautionary tale about the catastrophic consequences of dehumanizing, degrading, and abusing children. The world pays a horrific price for such actions, as seen in the legacy of lynching. When societies fail to protect and cherish their children, they perpetuate cycles of violence and hatred, leading to unimaginable suffering and loss. The stories within these pages underscore the urgent need to nurture and protect all children, recognizing their inherent humanity and potential.

If Black Americans do not learn from this long history of the West's anti-child violence that began with the degradation of white children, if we do not decolonize our parenting, if we do not purge our culture of childism and internalized racism, and if we refuse to abandon physical punishment, our children may be at risk of perpetuating cycles of violence that cascade across generations, maybe even becoming future lynchers themselves.

Now, take my hand. We're going into the dark.

CHAPTER 1

“The Fun We Had Burning the Niggers”

How Love and Trauma Primed White Children to Normalize Collective Homicide

Reginald Marsh, This Is Her First Lynching, *1934, drawing*
Reproduced in The Crisis *42, no. 1 (January 1935): 13.*

If you really want to understand American lynching, don’t look at the blaze or the victim. Look at who’s watching it. Because lynching was not just about hate. It was about inheritance. It was about love. About what the fire passed down. The “fun” was not innocent joy but a learned response shaped by repetition, community reinforcement, and the normalization of cruelty. By normalization, I do not mean passive exposure alone but the repeated framing of violence as justified, necessary, and even communal. These are conditions that shaped how white children came to interpret what they were seeing.

Come closer. Not to the flames. Not yet. I want you to see something else. Draw your eyes to the center of the image above. *There*—do you see her?

A little white girl, no more than six or seven, is perched atop an older woman's shoulders. One small finger is pressed to her chin like she's studying the scene. She's not flinching. Not crying. She's just up there, looking like a calm, chilling witness. Her body language says: *I belong here.*

Now let your frame of view expand. Look at the writhing mob below her. A tangle of white faces, men in work boots and suspenders, women in dresses and heels, bodies crushed together in collective anticipation. Some are grinning. Some stare wide-eyed. Others seem lost in the trance of firelight. Their eyes glint, not with empathy, but with something colder: bloodlust, curiosity, pleasure, thrill. Can you feel their breath on your skin? Does the thought of that make you want to wince?

The flames cast a greasy light. The vent stacks above the houses release smoke that hangs like a shroud. The unseen Black victim, off the page but ever-present, is burning just beyond the frame. You can almost hear it: the hiss of fire licking skin, the pop of bone, the victim's screams, and the crowd's delighted howls.

Now, return to her. That girl. She is the still point in this feverish scene. *A child.* Watching a human being die.

She looks like she's watching a parade. Or fireworks. Or a puppet show. She's not confused. She's not afraid. *And that's the point.* She's not reacting in horror because *none of the adults around her are horrified.* Her nervous system is in tune with theirs and doing what it's been trained to do: Mirror the people she trusts. This is not an aberration of innocence. It is the choreography of white socialization.

And yet, imagine if this drawing didn't carry the caption "This Is Her First Lynching." Without those five words anchoring the scene, the meaning becomes slippery. The image would still disturb, still haunt, but the viewer might miss the full horror of what they're witnessing. The child might be misread as a bystander rather than a student. Her expression might register as curiosity instead of conditioning. The ritual unfolding might be interpreted as incidental, not *intentional.*

The caption doesn't just label; it indicts. It forces us to reckon not just with what is happening but with *who* is being made in the process. Without it, too many viewers might focus on the flames or the crowd and overlook a child being baptized in the fire of white supremacy.

The artist, Reginald Marsh, didn't just draw the violence in this 1934 image; he named its legacy. That caption is a warning: This is how American lynching starts and remains so resilient. This is what it looks like when a white child's formative lesson in belonging is watching a Black person being publicly burned alive. But lynching isn't just about Black death; it was a white parenting strategy and a centuries-long pattern of neurological grooming.

The first time I saw this drawing was while combing through lynching files at Howard University's Moorland-Spingarn Research Center. I recoiled. Naively, I had assumed that even the most sadistic lynchings were carried out beyond the view of children. That even families steeped in white-supremacist ideology would feel some obligation, however flimsy, to protect their young. To shield them from the psychological wreckage of witnessing a human being tortured and murdered. I thought they would at least pretend to preserve childhood innocence.

I was wrong.

I couldn't stop looking at the drawing. I grunted, "Umph. Look at this creepy little girl." I wanted to call her evil. But then I paused. I looked again and thought about all I had learned about developmental psychology and neuroscience, and realized this isn't a monster. Not quite yet. This is a child in the process of becoming. And what she is becoming is the result of what the adults in her life have taught her to see as normal. This drawing revealed a grim reality: White children were *deliberately* exposed to acts of racial terror as part of their socialization. That's because there is no child-friendly version of white supremacy. It destroys children so they can, in turn, destroy others.

There is something communal and shared happening here. A sense of belonging to a local community. A bonding. A release of anxiety. A culture reinforcing the learning of race through collective homicide. Lynchings were a moral lesson to children, a form of disciplining and instruction on what happens to "bad people," to childish people. The future of white supremacy depended on training the next generation to feel nothing—or worse, to feel *good*—in the face of Black suffering.

THE NEUROSCIENCE OF RACISM

Let's talk about what's happening inside this child's body.

Children are sensory gluttons, absorbing sights, sounds, smells, and textures in a single swoop. Their senses are their first tools for exploring and understanding the world. While genes provide the basic framework for brain development, other components—the environment, experiences, relationships, and sensory input—sculpt and strengthen the brain's architecture. In early life, the brain is exquisitely sensitive, changing its shape, size, and circuitry in response to everything it touches, sees, and feels.[1]

A child is born with a built-in alarm system in their brain, the amygdala. When danger is near, it sets off biochemical reactions. The heart races, hormones surge, muscles tense, eyes widen. The body prepares to freeze, fight, or flee.[2] But not everything dangerous *feels* dangerous. Children learn what to fear by watching and mirroring adults. In *This Is Her First Lynching*, the child's brain is linked to a network of other psychologically damaged brains in that crime scene, influencing one another's internal biochemistry, emotions, and behaviors. The mood and messages of adults at lynchings would regulate white children's initial anxieties and fears and inoculate them against the normal stress responses that would send their bodies into fight-or-flight mode.[3]

So, when a trusted adult smiles, lifts a child high above the crowd, points her face toward the flames, and says, *Look* . . . the brain does not panic. The brain says, *This is okay. This is good.* In so doing, it makes a memory etched not just in thought but in flesh and the developing architecture of the brain. It gets stored in the muscles. In the breath. In the synapses. A sensory imprint of belonging is born from brutality. That's what Reginald Marsh's famous drawing captures. This child's lack of fear isn't natural. It's not a flaw. It's training.

Now look again at the woman holding her.

She's possibly a mother, grandmother, a community elder. Look at her open mouth stretched wide in a grotesque exhale, somewhere between a cheer and a howl. Her body is teaching. She is saying with her face, her arms, her rhythm: *This is a good thing. This is what we do. This is who we are.*

That child's brain is adapting to racial violence in real time. Her stress response is muted. Her empathy is silenced. Her Default Mode

Network (DMN), the system responsible for reflection, compassion, and awareness, is being dimmed even more than it already has been. Children who grow up in high-stress states of arousal and exposure to violence and terror are at risk for underdeveloped DMNs and may eventually suffer from a lack of compassion for others and the self.[4] Young people who attended lynchings learned not to fear Black suffering but to absorb it as spectacle.

And this kind of training doesn't happen through disciplining—it happens through *love*.

Children are born with a biological imperative to attach to their caregivers. This is an evolutionary drive designed to maximize survival. When those attachments are secure, children feel safe enough to explore, learn, and develop autonomy. But when love itself is laced with violence, that same drive becomes a trap.

Because the brain is a social organ, it is built to adapt, attune, and mirror. So, the child's mind bends toward whatever brings safety and belonging. Here, that safety is fused with spectacle. That belonging is bathed in firelight and smoke. Her brain isn't just observing violence. It's calibrating to it and absorbing it through posture, tone, breath, temperature. Encoding it in her blood, her bones, and her brain. Her Default Mode Network, already dimmed, goes quieter still. Her amygdala likely doesn't flare in terror; it flickers in recognition. As neuroscience suggests, it tells her that this is not danger. *This is home. This is love.* And the child is learning in the only language that matters: the body's.

This girl is in a stage of development where she cannot yet form her own moral or political judgments. She isn't reasoning or rebelling. She is absorbing. Right now, her brain is a sponge, tuned to sensory input and the emotional cues of the adults around her. Her only job, biologically, is to stay close, to please, to survive. So, she mirrors. Even in abusive homes, children bond because attachment is nonnegotiable; it's instinctual. And that instinct is what makes this moment so chilling.[5]

Secure attachment is how children learn to love, to trust, to make meaning. When violence is delivered through those attachments by mothers, fathers, grandparents, what gets encoded isn't just ideology but sensation: warmth, pride, approval, even joy. That's how racism becomes not just something white children believe but something they feel in their breath, their heartbeat, their nervous systems. Racism becomes home.

This child's body and the elder's body—their breath, posture, emotional cadence—are in sync. The adult's joy becomes the child's calm. The elder's gaze directs the child's focus. Together, they form a closed circuit of normalized violence, a duet of dissociation. What the older woman exalts, the girl internalizes. What one performs, the other rehearses. In this moment, their nervous systems are braided together and tuned to the frequency of violence. White adults conveyed a direct message to children that the goal of lynching Black people was to protect white people from danger, or to exact revenge against those who were accused, typically with no basis, of harming one of their own. Either rationale is a celebration of white power.

The child may not understand what's happening because her brain is still under construction. The circuits in her frontal lobes that help a child process morality, reasoning, empathy, social behavior, and long-term consequence are immature. That part of the brain develops slowly, over years, and doesn't fully complete until around age twenty-five.[6] Right now, she's not interpreting this moment. She's just feeling it and being shaped by it. Her brain isn't asking, *Is this wrong?* It's asking, *Am I safe? Am I loved? Am I doing what they want?*

And in this moment, surrounded by smiles, lifted by a caregiver, flooded by heat and cheers and the chemical thrill of belonging, her internal wiring gets the answer: *Yes.*

She doesn't need to understand the logic of white supremacy or what a lynching is to be marked by it. Her developing brain is learning *how* to feel, *what* to normalize, *who* to trust, and what kinds of human pain are meant to be ignored, mocked, or enjoyed. This is not ideology. It's wiring. This is how a racist child is not born but made.

And this, *this*, is what happens when we bring developmental psychology and neuroscience into the archives. When we stop treating lynching as just a public crime and start analyzing it as a formative biosocial event in the life of a child.[7] When we shift our questions from *Who killed?* and *Who died?* to *Who watched and what did it do to them?* Lynching wasn't just spectacle; it was a multisensory, physiological ritual that neurologically conditioned white people. Their brains were sculpted by terror and approval, trained to associate white safety with Black death, bonding with brutality, and violence with the warmth of community. This is how terror became inheritance. This is how belonging was built.

This is one of the most profound insights that developmental psychology and neuroscience offers: that trauma can feel like comfort if it's paired with familiarity, praise, or touch. White children didn't just witness horror, they experienced it as a family ritual, a community celebration. This reframes lynching not as a breakdown of morality but as a perverse expression of it, and a distorted form of moral and emotional development that links care and love with cruelty.

History isn't just about what people did. It's about what *it did to them*—to their insides, their breath, their pulse, their future. So, we need to get beneath the spectacle of lynching and find the imprint and internal wounds. That's where history settles. Not in the facts but in the flesh and organs. This is the missing frame in our study of racial violence in America: *the developing brain*. The child, as sponge, as sensor, as site of transmission absorbing terror as texture, as truth, as touch. This is how white supremacy reproduces itself, not just through laws or hateful language and ideas but through bodies trained to find comfort and love in domination and belonging in collective homicide.

The child in this old drawing may forget this day. But her body will not.

Her sensory map will likely remember the smells, the crowd, the heat. Those sensations will live in her, shape her, maybe even soothe her quietly, beneath her conscious awareness. Not as memories with words but as reflexes. As ease. As familiarity. The memory won't need language. It will echo in her posture, flicker in her pulse, surface in her reactions to anger and touch, to difference and the sight of Black bodies. The damage is not only what she saw. It's how she was held while seeing it. It's who taught her to look.

You can't see the lynched body in Marsh's drawing. But you can see what it has already done to this child. Except it didn't start here. This wasn't the first rupture in her instincts. Her lack of fear, her poise, her finger pressed to her chin—these are the rehearsed gestures of a child who has already been emotionally groomed. By the time she is lifted above the crowd to watch someone burn, her brain has already been primed to stay calm in the face of Black suffering.

This "first" lynching is not a beginning. It's a culmination. Of what, we can't say for sure. We can only speculate. But something in her internal wiring has already been shaped to meet racial violence with calm. Something, or someone, taught her that the sight of a Black person in agony requires no panic. No protest. No fear. That kind of response doesn't appear fully formed. It's practiced. Conditioned. Preloaded.

And this is what I need you to understand: This isn't just emotional. It's neurological. And "neurological" doesn't mean "fixed." It means "shaped." And what is shaped can be reshaped. These moments burn themselves into the brain's wiring, though rewiring can still happen later.

The wiring didn't begin with firelight; it began in the home. In the church pew, at school, at the dinner table and in bedtime stories. The repetition of offhand slurs, the silence after news of a lynching, the belt used to enforce obedience, the warning not to cry, the hush when race was mentioned. All of it laid the neural scaffolding for this moment. Her brain is not reacting—it's confirming. Matching its rhythms to the violence around her. Her sensory system is building categories, and her body is learning racial hierarchy. The heat, the shouts, the smell of burning flesh all reinforce who counts as human, and who does not.

And crucially, she is learning that violence is care. That punishment is proof of love. Just as the belt teaches her obedience at home, the rope teaches her loyalty to whiteness. The lesson is clear: Disobedience—whether from children or from childlike, unruly Black bodies—invites violence, always in the name of protection, always under the banner of love.

This is why American lynching survived for so long. Not just because of hateful ideologies, white economic anxiety, fears about Black political power, the threat of interracial sex, or the myth of the predatory Black man. Not just because of a collapsing post-Reconstruction South grasping for control. Not just because of failed law enforcement or racist politicians. Yes, all of that is true. But it's not the whole or even the most significant story. Lynching endured because it was more than a spectacle. It was an inheritance strategy. A form of social learning. A *family event* engineered to mold white children physiologically, emotionally, and neurologically into future enforcers of racial terror.

It wasn't just about what the mob did to the Black body. It was about what the people in the mob did to *their own children's bodies* in the process. That's what made lynching sustainable. That's what made it sacred. This wasn't only ideology; it was biology shaped by ritual. Passed through breath, blood, and bone and turned into memory.

So, when you look at this child's face, don't just see "a creepy little girl." See a child undergoing a transformation. A child whose moral compass is being guided by firelight, community, family, bonding, and love.

We think of white children at lynchings as background figures or as peripheral in the story of racial violence. But they were the audience that mattered most. They were the future being shaped in real time. They were the reason the crowd brought cameras. They were the proof that the ritual had worked. Because if a child can stand calmly in front of a burning body and feel no fear, then the white-supremacist system is safe. Then the cycle will continue. This is how white supremacy replicates itself. One child at a time.

Reginald Marsh didn't grow up in the Jim Crow South. He was a white artist born in France and living in New York City. *This Is Her First Lynching* was atypical of his work, which included integrated urban scenes, the seedy side of city life, beaches, mass transit, dancehalls, theaters, and people enduring impoverished circumstances during the Depression.[8] But in 1934, he drew *This Is Her First Lynching* with a level of psychological insight most historians still haven't caught up to.

His work reveals that this wasn't about a single child or a single corpse. He captured something more dangerous: *the ordinariness of it all.* The way white childhood was being sculpted in public, with community consent. The way a culture could wrap horror in festivity and call it family bonding. There's no accident in the way Marsh centers that little girl. The way the light hits her. The way the crowd seems to cradle her, lifting her into moral clarity or ruin.

Why did Marsh center the child at all? Why not draw the lynched Black body? Why not show the violence directly? That choice matters. Maybe it was strategy. Maybe it was refusal. Maybe it was Marsh's way of indicting white America without turning Black suffering into spectacle. Maybe he knew the real horror wasn't just the burning. It was the gaze. The calm. The child. That's the unsettling image white America needed to reckon with: the child shaped by its fire. Not the Black corpse.

And that's what makes *This Is Her First Lynching* so singular, so haunting. Marsh didn't draw horror; he drew habituation. He bypassed spectacle and documented transmission. He showed us how white supremacy doesn't just kill Black people. It *grooms* white ones.

That little girl isn't the future of racism. She is its present tense. Its vessel. Its proof of concept. And for nearly a century, most people have looked at her without seeing her. Or worse, looked and felt nothing at all. Because to truly see her would mean acknowledging what white childhood has always been: not an innocent counterpoint to racism but its laboratory. Its soft entry point. Its testing ground. Maybe that's why it's easier to look past and dismiss her. Because she's *just* a drawing. Not a photograph. Not a fact in a textbook. Just charcoal and paper. And that makes it easier to say: *She's not real. She's not ours. She's not us.*

This is why Marsh's drawing remains so riveting. Not because of what it shows, but because of what it refuses to sentimentalize. There is no redemption arc. No shocked expression. No innocence shattered. Just calm absorption. And what unsettles white America most isn't the fire; it's the possibility that the child isn't broken by racial violence. She's built by it.

Of course, you may be inclined to point out this isn't a photograph. We cannot build an entire argument around a single drawing, especially one that is not photographic. The child at the center of Marsh's old drawing isn't a real girl with a name and birth certificate. She's a rendering. Charcoal and Conté on paper. But don't mistake that for fiction. This 1934 image is still a form of historical evidence. Evidence of what a white artist saw, what he knew, and what he was willing to expose. Marsh lived in a nation where lynchings were frequent, where newspaper clippings and postcards showed children at the scenes, where racial violence was a civic event. His drawing is not imaginative. It is observational, interpretative, and composed in an America where such a child was not just plausible but common. So, when we analyze this image, we are not projecting. We are excavating. The emotional truth of that drawing stands as indictment and artifact.

Now that we've seen what lynching did to one child, how it sculpted her empathy, dulled her fear, and wired her to mistake cruelty for care, we need to zoom out. What Marsh captured in that single girl was not an exception. It was a ritual. A generational project. A sensory pedagogy of domination.

This chapter turns now to the deeper question: How does a society create children like the girl in the drawing, not once, but again and again? Not just one warped little girl. Thousands. Tens of thousands. How is this racism reproduced in such a faithful manner, creating not monsters *but mirrors*.

THE DARK NURSERY OF WHITE SUPREMACY

Childhood has always been the dark nursery where white supremacy first takes breath, where it enters the bloodstream. Through bedtime prayers whispered in homes where cruelty masqueraded as love. Through belts passed off as affection. Through lullabies wrapped around silence, pain, and warning.

Most histories of lynching start at the tree and end at the corpse. They catalog the dead, the mobs, the myths about white womanhood, the economic anxiety, the panic over Black land, Black autonomy, Black life. But they rarely ask: How does a child become someone who grins beside a burning body? Who poses for a photo? Who pockets a fingerbone as a souvenir? Who kicks, scratches, and spits at a lynching victim? Who falsely accuses a Black boy or man of rape?

To answer these questions, we must return to the places where a child learns to tether love to fear, safety to dominance, God to punishment. Because before white children could grow into grinning spectators and ritual executioners, they had to be neurologically groomed to see terror as bonding, to experience cruelty as care. Their empathy had to be pruned. Their fear rerouted. Their moral instincts recalibrated. What white children were told mattered, yes, but as sensory beings, what their bodies absorbed mattered more.

I am not suggesting that white supremacy is *inevitable* or something embedded biologically in ways that cannot be undone. The damage is real, but the brain is not fixed in cruelty. What is learned through repetition and proximity, generation after generation, can also be unlearned through rupture, care, and conscious re-patterning. Neural pathways formed in firelight can be rewired in truth.

What does it mean to sit with the knowledge that white childhood, so often framed as vulnerable and deserving of protection, was routinely nurtured on violence? That the same small arms wrapped around teddy bears at night were hoisted for a better view of the noose by morning? That white parents didn't just *allow* their children to witness lynchings but *prepared* them for this communal violence?

To grapple with that truth would upend the comforting fictions of American morality and innocence. It would force museums to stop aestheticizing racial terror. It would require textbooks to center not just Black death but white *grooming*. It would demand that white families look at their own archives, their photo albums, their inherited silences, and ask not "What did we witness?" but "What did we celebrate?"

And it would ask something even harder: *What do we still carry in our bodies?*

"A FRESH PAIR OF EYES"

In his boarding school yearbook, Marsh quoted the abolitionist Thomas W. Higginson: "Originality is simply a pair of fresh eyes."[9] That's what Marsh brought to the American visual archive of lynching: a pair of fresh eyes. I don't know what he hoped to achieve by rendering this image. But what he gave us was more than art. It was an indicting visual record of how a nation teaches its children to watch lynchings and feel nothing. He may not have had the language of neuroscience. But Marsh knew what he was looking at. He saw what we must be willing to see: that white supremacy doesn't just terrorize the victim; it seduces the child witness.

Yet, in the years that followed, as Marsh's work was celebrated and anthologized, little mention was made of *This Is Her First Lynching*. His alma mater praised him. Museums collected his work. But the drawing that captured the psychosexual, intergenerational complicity and pathology of white supremacy was largely ignored.

Marsh never wrote about racism. He didn't publicly explain this piece. He'd graduated from the Lawrenceville School in New Jersey during an era of open racism on campus, when there were no Black students at the school and white boys played games like "Nigger Baby" for sport. There was no obvious reason to expect such a searing indictment from him. And yet, he created it. And left it behind without masking his critique in abstraction, cloaking it in sentimentality, or imbuing his composition with moral ambiguity.

For that, I owe him gratitude. Because Marsh's drawing gives me, nearly a century later, a powerful tool: a way to write children and neuroscience into the archive of racial violence. A way to make visible the scars lynching left not just on the body of its victims but on the minds of the white children who watched.

Marsh's drawing first appeared publicly in *The New Yorker* on September 8, 1934. A liberal magazine of urbane wit and satire placed a little white girl calmly watching a lynching in its weekly offering, without commentary. No white journalists gasped. No editorials unpacked the horror. No child psychologists issued warnings about trauma. No white parents asked what it meant to raise children who could watch a lynching with equanimity. And certainly, white readers likely didn't see their own families reflected in that image. Because to see her, *truly* see her, would have required seeing themselves. Their mothers. Their churches. Their own childhoods. Their complicity.

By 1935, the NAACP and its executive secretary, Walter White, were ramping up support for an anti-lynching congressional bill sponsored by Edward Costigan and Robert Wagner. Marsh may have been responding to the national climate: the black flag flying outside the NAACP's Manhattan office that read, "A MAN WAS LYNCHED YESTERDAY"; the gruesome images of mutilated bodies appearing in newspapers; the urgent moral pressure rising across the country.

Marsh donated the drawing to the NAACP. It was reprinted in *The Crisis* in January 1935. Walter White understood the image's power. He had personally secured it, reprinted it, and ensured it landed in a publication that knew precisely what it meant to center a white child at the edge of Black death. *The Crisis*, founded by W. E. B. Du Bois, had long used its pages to name and confront the brutality of American racism, and Marsh's drawing was no exception.

Black readers, attuned to the daily rituals of white terror, would not have missed the image's implications. They would have recognized the calm in that little girl's face. They would have known, perhaps from experience, what it meant to be burned alive before such an audience. They didn't need the caption explained. They didn't need a moral to the story. Because they knew that child. They had been spat at by her. Tripped by her on sidewalks. Called "nigger" by her in schoolyards and soda shops. They had watched her throw rocks, spew slurs, laugh at pain.

The children she represented were emboldened by adults who nodded in approval.Children who slapped Black maids, mocked Black elders, hurled insults with the ease of inherited language. Children whose cruelty wasn't punished but praised. Black people likely saw Marsh's drawing as confirming of what they have always known: The racial terror didn't begin with adult mobs. It began with white children learning how to normalize murder.

Shortly after its publication in *The Crisis*, Marsh's drawing was included in the first-ever national anti-lynching art exhibition, *An Art Commentary on Lynching*, organized by White and hosted at the Arthur U. Newton Galleries in Manhattan. It was the most prominent work in the show. Thousands of patrons, most of them white and monied and hailing from cities across America and Europe, flocked to see these ghastly images. The aim of this educational effort to combat lynching was to present "distinguished art with a social message" to white audiences that were either desensitized to racial violence or silently complicit.[10]

The collection of oils, sculptures, wood carvings, prints, cartoons, and photographs depicted dark bodies hanging from trees and telegraph poles, streaked in blood and twisted in knotty agonies of death as white mobs applauded. The show was meant to unsettle, to break through white denial, and to rally support for federal legislation. One critic from the *New York World-Telegram* warned patrons that the show would "tear the heart and chill the blood."[11]

Despite the ambition of the show, no federal anti-lynching law passed. There was no mass outcry about lynching. No collective guilt. No calls to dismantle the culture that produced the scene Marsh rendered in ink. Instead, Marsh's drawing was treated as an artifact that was interesting, provocative, and safely distant from the contemporary moment. Museums framed it as a glimpse into a darker time, without reckoning with how the emotional circuitry it depicted kept humming through white American childhood.

This image remains resonant because it wasn't merely a record of a lynching or a neurological document. It was a blueprint of how whiteness sustains itself through childhood. How empathy is amputated. How horror becomes heritage. Marsh's work outlived him. *This Is Her First Lynching* eventually made its way into more gallery retrospectives, museum collections, and history books, though was often stripped of its raw moral force. It was praised for its line work, for its composition, for the way it captured "American life." But that's the tragedy. It became form, not fire. Aesthetic, not indictment.

I cannot tell you that Marsh intended for viewers to walk away from his drawing with a lesson on child development, attachment and social-learning theory, neuroscience, or the intergenerational transmission of racism and trauma. But he powerfully illustrated how utterly devastating the practice of bringing children to lynchings would be on a culture, eroding its humanity from the inside out. At the very least, Marsh's visual commentary indicated a kind of preliminary awareness of what developmental psychology and neuroscience suggest to us today about how environment, trauma, and socialization shape developing brains.

"HER FIRST TIME"

A year after Marsh's drawing was published, a Black-owned Texas newspaper, *The Houston Informer*, offered its own rendering. On November 23, 1935, just eleven days after a lynching in Columbus, Texas,

Editorial cartoon published in The Houston Informer *after the lynchings of Ernest Collins and Benny Mitchell Jr. in November 1935.*

the paper printed a cartoon that echoed Marsh's visual grammar but sharpened its critique.

This was not abstract commentary. The cartoon was a direct response to the public torture and murder of two Black teenage boys: fifteen-year-old Ernest Collins and sixteen-year-old Benny Mitchell Jr., illiterate farmhands accused of raping and murdering a local white valedictorian, Geraldine Kollman, near her father's pecan grove. Both boys had allegedly signed confessions with an "X." That was all it took.

They were chained together, neck to neck, and loaded into a car for transfer to a distant jail. But the mob had other plans. Vigilantes intercepted the vehicle, overtook the sheriff, and dragged the boys to a rural intersection just a few miles from downtown Columbus. There, beneath the gnarled limbs of a live oak tree lit by the beams of car headlights, Collins and Mitchell were hanged before a mob of seven hundred white onlookers: men, women, and children.

According to a local newspaper, just before the ropes were fastened around the boys' necks, a white Episcopalian pastor, Rev. Charles Gresham Marmion Jr., climbed atop a car and implored the crowd to "let the law take its course." But the law didn't allow juveniles to be executed. And the crowd knew that. That was the problem. Shouts rang out: "Supposed it had been some of your women folks?" "Get another rope!" Marmion was booed off the car and disappeared into the darkness. Then the ritual resumed.

The boys were dragged to the tree still chained together, as mob members likely didn't have the key. Ropes were thrown over one of the tree's limbs. Twenty men pulled, raising the boys' kicking bodies into the air. Collins, larger for his age, grabbed the rope and tried to pull himself up, crying, "Oh Lord, help me." Several men sprang forward and yanked his legs down, snapping his neck.

A photograph was taken. It is faded now, but the horror endures. It shows their limp bodies hanging from the tree. The caption beneath it reads: "Colorado Co. Protects Womanhood." Copies of the image were passed around the community. The nooses used in the lynching were later displayed in the window of a local drugstore, where they were admired by passersby. The boys' families, terrified, refused to claim the bodies. Collins and Mitchell were buried in unmarked graves.[12]

The bodies of Ernest Collins and Benny Mitchell, victims of a mob lynching on November 12, 1935, in Columbus, Texas. The photo caption reads, "Colorado Co. Protects Womanhood."

The Houston Informer, steeped in the rage and clarity of Black witness, responded with a cartoon titled *An Introduction to Culture of the Southern Variety*. In the cartoon, two white women and a young girl stand before a lynching scene. The little girl is flanked by the adults. One woman, perhaps her mother, presses a hand firmly to the child's head. Is it a gesture of affection? Or is she seizing her daughter's face, turning it toward the hanged bodies, forcing her to look? The caption reads: "HER FIRST TIME."

There's no sentimentality. No shock. Just another rite of passage.

The phrase suggests that lynching was not an aberration but a tradition, one with a past as well as a presumed future. It implies that both women had seen this before. That the child would see it again. That *she must*.

The firm hand on the child's head carries centuries of meaning. She is pressed to directly face the horror so she will stop flinching. Stop feeling. Learn what it means to be white in a country that defines power through the spectacle of Black death.

And this depiction wasn't fiction. It was reportage by other means. Thousands of white children were made to watch and, in some cases, participate in these rituals. Encouraged to smile for photographs beside charred corpses. Encouraged to laugh. Encouraged to remember.

We can see it in the archival record if we know where to look. The photographs from the lynching of eighteen-year-old Lige Daniels in Center, Texas, in 1920. The images of Rubin Stacy, thirty-seven years old, lynched in Fort Lauderdale, Florida, in 1935. In both cases, white children appear in the crowds, some grinning, some with frozen expressions, blank stares, locked postures. You can almost see the conflict in their bodies. The dissonance. The terror they're trying not to feel. Because somewhere, in some of those children, the nervous system still knew this was wrong. But adults snuffed it out.

What we are witnessing in these images, both cartoon and photograph, is the spiritual and neurological destruction of children. White parents brought their young to the killing tree. Not in spite of their innocence but because of it. Because that innocence had to be reshaped into detachment. Because the future of white supremacy depended on it. These were not random exposures. They were lessons. Initiations. Messages delivered through blood and ash: *This is who we kill. This is who we are. This is what you are meant to protect.*

And it worked.

Modern neuroscience confirms what these rituals already knew: that repeated exposure to the suffering of an "other" deadens the empathic response. And that empathic narrowing, when combined with in-group bonding, becomes especially powerful. Children can grow into generous, loving adults within their own communities, while remaining indifferent or even hostile to those marked as outsiders. The brain does not struggle with this contradiction. It resolves it through fear. The amygdala flares in the presence of the "other." Compassion shuts down.

Yet none of this removes moral responsibility. Racism is not a neurological glitch. It's not destiny. It's design. And while the damage is real, it is not irreversible. The brain remains malleable, especially when met with care and truth. But those opportunities are rare, and often unwelcome. Because unlearning white supremacy requires confronting not just ideas but embodied memories, those early moments when belonging was fused with brutality.

The body of eighteen-year-old Lige Daniels hangs above the heads of men and boys on August 2, 1920, in Center, Texas.

At best, a child's "first lynching" taught her to feel proud of whiteness and indifferent to Black pain. At worst, it shaped her into a killer. Or a voter. Or a teacher. Or a parent. Or a juror. Because no matter how many years pass, those little white girls never vanish. They grow up. They vote. They teach. They legislate.

They raise children of their own. Unless something interrupts the cycle, they remain what they were made to be. Not monsters, but mirrors.

WHAT THE FIRE PASSED DOWN

Reginald Marsh's drawing and *The Houston Informer*'s cartoon were not abstractions. They weren't metaphors. They were records—precise, deliberate depictions of what actually unfolded across the American landscape. They captured the truth of white childhood in a white-supremacist state: that horror wasn't something children stumbled upon; it was something they were ushered to. Required to witness. Expected to absorb. Parents didn't drag their children to lynchings in spite of the terror. They brought them precisely *because* of it.

Kristina DuRocher wrote it plainly in *Raising Racists*: "The white community did not see having children witness racial killings as barbaric, but instead embraced the experience for their children as part of a larger protective duty."[13] Protective. As in, defense against softness. Against empathy. Against moral hesitation. It was protection against becoming human. And the most harrowing truth is that many white adults knew exactly what they were doing. They weren't confused. They weren't swept up. They were making a choice to mold their children into vessels of calm cruelty, to call it tradition, and to pass it off as love.

This isn't biology's fault. If racism were etched into the double helix, if it pulsed from the spinal cord like hunger, there'd be no fault to assign and no accountability. Racism isn't destiny. Racism isn't born; it's bred. Not in blood, but in a pattern of nurture that is ritualized, rehearsed, and repeated. Which means it can be broken if white parents choose not to give their children over to the fire.

The journalist and anti-lynching crusader Ida B. Wells-Barnett saw it more than a century ago. In 1892, in Memphis, she watched as a little white girl, just twelve years old, stood beside her parents, wide-eyed, as a Black man was tortured and burned alive. Wells understood what was being done to that child's psyche:

> Two or three white women, accompanied by their escorts, pushed to the front to obtain an unobstructed view, and looked on with astonishing coolness and nonchalance. One man and woman brought a little girl, not over 12 years old, apparently their daughter, to view a scene which was calculated to drive sleep from the child's eyes for many nights, if not to produce a permanent injury to her nervous system.[14]

Decades later, Walter White described a similar encounter in his book *Rope and Faggot*. In Florida, after a mass lynching, he came across three white schoolchildren—clean, bright-eyed, and excited—eager to share the memory of what they'd seen. White, light-skinned enough to pass, was mistaken for a fellow white man, and the children let their joy spill freely. He writes:

> In Florida some years ago, several lynchings and the burning of the Negro section of town followed the attempt of a Negro pharmacist to vote in a national election. One morning shortly afterwards I walked along the road which led from the beautiful little town to the spot where

> five Negroes had been burned. Three shining-eyed, healthy, cleanly children, headed for school, approached me. As I neared them, the eldest, a ruddy-cheeked girl of nine or ten, asked if I was going to the place where "the niggers" had been killed. I told her I might stop and see the spot. Animatedly, almost joyously as though the memory were of Christmas morning or the circus, she told me, her slightly younger companions interjecting a word here and there or nodding vigorous assent, of "the fun we had burning the niggers."[15]

White didn't recoil. He named the violence for what it was: not just the mutilation of Black bodies but the mutilation of white minds. He understood what was at stake:

> In a community where a lynching or perhaps a burning occurs, where thousands of participants and spectators include mothers and children of tender age among them, where there is morbid scrambling for charred bones or links of the chain which held the victim to his funeral pyre, where leaders of the mob are exalted as men of courage and action—the effect upon young minds is almost too appalling to be contemplated. It is entirely within the range of possibilities that such experiences may result in arrestation. In the unconscious of these immature minds are thus sown the seeds of lynching as a panacea which will correct all ills and especially those emanating from Negro sources. . . . Lynchings justified and extolled, lynchers exalted as men of bravery and forthrightness, efforts at punishment of the lynchers blocked and derided—such frequently repeated acts cannot fail to shape young minds in moulds which seem destined to demand more victims.[16]

Destined to demand more victims. What a chilling statement.

That wasn't just a warning. It was a diagnosis. A curse. A foreshadowing of what happens when a society trains its children not to cry at death but to cheer.

Both Wells's and White's emotional intelligence outran white America's scientific literacy by a century. They saw what white parents refused to confront: that early exposure to sadism, when paired with love, community, and moral framing, rewires a child's nervous system. They saw it before there were fMRI machines. Before trauma theory.

Before the term "neuroscience" was even coined. They understood what the white community could not or would not. And in doing so, they showed more care for the psychological well-being of white children than their own families ever did.

That is the great and terrible irony: White supremacy sustains itself not just through hate but through bonds of love. Through family. Through touch. Through bedtime stories and Sunday clothes and community gatherings where the cost of belonging was a dead Black body.

This is why rape became such a potent excuse for lynching, not because it explained the violence, but because it cloaked it in paternalism. It made the horror feel noble. Protective. Necessary. Even though most lynchings had nothing to do with rape, the myth endured because it gave parents a script to follow and children a reason to obey.

People want to believe that Jim Crow was built on ideas, on cartoons, on books, on stereotypes, on white supremacist rules of etiquette. And yes, those things mattered. But those were the symptoms. The root was deeper. The root was the broken bond between love and humanity. The root was the trauma that passed down not only from parent to child but from sensation to nervous system. It was never just a political project. It was a developmental one.

The real crime, the one historians have rarely confronted, is how white childhood itself was devoured by whiteness. How white parents taught their children that cruelty was sacred. That love required sacrifice. That the price of acceptance was the silencing of compassion.

And we keep missing it. Because we're still asking the wrong questions. We focus on adult beliefs instead of childhood formation. We study ideologies instead of the practices that shape them. We study men in hoods instead of toddlers on shoulders. We keep overlooking the fire that burned into the child before she even knew how to name it.

Walter White understood it, and so did Ida B. Wells and the Black editorial staff at a Texas newspaper. They saw that white communities didn't need neuroscience to understand child development. White Americans already knew the timing. They already knew the method. They baptized their children in blood before adolescence had a chance to intervene. They passed down terror as tradition. They didn't need theory. They had instinct.

Maybe you're thinking I've made this too much about white children. That I haven't said enough about Black victims. That I've veered too far into white pathology. Perhaps there's something to that critique. But to understand how Black children came to be lynched, we must first understand how white children were trained to become lynchers. That horror, too, was passed down.

And here is where we pivot . . .

Because what happened on American soil, what Reginald Marsh drew, what Wells and White documented, was not new. It didn't begin in the red clay of the South or the backwoods of Mississippi. This ritual of childhood and violence, of fire as pedagogy, of belonging shaped through brutality, is far older. It is a ghost story with roots in European soil. A transgenerational haunting that crossed the Atlantic, not in theory but in blood and bone.

The trauma sailed here in bodies already marked. Bodies that had long forgotten what safety felt like. Bodies that had been taught, over centuries, to find familiarity in blood spectacle, in punishment as justice, in cruelty as order. What we call indifference to the lynching of Black people was, in fact, recognition. A felt memory. What we call callousness was comfort and familiarity. It was a reenactment of scenes passed down through lineage, not just in story but in the architecture of the body itself.

This was epigenetic inheritance. The silent handoff of terror through generations, not just through stories whispered at night or sermons from pulpits but through cortisol-soaked wombs, through childhoods disciplined by fear, through touch that taught violence as love. What these white communities brought to the lynching tree was not just rage; it was ritual. Not just hatred but homecoming.

The reason they didn't flinch was because their nervous systems had been rehearsing this ritualistic violence for centuries. The fire didn't disturb them. It steadied them. It matched the rhythm of something ancient and unhealed inside them. And so, they brought their children to witness so they could be calibrated to the cadence of inherited cruelty and find calm in carnage.

In the next chapter, we cross back over the Atlantic.

We're going to the place where the blueprint was drafted and where the horrors were first made familiar. Where white children learned to cheer at gallows and public executions. Where the sacred and the sadistic became indistinguishable. Where this fire first flickered, long before it found kindling in the cotton fields of the American South.

From Greek and Roman antiquity, through the Middle Ages of Christian monarchy and feudalism, right up to the early modern period, European cultures conditioned children to witness and internalize public violence as a social norm. That legacy of ritualized cruelty laid the groundwork for slavery, colonialism, and the lynching tree. When we trace the long arc of white participation in ritualized homicide, it becomes clear that lynchings were never about real threats posed by Black people. They were about reenacting an older, deeper trauma—transferring generations of unprocessed ancestral pain onto Black bodies. What looked like racial terror was often something more primal: white colonizers, disfigured by centuries of violence, offloading the rage their own histories had carved into their nervous systems. What we call racial violence was often ancestral anguish looking for somewhere to land. Somewhere to burn. As Walter White once wrote, these were not just mobs. These were bodies "demanding more victims."

Stay with me. The wind is shifting.

CHAPTER 2

From the Nursery to the Gallows

How Europe Rehearsed Racial Violence on Its Own Children

It is said so plainly, like a weather report: "In the days of George II it was no uncommon thing for children under the age of 10 to be hanged."[1]

Common.

To hang children.

Not just one. Not just a few. Sometimes, as young as nine.

This chilling recollection appeared in a 1932 issue of the *Nottingham Evening Post*, under the headline: "Youth on the Scaffold." It listed the public hanging of a nine-year-old boy at Chelmsford in 1831 for arson. A pair of siblings, Michael Hamond, age seven, and his sister, eleven, were hanged together in 1808 in the village of King's Lynn, for the crime of stealing. There was even a mass hanging of ten children at once. No names. No outrage. Only the numerical fact of their deaths. These executions were not random. They were choreographed warnings: Disobey, and you too will swing.[2]

The tone was cold, clinical, and eerily similar to how American newspapers would later describe the lynchings of Black people: tucked between soap ads, weather forecasts, and announcements for county fairs. Devoid of any sense of mourning, the *Evening Post* story was just a nod that times had changed as if the ritual killing of children was an outdated policy, not a generational trauma echoing across continents and centuries.

But the child executions weren't just local British horror. They were part of a global script. A culture of violence that took root in white bodies, rituals, and institutions, then boarded ships and crossed oceans, ready to replicate itself on new soil and demand new victims. The children who once gathered at the gallows in London became the progenitors of those who gathered at the foot of lynching trees in the American South.

Before white supremacy was a political regime, it was a parenting style. Before it organized nations, it organized households through fear, control, punishment, and the systematic breaking of children's spirits.

Long before the plantation, there was the parlor.

Before the rope, there was the rod.

The earliest experiments in domination did not unfold in foreign lands. They began in European homes, where small, weak bodies became the first test subjects in a long, unbroken rehearsal for empire. Long before Europeans turned their violence outward, they perfected it inward—on their own children—through infanticide, beatings, burnings, drownings, and public hangings.

The spectacle stayed the same. Only the scenery changed. And at the center, always, were children: watching, learning, absorbing. So, lynching in the US was not simply about race. It was the replication of power through a deeply internalized pedagogy of cruelty, and the continuation of Europe's long-standing legacy of anti-child violence. The violence inflicted on Black children in Jim Crow America was not an anomaly. It was the next chapter in a much older story.

Yes, other civilizations explored, warred, and enslaved. In a similar vein, childhood abuse existed elsewhere too; no culture is innocent. But no civilization constructed global systems so thoroughly rooted in dehumanization, extraction, and genocidal logic as Europe did. And while violence against children in many non-European societies was localized, inconsistent, or ritually limited, in Europe it was systemic and wide-ranging.

Europe was different. It systemized, normalized, and ritualized cruelty toward children on a mass scale in service of a global ideology. Public executions of minors. State- and church-sanctioned beatings.

Starvation as moral training. Emotional detachment as virtue. Shame as theology. Obedience as salvation. Parenting that trained children out of empathy and into domination or submission. Childhood itself was despised. These were not isolated customs. They were core pillars of cultural identity, sustained across generations, and became the emotional infrastructure of empire.

Colonization didn't begin with ships. *It began in the nurseries of Europe.*

From their first breath, children in Western cultures enter a world shaped by thousands of years of violence—where care and cruelty coexist in a fragile, often brutal balance. This legacy isn't an anomaly. As Lloyd deMause wrote: "The history of childhood is a nightmare from which we have only begun to awaken. The further back in history one goes, the lower the level of childcare, and the more likely children are to be killed, abandoned, beaten, terrorized, and sexually abused."[3]

If deMause mapped the nightmare, then Du Bois named the stakes. In *Darkwater: Voices from Within the Veil* (1920), he offered a haunting reflection: "In the treatment of the child the world foreshadows its own future and faith. All words and all thinking lead to the child,—to that vast immortality and wide sweep of infinite possibility which the child represents."[4]

Du Bois wasn't being sentimental. He was warning us.

When a society brutalizes its children, it does not merely injure individuals; it carves violence into its cultural bedrock. Generations of neglect, terror, and ritual cruelty didn't just leave scars. They cultivated a moral numbness and a psychic disfigurement that helped condition Europeans to enact colonial conquest, centuries of enslavement, and the lynchings of thousands of Black Americans. All of it foreshadowed by "the treatment of the child." The environments that shape children don't stay in the nursery. They reverberate outward, seeding the conscience of families, nations, and empires. And the world still lives with the consequences.

Du Bois wasn't just mourning the lost potential of children; he was inviting us to reconsider the moral architecture of the world built upon their backs. His insight compels a broader excavation, not just of what white people did after slavery but of what was done long before it. Most scholars trace lynching through a racial lens that begins with the aftershocks of the Civil War and the end of slavery. But I'm arguing something deeper. Older. The very capacity for racial violence was forged through the emotional, neurological, and ritual conditioning of white children, beginning thousands of years ago in Europe. Before they ever stepped foot on colonized soil, white children were already vessels of domination shaped by intrafamilial cruelty and sanctioned violence from the state.

We shouldn't just ask what white people did to others. We must ask what they did to each other, and how those internalized practices were later exported as empire. This approach destabilizes the neat binary of victim and perpetrator and forces us to confront inherited violence as ideology, as pedagogy, as emotion work. The argument is simple, but radical: *Child-rearing is the foundation of empire.* Because all people are children first. And what we do to children, we do to the world.

To understand the story of American lynching, we must excavate the psychological and cultural soil in which this violence took root. Without that foundational context, people may wrongly assume that lynching was a sudden eruption of racial violence after slavery, a Southern pathology, an American anomaly, or a reaction to emancipation. But lynching was the *continuation* of a much older tradition: the ritualized breaking of children as a form of social control.

Europe's gallows weren't just for criminals. They were pedagogical theaters. The home wasn't just domestic; it was *a training camp for domination*. Lynching, then, isn't the origin point. It's a transposition of a method already long rehearsed.

This chapter traces how European societies used stories, rituals of violence, and institutional power to normalize brutality and drill obedience into children through terror. These early emotional lessons became the blueprint for colonial violence, rendering it moral, inevitable, even divine. The emotional mutilation of those children became the psychological machinery of empire.

Most historians begin the story of American lynching in the aftermath of slavery and the rise of Jim Crow. But as we saw in the previous chapter with Reginald Marsh's *This Is Her First Lynching*, the violence of lynching was also a formative experience for white children. It was a ritual of emotional training, embodied, practiced, and passed down.

To understand how a child could witness such horror with calm curiosity, we must go back to Europe. To the nursery. To the scaffold, and the catechisms of cruelty where the child's apprenticeship began. Long before Africans were enslaved, European children were sacrificed on the altar of discipline, obedience, and patriarchal control. The child was the first body the state subdued. The tools used to break them, ranging from emotional detachment to public punishment and theological terror, became the blueprint for racialized domination in the New World.

This is the part of the story rarely told. Before whiteness was a racial project, it was a project of domination trained into the flesh of white children. By the time Europeans arrived in America, they had already been conditioned to torture and kill with moral conviction. That training didn't happen in secret. It happened in the town square, with children watching. Sometimes cheering. Sometimes crying. Sometimes playing. *Always learning.*

By mapping how fairy tales, religion, nursery rhymes, and public punishments shaped children's nervous systems, we will see how the emotional callousness required to attend (or perpetrate) a lynching was *not natural.* It was manufactured. Cultivated. Conditioned. In other words, white people didn't just wake up one day able to cheer for a hanging. They were neurologically groomed to be lynchers. This is the logical, horrifying culmination of generational emotional conditioning.

We will also see how empire begins in the nervous system. And when entire populations are emotionally mutilated in childhood, they build nations that mutilate others. Lynching isn't just a product of racism; it's a downstream consequence of an entire emotional regime that equates love with fear and obedience with worth. A culture creates executioners, lynch mobs, and spectators by breaking its own children first. Lynching was not an aberration but an escalation and a blood-soaked climax to a lifelong process of slow indoctrination.

Some people may see lynching as the collapse of civilization. No, lynching *was* civilization. A civilization built on early exposure to cruelty, spiritualized terror, and stories that taught that suffering is necessary, deserved, and divine. By the time a child watched a Black body burn or swing from a tree, they weren't shocked. They were witnessing what they had been taught to expect.

BOOGEYMEN AND CHILD-GUZZLERS

The transition from the nursey to the gallows was seamless.

In Europe, the seeds of violence weren't just planted in the town square—they were buried deep inside the home. Nursery rhymes and fairy tales—seemingly harmless—were actually the first lessons in a lifetime of violence. These stories, rooted in religion and folklore, carried messages that were darker than they seemed at first glance. This was educative violence: Children were terrorized into obedience by bedtime stories disguised as moral lessons. Steeped in fear and foreboding, these ghoulish tales trained children to associate disobedience with doom, preparing them for a lifetime of submission to harsh moral codes. And much of this messaging had already been laid down in the Bible.

Take, for instance, Adam's sin in the Book of Genesis. As Joseph Zornado notes in *Inventing the Child*, this wasn't just a garden mistake. It marked humanity as fallen, embedding in Western culture the belief that children are disobedient by nature. It's a foundational myth with a brutal moral: Disobey the father, and all humanity suffers. In this telling, death itself is the punishment for a child who won't obey.[5]

Obedience wasn't just a virtue. It was the spine of European childhood. Folklore didn't just reflect this. It reinforced it. The Brothers Grimm didn't just collect stories; they canonized Reform Calvinism for kids. Work. Cleanliness. Order. But above all: obedience. Obedience could save your soul. The ideal child was silent, obedient, invisible. That was the path to success. The stories were not just about obedience. They were about the consequences of defying it. Even nursery rhymes were early conditioning tools, teaching children that violence was normal. They were catchy lullabies wrapped in threat.

After the invention of the printing press, the monsters multiplied. Marina Warner describes how "child-guzzlers" (*Kinderfresser*) and "child-frighteners" (*Kinderschrecker*) spread across Germany on grotesque broadsheets. Their sole purpose was to terrify children into compliance. Even the Sandman, the sleepy bedtime figure, was a threat in disguise. Across cultures, his cousins were everywhere: Wee Willie Winkie, the Wolf at the Door, Tuatha Dé Danann, and the Man in the Moon. All whispering the same message: *Sleep, obey, or else.* Ogres that eat children. Death hiding in lullabies. These weren't just bedtime stories. They were weapons. Stories as tools of aggression, shaped to control. Bluebeards, ogres, and child-snatchers share a kinship with other malevolent spirits, forming a repertoire used by nurses, mothers, and fathers to either scare, cajole, or bully children into obedience and quiet. The fear of a child's demise becomes a dual-edged sword, simultaneously invoked as a threat and a means of control within the nursery environment.[6]

And when monsters weren't enough, adults used people. Gypsies. Jews. Turks. Blacks. Turned them into threats to keep white children in line. They became stand-ins for punishment. They were disciplinarian ghosts and a way for adults to outsource fear without getting their hands dirty. These groups serve as disciplinarian alter egos or stand-ins for harsh punishment, allowing adults to enforce rules without taking direct responsibility. The racialized bogeyman, with their diabolical practices, planted the roots of modern racism and xenophobia. Folklore didn't just entertain. It trained. It taught children who to fear and why. So, lynching didn't need new tools. It used the same psychological machinery that had long been used to terrify white children into obedience. It just aimed that machinery outward.

The Brothers Grimm turned fear of monsters into bedtime law. In their cautionary tales, disobedience didn't end in a lecture; it ended in blood. As Maria Tatar argues, true horror in *Grimm's Fairy Tales* isn't in revenge or monsters but in the warnings. Collected in the early 1800s, the Grimms' tales were violent morality plays, where good and even were split clean—no mercy, no nuance. The formula was simple: Break a rule. Get punished. Immediately. The moral? Adults are right. Children pay. Curiosity, disobedience, even questions were punished. The ending was almost always the same: The child suffers, the rule stands, and obedience wins. Power belonged to adults. They used it to crush deceit, curiosity, and defiance, often with glee. The Grimms made sure every child got the message.[7]

Nineteenth-century children's literature preached discipline like gospel. Lazy? Defiant? You'd be punished on the page and in real life. Some stories, like *Struwwelpeter*, went full horror, with bad kids losing fingers or burning to death. But even the tamer tales drilled the same image: The good child is obedient, quiet, and clean. In *Off with Their*

Heads!, Maria Tatar shows how British fairy tales joined the chorus, punishing disobedient children just like Grimms did. Disobedience was a vice. Curiosity, a danger. Punishment, inevitable. Every story was a setup: A rule is given, a child breaks it, and then the hammer falls. These were morality plays soaked in violence. These were two kinds of lessons: cautionary tales (break a rule, get hurt) and exemplary tales (follow orders, get rewarded).[8]

The moral was always the same: Obey or suffer. If a wolf eats you, it's not bad luck. It's because you didn't listen. If you turn into firewood, that's what you get for disrespect. Meanwhile, the good kids obeyed and were praised for staying silent, small, and obedient.

Violence wasn't just heard; it was seen. Medieval art blasted it onto walls and altars. Children appeared not just as innocents but as witnesses, and sometimes as victims, in a world built to glorify suffering. Scenes of crucifixion. Infanticide. Torture as devotion. Pain as piety. These weren't just paintings; they were lessons in holy violence. Artists called it spiritual instruction. But the scenes were blood-soaked. Christ in agony. Onlookers weeping. Children painted as cherubs or mourners, learning that godliness looks like suffering. Their presence wasn't decorative; it was didactic. Children in pain made the message unforgettable. Historian Mitchell Merback puts it plainly: "Children are brought [to public executions] for discipline, to have their wild impulses tamed by the spectacle of punishment."[9]

And then came the babies.

Infants slaughtered in paint and fresco—sometimes biblical, sometimes mythological, always brutal.

The Slaughter of the Innocents. Herod's blade in Bethlehem. Or mythic mothers throwing babies into rivers. These weren't stories for sleep. They were stories to shape the soul. You'll find it all: drowned babies, broken skulls, infants bashed and stomped, throats slit with knives and swords, little bodies flung against stone and walls. Whether the subject was war, religion, history, it didn't matter. If it involved children suffering, it made it to canvas.

As we'll see again and again, children didn't need to be killed to be broken. They just had to watch. Executions were staged to terrify them into compliance, showing what happened to those who dared to disobey, childishly or not. And for the children who didn't make it to the gallows, bedtime stories took care of the rest.

Historian V. A. C. Gatrell, in his book *The Hanging Tree*, tells of how Elizabeth Fry, who was later a famed prison reformer, was haunted by holy terror. After hearing the story of Abraham and Isaac, she feared her parents might sacrifice her too. "'Fear was so strong a principle in my mind, as greatly to mar the natural pleasure of childhood' and 'I believe my nervous system was injured in consequence of it.'"[10] Nothing says "Welcome to childhood" like thinking your parents might tie you up and kill you if God asked them to.

For children exposed to violent religious stories, the damage wasn't just spiritual; it was neurological. The developing brain is especially vulnerable to fear. These violent stories, such as the one where Abraham is willing to kill Isaac, didn't just live in the imagination; they lodged in the amygdala, the brain's fear center. Repeated exposure to terror, especially when it's framed as holy, can hardwire the nervous system for hypervigilance, disrupt emotional regulation, and compromise a child's ability to develop trust and feel safe. These aren't just bedtime stories. They're brain-altering events.

Picture it: a child in church, listening to the preacher praise Abraham for his unwavering faith. What they hear is, "God told a father to kill his son—and the father said yes." The child might wonder: *Could my parents do that too? Would they?* Suddenly, spilled milk and bad grades don't feel like the worst things that could happen. And sure, Isaac survives in the end. But what some kids remember isn't divine mercy; it's the moment Isaac realized his father was holding the knife. That trust doesn't easily return.

We know now what centuries of parents didn't: Fear changes the brain. Trauma, whether from real-life violence or stories soaked in dread, trains the nervous system to expect danger. Children raised in fear-based environments often carry that burden for life: anxiety, dissociation, damaged stress responses, difficulty trusting others. When children are taught that love equals sacrifice, that safety comes with a knife hovering overhead, it warps the very architecture of connection. And that distortion doesn't stop with them; it cascades across generations.[11]

This wasn't just fear—it was training.

Early exposure to violence in "innocent" narrative forms, through fairy tales, scripture, and nursery rhymes, primed children for more brutal lessons later. By the time they saw a real body swinging from a rope, it didn't shock them. It confirmed everything they'd been taught. Disobedience brings pain. Curiosity leads to death. Violence isn't just inevitable; it's righteous.

In every recorded epoch of Western history, exposing children to violence was seen as necessary for ushering them into adulthood.[12] Public executions were designed not just to punish the guilty but to send a carefully orchestrated message to the younger generation, shaping their beliefs and behaviors through fear. Those who did not attend these spectacles were still exposed to physical, sexual, and psychological voilence at home. Children were inundated with narratives of torture and death that reinforced the lesson that disobedience would not be tolerated. The cultural conditioning of European children, through stories, art, and public spectacles, laid the groundwork for the unimaginable brutality that would follow in the centuries to come. The legacy of these early lessons in violence and obedience continues to shape our world, perpetuating cycles of fear and control that began in the nursery and extended to the gallows.[13]

"A HOLIDAY SIGHT"

Lynching did not begin with Black death. It began with white childhood. The forgotten root system that nourished American lynching was European child-rearing practices soaked in spectacle, cruelty, and terror. Public executions weren't fringe events. They were cultural rituals. And more than that, they were *family-friendly*. Mothers lifted babies high so they could see. Famous poets and writers captured it. Doctors dissected the corpses. It was a society so desensitized that children learned their first moral lessons while watching bodies swing.

The public mutilation, the bloodlust, the eroticization, the crowd frenzy. The souvenirs made from skin. Fingers taken as trophies. Blood collected in cups. Audiences cheering. These aren't the twisted inventions of the American South. They're hand-me-down horrors from European forebearers. These practices migrated after they were tested first on white flesh and then perfected on Black people.

It was important that the children of Europe attend or even participate in the public executions of those who violated patriarchal rule. As legal historian Stuart Banner describes, this kind of punishment specifically aimed to terrorize young people in public. Popular belief held that for the death sentence to have its maximum impact, it had to be *seen*. "Not just seen, but seen properly," he writes. "An execution needed to be 'accompanied with circumstances of solemnity,' because solemnity 'would make a lasting impression on all ages, ranks, and characters—particularly on children and youth,' who turned up in large numbers, and who could be expected to take the lesson of terror most to heart."[14]

Victorian poet Coventry Patmore captured the chilling spectacle of children at executions in stark, unsparing verse:

They brought the man out to be hanged
Then came from all the people there
A single cry, that shook the air;
Mothers held up their babies to see,
Who spread their hands, and crow'd for glee . . .
A baby strung its doll to a stick;
A mother raised the pretty trick;
Two children caught and hanged a cat;
Two friends walk'd on, in lively chat;
And two, who had disputed places;
Went forth to fight, with murderous faces."[15]

Patmore's poem lays bare the brutal reality of children at executions. It exposes a society so steeped in violence that even infants absorb its logic.

The poem opens with the condemned man led to the gallows and a crowd buzzing with morbid excitement. As the man approaches his fate, there's an eerie sense of anticipation in the air. The line "A single cry, that shook the air" demonstrates the people's chilling, collective thrill at the coming death.

Children clap. Mothers lift up babies for a better view. A girl reenacts the killing with her doll. A cat is hanged. Children cheer. Patmore warns us: Exposure like this doesn't just warp individuals. It molds generations.

The children's play mirrors the execution. They aren't horrified; they're entertained. Violence was ordinary. Imitation was inevitable. There's no space for empathy in a world where killing is a family outing.

But this wasn't just cultural rot; it was strategy. Oppressive systems used violence to train children in complicity. The message was clear: This is justice. This is order. This is how we keep power. And once embedded in the child's mind, that logic didn't need repeating. It carried itself forward, generation to generation. As one study of white supremacy puts it: "Race fantasies are applied only at second hand to races; they are actually generated in the universal human setting of childhood and used by culture to handle its historical problems." To understand racism, we must first look at the psychic soil where it grows, "the infantile roots of mental experience."[16]

Oppressive systems have long used violence to instill fear, enforce obedience, and protect the powerful. This is why watching a woman hang became, for many men, a twisted sexual rite of passage.[17] The use of fear is particularly effective when applied as part of the process of socializing children into an unequal order. That is why attacks on childhood aren't accidental; they're foundational to race, class, and gender domination. Children watched the mutilation and drowning of the marginalized—poor thieves, drowned "witches," and foreigners—whose bodies were used to stage the limits of state power.

The carnivalesque ambiance commonly featured boisterous spectators partaking in various activities like drinking, fiddling, dancing, picking pockets, telling fortunes, having sex, sharing health remedies, and performing purification rituals and even touching the corpse for good luck. At some executions, surgeons waited nearby to collect bodies for dissection, the corpses' skin turned to book covers, skeletons scrubbed clean for hospital display.[18] Under the 1752 Murder Act, bodies were either dissected in public or left to rot in chains.

Elizabeth Hurren documents cases of hanged people waking up on the dissection table—only to die again under the surgeon's scalpel.[19] Rachel Bennett calls out the true purpose of this gruesome practice: The "post-mortem evisceration of the criminal corpse" in Scotland was designed to "add some further terror and peculiar mark of infamy to the punishment of death."[20] The goal was clear: Frighten the crowd, humiliate the dead. This culture of public torture, punishment, and desecration not only accepted and normalized the destruction of living human beings; it also sought to enhance the brutality of punitive measures by denying sanctity to the souls of the dead.

Judges handpicked surgeons. Corpses became teaching tools—for doctors and gawking spectators alike. In Scotland, many were sentenced not just to death but to dissection, performed in lecture halls before elite medical audiences. Between 1752 and 1832, Scotland dissected 110 executed murderers—85 men, 25 women. But demand outpaced supply. Some years yielded fewer than ten legal cadavers. And so began the body-snatching economy.[21]

William Burke and William Hare killed sixteen people to sell their bodies to a famous anatomy lecturer. Burke was hanged in 1829. In poetic justice, Burke's own corpse was dissected and turned into souvenirs.[22] Body parts were collectibles. So were bits of rope, tree bark, and blood-soaked dirt.

After James McKean was executed in Glasgow in 1797, his skin was flayed, tanned, and sliced into small circles, souvenirs for local gentlemen eager to own a piece of the killer. Burke's skin became a pocketbook, proudly displayed by Edinburgh police.[23]

In Europe, body parts of the executed were believed to hold magical powers. A fifteenth-century Franciscan preacher claimed that touching a rotten tooth with one from a hanged man could cure the ache. In seventeenth-century France, the power of invisibility was said to come from wigs made of a hanged man's hair, soaked in bird blood. In Germany, fingers from the executed brought luck to homes and businesses. If they were placed in stables, some claimed, the body parts soothed horses and improved their general well-being. The demand was so great it spawned fraudsters like Hans Moller von Dippertswald, who was caught selling fake thieves' thumbs.

In Spain, Inquisition records describe secret plots to steal body parts for use in spells. Corpses couldn't be touched until nightfall, so thieves waited for darkness to strike. A woman named Ana de Yuso confessed she tried to snatch either a finger from a hanged man or the rope that killed him, but someone showed up and spoiled her scheme. Others tried to steal hearts or hands but were interrupted—by passersby, scaffold guards, or nosy neighbors.[24]

Pause for a moment.

Does any of this sound familiar?

What you just read reveals a long, morbid obsession with death, where violence bled into folklore, superstition, and even shopping. The mutilation of Black bodies at American lynchings, the severed limbs, auctioned souvenirs, crowds pocketing ears and fingers, wasn't new. It was an echo. What was once done in Europe to white bodies—dismembered, fetishized, claimed as trophies—was perfected on Black flesh in America. These execution stories remind us that this brutality traveled. It crossed oceans. It took root in American soil.

These rituals left deep scars on child witnesses—on both sides of the Atlantic.

In early modern Europe, public executions weren't just tolerated; they were woven into everyday life, especially under Britain's "Bloody Code" from the late 1600s to the early 1800s. Lurid newspapers, cheap prints, and public gossip turned executions into spectacles that declared state power, bred fear, and rehearsed moral hierarchy.

In fact, the account of a four-year-old British child who saw the terrifying aftermath of a public hanging in 1804 illustrates this historical truth. At Hounslow Heath, on the outskirts of London, a man lured Charles Knight, a white boy on a routine walk home, by promising to show him "something curious." Knight was unaware of the horrors that awaited him, and he had no idea that the grim scene he was about to experience would permanently damage his impressionable mind for years to come.

In the pages of his memoir *Passages of a Working Life*, published six decades later, the now-famous novelist and publisher Knight described that terrifying event. Knight recalled the unsettling sounds of chains clanking and creaking through the air as the rusty iron plates of human-shaped gibbet cages revealed their grisly contents. There, before his eyes, were the tattered remnants of garments still clinging to the partially fleshed "horrible skeletons" of two individuals who had met their end through execution for crimes that likely entailed robbery, piracy, or murder.[25]

Instead of being buried, those criminal corpses languished in an eternal dance with death, suspended some thirty feet skyward for maximum visibility and studded with thousands of nails to keep them from being torn down. Their haunting presence served as a stern warning to passersby and nearby residents, who likely had to close their windows to avoid the horrible stench of decaying bodies. Over days, weeks, and months, those skeletal remains swayed in the breeze, acting as a shocking spectacle for all who beheld them.[26] This macabre scene was the playground of America's ancestors.

"That was a holiday sight for a schoolboy sixty years ago," Knight wrote in his memoir.[27]

A holiday sight?

Why do you think Knight described the rotting, putrid-smelling dangling skeletons of two criminals in such a peculiar manner?

As Gatrell puts it in *The Hanging Tree*, young Charles Knight and so many other European children grew up when the "grimy business of hanging" was ordinary.[28] Rotting corpses on display were as common in nineteenth-century Europe as church bells. These events were carnivals of cruelty—rowdy, joyful, and not unlike American lynchings of Black people a century later. Tens of thousands gathered at gallows, gibbets, and guillotines to watch bodies be torn apart.

Who died, and in what ways, illustrated the social order, organized by class, power, and religion. The condemned individuals were viewed not as inhuman but as sinners and lawbreakers who had forfeited their right to live. The state's power to kill was both feared and sanctified.

Imagine young Charles Knight being led toward the rotting corpses swinging in the breeze, an encounter that might have seared terror into any child's mind. Yet he would later remember it not with horror but as a "holiday sight." This unsettling recollection reveals something deeper than personal desensitization: This is the world Du Bois warned about—a world in which the seeds of collective violence are sown in the soft soil of early consciousness, cultivating moral numbness from the earliest years.

Knight's ability to reframe a scene of decay and death as something curious or quaint likely represents a psychological accommodation to the expectations of his society—one in which children were not merely permitted but encouraged to observe death as spectacle. His recollection lays bare the lasting effects of early exposure to public cruelty. It signals not only a loss of empathy but also a broader cultural lesson: that fear, pity, and moral revulsion can be displaced by fascination, detachment, or even pride. Knight's story offers a window into a society that ritualized violence as a means of shaping the next generation. It reveals how children, exposed repeatedly to suffering and death, came to see such spectacles as normal, even necessary. These children were not bystanders. They were apprentices. The rope around one neck taught a thousand eyes how not to look away. And they would grow into adults who carried forward the emotional logic of domination, reproducing its patterns across colonies, institutions, and racial hierarchies. As Du Bois understood, the treatment of the child foretells the character of the world that child will help build.

Knight's description may have been a psychic shield—a child's fragile barrier against horror. Or maybe time softened it, nostalgia tinting rot with warmth. Either way, the language betrays what the memory cannot hold: This was a trauma dressed as tradition.

As we read Knight's account today, we may find ourselves recoiling, our modern sensibilities shaken by the casual brutality he described. But to truly understand the world we live in, we must immerse ourselves in the world he knew—a place where the specter of violence loomed large, and life's harsh realities were impossible to ignore. Only then can we begin to grasp the complex emotions and experiences that wove together to create Knight's unique perspective on a moment frozen in time. His reaction to the decomposing carcasses on public display is consistent with the societal mores of the day. His was a *normal* childhood.

Historian Gatrell shows how British children reacted viscerally to the scaffold. He writes, "The scaffold's horror was seen freshly, and it was also unambivalently affirmed. It does not take dreadful stories like that of the 16-year-old in 1790 who, having watched a Bristol execution, hanged himself that day, his mind 'unhinged,' to make us realize that responses to the scaffold of the young were immediate as any we might encounter."[29] White children's well-being was never a priority in crime and punishment because they were used as dispensable tools for securing class and racial order for future generations. The elites and racists cared more about preserving whiteness and privilege than about the welfare of children.

Memories of public executions haunted Britons who witnessed them as children. In 1783, more than twenty years before Charles

Knight's encounter at Hounslow Heath, a young boy in Winchester witnessed the grim execution of a woman and her marine lover, hanged for murder:

"I was there along with the crowd. I sat on my father's shoulder and saw them bring her and the marine to the field. They fixed her neck, by a rope to the stake, and then set fire to the faggots, and burnt her."[30]

Similarly, on May 30, 1832, fourteen-year-old William Kelly's father took him and his cousin to see a murderer hanged in chains. "The scene around the gibbet was certainly most disgraceful, and truly 'like a fair,'" he recalled as an old man.[31]

Hans Christian Andersen, the Danish fairy-tale author who crafted tales about child abuse and other forms of violence, recalled an unsettling event from his adolescence. He witnessed a father collecting "a cup of dead man's blood" after an execution and administering it to his epileptic child, believing in its supposed healing properties.

This peculiar belief stemmed from widespread superstitions that drinking the blood of executed people could remedy an array of sicknesses and diseases. Monica-Maria Stapelberg notes that "for epileptics, this form of treatment was so popular that executioners routinely had their assistants catch the blood in cups as it spurted from the neck stumps of dying offenders. Epileptics waited at the scaffold as a beheading took place and drank the poor sinner's blood immediately while it was still fresh and warm." People stood in the crowd with "their faces smeared with blood like vampires."[32]

This appetite for blood wasn't limited to epileptics or the desperate. It bled into culture, into how people saw, remembered, and even eroticized death. Public executions weren't just rituals of punishment; they were stages upon which horror, wonder, fear, and desire played out before the eyes of children. And some of those children grew up to write about what they saw.

In 1856, sixteen-year-old Thomas Hardy, the famous novelist, climbed a tree near the gallows to watch a woman hang. In a letter many years later, he recalled how her face was barely visible through the rain-soaked hood, describing her with eerie eroticism: "What a fine figure she showed . . . against the sky as she hung in the misty rain. Her tight black silk gown set off her shape as she wheeled half-round and back."[33]

Across centuries and countries, European writers reflected on public executions they had witnessed in childhood or adolescence. Many of these accounts preserved memories that had remained vivid for decades. This wasn't limited to one region or era. Public executions were a shared childhood experience across Europe. The writers' letters and diaries preserve vivid memories of hangings, burnings, dismemberments, and beheadings. Dante, Pepys, Boswell, Goethe, Thackeray, Dickens, and Byron all wrote about what they saw—often in disturbing detail.[34]

Lord Byron, for one, was drawn to the spectacle. During a visit to Rome in 1812, he observed the simultaneous guillotine deaths of three robbers. He described the terror, the blood, the severed heads.

The first execution "turned me quite hot and thirsty, and made me shake so that I could hardly hold the opera glass (I was close, but was determined to see, as one should see everything, once, with attention)," Byron wrote. By the second and third executions, he felt nothing. "I am ashamed to say that [they] had no effect on me—as a horror."[35]

Byron's reaction offers a case study in how children become numb to violence. At the outset, he experienced both physical and emotional agitation during the first execution. Yet, as he continued to observe subsequent executions, his emotional response diminished, and he eventually admitted to feeling indifferent to the violence. His numbness reveals how repeated exposure dulls empathy. As Byron grew less horrified by the successive beheadings, he began to treat them as routine occurrences. Violence became ordinary. Moral boundaries blurred.

These cautionary tales are proof that early exposure to violence warps children's emotions and beliefs. These insights become even more poignant when considering the events that transpired two decades before public executions were finally outlawed in Britain. In his 1845 poem "The Murderer's Sacrament," written in response to the widely attended execution of François Courvoisier, Coventry Patmore captured this disturbing reality: Even babies were there.

TRANSATLANTIC INHERITANCE

The story Americans are told about European colonizers is tidy: They were fleeing persecution, escaping tyranny and religious repression in search of freedom. That master narrative casts them as victims-turned-heroes, saints in search of sanctuary. But what it omits, what it refuses to examine, is what they carried inside their bodies. Not just infectious diseases that would decimate Indigenous populations but something more enduring: a psychological inheritance. A nervous system wired by pain. A theology of obedience. A memory of the lash. A compulsion to repeat—what Freud described as the mind's drive to reenact old, unresolved trauma that's hardwired in the psyche.[36]

Their flight did not erase the imprint. Escape does not undo conditioning. The systems that oppressed the colonizers had already done their work. They brought with them the rituals of domination: sermons and straps, gallows and catechisms. Whippings delivered in silence. Obedience mistaken for love. Violence mistaken for virtue.

As Resmaa Menakem argues in *My Grandmother's Hands*, white Americans carry deep, unhealed trauma that originates not in slavery but in the centuries of brutality, war, class oppression, and rigid religious dogma that scarred European history: "Well before the United States began, powerful white bodies colonized, oppressed, brutalized, and murdered other, less powerful white ones. The carnage perpetrated on Blacks and Native Americans in the New World began, on the same soil, as an adaptation of longstanding white-on-white practices."[37]

This legacy of embodied terror traveled across the Atlantic with white immigrants, etched into their nervous systems. And as Mark Wolynn explores in *It Didn't Start with You*, that trauma didn't vanish with time or distance; it replicated. Passed down epigenetically and emotionally, it shaped behavior, stress responses, and worldviews, often without people's conscious awareness. Rather than confronting or healing these wounds, many white settlers displaced them and reenacted their ancestral pain through participation in white-supremacist violence.[38]

The colonizers of the Americas, men and women alike, had been broken in as children. Their emotional circuitry had been rewired to feel safest under submission, to mistake control for care. Before they ever dominated racialized others, they had been disciplined into submission by their own families, communities, and governments. So, when they arrived on new shores, they didn't need to invent cruelty. They simply needed new bodies to practice it on. The early lessons in domination didn't just vanish—they metastasized into American schools, courtrooms, prisons, and policing practices. The same pedagogies of control that broke European children were institutionalized in the colonies, now aimed at Black and Indigenous populations.

What had been rehearsed on generations of Europeans? A script of domination so brutal, so precise, that it would one day be exported and renamed "civilization." In a world where children might have symbolized possibility, Europeans rendered them as problems, irrational, sinful little beasts in need of subjugation. That subjugation was sacred, ritual, institutionalized. The gallows, the guillotine, the gibbet, the breaking wheel, the pyre, the whip, the locked cellar—these were pedagogical instruments and generational tools of "correction."

And the correction began early.

This treatment, rooted in the systematic dehumanization of the most vulnerable, laid the groundwork for entire civilizations of domination. It stripped childhood of innocence, leaving scars, traumas, and moral injuries that calcified into the psychic infrastructure of empire. Europe's brutality toward its own children wasn't just a private cruelty. It was a public rehearsal. A harbinger. A foreshadowing of the social hierarchies and institutions that would come to define the Western world: systems animated by inequality, calloused by repression, emptied of empathy. And so, the child who was beaten in the name of righteousness grew up to build nations on the backs of other people's children. This is how violence made its way into the bloodstream of modernity.

Unlike precolonial societies around the world that viewed children as deeply spiritual, as beings full of potential who should be guided *gently* into adulthood, European religious and philosophical traditions cast the child as innately lawless, ruled by appetite, immorality, and the devil. Childhood was not a time of wonder. Elites, anxious about the disruptive force of those left undisciplined, have historically viewed children as existential threats to the social and economic systems they benefit most from and seek to preserve.

This fear of the child's innate wildness fostered a sadistic tradition of cruel punishment and execution, where the "childlike" lawbreaker was publicly disciplined. These public events played an edifying role for spectators, especially for actual children, for whom public displays of torture and death served as a reminder of the mortal danger of remaining in their natural state of playful spontaneity and impulsiveness.

It was not enough to punish the offender; the real target was the child watching in the crowd. These spectacles taught obedience through horror and sent the following message to children:

Grow up fast.
Be quiet.
Be good.
Or hang.

The terrorization and degradation of European childhood, both conceptually and practically, involved the abuse of children's physical, emotional, and psychological well-being through exposure to violence. It unfolded in two forms. The first, what we might call *educative violence*, occurred in the home, the church, the classroom, delivered by those closest to the child and masked as love, discipline, salvation. The second form, *corrective violence*, was administered by the state through the courts, the police, the penal system, and the gallows. These forms were a public demonstration of what happens when education had failed and punishment took over. In Western cultures, both social and state brutalization were long conducted in public and have only recently become private.

Virtually every child raised in a European society for the past two thousand years of recorded history was subjected to some form of violence at the hands of parents, teachers, or slave owners.[39] Lloyd deMause and other historians have painted a grim and brutal picture of childhood in Western societies. European parents historically inflicted severe physical punishments on their children, using weapons like cat-o'-nine-tails, shovels, canes, iron rods, and sticks. Infanticide was widespread owing to poverty, the desire to control family size, the elimination of political rivals, and the belief that children with physical or mental disabilities were the result of demonic influence, and the act often went unpunished. In ancient times and throughout the Middle Ages, roughly between 5 and 10 percent of newborn children were killed by those meant to care for them, with both the poor and the ruling elites engaging in the practice.[40]

In addition to being directly subjected to violence, children bore witness to a grim tableau of public atrocities including torture, disembowelment, burning, hanging, and other forms of government-sanctioned murder. The main lesson of public execution was that if a child did not do their best to work toward civilized maturity, they would be dealt with. Historian Louis P. Masur highlights multiple examples of the solemn warnings that were articulated to youthful witnesses at the hangings of other condemned youth. Masur recounts the 1805 execution of seventeen-year-old James Hall in Dedham, Massachusetts, before which the condemned youth delivered a scaffold warning to the crowd of young spectators: "Do not CHEAT—DO not STEAL—Do not LIE—Do not commit ADULTERY—Especially, do not destroy VIRGIN INNOCENCE—and, above all, do not KILL."[41]

White societies have always been concerned with ensuring the quality of its generational successors, the inheritors of national, and later racial, identity and privilege. Violence was a necessary educational tool. To maintain authority and order through time, this violence needed to be intergenerational. It was essential that children be disciplined both as witnesses and as potential victims of capital punishment. This socialization and habituation would normalize and naturalize the subordination of the vicious, sinful, and irrational to the virtuous, pious, and rational.

The civilizing process leaves its mark. As Norbert Elias observes in his classic work, *Power and Civility*:

> The wounds of the civilizing conflicts incurred during childhood may heal; the scars left by them may not be too deep. But in less favourable cases the conflicts inherent in the civilizing of young humans—conflicts with others and conflicts within themselves—remain unsolved, or, more precisely, though perhaps buried for a while, they may open up once again in situations reminiscent of those of childhood. In these cases, the suffering, transformed into an adult form, repeats itself again and again, and the unsolved conflict of a person's childhood never cease to disturb his or her adult relationships.[42]

Elias's insights into the civilizing process of white children in Western cultures help illuminate the roots of racialized violence in America. The coercive systems he describes were embedded into the fabric of everyday life, beginning in antiquity and stretching forward through medieval and early modern Europe. Children were routinely subjected to brutal punishments and degradation, both in private and in public.

The archive of historical child-rearing practices reads like a manual of torture. Children were burned, shaken, thrown into rivers, buried in manure heaps, starved, castrated, thrown into fires as sacrifices, cooked and eaten in fertility rituals. Some were poisoned. Others were rolled in snow until they froze. Some were sealed within walls or foundations of buildings and abandoned in forests to be scavenged by animals.

In ancient Greece, a disobedient son could be mutilated, his tongue, eyes, or fingers cut off. Infants born with deformities were often killed to preserve "ideal" racial characteristics. Sexual abuse was also pervasive. Young boys and girls were kept as "pets," sold into slavery, or prostituted by their parents to pay off debts.[43]

The history of childhood in the West is a history of discrimination, dehumanization, exploitation, and violence.

You might be thinking, Certainly *not all Europeans* treated their children terribly throughout history!

As in any society, there were surely exceptions and variations in how children were treated. But my goal is not to demonstrate that *every* culture in European history abused children. Instead, what I want to show you is that the dominant philosophical, legal, and social frameworks of the primarily white Christian culture, which shaped European attitudes and informed the New World project, did systematically abuse children. This is a matter of public record, documented by countless historians before me.[44] Maybe there was a Celtic tribe or cuddly pagan family culture unrecorded by anthropologists or historians that existed in peaceful kinship with children, *but none of these folks settled in the colonies or became the founding fathers of America.*

The lynching of Black children in America is the predictable outcome of the practice of killing children in the European cultures that informed the American racial project. I use the term "Europe" as shorthand for various European societies that were cruel to children, with a particular focus on northern and western cultures. While I am primarily referencing the brutality documented within the British Isles, since this is the most direct cultural and legal predecessor of American racial violence, in no way was such cruelty exclusive to British societies. Looking as far back into the history of Britain as we can, you'll find no record of peaceful parenting. Anglo-Saxon youth, like Irish, Celtic, and Viking youth in ancient times, were enslaved or offered as servants to other families and, even when raised by their own families, were "raised with great severity" and regular beatings.[45] All available evidence suggests that violence toward children was ubiquitous across Western time and geography, from ancient Mediterranean society through subsequent medieval European civilizations structured around the Abrahamic religions: Christianity, prevalent in northern and western Europe; Islam in North Africa, the Iberian Peninsula, and the Middle East; and Judaism in Eastern Europe.

Looking south from Britain, life was no better for kids there. The Moors massacred children in their conquest of what is now Spain. Later, during the Spanish and Portuguese Inquisitions, officials terrified, imprisoned, tortured, and publicly executed children for over four hundred years. Nor was there any refuge to the east during the thousand-year reign of the Byzantine Empire, in which children were treated like servants just as they had been in ancient Greece and Rome.[46] Nor was there any during the next five hundred years of the Ottoman Empire; even as Qur'anic scripture extolled the sanctity of youth, still children in large sections of Muslim Europe endured sex slavery, military slavery, and general cruelty in almost all facets of life, especially in the domain of education.[47] Like the Moors and their ruthless conquering of the Iberian Peninsula, the Abbasid Caliphate did not seem bothered by the task of cruelly executing children during the sack of Thessalonica in AD 904. Whatever disagreements regarding Christian child-rearing, Islam hardly presented a check on the prevailing culture of violence toward children.

Again, not every European society that was cruel to children became a colonizing force in America or elsewhere. The Polish-Lithuanian commonwealth did not engage in colonial expansion, as it was regularly under siege from the Ottoman Empire, Russia, and Sweden. Likewise, landlocked Switzerland launched no fleets of colonial ships, though it certainly funded them. These and other European nations may not have established far-flung imperial claims, but they nevertheless shared the same culture of child maltreatment with England. This is important to note because although America began as a British colony complete with inhumane British institutions, American slave owners traced their ancestry to virtually every city on the European continent. Men from Warsaw and Geneva may not have amassed colonial fortunes, but once in America, they had no qualms about trading African slaves with the descendants of Englishmen.

Why?

Because despite cultural differences, they all shared a common conventional ethos of intergenerational violence and cruelty toward the child and, by extension, the "child races." There is simply no history of a safe place for children among the large majority of these cultures.

This widespread culture of cruelty toward children took root in the homes, schools, and churches of Europe, shaping how childhood itself was imagined and governed. Before we can understand how this violence evolved into colonial policy and racialized terror, we must first understand how Europe came to define childhood in the first place.

When exported abroad, these ideologies didn't just animate slavery or military conquest; they reshaped education itself. Colonial and missionary schools became violent laboratories for imposing European notions of discipline and civility onto child victims of colonization. Generations of Indigenous and African children were stripped of language, identity, and autonomy, their minds and bodies subjected to the same regimes of control that had been perfected on European soil.

The goal here is not to paint every European household as a horror show, but to expose how the normalization of childhood subjugation laid the psychological groundwork for global domination. This is where we move from memory to method—from the emotional residues of intergenerational trauma to the documents, debates, and omissions that have shaped our historical understanding of what it meant to be a child in the so-called civilized world.

When historians refuse to examine how children were treated in Europe, they leave the roots of white supremacy untraced. They tell a story of empire without telling the story of how empire was first practiced. And without that story, the violence that followed can too easily be seen as a deviation rather than the logical consequence of centuries of sanctioned cruelty.

We can tell a different story if we view Europe as a place where the concept of childhood as innocent or protected did not yet exist, where children were worked, beaten, and killed. These abuses were not tragic exceptions but expected rituals of social order. What happened later in the colonies was not an invention. It was an export.

According to some historians, the modern concept of childhood as a distinct and protected phase of life, characterized by innocence and freedom from violence, did not begin to take hold in Europe until the early seventeenth century. Before this period, children generally did not possess the right to be free from violence. This was a right that was reserved for adults, who viewed themselves as morally superior and free, while children were immoral and unfree. Historical records, including diaries, letters, autobiographies, and medical reports, provide ample evidence of the routine mistreatment of children throughout history.[48]

The terrorization and degradation of European childhood was both a conceptual and material process rooted in sustained violence against children's bodies and minds. The two forms of violence against children's bodies and minds—educative and corrective—reinforced one another. What began in the intimate spaces of home, church, and classroom was echoed in courts, prisons, and at the gallows. Private discipline rehearsed the logic of public punishment, and public spectacle legitimized everyday domination. There was little pretense that this brutality needed to be concealed.

In both domains, children were not protected from violence; they were trained by it. Violence did not simply terrorize children—it prepared them for usefulness. Discipline shaped bodies that could be controlled, deployed, and exploited. Archaeologists have determined that "children formed an important constituent of the Late Bronze Age economy." They were identified as servants in the classical era and, in the Middle Ages, were sent away to serve in elites' residences, preferred "because they were cheaper to hire, had no dependents and could be trained up into whatever capacity was needed." It is instructive to note that between the sixteenth and nineteenth centuries, "60 per cent of the English population aged between fourteen and 25 were servants."[49]

Even though children in England were not regularly executed, their sentences often reflected their status as expendable labor. In one late eighteenth-century case, after a ten-year-old English boy was condemned to death and the "crowd in court 'expressed their horror of such a child being hanged,'" officials commuted his sentence and instead ordered him to be transported to the British colony for fourteen years of labor.[50] Historically, much of the instructive violence enacted on children was private and enforced by members of the household, but in exceptional circumstances officials would condemn children to death. Though relatively few were executed, the threat of execution hung over the heads of disobedient children in Europe.

For many years, historians have debated about how children were conceptualized in ancient times. A landmark contribution to the debate was the 1962 book *Centuries of Childhood*, in which author Philippe Ariès argued that the idea of childhood, as we understand it today, is a relatively recent development, an attitude about the young unknown to the ancient Europeans. Children were not viewed as special or vulnerable, so they were treated poorly. Perhaps the most cited counterargument is Linda Pollock's 1983 *Forgotten Children: Parent-Child Relations from 1500 to 1900*, which argues that violence against children was already rare by the Middle Ages. She bases this claim almost exclusively on the absence of accounts of such violence in the diaries of adults, suggesting that since the historical documents we would normally consult—such as artistic depictions of children, parenting manuals, educational manuals, travelers' accounts, children's dress, and infant mortality records—don't really tell us how people actually raised their kids, we must rely on diaries written by adults about their childhoods. Pollock also makes the argument that in cases where violence against children occurred or when parents chose to abandon their children, we must consider the historical, cultural, and economic circumstances that likely left otherwise loving parents with few alternative options.

Forgotten Children would go on to be widely cited. However, this argument didn't sit well with some critics who immediately pointed out that Pollock's methodological approach suffered from adult-centrism, meaning it was too focused on what grown-ups thought and ignored the actual lived experiences of children. All Pollock could demonstrate, given her restrictions on evidence, is that adults who were well-heeled enough to keep a diary (mostly in the eighteenth century) didn't see violence against children as remarkable enough to bear mention.

Barbara Hanawalt observes that, in the Middle Ages, "corporal punishment was normal in dealing with children who misbehave."[51] And, of course, it is simply a fallacy (specifically, that of *argumentum ex silentio*) to deduce from the absence of comment in the diaries of eighteenth-century elites that, therefore, children were rarely hit. The absence of evidence is not evidence for absence. Furthermore, studies like Pollock's often downplay certain less severe forms of physical discipline against children as so commonplace and conventional as to be inoffensive. Such discipline is sometimes depicted as benign because it is part of a comprehensive parenting approach in which adults also recognize the importance of reasoning with children.

Pollock's work is typical of the revisionist apologetics sometimes found in childhood history studies, works that tend to excuse past adults as constrained by tradition or circumstance while disregarding the voices and experiences of the child victims. We would never apply similar leniencies when examining the historical abuse of women by men. We would never claim that the lack of violence against women in the diaries of men proves that women were rarely abused. Nor would we claim that men were so constrained by patriarchal norms that they had no choice but to be reluctant abusers. We would also never claim that because it was considered normal to use violence against women "at the time," it would be anachronistic for us to claim that such women were actually "abused."

Scholars do not always extend this same level of consideration to children, whose harsh treatment in the past has been marginalized or overlooked. Whereas women could prove their rationality and, therefore, their full humanity, children would remain powerless and categorically excluded. It is essential to recognize this disparity in historical approaches to abuse, and to offer children the same level of consideration and empathy granted to other marginalized groups who have suffered throughout history.

When scholars neglect to recognize the mistreatment of children, both public and private, we come up short in gaining a comprehensive understanding of the evolving dynamics between children and adults, a crucial foundation for perpetuating all kinds of toxic ideologies, behaviors, and oppressive systems across successive generations.

Although public executions of children were far less common than those of adults, they did occur, and their ritual significance cannot be dismissed. As V. A. C. Gatrell demonstrates, English courts did not categorically exempt minors from capital punishment, even if the fact of their youth sometimes prompted clemency or commutation.[52] Archival execution records compiled by researchers such as Dave Mossop confirm that children were executed in Britain from at least the mid-sixteenth century (beginning with Alice Glaston in 1546) through the nineteenth century (ending with Charles Robinson in 1866).[53] These cases include children ranging from the youngest (John Dean, aged eight or nine) to those who were nineteen at the time of their execution. Though statistically rare, the cases reveal a legal culture willing to subject children to the full symbolic machinery of the gallows. The record of official public executions of children is far from exhaustive in light of the innumerable children who were unofficially killed by adults who took justice into their own hands. There is no official record of their brutal ends.

This record reveals a society grappling with notions of criminal responsibility, deterrence, and the value placed on young lives. The public nature of these executions served in a minor sense as punishment for the condemned, but far more important was the stark warning they issued to other youths and the broader community.

As public attitudes began to shift in the nineteenth century, we see a gradual reduction in child executions and an increasing tendency to commute death sentences for younger offenders. This evolution reflects in part the changing perceptions of childhood, criminal responsibility, and the effectiveness of capital punishment as a deterrent, but even more, it was the desire to maintain order in the streets, which ultimately led to legal reforms in the twentieth century, that would drive the prohibition of executing criminals in public.

The public execution of white children in Europe was not merely a form of sanctioned punishment; it was a spectacle designed to instill fear, maintain control, and solidify societal hierarchies. As these practices were carried across the Atlantic to North America, they evolved within the context of colonialism, slavery, and racial terror. The normalization of violence, once used to control and discipline European children, found new targets in the racialized violence against Black children. The deeply ingrained cultural acceptance of public punishment and execution, learned and internalized in Europe, set the stage for the horrific practices of lynching that would later terrorize Black communities in America.

So, what became of those children?

The ones who watched bodies sway from ropes like wind chimes of warning. Who saw blood turned to medicine. Who played executioner with dolls and cats. Who were handed fear as inheritance and told it was law, told it was right.

They did not forget.

They carried it across borders, across generations, across oceans. And when they arrived in America, they did what they had been taught: They turned spectacle into doctrine. They traded gibbets for trees. They found new children to hang.

In the next chapter, we cross the Atlantic and descend into the Jim Crow South, where the brutal lessons once rehearsed on white bodies were perfected on Black ones. Where Black childhood itself became a target, a threat, a pretext for terror. What Europe called justice, America called tradition.

The rope was the same. Only the victims changed.

Don't look away. That's the luxury they had. You don't get it. Turn the page.

CHAPTER 3

"My Son Can't Learn Too Young the Proper Way to Treat a Nigger"

The Transatlantic Legacy of Public Execution and the Lynching of Jesse Washington

Day dawned, and soon the mixed crowds came to view
The ghastly body swaying in the sun
The women thronged to look, but never a one
Showed sorrow in her eyes of steely blue.
And little lads, lynchers that were to be.
Danced around the dreadful thing in fiendish glee.

—CLAUDE MCKAY, "The Lynching" (1922)

We leave behind Europe's haunting scaffolds, creaking guillotines, weathered nooses, and iron gallows. We move past the iron chains of gibbet cages, where bodies once swayed like eerie lanterns above jeering crowds. These were places where bloodthirsty crowds—men, women, and children—once roared in approval at public killings. Their cheers are now distant ghosts. But we cannot leave behind the child who witnessed these atrocities.

For while these horrific scenes may have faded from Europe's landscapes, their echoes reverberated across the Atlantic. They traveled in the minds and bodies of settlers, carrying centuries of intergenerational trauma and violent lessons learned in childhood. They brought ancestral memories of brutality—wars, executions, inquisitions—etched into their bones from childhood.

Early European settlers came from societies that had systematically trained them, from the nursery onward, to see violence as moral instruction and domination as duty. Conflicts like the Thirty Years' War, the Spanish Inquisition, and the English Civil War weren't just episodes of bloodshed. They were eras when generations of children were raised amid terror, witnessing punishments designed to drill obedience. These memories, collectively internalized, inevitably shaped how colonizers imagined order, punishment, and racial hierarchy in the New World.

While some colonizers arrived with a superiority complex the size of the Atlantic, many early settlers were poor, persecuted, or fleeing harsh conditions, not seeing themselves as oppressors. But they were not blank slates. Many were convicts who might have faced execution in England had they not been transported to the colonies of North America and Australia. Banishment was the better option.

They carried not just smallpox and disease but the culture of oppression beaten into them as children: religious zealotry, a ruthless drive for conquest, and blind faith in punishment as social glue. As they built new lives in America, those traumas and lessons bled into their laws, rituals, child-rearing, and the violent enforcement of racial hierarchies. They embedded dehumanization into American life, carrying childhood conditioning they could never escape.

They enacted that violence on the most vulnerable—indentured servants, women, children—as well as on Indigenous peoples, enslaved Black people, and other colonized populations. Practices of domination honed in Europe were carried into colonial expansion, where they were institutionalized within racial hierarchies and legal regimes. The violence of their past became the violence of their present, spilling over into the colonized world, where old traumas gave rise to new systems of oppression. The scars of violence learned in Europe became the tools to build and maintain control in America, shaping racial hierarchies and institutions.

We now move across space and time, from Europe's gallows, guillotines, and scaffolds to the heart of Waco, Texas, from early modern Europe's bloody rituals to the early twentieth-century American South, focusing on the 1916 lynching of Jesse Washington.

Our subject shifts from European children watching state executions as moral lessons to white American children eagerly attending community lynchings as lessons in racial terror. The victim changes too, from condemned criminals and heretics in Europe to a Black teenage boy. The mechanism of violence evolves from state-enforced obedience to mob-orchestrated racial domination. And the ultimate principle transforms—from loyalty to monarch or church to the enforcement of white supremacy and Jim Crow's racial hierarchy. Now, in the heart of Jim Crow America, those brutal Old World child-conditioning rituals have found new life. And once again, we see children at the center of this evolved colonial inheritance.

"A NECKTIE PARTY"

Waco, Texas. May 15, 1916.

This wasn't the Middle Ages, with cheering crowds at burnings and beheadings. It wasn't the Spanish Inquisition, with institutionalized torture in the guise of religious purity. It wasn't the witch hunts of early modern America, where women were drowned or burned at the stake for imagined sins, nor the guillotine executions of revolutionary France. No, this was twentieth-century America, a nation that prided itself on progress, civilization, and democracy.

And Waco was no backwater town. It was prosperous, with telephones, flushing toilets, good schools, libraries, and modern amenities. Waco was home to several institutions of higher education, including Baylor University, a self-described Christian college, and one historically Black college, Paul Quinn College. This was the time of our grandparents or great-grandparents, much closer to us than the era of medieval atrocities. Yet the same capacity for savagery burned beneath the surface of "modern" America. In Waco, the instruments of death evolved, but the thirst for torture remained unchanged.

Beneath the relentless sun, somewhere between fifteen thousand and twenty thousand well-dressed, straw-hatted merrymakers clustered around the red-brick city hall in this thriving middle-class "progressive" community. Men, women, and children gathered to watch a "necktie party" for seventeen-year-old Jesse Washington, a "wonderfully built" Black farmhand who had allegedly confessed to raping and killing Lucy Fryer, his white employer's fifty-three-year-old wife.

Plans for the party had begun the day before, as crowds poured into town, swelling even more in the early hours of the morning. Local businesses closed shop for the day and thousands traveled in on trains, much like they had done in the Old World on hanging days when entire towns paused to witness public death.[1] A caravan of cars, trucks, buggies, and horses clogged downtown Waco's main streets.

The first guests to arrive that day were *children*. They charged into the grassy city hall plaza, "running, leaping, glancing back over their shoulders as they urged their comrades toward the square."[2] Their small feet pounded the dirt, their faces were flushed with excitement, eyes wide with anticipation. High-pitched laughter and eager shouts rang out as they raced toward a spectacle they were too young to fully understand and too conditioned to question. Their inexperience twisted into complicity as they rushed toward the site of racial terror.

Lured by yelling in the streets and the blaring of a fire alarm, students from Waco High School rushed out of their classrooms after being let out just before lunch to join the show. As the mob swelled with new arrivals, children climbed trees to get a clear view, while smaller children were lifted onto adult shoulders, held by their ankles as if they were at a ball game. These opportunities—for children to climb trees, leave school early, and get hoisted onto shoulders—all sent a clear message that this was a festive event for all ages.

The early arrival of these schoolkids shows how deeply embedded lynching was in the fabric of the community. Just like generations of European children before them, they were socialized into a voyeuristic culture of violence. A lynching wasn't seen as a grim event to be shielded from but rather as a form of familial and community bonding, a mass celebration. It offered not just instruction in racial hierarchy but a deeply perverse lesson in power: the thrill of controlling and desecrating another's body, a lesson in both violence and sexual domination passed down to even the youngest witnesses.

A small boy was paid an undisclosed sum to gather slats of wood, dry goods boxes, crates, and trash to build a pyre beneath a tree, ominously located just below the mayor's office window. What do you think may have been running through that child's mind as he set out to complete this ugly task? Was he simply focused on the coins promised for his labor, unaware of the horror he was helping to construct? Or was he so desensitized that it felt no different than fetching firewood for a family bonfire? One can imagine him feeling a quiet thrill, a sense of belonging in playing even a small role in something larger.

Perhaps, deep down, there was confusion as the pyre took shape, hinting at a purpose too dark for his young mind to grasp. His young brain, still developing moral judgment, may not have grasped the gravity of what he was doing. At his age, children are often motivated by simple rewards and may focus on the task, not its larger implications. And yet his developing mind might still have felt moments of unease. Children may lack abstract reasoning but begin recognizing fairness and empathy early. The pyre may have hinted at a darkness he could feel in the pit of his stomach but couldn't yet articulate.

Like many children, he might have trusted that because adults directed him, the task was acceptable. Or perhaps he didn't see it as wrong because his family and community routinely condoned and celebrated such horrors. The boy's task wasn't just labor; it was part of his civic role in maintaining the racial order.

As thousands converged on the plaza, Waco's mayor, John Dollins, phoned local photographer Fred "Gildy" Gildersleeve, telling him that "the proper moment" had arrived to come capture the triumph and pleasures of this "spectacular" community event.[3]

A short while later, the impish photographer in his floppy golf hat rushed into City Hall and up three flights of stairs, where his cumbersome equipment was already set up: A big box camera. Tripod. Flash pan and powder. Plates of negatives and a black cloth. He planned close-ups of the Black boy under the tree, wide crowd shots, and an aerial view from the roof. Gildersleeve didn't just document the lynching; he framed the killing of a Black teenager as something akin to art.

Mayor Dollins and Police Chief Guy McNamara waited by the open window as Gildy arrived. Gildy set his camera in front of the window and focused his lens on the big tree ten feet below. He ducked his head underneath the black cloth covering his camera and waited.

"GET THE NIGGER!"

As we move forward, I must caution you—what follows is a graphic and deeply disturbing account of Jesse Washington's brutal murder. The details are harrowing. I urge you to brace yourself for the raw, unfiltered violence inflicted in one of the most horrific spectacles of racial terror in American history. And remember: Children were actively involved.

A few blocks away from the mayor's office, Jesse Washington's hurried trial, which began at 10 a.m., was wrapping up in the 54th District Court of McLennan County. The courtroom was packed beyond capacity. The muscular, developmentally delayed teen lived in Robinson, a small farming community seven miles from Waco, with his parents and eleven siblings. A week earlier, Washington was accused of raping Lucy Fryer and beating her to death with a blacksmith hammer. A confession was obtained, likely under duress. Washington, who could not read or write, signed the document with an X.

When word spread of the teen's alleged confession, the *Waco Morning News* warned it would "cause the hot blood of the Robinson countrymen to flame and cry for protection of their women and homes against the lust of the brute."[4] This statement shows the media's crucial role in inciting and justifying racial violence. With inflammatory, dehumanizing language, the press turned Washington into a monstrous threat to the white community. The description of his alleged crime as "the lust of the brute" served as a dog whistle, provoking public outrage. The paper's rhetoric, which linked Washington's alleged crimes to a broader threat against white women and homes, went beyond reporting. It actively fanned the flames of racial terror. The phrase "hot blood of the Robinson countrymen to flame" called for vigilante justice and preemptively justified the violent mob action that followed. The media became complicit in shaping the public fury that ultimately led to Washington's lynching. At the time, newspapers wielded enormous power as moral and social authorities within their communities. The *Waco Morning News* carried significant weight, shaping public opinion and guiding the community's response. The paper abandoned all journalistic responsibility to report facts impartially, opting instead to stoke fear and justify violence.

At 11:22 a.m. the verdict was read.

"We, the jury, find the defendant guilty of murder as charged in the indictment and assess his punishment at death."

"Is that your verdict, gentleman?" asked Judge Richard Monroe.

They answered yes.[5]

Among the all-white jury that found Washington guilty after just four minutes of deliberation was a convicted murderer with a suspended sentence. Washington's appointed attorneys made no effort to cross-examine witnesses or present any meaningful defense. This was no surprise: Lawyers and police often withheld exculpatory evidence to ensure easy convictions, especially for Black defendants. Washington's trial was rigged from the start, with everyone complicit in a deliberate miscarriage of justice. It was never meant to be a legitimate pursuit of justice but rather a procedural formality to rubber-stamp a predetermined outcome.

Judge Monroe turned to the 1,500 spectators jammed in the gallery and said, "The prisoner has been given a fair trial, as fair as any ever given in this court."[6] By declaring the process fair, the judge ensured the violence could be framed as justice rather than as a deviation from it. His declaration was met with applause. The white audience didn't see the trial as a farce but as a rightful proceeding reinforcing racial order.

A hush fell over the courtroom as Judge Monroe wrote in his docket: "May 15, 1916: Jury verdict of guilty—" The entry stopped midline as shouting exploded from the back of the courtroom.

An aerial view of the torture and lynching of Jesse Washington, photographed by Fred Gildersleeve.

"*GET THE NIGGER!*" a big fellow in the back of the courtroom yelled.

The stenographer quickly packed his notes and slipped out a side door with the sheriff. They knew what was coming. Though Judge Monroe had firearms at his desk, he made no effort to stop the mob. When asked to intervene, he coldly replied, "Do you want me to spill innocent blood for a nigger?"[7]

The mob rushed so quickly they knocked over reporters and court staff. They dragged Washington out the back door and down an iron staircase into an alley where bloodthirsty men and youths attacked. The teen shrieked and struggled as a chain was tied around his body and hitched to the back of a car. His attackers cut off his overalls and calico shirt with pocketknives. They pelted his naked body with bricks and stones and distributed pieces of his clothes as souvenirs. There weren't enough pieces of clothing, so someone cut off an ear as a keepsake. A young girl watching from an office window saw a man sever Washington's penis; others said they saw a member of the mob "carrying the proof around in a handkerchief as a souvenir."[8]

Why did they cut off his genitals?

It is almost unthinkable to ask, but necessary. This sadistic mutilation was more than an act of racial hatred. It was driven by fear, control, and a perverse sexual fascination that cannot be divorced from the underlying pedophilic dimensions of lynching. By "pedophilic dimensions of lynching," I mean the way mobs targeted Black boys with sexualized violence that was both normalized in these rituals and taboo in wider society—a perverse contradiction that made the cruelty even more transgressive.

A severed penis was a highly prized souvenir at lynchings. Crowds hated, envied, and desired it for its perceived potency and threat. But it's more than that. White men were sexually fascinated with the bodies of those they subjugated: women, children, enslaved and newly freed Black people. White men sought mastery over Black bodies, nothing illustrating it more than the practice of keeping them as tokens. It's a serial killer mentality.

By casting Black boys as hypersexualized threats to be dominated, lynching mobs engaged in a form of racialized pedophilia. The sexual mutilation of Black boys was both an expression of their dehumanization and an assertion of white male control over Black reproductive life. The violence was not just about the physical destruction of a body but about reinforcing white supremacy through a ritual of sexual and racial power. Castration, particularly of young Black boys and adolescents, was a ritualized act of sexual fascination and domination. The act of stripping away their masculinity before they could fully embody it asserts control over Black bodies, futures, and reproductive potential.

It wasn't enough to kill Jesse Washington. This was about sending a terrifying message to Black parents and the broader Black community about generational eradication. It sent the message that Black boys would never be allowed to grow into men capable of having and protecting their families, asserting their autonomy. It was a reminder to Black parents that the aspirations they held for their children could be violently and irrevocably destroyed at any moment. There will be no grandchildren. There will be no future.

For Black children witnessing or hearing about this kind of violence, the psychological toll would have been profound. Hearing of a Black boy mutilated signaled they too were vulnerable—that no matter how much they aspired to grow, succeed, or protect loved ones, they could be rendered powerless. It sent a haunting message to Black youth that their bodies weren't their own, that their genitals could be taken and passed around among white strangers, and that society would go to any length to control them. It was a brutal way of saying that their lives could be dismantled with the same ease as their elders' lives were.

Ordinary people participated in the brutalization of Jesse Washington and turned the event into a collective, violent ritual. The *Waco Times-Herald* reported:

> On the way to the scene of the burning, people on every hand took a hand in showing their feelings in the matter by striking the negro with anything obtainable; some struck him with shovels, bricks, clubs, and others stabbed him and cut him until when he was strung up, his body was a solid color of red, the blood of many wounds inflicted covered him from head to foot.[9]

The article didn't shy away from describing the grotesque and excessive violence. Black suffering was consumed and reported as spectacle, further dehumanizing the victim. We have these hideous details of lynchings because of the work of reporters. But what of those reporters? What were they thinking?

Editors became increasingly profit-driven, recognizing that lynching coverage attracted large, voyeuristic audiences. By publishing such graphic accounts without condemnation, the *Waco Times-Herald* helped perpetuate a culture of racial terror. Instead of critiquing the brutality, the report's factual tone reinforced lynching as a normalized method of racial control.

"PEOPLE GONE MAD"

Twenty-five. That's how many times Washington was stabbed before reaching the tree where the pyre had been prepared earlier by that young boy. Gory stains marked the foot trail left behind by the victim. According to one report Washington, with tears reportedly rolling out of his eyes, prayed and cried out to "God Almighty to have mercy on his soul, that he was innocent."[10]

Do you believe that Washington uttered those words?

I ask because although this statement was widely circulated by the white press, such an account must be approached with skepticism; the press often ventriloquized victims, attributing words they may never have spoken. The purpose of putting these words in Washington's mouth, or that of any lynching victim, served multiple functions in controlling the narrative. By portraying Washington as desperate and repentant, the white press reinforced existing stereotypes of Black males as guilty and sinful, even when they claimed innocence. His supposed plea for mercy fit a script that portrayed Black people as spiritually inferior or inherently deserving punishment, with prayers framed as admissions of guilt.

By the time Gildy's camera framed the half-conscious, writhing boy in the eye of that giant jostling circle of angry spectators, his naked body was drenched and glistening red with blood. The mob had decided that a hanging was too good. It baited the lynchers for a drawn-out show.

"BURN HIM! BURN HIM!" the crowd chanted.[11]

While Washington's parents and brother William sat in a local jail "for safe keeping," the teen desperately grabbed at the chain in a futile attempt to escape. Such resistance was not uncommon in lynchings. Some victims threw pieces of wood and rocks at the crowd, while others cursed their captors and the white people around them. In rare instances, when victims summoned "superhuman" strength to break free, the mob would drive them back into the flames with metal rods and shovels. Despite the near impossibility of escape, these victims fought back however they could—cursing, resisting, asserting their humanity. White mobs sought not only to kill but to crush the will to fight back, ensuring any hint of rebellion was smothered.

Jailing Washington's parents and sibling during his lynching was a calculated act of psychological and racial control. It isolated his family, reinforcing their powerlessness by forcing them to experience the helpless terror of being unable to intervene. It also sent a chilling message to the Black community: Not only could their loved ones be executed without justice, but they themselves were subject to arbitrary detention.

As Washington twisted his body and gripped a nearby chair, members of the mob stepped forward and cut off a few of his fingers. The crowd cheered wildly. Kerosene oil and gasoline were splashed onto the boy's body. "People pressed forward, each eager to be the first to light the fire," a reporter from the *Waco Morning News* wrote. Matches were thrown. Flames shot high and licked around his body as the crowd gasped with delight. Their cheers mingled with Washington's agonized shrieks. "As smoke rapidly rose in the air, such a demonstration as of people gone mad was never heard before."[12]

As Mayor Dollins watched the savage spectacle from his office window, he complained about the mob ruining the beautiful foliage on a good tree.

To prolong the sadistic torture, a large white man with a rag in his hand gathered the hot chain wrapped around Washington and threw it over a tree limb, then jerked Washington's gasoline-soaked body into the air. The boy's tongue shot out of his mouth like a jack in the box. His eyes bulged from his sockets and rolled from side to side. His body was lowered again into the fire—up and down, up and down, up and down. Washington's choking cries and groans cut through the smoke rising to the sky as his skin sifted down through the coils of the chain and his arms and legs curled back. The odor of burning flesh did not stop the crowd's cheers or make them flee the scene. According to a few reports, the large white man who kept up this maniacal torture for about an hour or so was William Henry Frazier, a hard-drinking farmer known for beating his sons with a buggy whip as they worked the fields.[13]

I want you to think about these questions: What kind of man could take part in such sadistic violence, lowering and raising the body of someone else's child into flames, over and over again? How does a father's brutality within the confines of his family shape his capacity for public violence? Should we be surprised that the same hands that whipped his own children in the fields also lowered the body of somebody else's child into flames?

The fact that Frazier was known for beating his sons is far from incidental. It's part of a deeply entrenched pattern where cruelty in the white family's private sphere extended seamlessly into public racial terror. Frazier's violence toward his children was of a piece with the brutality he inflicted on Jesse Washington. His role in this atrocity was not an isolated act but part of a larger culture that normalized violence within white patriarchal families. The pattern is clear: The violence Frazier inflicted on his sons—those under his direct authority—was a precondition for the sadism he exhibited in Washington's lynching. Beating his children with a buggy whip wasn't just about punishment—it was about power and control. His pleasure in controlling and harming others was evident in both private and public spheres, as the boundaries between family violence and racial violence blurred. His domestic violence wasn't a separate issue; it was part of the very same mindset that justified lynching—a mindset rooted in sadism, domination, and dehumanization.

In the crowd of thousands, a white father hoisted his young son onto his shoulders to ensure the child had a clear view of the gruesome spectacle. When asked if it was inappropriate to let his child witness such violence, the father reportedly replied, "My son can't learn too young the proper way to treat a nigger." The deliberate exposure of Black suffering to white children, coupled with the casual attitude displayed by this father, made this violence an educational tool.

Meanwhile, young boys remained perched in the trees for a clearer view of the horrific display. If you examine the old black-and-white

A crowd of men and boys gather around the charred body of seventeen-year-old Jesse Washington as other adolescents watch from trees.

photos closely, you can see shadowy figures of adolescent boys mingling with the branches, eager for a front-row seat to the brutality. According to a report published in *The Crisis* magazine, "A little boy was in the top of the very tree to which the colored boy was hung."[14] He went unnoticed by the massive crowd until the thick smoke began to overwhelm him. Firefighters eventually rescued the boy from the branches, where he sat transfixed by the sacrifice below.

A Black youth was being burned alive and white people didn't even notice that one of their own children was choking on the smoke and was only rescued at the last second! The moment was truly emblematic of America.

As we continue scanning the haunting scene in Gildersleeve's aerial photograph of the lynching, something else stands out among the sea of white faces: the presence of a few Black people scattered in the crowd. Does it surprise you that Black people were there that day, witnessing this brutal spectacle? What could have drawn them to this unimaginable horror? Were they there because they believed in Washington's guilt, or were somehow complicit in the punishment? Or were they forced to attend, compelled by the white community to stand silently as a warning to others—to reinforce the ever-present threat that white people held absolute control over their lives?

Another photo taken that day shows white attendees with their heads turned, eyes fixed on the Black onlookers. What were they watching for? Perhaps they took perverse pleasure in seeing terror on Black faces, knowing the fear of lynching simmered just below the surface. For some whites, it wasn't enough to simply participate in the ritualistic violence; it magnified their pleasure to see Black people's horror, to make them feel small and powerless under the weight of white supremacy.

But perhaps those Black faces had other reasons for being there. Maybe some were standing in solidarity with Washington, ensuring that he wouldn't die alone, bearing witness to his suffering in a quiet act of resistance. They might have known, deep in their bones, that this was not justice but terror in its purest form—a display of power masquerading as punishment. They might have been there to carry that story to Black newspapers, to NAACP offices, ensuring the world knew of the atrocity, setting in motion activism to challenge lynching.

There's also the possibility, as chilling as it is heartbreaking, that some of those people were Washington's own family. Maybe they were his kin, there to claim what was left of his body once the mob had finished. To stand there and watch, helpless and grieving, knowing they would soon be retrieving the charred remains of their loved one—such a thought is almost too painful to imagine, but the possibility looms large.

We can only speculate. The voices of those Black witnesses have been erased from the historical record, silenced in a way that mirrors Washington's own fate. Their presence, however, forces us to confront the complexity of this moment. These were not passive bystanders. Whether there in fear, solidarity, resistance, or grief, their attendance makes the scene even more unbearable—a testament to how lynching functioned not just as violence but as psychological terror, silencing some while forcing others to bear witness and carry the weight forward.

The photos taken that day would be quickly duplicated into postcards, stamped by Gildersleeve, and sold for ten cents as celebratory souvenirs to be collected or passed along as gifts. Ultimately, they were a way for all of America to relive and enjoy the terror. They were cultural artifacts that preserved the memory of the lynching for generations. They, like the illustrated fairy tales of the Old World, were more than mementos; they were tools for indoctrinating future generations of young whites into a culture that celebrated racial violence and turned a heinous act into a source of profit and pride for America.

"ANSWERING THE SMILE OF HEAVEN BLUE!"

While conducting research for this chapter, I came across an old, yellowed copy of the Waco High School yearbook from 1916, the same year seventeen-year-old Jesse Washington was lynched before a crowd of thousands at City Hall. Remember, the students of this class were let out of school to witness the lynching.

Its brittle, fragile pages smelled of mildew and time—a musty reminder of Waco's long-forgotten past. As I turned the crumbling pages, I wondered what stories lay hidden in its fading ink—stories from the same students let out of school to witness one of America's most brutal lynchings. Turning the pages of the book is a chilling experience, each page seeming to carry the weight of both innocence and horror, beauty and brutality. The irony, hypocrisy, and contradictions within this context are profound.

Let's begin with the class poem by student Reba Renick:

Daisies growin in Time's memory garden,
Loved by laughing sun and cooled by dew,
Flowrets from a mystic, magic Arden,
Answering the smile of heaven blue!

See, we pluck you for our festive garlands,
Petals white, of promise, pure and fair,
Clustering round the center, golden-hearted,
Honesty and truth are hidden there.

Winding, weaving, twining each loved flower
With immortal blossoms of the past,
Thus the chain forever and forever,
Grows and lives with each succeeding class.

Daisies growing in Time's memory garden,
Loved by laughing sun and cooled by dew,
Flowrets from a mystic, magic Arden,
Answering the smile of heaven blue![15]

Renick's poem takes on an eerie, unsettling quality when read in the context of Jesse Washington's lynching. At first glance, its focus on nature, beauty, and innocence seems harmless, even idyllic. Daisies, sunlight, dew, and a "magic Arden" suggest a celebration of youth and time. Yet when considering these same students witnessed Washington's lynching that year, the poem becomes disturbingly out of place, even grotesque. The line "Answering the smile of heaven blue" is particularly jarring. It's difficult to reconcile this image of a smiling heaven with a crowd cheering the torture and murder of a Black teenager. What strange fruit was this heaven smiling at? The sky these students saw that day wasn't peaceful; it was filled with smoke and the cries of a lynched boy. The beauty described in the poem feels like a willful distraction from the violence embedded in the culture of Waco at the time.

The description of "honesty and truth" being "hidden there" deepens the unsettling tone. How could these words be written in a place steeped in racial terror and hypocrisy? The reference to "honesty and truth" seems especially hypocritical when juxtaposed with the deep dishonesty of justifying Washington's death as "justice." The poem's idealization of nature and purity seems designed to sanitize, ignoring the brutal realities of the time. In the same semester that students witnessed a lynching, their yearbook celebrated "immortal blossoms" and "festive garlands," as if poetic nostalgia could erase the ugliness of the world around them. The line about a "chain forever and forever" that "grows and lives with each succeeding class" takes on a grim undertone.

In the context of 1916 Waco, this poem reads less like a nostalgic tribute to youth and more like an eerie, oblivious denial of the horrors unfolding around these students. It reminds us how easily beauty and innocence can be invoked to distract from violence and injustice, creating a dissonance between the words on the page and the dark reality those words attempt to mask.

Then there's the photograph of William Poage, a fifteen-year-old sophomore at Waco High School who went on to serve forty-two years in Congress. Was Poage, like his classmates, in that crowd watching Washington's murder? What did witnessing such brutality do to the minds of the young people in that town? Future leaders and lawmakers might have been shaped by this experience before graduating to the nation's halls of power.

Even more troubling is the image of a teacher, captured in both the yearbook on a page titled "Faculty Snaps" and in one of Gildersleeve's photographs, standing near Jesse Washington's charred body. A figure tasked with guiding and educating young minds was close enough to the lynching to pose in photos afterward. He and others responsible for shaping young people's moral and intellectual development were complicit in acts of racial terrorism.

Gildersleeve took many of the photographs that fill the pages of this yearbook, crafting carefully posed scenes of white students basking in moments of trivial joy—smiling, playing, and learning. These were the same students who, only a month earlier, had stood in a jeering crowd to witness the public lynching of Jesse Washington. His camera frames them as innocents, yet their participation in Washington's brutal murder stains every candid smile. What makes Gildersleeve's work even more grotesque is its breadth: He also captured Black life through his lens, documenting local church choirs, joyful mortgage-burning ceremonies, and even students at Paul Quinn College, the oldest historically Black college west of the Mississippi. Gildersleeve made money photographing these dignified moments—moments of pride for Black families—yet he showed no hesitation when it came to photographing the sadistic degradation of a Black youth from that same community. A contradiction at the heart of America.

The same man who earned a living off documenting everyday Black humanity also immortalized Jesse Washington's dismembered body. Gildersleeve's camera continuously clicked through the obliteration, treating the charred corpse as just another scene to be captured and sold. There was no moral dilemma, no second thought—whether it was choir members lifting their voices in praise or a burning corpse surrounded by thousands, it was all just another photograph, another payday. His lens did not discriminate between life and death, between beauty and horror; it captured both with the same cold detachment. Gildersleeve's photographs served two purposes: to affirm the humanity of Black people through joyful images while also profiting off their dehumanization through gruesome spectacle. It's as if his camera held a perverse duality—offering recognition on one hand and annihilation on the other, while never once flinching. A grim reminder of the sinister economy built on racial violence and spectacle.

The yearbook doesn't just reflect a class of students; it reflects a society that used beauty to mask brutality and raised its children to accept, participate in, and even celebrate unspeakable acts of violence. The smiles in the yearbook stand in stark contrast to the cries of Washington, and the flowers in the poem wilt under the weight of a lynching tree.

Gildy got the shots he wanted—close-ups and aerial. A shot of men and boys smiling, gazing at the hideous crisp and calmly considering their handiwork. His photos proclaim: *Here is a dead nigger!* They communicate to other viewers that those in attendance had done their civic duty to preserve white supremacy. In their faces, you can see the solidarity and pleasure over their cruel work.

"ENOUGH TO MAKE THE DEVIL GASP IN ASTONISHMENT"

It wasn't unusual for spectators to debate shooting the victim to end his agony. Sometimes armed men would riddle the body with bullets. But not this time. The Waco crowd opted to let Washington suffer as much as his life allowed. Can you imagine that the last thing Washington heard in his short life was the monstrous jeers, laughter, and applause of thousands of wild-eyed white people all around him?

Washington had been dead for hours as spectators milled about. The men parted to let giddy women and children get a closer look and take turns spitting on his smoldering, creepily cooked remains. The *Chicago Defender*, a leading Black newspaper, reported that when the flames subsided into glowing embers, the spectators "hacked with pen knifes the fingers, the toes, and pieces of flesh from the body, carrying them as souvenirs to their automobiles."[16]

Links from the chain used to string up Jesse Washington were sold for twenty-five cents. This tokenizing of Black bodies was not unusual. Crowds sometimes crushed victims' bones into fragments to sell for a quarter or auction off to the highest bidder. Like their European ancestors, white lynching spectators would chop off pieces of the hanging tree, collect blades of grass with the victim's ashes, and strip the entire scene for mementos. As Harvey Young notes in "The Black Body as Souvenir in American Lynching," obtaining body parts provided "material evidence of your presence" and a testimony of your participation at a lynching.[17]

When the crowd finished pawing and hunting for souvenirs, Washington's body was strung up again and set on fire until all that remained was a charred torso. He suffered one final indignity when his charred corpse was placed inside of a canvas sack, lassoed to the back of a car, and dragged through the main streets of a Black neighborhood as young boys ran behind. At some point, the teen's head came off. The boys scooped it up, sat it on steps, extracted his teeth, and sold them for $5 each. They weren't horrified or afraid to pick up a severed head and reach into its charred mouth to pull out teeth. Instead, they seized the moment as an opportunity to engage in commerce.

As chilling as this moment was, those boys did exactly what untold numbers of white children were expected to do at a lynching: Cheer on the men, gather kindling, keep the fire going, and auction body parts.

Enslaved people were subject to similar brutality, as their teeth were extracted either for punishment or profit.[18] In Europe and early America, the teeth of soldiers killed in battle were often collected from the fields after wars. Scavengers harvested teeth from the dead to sell to dentists, who crafted dentures from them. By the time those Waco boys pulled Washington's teeth in 1916, they were participating in a centuries-old economic practice that taught them, on a subconscious level, that human remains could be sold or traded like any other commodity. The boys' act was not simply a spontaneous moment of cruelty but the culmination of a long lineage of white entitlement with regard to Black bodies, which existed for white use, whether for labor, entertainment, violence, or profit. The adults who purchased Washington's teeth sanctified white children's participation in racial terror and murder. For the boys, the exchange was their baptism into the fraternity of whiteness, which requires the systemic, intergenerational, ritualistic destruction of Black bodies.

For some, eating or socializing after a lynching was a form of emotional distancing—normalizing or trivializing the unspeakable, signaling it wasn't a deviation but an accepted, even sanctioned, part of daily life.

But I wonder, what kind of conversations took place in the homes of the boys who sold Jesse Washington's teeth that evening? When they sat at their dinner tables, what did they say? Did their parents—if they hadn't themselves been part of the bloodthirsty crowd—ask them how their day went? Did those boys casually mention they had spent the afternoon profiting off a murder? Did they empty their pockets, proudly displaying their gruesome loot like prizes won at a fair?

Can you picture it? After the excitement, they were likely fed supper, maybe given milk, then tucked into bed as if nothing extraordinary had happened. Their hands, still tainted with the horror of the day, folded neatly under their pillows, while their minds drifted to sleep in the same peaceful homes that had incubated such indifference to the violence inflicted on Black bodies.

And what of Jesse Washington's parents and siblings? What was the mood in their home that night? Was it one of shock so deep it stilled the air?

Did silence hang like a heavy fog, too thick to break with words?

Or were there bursts of anger, the kind that boils over into trembling hands and clenched fists?

Were there tears—hot, endless tears—or the kind of deep, guttural wailing that only the heart of a grieving mother can summon?

Did they fall to their knees in prayer, or were they frozen in place, paralyzed by a grief too immense to comprehend?

Did vengeful thoughts flicker behind their eyes, or was their sorrow too consuming for anything but the weight of loss?

We will never know the answers to these questions, because the voices of Washington's kinfolk have been permanently muted in the historical record. The silence of the parents, siblings, and family members of lynching victims like Jesse Washington speaks volumes about the profound trauma and fear that permeated Black families during these periods of racial terror. This silence is a testament to the oppressive weight of white supremacy, a forced muteness that reflects the unimaginable grief and powerlessness Black families endured in the face of violent retribution. The lynching of a Black youth was an act of terror meant to traumatize and subdue the entire Black community.

The absence of these narratives perpetuates a void in understanding the psychological warfare waged on Black households, the erosion of safety, and the enduring scars of witnessing a child's humanity erased in a spectacle cheered by neighbors. Without centering these perspectives, we fail to grasp lynching's true aim: to traumatize generations, embedding a legacy of racialized terror that reverberates in unanswered questions about survival, memory, and the unspoken resilience required to endure.

It's hard to fathom such communal barbarism meted out onto a young person, isn't it? The famous Black Harlem Renaissance writer

James Weldon Johnson summed it up best when he wrote that Washington's lynching was "enough to make the devil gasp in astonishment."[19]

I am not the first historian to reconstruct the lynching of Jesse Washington. His murder is famous among historians and stands as one of the most iconic and scrutinized lynchings in American history because it was captured in photos as it unfolded. The *Chicago Defender* noted that "the crowd was made up of some of the supposed best citizens of the South. Doctors, lawyers, businessmen, ministers, and Christians (posing as such, however), looked upon the scene with approval." Idaho's *Blackfoot Optimist* newspaper said, "Citizens of Waco, Texas broke through the thin crust of civilization and fried another nigger." *The New York Times* said the "lynching had been carried out apparently by the whole population of the place."[20]

Waco's leadership and white residents tried to quickly forget the horrible event, which hurt the city's reputation and proved bad for business. "Yesterday's exciting occurrence is a closed incident," declared the *Times-Herald*. But Washington's lynching drew denunciation across the country and became a cause célèbre for the NAACP, which raised thousands to expand its anti-lynching campaign and pressed for federal anti-lynching legislation. The NAACP's *Crisis* magazine ran an eight-page investigation featuring Gildy's photos and dubbed the event "The Waco Horror."

THE COMMODIFICATION OF BLACK DEATH

It's important to acknowledge that many of the photographs of lynched children featured in this book are images I had to purchase from digital news archives, often for significant sums of money. Even decades after their brutal deaths, these children are still being commodified. I wrestled with this deeply. Every time I acquired one of these photographs, I was forced to confront the uncomfortable reality that, in a way, I was participating in the same system that continues to profit from their suffering. These images—originally sold as souvenirs to white spectators—now carry a different kind of price tag, but the transaction still feels wrong.

I grapple with knowing I'm purchasing images capturing the last horrific moments of these children's lives, their dignity stripped away in death as in life. Yet I recognize that to tell their story—to remember them, not just as victims but as children full of potential whose lives were stolen—I must confront this brutal history. These images, as disturbing and heartbreaking as they are, hold a necessary place in the fight to document and honor the truth. Still, the fact that they remain a commodity in any form is a reminder of how little has changed in the way Black pain is consumed and profited from.

On one hand, we should be grateful that Gildersleeve and other photographers and journalists captured and preserved this awful history. Their images serve as undeniable evidence of the brutality and racial terror that lynchings inflicted on Black communities, a reminder of the violence that shaped America. Without these photographs, it might be easier for some to dismiss or downplay the extent of these atrocities. These visual records force us to confront the ugly truth head-on, ensuring that the horrors of lynching cannot be erased or forgotten.

But even in that gratitude, we are left with an inescapable bitterness, a deep disgust for these same individuals. They weren't acting as neutral observers or moral witnesses; they were often part of the spectacle, complicit in the dehumanization of Black bodies. Gildersleeve and others didn't capture these images out of a sense of justice or empathy—they did it to profit from the suffering, to offer a gruesome souvenir for white spectators to collect and pass down. They turned Black death into a commodity, reducing human lives to spectacles for white pleasure, and preserved these moments not out of a sense of moral responsibility but because there was a market for Black suffering.

We are left wrestling with this contradiction: recognizing that these images are necessary for confronting the truth of America's violent history while despising the motives and cruelty behind their creation. It is the paradox of needing the proof but hating how that proof came into being, knowing that even in death, Black bodies were exploited, captured, and consumed for the entertainment and satisfaction of others.

One thing that stands out about the news coverage and scholarly analysis of Jesse Washington's lynching is how often the seventeen-year-old is described as a "man." Reporters, police officers, and coroners frequently "aged up" Black victims, labeling children as adults, even after their parents corrected them. By framing Washington's murder as a crime against an adult, the narrative erases the deeper reality: Black children were frequent targets of racial terror, with white children participating in that violence.

This distinction is significant because it distorts our understanding of the true nature of racial violence. Treating Washington's lynching as a crime against an adult removes the context that this was an atrocity rooted in the terrorization of Black youth as part of a broader strategy to maintain white supremacy. By repeatedly describing Black teenage victims as "men," the media and official reports justified the violence, subtly reinforcing racist notions of Black youth as threatening and mature beyond their years.

Moreover, failing to recognize Washington's youth covers up the role childhood played in the violence, both in terms of who was targeted and who actively participated in these spectacles of cruelty. By ignoring this, we miss how violence against Black children, and the culture of violence that made white children cheer it on, were central to the racial indoctrination that maintained Jim Crow's social order.

I want to make clear that Jesse Washington merits more than a passing mention when we tell the tragic history of lynching. He is more than just another victim in a long list of brutalized Black bodies, more than a symbol of racial terror. Jesse was a seventeen-year-old boy with a life full of potential—someone who should have had the chance to grow, dream, and live beyond the boundaries that Jim Crow society imposed upon him. His name, his story, must stand as more than a grim footnote in the history of American violence.

In telling Jesse's story, I want to restore him to his rightful place in history, not as a faceless victim but as a human being whose life was violently stolen. I want to honor him, to remember that he was a son, a brother, and a teenager with hopes and fears like any other young person. His death was not just a singular act of cruelty; it was a wound inflicted on an entire community, a reminder of the everyday terror Black people faced simply for existing. Jesse deserves to be remembered for more than the horror of his death. We must see him as the person he was and the person he could have become had he not been torn from this world in such a monstrous way. In writing about him, I hope to lay him down to rest peacefully, to give him the dignity and recognition that was denied to him in life.

As I close this chapter, I want to make something unmistakably clear to white readers: I have foregrounded *your children* in this story because they are not innocent bystanders. They were active participants in the violence. The boys who laughed, cheered, and collected pieces of Jesse's body as souvenirs weren't just the byproduct of a cruel society. They were intentionally nurtured by it. This was the behavior modeled to them, and they absorbed it with terrifying ease. These were your sons, your nephews, your grandchildren, your students—children molded into monsters by a culture that celebrated racial violence.

We witness in this moment the warning W. E. B. Du Bois gave us, a caution against the mistreatment and moral corruption of children. We witness the imperative that James Baldwin gave us: "These are all our children, we will all profit by, or pay for, what they become."[21] What becomes of a society that allows its children to be victims of, bear witness to, and participate in acts of sadistic brutality? It's not just Black bodies that suffer but the very souls of white children. By feeding them hate and racism, you turn them into murderers in the light of day, unashamed, emboldened, and deeply damaged by the violence they are taught to enjoy. Let Du Bois's warning ring loud and clear: When you mistreat and corrupt your children in the name of hate, you create a future defined by violence, where the next generation of white children is just as dehumanized as the Black victims they're taught to brutalize.

I center these white children not just to indict the past but to offer a reminder of what happens when a society dehumanizes its children: We destroy our future. Generations of white children were groomed to become the enforcers of white supremacy, to uphold a brutal system of dehumanization. And in doing so, they showed up in public spaces acting like monsters, without a shred of compassion or humanity. This is the legacy you must confront: the normalization of racial terror by children who were witnesses and accomplices to the horror.

To understand how a nation produced such horrors, not as aberrations but as civic rituals, we can't look only at the blood-soaked stage in Waco. We have to go back. Back to the older stories that reveal how this culture was built piece by piece, life by life, law by law.

In the next chapter, we will leave behind the Jim Crow South and return to colonial New England, to examine the hanging of Hannah

Ocuish, a twelve-year-old mixed-race girl executed by the state. Because the story of American lynching doesn't begin with mobs in Texas. It begins with a scaffold in Connecticut, where even children were taught that death could be righteous punishment, and that some lives could be disposed of to maintain social order. To see the roots of the tree, we must dig deeper into the soil in which child-killing first took root in America.

You may ask, why didn't I begin this story in colonial New England and the hanging of Hannah Ocuish? Because I needed you to see first, without flinching, just how complete and perfected the ritual of racial violence became by the time it reached Jesse Washington. I needed you to see the blood and smoke of Waco before we trace the roots back to the scaffold in Connecticut. Because these spectacles did not emerge fully formed from the American earth. They grew from older traditions of public punishment, from the quiet conditioning that trained children to see death as justice.

In the next chapter, we will see how that seed was planted, to watch the moral lessons of execution take shape in the killing of a child by the very institutions sworn to protect her. Only by understanding that beginning can we truly grasp the depth to which America sank and how white children in Waco could one day sell charred teeth and pass around genitals in a handkerchief without a flicker of remorse.

CHAPTER 4

"The Time for You to Die Is Come"

White Christianity, Profit, and the Ritualized Killing of Children in Colonial America

It began in the cold, stern quiet of a colonial courtroom. Judges and ministers invoked God's justice. Juries decided even a child could be condemned to die to preserve order. This was the root system beneath the lynching trees of the Jim Crow South.

Long before Jesse Washington was burned before thousands in Waco, a twelve-year-old girl named Hannah Ocuish was hanged by the state of Connecticut. Of Black and Pequot descent, she was marked as an outsider—easy to scapegoat, impossible to save. Her execution wasn't a riotous spectacle; it was a civilizational performance. A sermon was preached. Justice was declared. White society walked away certain it had preserved moral order.

This is where we must go next: the scaffold in New London in 1786. A nation that would burn Black boys alive first taught itself to kill its children quietly, righteously, and with God's blessing. Child hangings in colonial Connecticut prove Jesse Washington's lynching wasn't uniquely Southern or postbellum. It was an inherited ritual, perfected in the colonies—execution, public pedagogy, religious justification, and racial scapegoating, teaching entire communities to see some lives as disposable.

"YOUR EYES WILL BE SHUT BY DEATH"

December 20, 1786.

A bitter morning in New London, Connecticut. The noose hung still. The silent promise of what everyone had come to see. Hannah Ocuish trembled beneath the gaze of her executioners, about to become a cautionary tale.[1]

To them, she was sin incarnate.

Beneath the gallows, the preacher's voice dripped with sanctified cruelty. "The time for you to die is come," he intoned, final and merciless. Her life, marked by poverty, abandonment, "heathenish ignorance," and petty crime, was declared unworthy of saving.

"She did not even know there was god," he spat to the waiting crowd.

Months earlier, Hannah had allegedly killed six-year-old Eunice Bolles in a fit of rage after being scolded for stealing strawberries. "The head and body were mangled in a shocking manner, the back and one arm broken, and a number of heavy stones placed on the body, arms, and legs," according to *The Connecticut Courant and Weekly Intelligencer*.[2] Years before, she and her brother were accused of beating another child in Groton.[3] Connecticut law allowed executions of children as young as seven, but hanging was rare. This time, they wanted to make an example: One child's death to avenge another's was a grotesque arithmetic only colonial justice could sanction.

In the crowd, mothers clutched their children close. Rev. Henry Channing's words lashed like a whip. "Your eyes will be shut by death, and you will not see the light of this sun again, forever." Final words, as irrevocable as the impending snap of the execution rope.

When the executioners stepped forward, Hannah broke. She wept, clinging to anyone within reach, begging for mercy. Channing remained unmoved. "You are going where I cannot see you; where I cannot instruct you or even pray for you," he intoned, smug and cold. "Soon you will know what I cannot tell you now, you will stand before the Judgement-Seat, where there will be no mercy if you do not repent."

Repent? How?

At twelve, she could grasp immediate consequences but not the moral reckoning demanded of her. But they didn't know—or care—about child development. They didn't see a confused child trying to understand right and wrong. They saw a menace to be purged.

Her developmental delays were proof, in their eyes, of moral defect. Any call for repentance was a cruel charade demanding submission she couldn't give. In those final moments, Hannah wasn't a soul to save. She was a scapegoat to sacrifice.

Channing's parting words were not a blessing but a curse: "You are now going to be hanged until you are dead . . . after that, you will know better than I can tell you the joys of Heaven, or the miseries of Hell." With feigned pity, he finished: "Poor girl, may God in his abundant goodness give you repentance unto life and have mercy on your soul. Amen and Amen."[4]

The noose tightened around her small neck. The crowd watched, hushed, as the ritual reached its climax: The rope snapped, and her body swung beneath the cold, gray sky. Her last breath stolen by those who claimed God's authority.

She wasn't a twelve-year-old girl anymore. She was a lesson. A warning. A body sacrificed on the altar of America's white Christian order.[5]

To the preacher and the crowd, her life ended the moment she took Eunice's. The hanging was just a necessary formality, the blood price for restoring order. His sermon wasn't guidance. It was a death sentence clothed in scripture, a justification for the killing of a child. Hannah's death wasn't an aberration. It was part of a tradition of public execution meant to purge society of "unwanted" bodies, especially those deemed unruly or inferior.

This wasn't some colonial footnote. It was a template. Hannah's execution wasn't just one child's death. It was a dress rehearsal for centuries of racial violence.

The religious ideology behind it wasn't generic Christianity. It was a carefully crafted colonial theology designed to maintain social hierarchies. The same faith that blessed the Inquisition and public burnings in Europe found new purpose in America, trading papal robes for Puritan bonnets and turning gallows into pulpits. Order demanded sacrifice. Even the life of a twelve-year-old girl.

Hannah Ocuish embodied everything contained in America's debased view of childhood. A girl, a servant, Black, Indian, "Mulatto"—each category marked her as inferior, irrational, criminal. But her trial and execution didn't treat her like an adult, as some scholars have argued.[6] It did the opposite.

She was twelve. But in colonial society's eyes, she was always a child in every way that made her vulnerable to violence, and in every way they needed her to be when they tightened the rope around her neck.

Marginalized people were always viewed as children: irrational, needing paternalistic control, perpetually open to violence. These children weren't victims of "adultification." America practiced permanent social infantilization, stripping them of legal protection.

Ocuish's marginalized identities were historically equated with childhood, regardless of age or size. Saying Ocuish was executed because she was "adultified" misreads the violent norms of colonial America. She was twelve, and she was treated precisely as children have always been treated.

This readiness to hang a child of color wasn't just about race; it was rooted in how white society trained itself to treat children as expendable. Ocuish's execution was the predictable flowering of a system that maintained its moral and racial order by killing children in public, with God's name on its lips.

FROM CHILD LABOR TO CHILD SACRIFICE

When we think about American lynching, we often see it as a uniquely Southern horror used for disciplining Black bodies. The truth is more unsettling. White children weren't born into innocence or protection. They were worked to death, whipped, abandoned, and even hanged, teaching communities to view young lives as expendable for power's sake. While we must recognize the specific racial violence Black and Indigenous children faced, we also need to confront the cultural foundation that normalized killing children as public ritual. The abuse of white children laid the groundwork for even more vicious systems codified in service of white supremacy.

I make this distinction not to say "white children had it bad too," but to show that child dehumanization was deeply rooted in European colonial practices that shaped American society. The so-called protections later granted to white children weren't benevolent gifts. They were deliberate choices about who was deemed worthy. White childhood became a training ground for producing the next generation of economic and social power, while Black and Indigenous children remained trapped in cycles of violence, exclusion, and death.

The harsh treatment of white children became the scaffolding for even more brutal racial hierarchies. These hierarchies framed Black and Indigenous children not merely as barbarians or savages but as permanent children—irrational, inferior, and always subject to violence. That's why Hannah Ocuish's story isn't an anomaly. Her execution belongs to a long tradition founded on children's disposability that went beyond race once whiteness, not children, became what was protected.

It was a grueling apprenticeship in survival. Only the lucky few reached adulthood. Poor white children—those chimney sweepers, street beggars, and factory fodder—were treated as expendable tools. Indentured white children were beaten, starved, abandoned, hanged, or sent off to war.

The brutalization of *all children* was foundational for a system that ultimately focused on protecting whiteness alone. Whiteness became synonymous with adulthood, with all its sacred privileges and protections.

The harsh reality is that childhood in America was never guaranteed sanctuary. It was a battlefield where young lives were sacrificed to maintain order. If anything, the brutal treatment of Black children reveals not that white childhood was once sacred but that *no child* was truly safe in a system built on violent control.

While the lynching of Black children was an expression of Jim Crow racial terror, Hannah's execution reflected an older belief: that children were inherently sinful.

Sixteen-year-old Thomas Granger, hanged in 1642 for bestiality, was among the first juveniles executed in Plymouth Colony, showing the era's rigid moral codes. Bathsheba Spooner and sixteen-year-old Ezra Ross conspired to murder Spooner's husband and were executed in 1778. Ross had been recruited as a child soldier for the Revolution, and Spooner was pregnant with their child. Ross survived America's nation-building escapades once but not twice.

Between 1776 and 1971, the UK and America formally executed more than 425 white children and over 480 Black children. Throughout those two hundred years, white children were executed regularly, with the raw number of cases increasing as the overall population expanded and peaking in the early twentieth century. In early colonial years, it wasn't unusual for white settler children to die from abuse or neglect, or to be used as cannon fodder in wars fought for wealthy men's profit.

Black children, meanwhile, were murdered with near-total impunity under slavery. After gradual emancipation, states began formally executing Black children as well. Examples include James Guild (in 1828), Judah (1834), an enslaved girl from Maryland who by age fourteen had killed three of her master's children, Jane Huff (1837), and Roseanne Kenn (1844). After abolition in the late nineteenth century, executions of white children dwindled, while both state and mob executions of Black children expanded.

We need to confront something that goes beyond the obvious horrors of slavery and lynching. From the start, white society brutalized its own children in the name of labor, obedience, and divine control. Europeans treated their own young as disposable—whipped, hanged, sacrificed for power. So, what hope did Black children have, who were denied even the illusion of belonging or protection?

What does it mean to live in a world where childhood itself was always dangerous—even for those closest to power? If white people did this to their own children for centuries, what chance did that give to ours?

The brutality was democratic in the worst way, doled out to children regardless of race, though over time Black children bore the brunt. For anyone nurturing a Black child, it raises chilling questions recognizing that white supremacy was built not just on the dehumanization of Black people but also on the violent sacrifice of white children. It reveals that the same system that justified and rationalized slavery and lynching operates on control, not care, where all children, but especially Black children, become tools of discipline and dominance.

This understanding forces a reckoning: If the protection of childhood was never an inherent value in white society, Black parents face the terrifying reality of trying to keep their children safe in a world built on punishment and control. So, how do you protect your children from a world that has normalized cruelty toward its *own* youth, and turned that cruelty toward yours in even more vicious ways? This is the grim continuity of racialized violence, where the disregard for Black life extends from a colonial ethos that treated even white children as disposable labor and bodies for discipline and sacrifice.

It's a haunting truth: When violence is foundational, it metastasizes. Children, white and Black alike, become casualties of that logic, but Black children always remain children, even into adulthood.

THE FALSE PROMISE OF A NEW WORLD

Wasn't America supposed to be different?

How could the so-called New World, sold as a land of freedom and fresh starts, so quickly become a stage for ancient cruelties?

Weren't the Pilgrims fleeing persecution and the brutality of Old World class hierarchies?

Didn't America promise republican autonomy, individual rights, and democratic participation?

Hannah Ocuish's death shatters any idea that early America held space for innocence or redemption. Her body swinging beneath a gray sky was not a mistake but the system working exactly as designed. For all the talk of freedom and new beginnings, this "New World" arrived with the same old nooses, torches, and sermons cloaking cruelty in righteousness. The promise of liberation and equality began to collapse under the weight of these rituals.

Brutality in child socialization, especially the socialization of Indigenous people and marginalized groups, wasn't unique to the American colonies. Australia, Canada, and other British colonial projects imposed their own violent systems of control, especially through boarding schools and forced removals. But America, before and after it became the United States, stands apart.

First, unlike Australia or Canada, the United States marketed itself as a revolutionary departure from Europe, a "new birth of freedom." This mythology of exceptionalism was central to the American project, making its continued European-style violence not just cruel but profoundly hypocritical. It wasn't simply brutality, then; it was brutality wrapped in lofty promises of freedom and equality, which compounds the psychological violence. The rhetoric of liberty that accompanied US nation-building created an illusion of moral superiority even as the nation continued practices inherited from its colonial forebears.

Second, where Australia and Canada focused much of their violence on Indigenous populations, the US layered racial hierarchy through slavery, building its economy on the backs of African laborers. This double exploitation, of Indigenous dispossession and African enslavement, meant that America's brutality was not only more expansive but also more deeply entrenched in its economic and legal systems. As a result, both Black and Indigenous children became the focus of uniquely dehumanizing and violent control in the American context. So, while Australia and Canada were undeniably brutal, those colonial powers never promised to be anything but colonies within the British Empire. In contrast, the United States cloaked its colonial violence in the language of freedom, creating a peculiar form of cognitive dissonance that endures to this day. Still, despite the differences between the various colonial contexts, they all reveal a larger pattern: Children, whether Indigenous or enslaved, were always the first to be targeted by systems of control.

Perhaps America simply needed some time to iron out the wrinkles, but how, even a century after the formation of our country, could its children still be hanging from gallows and bridges, or rejoicing in torture and clawing at the charred bodies of the dead?

If this new nation was a blank canvas, it didn't take long for it to be stained with blood. The same hands that penned declarations of inalienable rights also sanctioned the fastening of nooses around the necks of kids. This public killing of children tears apart the comforting lie of American exceptionalism: the myth that America left Europe's barbarism behind. The story we've told ourselves—about American progress, freedom, and moral virtue marking a break from the oppressive traditions of the Old World—collapses. How could a nation supposedly founded on life, liberty, and the pursuit of happiness be a place where children became sacrifices to maintain order and hierarchy?

The fact that children, who are often imagined as society's future, were publicly murdered reveals the sham of "American progress." These rituals weren't relics or mistakes; they were *fundamental* to the logic of our system.

America didn't just inherit Europe's barbaric practices, *it perfected them.*

The rhetoric of freedom and new beginnings masked a continuity of violence that showed no regard for the young. The myth of a moral awakening on American soil is undone when we realize that "progress" always depended on someone being thrown to the wolves, whether on gallows, on a plantation, or beneath the branches of a lynching tree.

So, what does this say about the America we've built?

It says that freedom was never universal, that law was always racialized, and that our progress has been a carefully curated illusion. Every time a child was sacrificed, whether it was Hannah Ocuish or George Stinney, the message was clear: Control matters more than humanity, and power trumps even the sanctity of life. The same mechanisms that justified enslaving Black children justified executing poor children and lynching them with impunity. In America's brutal ledger, children's lives, whether Black, poor, Indigenous, or otherwise marginalized, were never debts worth paying back.

To understand how a nation ostensibly built on promises of freedom so easily descended into rituals of cruelty, we must examine the religious practices that shaped its soul. The ritualized killing of children didn't emerge in a vacuum; it was sanctified, justified, and perpetuated by faith traditions that arrived on America's shores and took root in its soil. Each denomination, with its own doctrines and dogmas, played a role in creating a moral framework where violence against children was not just tolerated but demanded. If we want to make sense of how these executions and lynchings became embedded in the fabric of American life, we must dive into the theology that made them not only possible but also morally righteous.

THE GHOSTS OF ROANOKE: A NATION'S INTRODUCTION TO DISPOSABLE YOUTH

Early American society was a perfect storm of religious dogma and colonial desperation. If you thought crossing the Atlantic might wash away Europe's blood-soaked traditions, think again. The Old World's penchant for public executions didn't fade away on new shores. Rather, it played out Europe's worst instincts. Colonial life demanded labor, obedience, and fear, and it found in children the perfect targets for its harshest doctrines. Christianity provided the moral cover, reinforcing the idea that violence was not only justified but necessary to ensure salvation and maintain order. This was not about nurturing innocence but about breaking spirits.

At the time when Europeans were scrambling to plant their flags in the Americas during the late fifteenth century and early sixteenth century, Europe was defined by hierarchies maintained through violence, rigid class structures, religious control, and the routine marginalization of the most vulnerable, including children. In England, for example, under the Tudor Poor Laws and other labor regulations, children from impoverished families were often forced into apprenticeships or labor, sometimes facing slavery-like conditions.[7] Religious doctrine emphasized corporal punishment, as children were seen as inherently sinful and in need of correction. A few hundred years later, the infamous "Bloody Code" of eighteenth-century England would reflect a continuity with these earlier European norms, where severe punishments, including for juveniles, were meant to maintain social order. Like Abraham dragging Isaac up the mountain, adults were already practicing the fine art of child sacrifice, for God, gold, or whatever glory was on the table that day.

While Britain was still tangled in political infighting during the fifteenth century, the Spanish and Portuguese had been touring the globe in search of gold, murdering and enslaving Indigenous communities wherever they were encountered. When the British finally got into the imperial game, one of their first ventures was an ill-fated community called Roanoke, established in 1585, in what would become North Carolina. As if portending the dismal future of childhood in America, among the settlers were a dozen young boys and girls, including Virginia Dare, the first English child born in America. There is no historical record of what became of the children. Virginia became a ghost story, a fitting start for a nation that would treat children as expendable.

A couple decades earlier, Britain had passed the Artificers and Apprentices Act, which, among other things, gave the government the power to regulate the apprenticeships of children, and the colonies soon followed suit. The law would serve as the model for American regulation of child labor.

Jamestown's founding in 1607 marked the next chapter in the grim future of childhood in America. The profit-driven Virginia Company of London financed hordes of settlers who were ill-prepared for the harsh realities of colonial life. Among them were child servants like twelve-year-old Samuel Collier and two eight-year-olds, James Brumfield and Richard Mutton. These children of Jamestown either disappeared or died in war. None of them had much of a chance in the New World, as they weren't sent as future leaders of the colony or as valued members of society. They were sent to work or die, with war, disease, or neglect often making sure that death came soon.

The Pilgrims, a group of religious exiles fleeing what they felt to be England's corrupt and oppressive political system, arrived in 1620 on the *Mayflower* with more than thirty children. Are you surprised to learn that dozens of children were on the *Mayflower*? This detail is often overlooked, as much of the popular narrative surrounding the Pilgrims tends to emphasize adult religious leaders and key figures like William Bradford. Children were key to the Pilgrims' community-building efforts, for they were not just passive passengers but integral to the establishment of the new society as both laborers and future leaders of the colony.

The Pilgrims were tied to their own form of capitalist hell. Their voyage was funded by a group of wealthy investors called merchant "adventurers," who saw an opportunity for profit in establishing a colony of hard-working zealots in the New World. The financial backers didn't care about the Pilgrims' religious freedom or the future of their children; they wanted a return on investment! The Pilgrims were given seven years to repay what they owed, thrusting them into a dire economic arrangement from the start. They weren't just building a new life; they were building wealth for others, and their children were necessary tools.

Because these children were born into the rigid doctrines of separatist Puritanism, even if they survived to see the debt repaid, their days were still filled with work and fear. Fear of God. Fear of punishment. Fear of the unknown around them. They were human capital necessary for the establishment of a Puritan society characterized by devout industriousness.[8]

The arrival of more children on ships like the *Anne* and the *Little James* in 1623, and the *Charity* in 1629, added to the growing population of child laborers and servants. Tens of thousands more would follow in the next decade, not as free individuals but as young bodies condemned to suffering and sacrifice for the success of the faith and profit-driven colonies. Children like Virginia Laydon, whose birth in 1609 marked her as the first child born in Jamestown, entered a world where the objective was to work for the glory of God or die. There was never a guarantee of something different, something more humane; that was a promise read back into the era by romantic modern historians.

CALVINIST LOVE: BREAKING WILLS AND SAVING SOULS, ONE BEATING AT A TIME

Fleeing persecution, the Dutch (in 1624) and the French Huguenot Calvinists (in 1685) brought their reformed version of draconian child-rearing to New York and the Carolinas. Both the Pilgrims in the Plymouth Colony and the Puritans in Massachusetts Bay Colony imported Calvinism like it was divine truth wrapped in barbed wire. A Protestant movement founded by the theologian John Calvin during the sixteenth century offered a distinct and theologically grounded view of children, sin, and discipline. Calvin's teachings made it clear: Children were born sinners, and only violence could straighten them out. This belief was deeply rooted in ancient European philosophies and Christian theology, tracing back to St. Augustine's doctrine of "original sin." Augustine viewed children as carriers of Adam's sin, inherently inclined toward selfishness and disobedience, requiring correction from the moment they entered the world.

Discipline became an act of spiritual care, where violence wasn't cruelty but love, a divine obligation to purge sin and maintain order. The logic was airtight: If a child's nature is sin itself, then it's the parent's job to beat that sin out of them. Calvin left no room for ambiguity: "For our nature is not only utterly devoid of goodness, but so prolific in all kinds of evil, that it can never be idle." Work is what kept those idle hands busy. And any refusal to work was to be corrected with violence. Calvinist communities interpreted passages like Proverbs 13:24 (the infamous "He who spares the rod hates his son, but he who loves him is diligent to discipline him") as a divine mandate for parents to employ painful correction. According to Calvin:

> Even infants bear their condemnation with them from their mother's womb; for, though they have not yet brought forth the fruits of their own iniquity, they have the seed enclosed within themselves. Indeed,

their whole nature is a seed of sin; thus it cannot but be hateful and abominable to God.[9]

Rather than view discipline as the absence of care, Calvinists believed that it was an expression of love aimed at saving children from their sinful natures and leading them to righteousness. In fact, Calvin emphasized that failure to discipline was tantamount to neglecting the child's soul.

This perverse vision of violence flourished in young America, which needed a lot of young workers and, accordingly, a lot of compulsion. American Puritan ministers like Cotton Mather didn't hold back. As he laid out in *A Family Well Ordered* (1699), disobedient children were one step away from the gallows: "I tell you, O Undutiful Children; There is Danger, Lest you be so Cursed of God, as to be Hanged on a Tree, at the Last. . . . It seems, an Untimely and a Tragical Death, often Exposes the Carcasses of those Children, to the Carnivorous Fowls of Heaven."[10]

Back in England, Richard Baxter chimed in with his *Christian Directory* (1673), telling children their parents' beatings were tough love: "Patiently submit to the correction which your Parents lay upon you. Consider, that God hath commanded them to do it, and that to save your souls from Hell; and that they hate you if they correct you not when there is cause, and that they must not spare for your crying. . . . It is not their delight; but for your own necessity. Avoid the fault, and you may escape the correction.[11]

Discipline was considered spiritual care to ensure children grew up obedient. John Robinson, in *Of Children and Their Education* (1628), compared children to stubborn horses needing a bit and bridle: "And surely there is in all children, though not alike, a stubbornness, and stoutness of mind arising from natural pride, which must, in the first place, be broken and beaten down; that so the foundation of their education being laid in humility and tractableness, other virtues may, in their time, be built thereon."

The child, here, is posed not just as a beast of burden but as a beast that must be tamed to save its life: "For the beating, and keeping down of this stubbornness parents must provide carefully for two things: first that children's wills and willfulness be restrained and repressed, and that, in time; lest sooner than they imagine, the tender sprigs grow to that stiffness, that they will rather break than bow."[12]

If a child is so spirited that she simply refuses to bend, then she must be broken: Break the will, save the soul, or else. As Robert Schnucker's study on Puritan attitudes toward childhood discipline reveals, these brutal ideas persisted from 1560 to 1634, saturating the American colonies with a parenting philosophy that treated children as livestock waiting to be tamed. Whether the objective in this parenting approach was to honor God, create wealth, or secure a nation, what is clear is that the violent coercion of children was central to the American colonial project.

Schnucker writes that "by 1635, [the Puritans] had written close to two dozen such books plus pamphlets, treatises, and sermons touching on child rearing." They saw the family as central to both religious life and the moral upbringing of children, and they placed great emphasis on the father's role as a figure of authority, representing God within the household. The mother, while subordinate to the father, played a significant role in maintaining the family order. Although the Catholic Church had argued that children were not capable of mortal sin until the age of seven, many Puritans argued that original sin manifested itself while the children were at their mothers' breasts. It was, of course, small consolation to children that their parents only beat them out of love and did not beat them so badly as to leave them incapacitated. Perhaps they would have preferred a Catholic doctrine of beatings only after the age of seven.[13]

Throughout the seventy-five years covered by Schnucker's study, Puritan attitudes toward childhood discipline consistently remained remarkably brutal. Even though some ideas, such as the dangers of overindulgence or "coddling," became more pronounced over time, the overall approach remained the same. Puritanical parenting thus persisted as the population of white settlers exploded in the New World during the eighteenth century. By the nineteenth century, slavery was in full swing, and the children of white families were exposed to increasing amounts of violence. We can reasonably assume that early American child discipline was not concerned exclusively with executing godly punishments, or economic control, or a new legal regime, since it is likely that all these motivations were at play.

This was the founding of America.

QUAKERS, METHODISTS, AND BAPTISTS: FINDING GRACE IN THE BEATINGS

If fear of hell didn't keep kids in line, colonial statutes like the Massachusetts Bay Colony's Stubborn Child Law of 1646 did. The law laid out a chilling ultimatum: If a child over sixteen refused to obey the colony's laws, their parents could drag them to court to be sentenced to death. Plymouth's laws echoed the same sentiment in 1671, threatening any child who struck or cursed a parent with execution, unless, of course, the parents had been "unchristianly negligent" in their beatings.[14] How generous. The killing of disobedient children was written into the very first American legal systems. Reiterating Deuteronomy 21:20–21, the law proclaimed:

> If a man have a stubborn or rebellious son, of sufficient years and understanding (viz.) sixteen years of age, which will not obey the voice of his Father, or the voice of his Mother, and that when they have chastened him will not harken unto them: then shall his Father and Mother being his natural parents, lay hold on him, and bring him to the Magistrates assembled in Court and testify unto them, that their son is stubborn and rebellious and will not obey their voice and chastisement, but lives in sundry notorious crimes, such a son shall be put to death.[15]

The laws functioned more as a deterrent than a legal certainty, but the psychological terror of imminent murder by one's own parents and community was harrowing for defenseless children.

The view of children as inherently sinful demons wrapped in baby skin and in need of violent coercion, etched in law, produced a new kind of deviant, the "delinquent." According to John Sutton, writing in his book *Stubborn Children* (1988), "Child control reformers did not 'invent' the concept of delinquency *de novo*. Rather, they built their programs on a fairly stable and broadly legitimate set of assumptions about childhood and deviance that originated in the Puritan ideal of family discipline."[16] The juvenile delinquent was simply the Puritan fabrication of the community's own worst nightmare, a boogeyman of idle and sinful youth.

Calvinist beliefs about discipline were also shaped by the doctrine of predestination, which held that God had already determined who would be saved (the elect) and who would be damned. While parents could not know whether their children were among the elect, they were nevertheless obligated to raise them in fear of the Lord. Perhaps a child was doomed from birth, but who could know? Better to beat the sin out of them just in case. American parents were encouraged to exercise strict discipline in the hope that their children might *prove* to be part of the elect, though their ultimate fate was left in God's hands. This uncertainty added a sense of urgency to child-rearing, as parents could not afford to neglect the spiritual training of their children, even if they could not guarantee their salvation. This reinforced the view that discipline was a vital part of preparing children for God's judgment.[17]

The American family and its regime of Puritan discipline became a model for collective legal obligation. In Pennsylvania, if a parent or guardian wasn't properly discipling a disobedient child, the youth could be whipped by a constable. The hierarchy and order of the family became the paradigm for understanding legal and political life.

Reformed churches were not the only form of Christianity to arrive on the shores of the New World. Catholics, Methodists, Baptists, and Lutherans all had their own spins on corporal punishment, each believing that discipline was the key to salvation. Even Quakers and Anabaptists, despite their famous moderation, couldn't resist entirely. Catholicism arrived in America with English settlers who founded Maryland in 1634, alongside French and Spanish Catholics establishing colonies in Louisiana and Florida, respectively. Catholic teachings on child discipline were more moderate than those of reformed Protestant denominations, urging a balance between reason and violence. Some Catholics believed that Protestant approaches to discipline lacked the compassionate grace central to Catholic doctrine. They viewed Protestant practices as overly focused on punishment and lacking the sacramental understanding of childhood innocence and moral guidance. That said, the pedophilic legacy of the Catholic Church and its abuse of children should not surprise us. Protestant children faced a great deal of very public abuse, but Catholic children experienced abuse behind closed doors.

Lutheranism arrived in America with Swedish settlers who established the colony of New Sweden in the Delaware Valley in 1638, followed by later waves of German Lutherans who settled in Pennsylvania during the eighteenth century. Martin Luther's approach to child discipline, while firm, also emphasized the importance of balancing punishment with rewards.

Methodism arrived in America in the mid-eighteenth century, largely through the efforts of John and Charles Wesley. It grew rapidly after the establishment of the Methodist Episcopal Church in 1784, with John Wesley's teachings on child discipline playing a significant role in shaping the community. Wesley stressed the importance of early discipline, focusing on breaking a child's will to foster obedience and moral behavior.

Quakers arrived in America in the mid-seventeenth century, with William Penn establishing Pennsylvania in 1681 as a haven for religious minorities. Unlike other Christian denominations, Quakers rejected severe punishment in child-rearing, emphasizing nonviolence and moral example instead. They critiqued other Christian denominations, particularly the Puritans and Calvinists, for their reliance on physical punishment, which they viewed as being in tension with the Gospel's message of love and peace.[18] Quakers believed that violent discipline undermined a child's ability to develop a personal connection with God, though they did not prohibit it entirely.

Similarly, Anabaptist traditions, such as the Mennonites and Amish, embraced a more moderate approach to child discipline. Mennonites began migrating to Pennsylvania in the late seventeenth century, seeking religious freedom, followed by the Amish in the early eighteenth century. These more qualified and moderate doctrines of child discipline would not influence American parenting practices until the late nineteenth century, and at that time they only applied to white children. Given the need to compel children to work, moderation was quickly replaced with the tougher practices.

Evangelicals, including Baptists and Pentecostals, became prominent in American religious life during the twentieth century, particularly in the South and Midwest. Modern evangelical thinkers today continue to promote physical discipline, drawing on traditional Protestant views. And by the twentieth century, evangelicals like James Dobson and Michael Pearl were still beating the same drum (and their kids) in the name of order and discipline in America.

LESSONS IN SUBMISSION: CHRISTIANITY'S INFLUENCE ON BLACK PARENTING

The white Christian ideas I've summarized in this chapter were integral to the practices of American slavery, and through that dismal institution influenced how Black people would raise their own children. As European settlers imposed Christianity on enslaved Africans in colonial America, they transmitted disciplinary practices tied to religious instruction. Although some African traditional religions persisted, the spread of Christianity, primarily through Anglicanism, Methodism, and Baptism, gradually came to dominate religious life in Black communities. The violent religious instruction administered to enslaved Africans and their descendants emphasized obedience and submission, with child discipline becoming a central part of this teaching. Over time, African American communities absorbed the notion that harsh discipline, often based on the teachings of white masters and ministers, was necessary for raising obedient and godly children.

Early Black religious writers in these traditions echoed the injunctions to discipline children through corporal punishment, adapting them to their communities' needs and realities. The Anglican Church was one of the earliest denominations imposed on enslaved Africans in the Southern colonies, particularly in Virginia and the Carolinas. Although the Anglican Church itself promoted moderation in child discipline and avoided encouraging extreme forms of punishment, plantation owners saw the religious instruction of slaves as key to ensuring compliance and control; consequently, an emphasis on authority and submission became central to their religious instruction. Anglican teachings about the need for children to respect authority figures infected Black religious contexts, contributing to the idea that physical discipline could be a necessary tool to ensure obedience. Early Black Anglican writers, such as Jupiter Hammon, an enslaved preacher and poet, reflected this emphasis on obedience. His works urged the importance of submission to authority and the moral development of children. He wrote:

> Now whether it is right, and lawful, in the Sight of God, for them to make slaves of us or not, I am certain that while we are slaves, it is our duty to obey our masters, in all their lawful commands, and mind them

unless we are bid to do that which we know to be sin, or forbidden in God's word.[19]

Methodism gained prominence in Black communities during the late eighteenth and early nineteenth centuries, as white Methodists actively evangelized enslaved Africans. John Wesley's emphasis on discipline, particularly his teaching that parents must "break the will" of children to ensure their salvation, was widely absorbed. Early Black Methodist leaders, such as Richard Allen, founder of the African Methodist Episcopal (AME) Church, echoed some of these teachings. While Allen's writings focused more on spiritual guidance and self-discipline, later Black Methodist preachers incorporated the idea of firm child discipline into their sermons. Daniel Payne, a leading figure in the AME Church in the mid-nineteenth century, advocated for the necessity of discipline in both the school and the home, viewing it as critical for moral development and proper behavior. While Payne also emphasized education and self-restraint, the broader Methodist influence on Black communities included a belief that physical punishment could help children avoid sinful tendencies and ensure their obedience.

Baptists became the most widely embraced Christian group among Black people in America, particularly after the Second Great Awakening, as Baptist congregations spread throughout the South. The Baptist emphasis on the sinful nature of humanity and the need for moral correction reinforced the idea that children required firm discipline. Early Black Baptist preachers, such as John Jasper, integrated teachings on discipline into their sermons. Jasper, though primarily focused on spiritual salvation, believed that children's sinful tendencies must be corrected through strong parental guidance. By the mid-nineteenth century, Black leaders like Henry McNeal Turner echoed the broader Baptist call for strong moral discipline within the home. Turner, who became a key figure in the AME Church as well, strongly believed in strict discipline, urging parents to prevent their children from falling into sin by maintaining authority. The broader Baptist message about discipline, which included the belief that "sparing the rod" meant "spoiling the child," permeated African American Baptist churches, leading many Black preachers to advocate corporal punishment as a necessary tool for raising godly children.

The same system that saw white children as beasts of burden saw enslaved people as nothing more than tools for pleasure and economic gain. Both groups were subjected to a dehumanizing logic: They existed to serve the colony, to work, to survive in conditions that disregarded their humanity. White children, while exploited and abused, still had the possibility of a future free from servitude. Enslaved people, on the other hand, were trapped in a cycle of childhood brutality from which there was no escape. Both groups were exploited, though, as Fredrick Douglass lamented, the scale and severity of the abuse inflicted on Black people (conceptualized as permanent children) consumed the lifespan of the slave. Douglass decried that as a slave, he was never allowed to become an adult and escape the subjugation and violence of childhood servitude.

Puritanical parenting set the tone for American child-rearing from the moment the first settlers stumbled off their boats, clutching Bibles in one hand and whips in the other. Immigrants from across Europe flocked to the New World, eager not just to own land but to own people. And though not every immigrant was a Calvinist, nearly all of them were devoutly Christian, finding common ground in the belief that discipline, preferably the painful kind, was essential to keeping everyone in line. America may have inherited much of its cultural and legal personality from Britain, but it also managed to cling to slavery long after Britain had abolished it. And though Catholic and Protestant communities occasionally squabbled, they united under a slave economy that ran like clockwork.

But cracks began to show, primarily over the impact of slavery on white children, who grew up amid horrifying violence and were twisted by the experience.

THE ANTEBELLUM PERIOD: A NATION OF SIN AND WHIPPING

White children in the antebellum period fared no better than their colonial-era predecessors, their souls ruined by witnessing, and sometimes participating in, brutality. In *They Were Her Property*, Stephanie Jones-Rogers recounts the 1857 story of the Martin sisters, two white girls in Washington County, Georgia, who watched their father and brother torture a thirteen-year-old slave named Alfred. Alfred allegedly told his master's son, Godfry Martin, to kiss his ass. Over three excruciating hours, Godfry and his father beat Alfred to death. Godfry made sure Alfred stayed conscious during the beating by pouring water on him. For good measure, he placed a saddle on Alfred's back, ordering him to crawl like an animal. They bludgeoned and dragged the boy until he died.

The Martin sisters watched the whole thing and didn't lift a finger to stop the killing. Whether they were desensitized or paralyzed by fear is anyone's guess, but their silence speaks volumes. White children in the antebellum South were trapped in a nightmare of their own—witnessing violence they could neither challenge nor escape. Participation in brutality wasn't unheard of; sometimes children were even encouraged to practice "bloodletting discipline" to prepare them for future slave ownership. A visiting fifteen-year-old white boy named John A. Bedgood also witnessed Alfred's torture. He was so horrified that he fled to a neighboring plantation to escape the spectacle. For children like the Martin sisters, flight wasn't an option. The only choice was to freeze in terror or somehow accept the horrors as normal and necessary. Alfred was lost, and the souls of the children who bore witness were mutilated.[20]

Women found themselves in much the same predicament as children: They were victims of violence one moment, perpetrators the next. In *Out of the House of Bondage* (2008), Thavolia Glymph explains how white women who beat their slaves were often beaten by their husbands and, in turn, took out their frustrations on their children. Similarly, in *Within the Plantation Household* (1988), Elizabeth Fox-Genovese describes how white mothers struggled to balance child-rearing with the management of plantation life. Mahala Roach was a white mother who begrudgingly whipped her daughter, Sophy, when the girl misbehaved. "I hate to do it," Roach admitted, but that didn't stop her. On one particularly bad day, she confessed: "Sophy has been very bad today, have had to whip her three times . . . so I think she can't be well." Even maternal affection was twisted by the need to maintain order through violence.[21]

Toward the end of the antebellum period, some Southern fathers began to worry that exposure to the violence of slavery might morally corrupt their children. In *Southern Sons: Becoming Men in the New*

Nation, Lorri Glover recounts how wealthy slaveowners like Robert Carter III sent their sons away from plantations, hoping to shield them from the corrupting influence of tyranny.[22] Thomas Jefferson shared similar concerns in his *Notes on the State of Virginia* (1784). He warned that children learn by imitation, absorbing their parents' worst behaviors: "Our children see this, and learn to imitate it. . . . The parent storms, the child looks on . . . gives a loose to his worst passions, and thus nursed, educated, and daily exercised in tyranny, cannot but be stamped by it with odious peculiarities." Some fathers believed the future of whiteness depended on distancing young men from the day-to-day brutality of slaveholding. Better to send them to the city to cultivate a civilized demeanor, leaving the dirty work to be outsourced to hired managers at home.

When the Civil War eventually erupted, children were caught in the crossfire, some as soldiers, others as refugees, and many more as casualties of hunger and disease. James Marten reveals that at least ten thousand boys, aged thirteen to seventeen, fought for the Union army, their deaths romanticized in obituaries that framed them as heroes. Charlie King, just twelve years old, was the youngest to die on the Union side, killed during the Battle of Antietam. On the Confederate side, David Bailey Freeman enlisted at age eleven. But the true cost of war was borne by non-combatant children, many of whom became refugees. At the same time, thousands of enslaved children, classified as "contrabands," fled plantations, seeking refuge behind Union lines. War left these children psychologically shattered. Families were torn apart, and the trauma of separation and loss haunted those who survived.[23]

The legacy of violence that shaped American childhood left behind a profound and complicated inheritance. Whether on the plantation, in reform schools, or on the battlefield, children were molded by American discipline. Those who witnessed or participated in brutality carried the weight of it into adulthood, perpetuating cycles of harm that would become deeply ingrained in American culture. Even when parents tried to shield their children from the worst of these realities, the undercurrent of violence remained, an unavoidable feature of the world they were growing up in. For children, the lines between love, discipline, and domination were blurred, leaving them to navigate a social order where survival often meant accepting or reenacting cruelty.

The trauma of these experiences didn't end with childhood; it became a generational burden, quietly passed down in homes, institutions, and systems that would continue to privilege violence over compassion.

In 1630, John Billington, one of the original *Mayflower* passengers, became one of the earliest colonists executed in North America—and the first in Plymouth Colony to be executed for murder—when he was publicly hanged. Children likely stood among the crowd that day, absorbing the brutal message of colonial justice. Public executions like these served as grim reminders that death was a constant threat, whether delivered by nature or by the law. A century later, little had improved in the so-called New World. During the "Negro Conspiracy" of 1741, a rebellion organized by enslaved Africans and poor whites in New York was uncovered, leading to deadly reprisals. A poor white child who was caught stealing betrayed the plot, resulting in the execution of thirty Black people and four white people. Thirteen of the Black conspirators were publicly burned at the stake, an event witnessed by children standing among the spectators. Even when not formally executed, children lived under a legal regime that did not categorically exempt them from capital punishment, and they absorbed the lesson that colonial justice could consume entire communities.[24]

LYNCHING AND THE SOCIALIZATION OF WHITE CHILDREN

In the post-slavery era, white children were increasingly shielded by reforms like juvenile courts, while Black youth remained exposed to lethal violence—lynchings replaced slaveholder whips, and segregation-era policies codified Black youths' vulnerability. The fusion of religion, patriarchy, and racism created a culture where racial terror was divinely justified, embedding violence into the nation's social fabric. From Ocuish's gallows to Waco's lynching photos, this legacy persists, shaping policies that disproportionately target Black children today. The tragedy lies not only in the lives lost but also in America's enduring failure to imagine justice beyond punishment—a nation that taught itself to kill its children now faces the imperative to unlearn that practice.

White children were often raised by Black women and played alongside Black children. It is this close interaction and the potential for solidarity that would eventually make wealthy white-supremacist Americans nervous, and lead to a sea change in the conceptualization of white youth as proto-adults. By the 1800s, state governments were getting more and more involved in the management of white children. Delinquent children would no longer be left to die on the street; they would be forced into reform institutions. In 1839, the Pennsylvania Supreme Court, invoking the principle of *parens patriae*, decided that the practice of holding children against their will in a school (in this case, a House of Refuge, or juvenile reform school) did not violate habeas corpus because any child in such an institution was there for being delinquent from school, which is technically not a crime and thus that school was technically not a prison. The principle of *parens patriae*, meaning "parent of the nation," was invoked to justify the state's role in controlling and disciplining children. It allowed the state to act in a parental role, asserting its responsibility for white children's welfare. Indeed, the legal system constructed multiple paths to adulthood for white children, who were being disciplined into the social order and prepared for the responsibilities of citizenship. For children of color or marginalized groups, however, such institutions would one day function as a mechanism of exclusion or punishment—of permanent childhood delinquency—rather than preparation for full participation in society as citizens.

But the end of slavery didn't end the exposure of white children to racial violence. Instead, during the Jim Crow era, lynchings became part of their socialization. White children didn't just witness these acts, they were often active participants. As Kristina DuRocher explains in *Raising Racists*, white parents believed such exposure was necessary to preserve racial hierarchies. H. L. Mitchell, just eleven years old, attended a lynching in Arkansas, initially eager to witness the spectacle. But the sight of Scott Lingon's corpse and the stench of burning flesh shocked him to his core, sending him running back to the railway station.[25]

While traditional historians often focus on economic or ideological motivations for slavery and segregation, we must attend to the deep psychological scarring that occurred in these contexts. For white Americans, these brutal systems did not just impose economic and political hierarchies; they also inflicted deep psychic and emotional wounds that became embedded in family life and parenting practices. Southern family values during slavery revolved around racialized patriarchy, with parenting itself often outsourced to enslaved people, which not only shaped white children's emotional development but also trained them to absorb the logic of domination and submission. Boys were groomed for hyper-masculinity, learning that power and violence were necessary tools for asserting authority.

As Gilda Graff explores in her article "The Intergenerational Trauma of Slavery and Its Aftermath," trauma persisted within Black communities through systems like Jim Crow and convict leasing; however, the psychological impact of these systems also extended to white families, where patterns of emotional repression, hyper-discipline, and control were perpetuated across generations.[26] Girls were prepared for lives of compliance, trained to accept subjugation in the domestic sphere. Kenneth Alan Adams, in "Lynching, Sacrifice, and Childrearing in the New South," draws a direct connection between violent child-rearing practices and the normalization of lynching, arguing that these traditions were deliberate mechanisms for passing down both corporal punishment and white supremacy from one generation to the next.[27]

Fathers, disconnected from emotional intimacy, disciplined their sons into becoming enforcers of the racial and social order. Mothers, consumed by the burdens of both child-rearing and plantation domesticity, perpetuated cycles of harsh punishment to maintain control in a world that offered them little autonomy. Children, whether they froze in fear, fled in horror, or actively participated, were irreparably marked by the violence they encountered. The trauma was not acknowledged, let alone addressed. Instead, it became the foundation of Southern family values, ensuring that white supremacy permeated each new generation.

The violence white children witnessed was woven into the fabric of their emotional and social development. Children raised in homes where power was enforced through beatings, and where enslaved people were treated as subhuman, learned to equate order with violence. The spectacle of public executions and lynchings only reinforced these lessons. As Adams argues, white parents passed down not just family heirlooms but also an inheritance of cruelty, a belief that order could only be maintained through punishment and dominance. Whether on the plantation, at public hangings, or in their own homes, these traumatic experiences became part of the psychological inheritance of white families—a generational loop of trauma, where white parents raised children to reproduce the very same structures of violence that had shaped their own lives. Religiously sanctioned cruelty laid the groundwork for systemic racial terror, as seen in the Jim Crow era's lynchings. State-sanctioned lynchings, like Ocuish's hanging, became public spectacles of dominance, where white children—conditioned by generations of violent discipline—learned to equate whiteness with the right to punish and kill. Their presence at these rituals would reinforce a racial order where Black suffering was both entertainment and instruction.

CHAPTER 5

Birthing Racism

White Women as Biological Gatekeepers of Intergenerational Violence

Historians have long chronicled lynching through photographs, court documents, and demographic data, evidence that can be cited, footnoted, and preserved. But what gets lost when we privilege the record over the body? When we treat white supremacy solely as a legal phenomenon, and not also a sensory one?

This chapter takes a different approach. It reads lynching not just as a political act but as a neurological, hormonal, and intergenerational event, one that shaped the bodies, brains, and behaviors of those who witnessed it, especially white children and pregnant women. This is not a departure from history. It is a refusal to let the archive define the boundaries of truth. If terror was passed down through the womb, then the womb belongs in our analysis, not as metaphor but as fact.

Hannah Ocuish didn't just die on a scaffold in New England—she became the prototype. Her small, broken body marked the moment America learned to kill its children and call it a righteous act. What began with a noose evolved into a national ritual, woven into churches, courthouses, and the wombs of white women. If the previous chapter showed us how the rope trained a nation to sacrifice children in public, this chapter reveals what happened in private: how the violence was absorbed into bloodlines, passed quietly from body to body, until cruelty became hereditary.

WHAT THE ARCHIVE CAN'T HOLD

Come, look at an old famous photograph with me, as shown below. Not to gawk but to bear witness to the unspoken and overlooked complicity frozen in time.

This photo reveals how Jim Crow racism operated not just through visible acts of violence but also through quiet, insidious processes of biological preparation and cultural reproduction. The echoes of this violence found their way into the intimate and familial spaces of those present, traveling through bodies and memories.

It also offers a powerful visual demonstration of how racism is rooted in intimate, familial, and bodily experiences, challenging understandings of its transmission across generations. Racism is not just learned; it can be biologically primed, passed down where the womb and bloodline intersect with culture and society. The haunting truth captured in this photograph is in the unseen, enduring legacy it left, embedding itself in both body and history.

This photo transports us back into the smothering heat of the dark night of August 7, 1930, in the Northern city of Marion, Indiana. The atmosphere hummed with the sadistic celebration of the torture and hanging of two Black teenagers who were falsely accused of raping nineteen-year-old Mary Ball, who, according to everybody in town, was "no good." Decades later, a white woman who attended the lynching chuckled during an interview and said, "Nobody would rape her. They wouldn't have to."[1]

Marion, Indiana, August 7, 1930. The brutal lynching of Thomas Shipp and Abram Smith, falsely accused Black teenagers, drew a crowd of thousands.

Ball would later confess that she wasn't raped. White womanhood functioned in insidious ways within this system of terror. White women like Ball, who falsely accused Black males of rape, used lies to regain power. By accusing Black males of sexual violence, these women participated in a ritual that could temporarily restore their status as paragons of white purity and virtue, especially if their reputations had already been tarnished or their social standing compromised within the rigid moral expectations of white patriarchy.

White womanhood in this context was constructed as an ideal of purity and innocence, yet it was also precarious and perpetually threatened by moral or sexual transgressions that could render a woman "fallen" in the eyes of her community. By accusing a Black man or teenager of rape, a white woman could reframe herself as a victim of racialized predation. By doing so, she could gain societal sympathy and also be absolved of any personal failings, redirecting scrutiny and outrage toward the accused Black male. In doing so, she reaffirmed her position within the racial and gender hierarchy while bolstering the mythology of white womanhood as sacred and in need of protection.

This restoration of purity, however fleeting, had devastating consequences. It preserved the accuser's social standing and reinforced white supremacy and patriarchy. The lynching that often followed served as a ritualistic enactment of these systems, where white womanhood was re-centered as sacrosanct, and Black life, irrespective of age, was annihilated in the process. The violence validated the myth of the Black predator, justified the sanctity of white womanhood, and fortified the racialized terror that kept Black communities subjugated. In this way, the act of false accusation and the spectacle of lynching worked hand in hand, weaponizing white womanhood to uphold the brutal architecture of American racism.

The consequence of Mary Ball's false accusations is evident in the stark imagery of the two lynching victims, nineteen-year-olds Abe Smith and Tom Shipp, whose bodies dominate the upper part of the frame of this photograph, sturdy ropes draped over thick tree branches that arch over the scene like an unwanted stage curtain. They look like puppets that the mob discarded mid-performance. Their feet are stiff and twisted awkwardly, the ropes bite into their necks, and their heads tilt unnaturally, as if even the dignity of eternal rest has been denied to them.

Their clothes are grimy and stiff with dirt. One of the teens had been cruelly stabbed by a woman, who dragged the sharp end of her high-heeled shoe down his back. His bloodstained shirt is wrapped around his waist and legs. The fabric clings in a crude attempt to conceal that his genitals were severed. The humiliation didn't end with the castration, as their corpses were left out on display until the next day.

Take a deep breath with me. Hold it for three seconds. Now breathe out slowly.

Too often, the study of lynching collapses individual lives into numbers—thousands of souls strung together in grim statistics, their names buried beneath the weight of data. This aggregation obscures the specific function of lynching children, erasing not only their youth but also the intimate violence that marked their final moments. It turns horror into history, spectacle into spreadsheet.

We must resist this erasure.

Say the following sentence out loud with me: *Abe Smith and Tom Shipp were not abstractions.* Say it again.

Smith and Shipp were shoeshine boys, they had lives and families, they belonged to a community, they had connections, laughter, dreams, and promise, though we may never know the fullness of their stories. A third victim, sixteen-year-old James Cameron, who looked about eleven or twelve, was beaten senseless. A noose was tied around his neck, and just as he was about to be strung up, a voice rang out and declared that he was innocent. His life was spared. He lived to write a book about his traumatic experience and kept this story alive until his death in 2006.[2]

THE FACES BELOW THE TREE

Look away from the bodies of those murdered teens.

Shift your eyes downward to the bottom half of the photograph. Look at the crowd formed in a perimeter around the bodies. Somewhere between ten thousand and fifteen thousand people descended upon Marion that night, traveling from as far as Indianapolis. Cars were parked in chaotic angles across the scene.

The light from the camera's flash, bright and unrelenting, sliced through the darkness, throwing every face, figure, and expression into sharp relief and exposing the unsettling ordinariness of this horrifying scene. Look carefully at each face, every expression and posture, because it is here where the truth of this moment emerges—and with it, a fuller story.

The faces turned toward the camera show a range of expressions. Some are eerily calm while others smirk in quiet satisfaction. Some stare blankly, their eyes hollow, like dark pits. And others seem drunk with the thrill of the night, as if unaware they were standing at the edge of death. The detachment reveals how deeply normalized this ritualistic violence had become. There is no shock, no horror, no grief in sight.

The composition centers on a man with a Hitler-like mustache pointing his arm upward. His face is sharp and angular, filled with the arrogance of someone certain of his place in this hierarchy of life and death. His tattooed arm, extended directly at the boys, is both a declaration and a threat etched in air, a silent command to every Black person who might step beyond the boundaries of Jim Crow etiquette: *This could happen to you or your child*, this warning punctuated by the N-word.

Around him, the crowd buzzes with motion. Some faces blur in the photograph's exposure, hinting at the movement of people shifting their weight, leaning in, and craning their necks to catch a glimpse.

As you look at the crowd with me, you might be struck by the variety: well-dressed men in hats, women in simple cotton dresses, and all those widened bloodlust-heavy eyes. Do they call to mind the gaunt faces sketched in Reginald Marsh's famous cartoon? These aren't the rough characters of folklore mobs. No, they are ordinary people: citizens, neighbors, high school students, lovers, church folks. And the bright flash exposes the different moments of joy, drunkenness, and detachment among them, making their collective complicity all the more chilling.

This was no ordinary lynching, if such a thing could exist. This was communal homicide, performed with the same fervor their colonial ancestors once brought to public executions. The inheritance of violence echoed here, carried across generations from the European squares where thousands of men, women, and children gathered to jeer at the condemned, to these American fields and courtyards where death hung from trees instead of scaffolds and gibbets. In these gatherings, the act of killing was more than punishment; it was entertainment, ritual, and moral instruction. What we see here is a community being baptized in blood and unified by cruelty.

There are more details that deepen the horror. Stay with me.

At the lower edge of the photograph, the crowd thickens. A couple stands off to the left, their hands clasped amid the chaos. They had attended a local dance that night. Look at how their interlocked fingers, so casually intimate, seem untouched by the horror before them. It's a chilling reminder of how easily leisure and brutality slipped into the rhythms of ordinary life.

Behind the couple stands a woman smiling wide. Her light-colored simple dress falls loosely over her frame and conveys practicality rather than fashion. The fabric stretches slightly over what could be the curve of pregnancy—something scholars have suggested after reading eyewitness accounts but that has not been fully corroborated. Her posture is easy, almost carefree, standing in stark, jarring contrast to the brutal violence hanging above her head.

Not far from them, in the foreground, another woman draped in a white dress stands upright and separate from the crowd's movement. She is calm in the chaos. Her presence shifts the tenor of the photograph. While others revel in the spectacle, she becomes a haunting symbol—of something unspoken yet essential.

In most lynching studies, scholars tend to direct attention to the spectacle of violence itself, which typically centers on the immediate victims and the mobs that murdered them. The women situated just beyond the mob receive less attention. Lynching and other forms of racial trauma primed white women's bodies to biologically and psychologically transmit traumas across generations. Using the lens of pregnancy can help us see lynching as a reproductive and racial project.

Lean in and fix your eyes only on this woman.

Her arms rest lightly at her sides and her body language is neutral. She is framed neatly in the photographer's shot, illuminated by the harsh flash. She is neither horrified nor celebratory. Her face is closed, set in a blank expression that borders on indifference, though it's not quite that simple.

Does her expression remind you of the deadpan stare of the little girl in Reginald Marsh's famous cartoon?

Here is yet another face devoid of shock or emotion. She has come to this lynching to normalize, to accept, to pass down. She stands slightly off to the side yet is perfectly visible, as if she, too, were part of the performance.

Beneath her dress, a child stirs.

Can you see the faint curve of her belly, the quiet evidence of new life waiting to emerge? Do you wonder what thoughts she carries alongside that life—of fear, acceptance, or an emotion unspeakably indifferent to the lynching in front of her. How do you think the developing baby interacted biologically with its mother's body with respect to this terror?

With one hand cradling her belly, the woman absorbs the oppressive heat, the sights and sounds, the smell of sweat from the pressing crowd, and the metallic tang of death as she carries the next generation in silence, one that will bear physiological witness to this atrocity, even before taking its first breath.

Today, studies in epigenetics, fetal development, and prenatal influences provide us with a haunting lens through which we can begin to understand what might have been happening within this woman's pregnant belly and those of her peers. Steeped in the spectacle of racial hatred and violence, her body was not unaffected. The sensory chaos of that night, the tension, the sick cheering, the collective energy of that mob—all of it radiated through the scene. Her body became a conduit for its transmission. It traveled deeper, filtering through her body and into the quiet, aquatic world of her womb, influencing the unborn child's neural pathways.[3] These neural pathways might be primed for heightened fear responses, emotional numbing, or aggression.

What those pregnant women saw, felt, smelled, heard, and tasted set off a cascade of adrenaline, cortisol, and other stress hormones through their veins, crossing the placenta and influencing the fetus. The women's rapid heartbeats, like drumbeats of unease, echoed into their wombs, where their unborn children floated in amniotic stillness. The rhythmic rise and fall of their breathing, strained and shallow, carried chemical signals that shaped the fetuses' developing brains, priming them for a world of fear and threat.

The fetuses' tiny, unformed sensory systems tuned in, absorbing the stress, the vibrations of their mother's voices, the pulse of their blood, and the tension in their muscles. Even the air they breathed, laced with the residue of smoke and sweat, was processed and broken down. The molecular imprint crossed the placentas and left faint, invisible scars on the cells of their growing children. These stress signals didn't simply vanish. They inscribed themselves into fetal nervous systems, laying down pathways that would shape how these unborn lives might respond to danger, fear, and even human connection.

The camera's focus traps the Marion woman in this moment—a mother-to-be, standing between death and life, beneath a tree heavy with corpses.

The way the crowd surrounds her, pressing in without fully noticing her, makes her belly almost invisible, much like the Black unborn lynching victims of this era, who haven't been fully acknowledged, counted, or remembered. She is an anomaly, yet she belongs here, her silence reflecting the quiet violence that will soon shape the mind of her unborn child. And so, in this photograph, this pregnant woman carries the legacy of this moment, its terror creating physiological changes that her lineage, for at least the next two generations, will absorb.

GESTATING WHITE SUPREMACY

Science tells us that pregnancy is never solitary; it is a mechanism (one of several) of intergenerational modulation, potentially priming the transmission of violence. In fact, in this biological process, three lives are intertwined: the pregnant woman, her fetus, and the faint, microscopic beginnings of her grandchild.[4] All these lives share this space, this moment, and this trauma of lynching. Within her womb, the fetus carries its own germ cells, the precursors to future eggs or sperm that form the building blocks of another life yet to be. This means that as the sights, sounds, and emotional weight of this lynching in Marion seeped into her senses, they did not stop at her unborn child. They likely rippled forward, potentially shaping the physiological and epigenetic expressions of the next generation.

In this way, a pregnant woman's experience at a lynching did not belong solely to her. It moved through her child and into the genetic expression and emotional possibilities of the future, priming the embedding of terror and violence into the architecture of life itself. Beneath those women's dresses, beneath the surface of this image, an intergenerational legacy was being forged, not just in memory but in flesh. It is a connection that tied these women to the past and to a future shaped by the biological residue and cellular memory of racial terror.

Here, in this photograph, the promise of new life mingled with virulent racism and the presence of violent death. The swollen bellies among the crowd tell us that lynching served to prime and shape the lives yet to begin, indoctrinating the next generation with the sights, sounds, and smells of racial supremacy. And yet, the mob itself, a seemingly disparate collective of men, women, and children, was not peripheral to this process. They were active participants in shaping the womb as a site of biological trauma. Even for those in the crowd who were not pregnant, their collective actions, their cheers, and their presence co-created an environment that influenced the unseen futures within these pregnant women's bellies.

I want you to see how racism operates not only as a social, cultural, or ideological construct but also as a biological foundation. White women have been traditionally portrayed as secondary or passive victims at lynchings who are constrained by patriarchal forces, and often as symbolic figures of purity and virtue whose honor was "protected" by racial violence. But they were more than that. White women were biological gatekeepers of racism. The violence of white supremacy infiltrated, and continues to infiltrate, the very act of human reproduction, priming the bodies and lives of both the oppressors and the oppressed. Pregnant white women who attended lynchings were complicit in normalizing and ensuring the continuity of a racist system across generations.

But what about the pregnant white women who stayed home, who did not attend lynchings but lived in homes and communities steeped in the ideologies of white supremacy? Their role cannot be dismissed. The stories they heard, the photographs they saw, the lessons imparted to them by fathers, brothers, and neighbors—all of these environmental factors entered into their bodies in the form of stress, as belief, and in the normalization of a world where racial terror was routine. For these women, the mob's energy did not need to be physically present to shape the futures of their children. The pervasive culture of systemic racism wove itself into the rhythms of their pregnancies, ensuring that the absence of direct participation in violence did not equate to freedom from its influence.

Neuroscience and epigenetics offer chilling insights into this cycle of violence, casting an even darker shadow over that summer night in Marion. The pregnant women in that crowd who watched with apparent ease as two Black teenagers dangled lifeless before them were not merely spectators; they were vessels through which the physical and psychological weight of that moment could be transmitted to future generations. Beneath the hanging bodies of Abe Smith and Tom Shipp, futures were being forged in silence. Futures shaped by the quiet, implicit acceptance that destroying Black lives was not only permissible but righteous. This is the world their children would inherit, as they were biologically and socially primed to perpetuate these horrors before birth.

Through these visceral physiological channels, the horrors of that night were not just witnessed, *they were biologically transmitted.* Those children, yet to take their first breath, were already learning the rhythms of a world where violence and detachment lived side by side. Each sensory fragment of that lynching became part of the architecture of their future selves—priming their neural, emotional, and epigenetic pathways. This is how the intergenerational legacy of white supremacy, perpetuated through violence, inscribes itself at the cellular level, linking histories of racial atrocities to the biology of the unborn.

These sensory experiences were paired with the cultural indoctrination that awaited those children after birth—stories told at family dinners, shared photographs of lynchings treated as keepsakes, and lessons on the perceived sanctity of white supremacy. The biological priming—the stress-hardened neural pathways shaped in utero—dampened empathy and heightened threat perception, making it easier for cultural indoctrination to override natural moral resistance. The result was a powerful reinforcement loop in which the body had already been conditioned to accept what the culture would demand: silence, complicity, and the capacity for violence.

The unborn children at that Marion lynching were not just forming in a physiological sense; they were also absorbing the emotional and psychological DNA of white supremacy. Their mothers were carrying forward a legacy, one etched into their children's biology, emotions, and worldview, ensuring that the rhythms of life and death remained forever inextricable in the service of systemic racism.

Let me be very clear: I am claiming not that racism is "genetic" or innate but rather that stress, trauma, and societal conditions have measurable effects on prenatal development. The science complements rather than replaces historical and sociological analyses.[5] Could this focus on the physiological pathways of trauma and priming for violence be misread as attributing an immutable inheritance to racism? The answer lies in understanding the dynamic nature of epigenetics. While environmental influences—such as the stress and sensory chaos of the Marion lynching—can imprint themselves on developing fetuses, these effects are not permanent. They are predispositions that are then shaped by context, not destiny. Just as the terror of that night could ripple forward in biological and cultural ways, so too could future healing, nurturing, or even resistance alter these pathways.

This raises an unsettling question about those gathered in Marion that night: Did they, too, carry the physiological remnants of their ancestors' violence and trauma, passed down through generations of racialized hatred and supremacy? Were their responses—calm, detached, or celebratory—not only cultural but also conditioned by the unseen forces of epigenetic legacies? And if so, does this suggest that cycles of racial violence could be disrupted through fostering conditions that undo these epigenetic marks? By understanding this interplay of biology, history, and environment, we move away from fatalism and toward intervention, where the cycle of hate can be interrupted both in the body and the world.

The pregnant white women present at lynchings like the one in Marion were, without question, directly immersed in an atmosphere of racialized violence. However, this chapter cannot ignore the many white women who were no less entangled in the machinery of white supremacy. Their absence from these overtly violent events does not absolve them from complicity; rather, it points to the quieter, more insidious environments where systemic racism thrived—and where it continued to shape the prenatal development of their unborn children.

Consider the "ordinary" racist environments in which many pregnant white women lived. These were likely homes filled with casual slurs over dinner conversations, segregated neighborhoods upheld by exclusionary policies, churches preaching racial hierarchies, and schools indoctrinating children into white superiority. In these spaces, the cultural transmission of racism was no less potent than at a lynching. Even without the visceral imagery of hanging bodies or cheering mobs, these environments dripped with the same toxins of supremacy, embedding them in the everyday rhythms of life.

The stresses of maintaining white dominance, the silent yet pervasive fear of social change, and the quiet acceptance of structural violence—all of these contributed to a similarly charged atmosphere. Pregnant white women absorbed these subtler stressors, and the hormonal responses in their bodies rippled into the quiet recesses of the womb. Their unborn children were exposed to the physiological echoes of their mothers' interactions with an inherently violent system, whether through elevated cortisol levels in utero or, after their birth, through the normalization of a worldview that dehumanized others.[6]

These "ordinary" environments did not create the same spectacle as the Marion lynching, but they were no less instrumental in sustaining the legacy of systemic racism. The children born into these homes and communities inherited the same social architecture, one that wove together biological priming and culture to ensure the continuity of white supremacy.

WHAT THE BODY REMEMBERS, A NATION REPEATS

The lynching in Marion was not an isolated event. It was part of a vast, orchestrated campaign of racial terror that stretched across the United States. Concentrated in the South but extending beyond, the campaign entailed the lynching of thousands of Black people between the late nineteenth century and the mid-twentieth century. Each lynching was a communal ritual and a public spectacle, carefully choreographed to enforce white supremacy and terrorize Black communities. These killings followed predictable patterns, occurring in areas where white dominance was most violently enforced and where Black people sought refuge and opportunity.

The persistence of lynchings over decades and across regions cannot be reduced to a series of isolated acts. They were a systemic phenomenon, sustained by law, culture, and biology. Racial violence was transmitted through the bodies of those who participated in, witnessed, or were born into environments steeped in terror and white supremacy. White communities that normalized and ritualized lynching were shaped by this inheritance as much as by the cultural ideologies that upheld it.

In regions where lynching was pervasive, its frequency ensured that its effects permeated entire communities. For Black people, the constant threat of violence generated cycles of trauma and vulnerability, encoded at the cellular level and passed on through generations. For white communities, organizing and witnessing lynchings, or simply living in proximity to them, left a legacy of biological residue and cultural transmission. Over time, the repeated exposure to racial violence dulled stress responses, recalibrated empathy thresholds, and embedded a physiological tolerance for brutality. That's why so many in the photographs appear calm, even joyful, smiling beneath swinging corpses, flirting in the glow of horror. If your nervous system has been conditioned to interpret domination as safety, and violence as order, then the sight of a lynching isn't disturbing. It's reassuring. The normalization of racial violence became embedded in white people's power, behaviors, and responses to fear, reinforcing the very hierarchies lynching was designed to protect.

Lynching's staying power as a practice, its persistence across decades, and its geographic spread underscores the biological argument in this chapter. This was a sustained campaign, woven into the rhythms of American life. Black bodies were mutilated and hanged as warnings to entire communities, while white bodies stood by or participated, absorbing the violence into their nerves, bloodstreams, and reproductive systems. In this way, lynching shaped the social systems of the United States and primed the biology of those who lived through it, ensuring that its echoes could reverberate across generations.

The Marion photograph is central to this chapter because of its harrowing specificity, but its implications stretch far beyond this single moment. The terror captured in Marion was replicated thousands of times across the nation, in towns and cities where the boundaries between life and death were blurred by the same forces of racial violence. The biological priming for racism extends beyond that crowd, that tree, or that night. It is a national phenomenon, a legacy of lynching that reveals how violence, reproduction, and ideology converge to shape history and generations to come.

What does this mean for white bodies today? Since white supremacy operates not just ideologically, but through the literal shaping of bodies and minds across generations, it means that white bodies still carry the lingering echoes of America's violent racial history, shaping how white people exist within it. These inheritances still manifest in subtle but powerful ways through maladaptive behaviors such as implicit biases, physiological responses to perceived threats, or the normalization of systemic inequalities. If the intergenerational biological argument holds, it suggests that the legacy of racial violence resides in the very cells and neural pathways of those whose ancestors were complicit in its perpetuation.

The Marion photograph, with its haunting interplay of life and death, forces us to confront its reverberations through time. Just as the swollen bellies in the crowd symbolize the perpetuation of racial violence, the bodies of Black women—and the unborn lives they carried—have long been targets of systemic brutality. This violence was not confined to the public squares where crowds gathered; it extended into the medical, legal, and scientific realms, cloaked in the language of progress and preservation.

This moment is part of a chilling continuum of ideas about power, reproduction, and racial control carried across the Atlantic through colonialism. These ideas shaped how Black life was valued, or devalued, before it even began, creating a legacy that lingers.

What makes this history so devastating is not only what it reveals about white violence but what it dares to say about white formation. Racial violence was never just a belief system; it was a biology, a ritual, a spiritual inheritance. It was rehearsed in the body before it was ever written into law. It endures because it didn't need books or speeches to survive. It needed breath. It needed blood. It needed birth.

What does it mean that white women, long mythologized as protectors of innocence, were the ones quietly transmitting terror to the next generation? When the womb becomes a weapon, there is no sanctuary left. The cycle didn't end with the last swing of the rope—it was baked into bodies, whispered into lullabies, passed down as nervous systems shaped by terror and nurtured in silence.

This is not metaphor. This is not exaggeration. The womb has always been political terrain—regulated, exploited, romanticized, and weaponized. What I'm describing is a system in which white women's bodies were not passive vessels but active sites of transmission. Through blood and breath and belief, they carried more than babies. They carried the rhythms of terror, the hormonal imprints of dominance, the sensory echoes of Black death. These transmissions didn't happen in spite of motherhood—they happened through it. This is not about genetics. It's about proximity. It's about a culture that made it possible—*normal*, even—for a pregnant woman to stand beneath a swinging Black body and feel no rupture. That is the inheritance. That is the violence. And that is what must be named.

Some historians will call this speculative. But what they often forget is that the absence of evidence is not the evidence of absence; it is a symptom of how power protects itself. The archive was never built to capture the chemical tremors inside a womb at a lynching. It was not designed to track how cortisol, adrenaline, or sensory overwhelm shaped fetal development or intergenerational emotional patterning. But those effects existed whether or not someone recorded them in writing. This is not conjecture. It is a methodological expansion. To read history only through documented speech and policy is to participate in the very erasure that made such violence possible. If the white womb was used to transmit terror, it must be studied as part of the machinery of white supremacy, not because the body is evil but because the body is a carrier. This is not a leap beyond history. It is history with its blindfold removed.

In the next chapter, we will shift our focus to the Black unborn, exploring how the European practice in which white women sentenced to death delayed their execution by "pleading the belly" evolved into a uniquely American convergence of racialized child-saving campaigns, which included racialized embryological research. These threads, seemingly disparate, illuminate how the Black unborn became targets of both physical annihilation and ideological erasure—a double lynching justified under the guises of science, morality, and progress. Understanding this history is about acknowledging the past while also interrogating how the echoes of these ideologies persist, shaping current discourses on race, science, and reproduction. This history demands that we confront the insidious dehumanization of Black life before it even drew its first breath.

CHAPTER 6

"My Lord, We Plead Our Bellies"

Lynching Black Pregnancy and the Scientific Racialization of the Black Unborn

Come go with me to Little River near Barney, sixteen miles north of Valdosta, Georgia. We are in Brooks County, long known for being the most mob-prone county in the entire South, carrying out lynchings with horrifying regularity.[1]

It's Sunday, May 19, 1918. Noon.

I want you to picture a cornfield along Ryalls Road, dense and tall, hiding a trembling ten-year-old boy. Rufus Morrison was crouched low, his small frame barely distinguishable among the shadows cast by the towering stalks. Or perhaps he was standing small enough not to need to stoop. His breath was shallow with fear.

Can you see him?

I can.

From his hidden vantage point, he was about to bear witness to an atrocity. A narrow, secluded road cut through the woods and was thick with trees on both sides. A small oak tree arching over the road set a gloomy and appropriate stage for what an angry white mob had planned: the lynching of Mary Turner and her unborn child.[2]

Turner's husband, Hayes, had already been lynched. His nose and ears were cut off and he was castrated by a local mob the day before. Eight other Black men were burned, mutilated, shot, and lynched in a racist rampage several days before him. Before Hayes was captured and jailed, his mother had hidden him in a foxhole.[3] This was an act of desperate maternal courage to preserve her son's life. Risking her own safety, she crept through the cover of night to bring him food and clothing. Her every step must have been burdened with the weight of love and fear. Her determination was a testament to the lengths a mother would go to shield her child from the clutches of merciless killers, even as the odds loomed impossibly against her.

Hayes and all the other men had been accused of planning and carrying out the robbery and fatal shooting of Hampton Smith, a prominent white farmer who had a notorious reputation in the Black community for brutally beating his workers, including a pregnant Mary.

The grief-stricken Mary reportedly made "unwise remarks" that inflamed the white community. According to an investigative report published by the NAACP's *Crisis* magazine, "Mrs. Turner made the remark that the killing of her husband was unjust and that if she knew the names of the persons who were in the mob that lynched her husband, she would have warrants sworn out against them and have them punished in the courts."[4]

A mob of white men and boys formed. They came in cars, buggies, and wagons from nearby counties. Turner took her two small children, Ocie Lee and Leaster, to family members' homes for safekeeping. Then, in her eighth month of pregnancy, Turner tried to flee but the mob captured her.

"The delicate state of her health, one month or less previous to delivery, may be imagined, but this fact had no effect on the tender feelings of the mob," according to *The Crisis* report.

They showed her no mercy.

Rufus kept watching, perhaps wishing his body into invisibility. But the scene before him demanded he watch. He peered through the gaps in the towering stalks, his eyes wide, unblinking, and fixed on the mob as they dragged Mary Turner to the oak tree. Gasoline and oil were siphoned from automobile tanks. Rufus probably heard the sickening splashes being thrown over her body.

"While she writhed in agony and the mob howled in glee, a match was applied, and her clothes were burned from her person." One man took a swig of moonshine from a jug and spat it on her.

The flames quickly consumed the woman and unborn child, sending up thin plumes of acrid smoke. The jeering faces of the mob were fully visible, their expressions of glee and rage clear in the sunlight. The acrid smell of burning flesh may have reached young Rufus even through the dense corn. He watched Mary writhe, her body convulsing in agony. Maybe he wanted to squeeze his eyes shut and block out the horror, but he couldn't. Maybe he wanted to cry. But he could make no sound because being discovered meant becoming the mob's next target.

The flames subsided.

Mary was still clinging to life.

The mob was not finished.

The man who spat moonshine on her was dared to slit open her pregnant belly. He gripped a blade meant for splitting hogs. Its cruel edge glinted in the sun. As he plunged it into Mary's swollen abdomen, Rufus watched in horror as "the birthing matter which provided nourishment to her unsuspecting baby, spewed over three of Mary's executioners."[5]

The bloodied premature infant fell to the ground, "gave two feeble cries," and then its head was stomped and crushed by the heel of this man's boot. Turner's body was then riddled with hundreds of bullets from high-powered rifles until she was no longer recognizable as a human being. She and her baby were buried a few feet away from the oak tree.

The scene was grotesquely commemorated with a grim token. At the head of Mary Turner and her child's shallow grave, an empty quart-sized whiskey bottle sat with the stump of a cigar wedged into its neck. One man used the cigar's scent to shield their "delicate nostrils" from the stench of burning human flesh—a final act of inhumanity. NAACP field officers later documented the scene with a photograph that served as a haunting visual record of a crime meant to fade into silence.[6]

"BLOOD-THIRSTY GEORGIA CRACKERS"

White-owned newspapers, including *The New York Times*, *Washington Post*, *Baltimore Sun*, *Chicago Tribune*, *Atlanta Journal-Constitution*, and others, made no mention that Turner was pregnant or that Hampton Smith had beaten her. In fact, her husband had been jailed for trying to protect her during one of Smith's beatings.[7] By omitting the disembowelment and infanticide, these outlets sanitized the barbarity and reinforced a systemic effort to dehumanize Turner and other Black lynching victims by portraying them as thieves and murderers.

This deliberate erasure muted the horror and preserved the white public's moral distance. The press often referred to the mob as "citizens." It was not just the physical lynching of Black bodies that silenced generations but also the cultural and narrative lynching perpetrated by institutions of power, including the press.

The Black press refused to let the humanity of Turner and the terror of her lynching be hidden in euphemism. Black newspapers such as *The New York Age*, *Chicago Defender*, *Cleveland Gazette*, and others did what the white press refused to do. They bore witness, providing an unflinching record.[8]

By calling the mob "man eating savages," "barbarians," "bloodthirsty," "fiendish," and "crackers" in blazing headlines and framing the week of violence as a "holocaust of lynching," Black reporters asserted the moral clarity of their outrage and refused to let white mobs be framed as protectors of societal order or passive participants in systemic terror. By stripping away any veneer of justification for the violence, the Black press reinforced the dignity and humanity of victims like Mary Turner and her unborn child and counteracted the moral erasure embedded in white media narratives.

Still, the deeper emotional toll of these atrocities often remained cloaked in silence, carried in the whispered memories of Black families. Within Turner's community, the lynching was spoken of only in hushed, fragmented terms. She was simply remembered as "the lady who had the baby cut out of her."[9] These emotional scars, like the ones whispered within my own adoptive and biological families, were rarely documented. In a nation that silenced the grief of Black families, the anguish of those left behind after lynchings like that of Hayes and Mary Turner and their unborn child has too often been omitted from the historical record.

Yet, in a rare and haunting account, C. Tyrone Forehand, the great-grand-nephew of Hayes and Mary Turner, broke this silence to chronicle the generational trauma that rippled through their family in a brief essay titled "A Place to Lay Their Heads."

Forehand wrote about how Hayes's siblings—Joseph, Mary, John Jr., George, Julia, Willie, Naomi, and Norman—"were tormented for many years by the memory of their brother's horrific murder. Questions posed by their children and grandchildren regarding the murder of their brother would always result in an overwhelming sense of sadness, accompanied by a distant and terrifying stare. A deafening silence would follow as tears began to flow."[10]

Mary Turner's siblings—Pearlie, Perry, Otha, and Etha—"were forever changed" as well, their lives shaped by the unspoken weight of that horrifying day. Through Forehand's words, we glimpse the unimaginable. We can witness the grief that lingers in quiet moments, the silences that speak louder than words, and the tears that fall for lives stolen, leaving families fractured and futures haunted.

"GET THAT NIGGER BABY OFF ME!"

Rufus Morrison, the ten-year-old boy hiding in the cornfield, is a witness whose voice has been largely overlooked in historical accounts of Mary Turner's lynching. This is shocking, given how much has been written about Turner's execution, the gruesome details of her unborn child's murder, and the rage of the mob.

Why?

How is it that a child who bore the burden of witnessing such horror has been rendered almost invisible?

We know what we know about this lynching because of this ten-year-old boy. I cannot imagine a white member of the mob stepping forward to confess, even though we know whites bragged about participating in lynchings and posed for photographs. This particular lynching, however, crossed a threshold of barbarity that even the most desensitized participants may have feared admitting to. The disembowelment of a pregnant woman and the brutal murder of her unborn child carried a level of savagery that, if spoken aloud, risked exposing the mob's actions not just to condemnation but to a deeper reckoning. The murder of Mary's child was something these good Christians refused to acknowledge. Even within a culture steeped in racial terror, there were some atrocities so grotesque that they demanded silence.

Nor can I imagine the remaining Black residents of Barney, terrified and under threat of further violence, speaking openly about what happened. Five hundred terrified Black people left that town after the lynching, while those who stayed were threatened with retribution if they dared to leave. This leaves us with Rufus.

Much like Forehand's essay on the Turner family killings, Rufus's account was preserved through the efforts of family descendants, passed down to his daughter, Ester, who later shared the details with author Audrey Grant. Grant, who did not even know that Mary Turner was her great-grandmother until 2000, learned the truth when a community organization began holding public meetings about the 1918 lynchings.[11] Despite the critical role Rufus played as a witness, his contributions have been ignored or largely relegated to footnotes.

What does it mean that historians and journalists have not fully acknowledged Rufus Morrison as the primary source? And what about the traumatic impact on this ten-year-old child who bore witness? Forehand writes that "the memory of a frightened and bewildered woman was forever etched in his mind." Rufus, in his recollection, noted that when the mob finished, "the sky became dark."

This haunting observation echoes accounts of the Jesse Washington lynching in Waco, Texas, where residents reported that a tornado swept through the downtown city center, retracing the very ground where Washington's mutilated body had been dragged. At other lynching sites, like Marion, Indiana, trees reportedly withered and died. For Black communities, these occurrences were seen as signs of divine justice, evidence of nature itself recoiling from evil.

Rufus's testimony extends beyond the immediate horror of that day. As quoted in Mari Crabtree's *My Soul Is a Witness*, Forehand recalled that "each of those members of the mob who the birthing matter from Turner's stomach had touched, they all died horrific deaths; one shouting on his death bed, '*Get that nigger baby off me!*'"[12] Such chilling accounts carry the weight of both divine retribution and intergenerational trauma, offering insight into the spiritual and emotional frameworks that Black communities used to process the unthinkable.

And yet, an important question remains: What does it say about the violence itself that its memory persisted in the trembling voice of a boy whose courage ensured that we would not forget? His story is a reminder of the cost of bearing witness and the silences that surround those who must live with such memories.

"YOU OUGHTN'T TO KILL ME!"

Take another deep breath with me.

And now, brace yourself again.

Let's travel 375 miles west of Valdosta, Georgia, and flash forward seven months after the ghastly lynching of Mary Turner and her premature baby. A few days before Christmas, the unrelenting tide of racial violence rose again. This time in Shubuta, Mississippi, on a cold Friday, December 20, 1918.

Four young Black siblings—Andrew and Major Clark, ages fifteen and twenty, and Maggie and Alma Howze, ages twenty and sixteen—were dragged from their jail cells and lynched on the Chickasawhay River bridge. They had been accused of murdering Dr. E. L. Johnston, a chronically drunk, failed white dentist who had repeatedly raped and impregnated the Howze sisters. Maggie was four months from delivery, and the younger Alma was just two weeks away from giving birth. At some point, Major Clark began "going with" Maggie and planned to her marry her, and this led to a violent confrontation with the dentist. According to a February 1919 report in *The Crisis*, Johnston warned Clark to "let her alone or he would kill him."[13]

The truth behind Johnston's death is murky.

Black residents whispered that the dentist had been killed by another white man who had a grudge against Johnston for "seducing" his wife and "felt he could safely kill the dentist and have the blame fall on the Negro." Even Johnston's parents, deeply aware of their son's reputation among the white community as "worthless" and "loose with women," doubted the Black siblings' guilt. His father, a wealthy former state legislator, begged the mob not to lynch the two pairs of siblings. But the mob, immune to reason and drunk on its own fury, was determined to carry out its grotesque justice.[14]

Major Clark bore the brunt of the mob's sadistic wrath. While jailed, he was stripped naked and forced to sit on a vise—a clamping tool with two jaws. His testicles were placed between the jaws and closed tighter and tighter, crushing them until he confessed to the murder. His coerced admission sealed the siblings' fates.

At the bridge, four ropes hung from a girder, waiting to claim the young lives and two unborn. Up until the last moment, the siblings protested their innocence and begged the mob not to lynch them.

Maggie Howze, the most defiant even in her terror, screamed and fought to the very end. Hear her voice: "I ain't guilty of killing that doctor, and you oughtn't to kill me!" she cried.[15]

Her resistance enraged the killers.

One member of the mob struck her across the mouth with a monkey wrench, the metallic crunch of breaking teeth mingling with her cries of pain. Another blow to her head left a deep, gaping wound so large that the side of a hand could fit into it. Her sister Alma, along with the Clark brothers, met their deaths swiftly.

Described as "strong and vigorous," Maggie's will to live shone through her agony, a flicker of hope that seemed almost unbearable in its futility. They threw her over the bridge once, but her hands caught hold of the edge. They hauled her up again, only to throw her over a second time. Still, she caught herself once more.

On the third attempt, Maggie's struggle ended. She and her unborn child died.

Yet, even in her death, her fight left a bitter mark on the mob. In town the next day, members of the mob laughingly told of how hard it was to kill "that Black Jersey woman."[16] Their mocking words were likely an attempt to dispel their unease at her unrelenting defiance and desperate will to fight for her life, her dignity, her right to exist and secure the future of her unborn child.

The bodies hung from the bridge all of Friday night and into Saturday morning. The family members and other Black folks in town refused to cut down the bodies and bury them, fearing they too would be lynched. And some refused to cut down the bodies because they felt that since white folks had lynched the four victims, they should be the ones to do the grisly work.

Witnesses noted that even in death, Alma's unborn baby "had not died but its movements could be seen in the abdomen of its dead mother."[17] However, from a medical standpoint, the baby's movement was not a sign of life but rather the result of postmortem physiological processes. The fetus, deprived of oxygen and nutrients following Alma's death, would have passed away within minutes. The movements in her womb were likely caused by uterine contractions. These contractions, combined with the physical position of the body and the effects of gravity, created the illusion that the fetus was moving independently. The horrifying image of a seemingly stirring fetus amplified the spectacle of violence and added another layer of cruelty to the mob's actions.

Now, pause and imagine being the parents of these siblings and the grandparents of those unborn children. The voices of the Howze sisters' parents were muted in the historical record, and so was the mother of the Clark boys. But Andrew and Major's father was described as "a deeply religious man, well-liked by all the white people of town in which he lives. . . . He is a perfect example of that type loved by the Southern whites—a good 'darkey' who knows how to 'keep his place'—a good nigger.'"[18] But his faith and submissiveness did nothing to shield him from the unimaginable grief of losing two generations of his progeny or the suffocating terror of living under a system that demanded their silence.

Picture those parents.

Imagine the unimaginable weight of knowing your children—two sons who likely tried to shield and protect the sisters, and two daughters, carrying not only their own lives but the fragile hope of new life within them—were hung together. On the same night. From the same bridge. Imagine the devastation of losing not just four young lives but the promise of the future generations they might bear. Imagine their lifeless bodies suspended in plain view and the echoes of their cries still haunting your ears. And yet, even in your grief, you are paralyzed by terror, knowing that if you dared to cut them down, to give them the dignity of burial, you might hang next to them.

What was the message to Black parents in Shubuta that December night?

It was a brutal proclamation of power, a reminder that your children, your lineage, your very future did not belong to you. It belonged to a system of white supremacy that sought to snuff out any spark of resistance, any flicker of hope. This was not just a murder. It was a generational assault, a warning etched into the hearts of every Black parent who watched in horror, too frightened to mourn aloud, too powerless to defy the mob. The bridge did not just hold four bodies that night; it bore the weight of a community's shattered faith and its trembling resolve to survive in a world that demanded their silence and submission.

If that wasn't enough, the cruelty extended its reach and didn't end with the siblings' lynching. Yet another young life would be snuffed out. Less than a month later, on January 3, a brother of the Howze sisters was returning to Shubuta after serving honorably in the US Army and found himself ensnared by the same monstrous force that had claimed his sisters. Walking along a lonely road toward his parents' house, likely filled with anticipation of their embrace, he was seized by a white mob and vanished. Some members of the community said he had been lynched and buried in the snow, while others said he was placed in a chain gang.

RACIAL TERROR IN THE WOMB

What was left for the Turner and Howze families was a silence so heavy it threatened to suffocate, an unbearable reminder that one by one, their children had been erased, leaving behind only shadows of lives that could have been. The void left by their absence seemed insurmountable, but it was not unique. Across the South and beyond, the specter of racial terror claimed not just individuals but entire futures. The unborn babies of Mary Turner and the Howze sisters were not the only ones murdered in acts of racial violence. At least six other documented cases reveal the horrifying extent to which the unborn became targets in the relentless campaign of racial terror. These stories demand that we broaden our understanding of lynching to include the brutal erasure of futures that never had a chance to begin.

In 1914, seventeen-year-old Marie Scott was lynched by a mob of a hundred masked white men in Wagoner County, Oklahoma, while eight months pregnant. Accused of stabbing a white boy, later revealed to be the father of her unborn child, she was dragged from jail and hanged. While white newspapers sanitized the event, Black press coverage exposed it as a brutal punishment for transgressing racial and sexual boundaries. Her death is yet another name in the ledger of unborn Black children extinguished in acts of racial terror.[19]

The unborn were not spared, even decades later.

Dorothy Malcom, a domestic worker who was twenty years old and seven months pregnant, was among four victims of the infamous Moore's Ford Bridge lynching in Georgia on July 25, 1946. Dorothy and her husband, Roger, along with her brother George Dorsey and his wife Mae Murray Dorsey, were ambushed by a mob of white men as they returned from posting bail for Roger, who had been arrested after stabbing a white man during a fight. The mob riddled their bodies with bullets, then cut Dorothy's unborn baby from her womb.[20]

In her book *Fire in a Canebrake*, Laura Wexler notes that local Black residents insisted that both male victims had been castrated. Roger Malcom's genitals were stuffed inside his mouth, and both women's genitals were "carved out and tossed into the trees by the Apalachee River. And others said that one or both of the women had been pregnant, and that their babies had been ripped from their wombs and murdered too." But then Wexler adds, "There was no proof of these things—neither the newsmen who reported on the viewing" nor others said anything about castration or pregnancy.[21]

No newsman had reported these details. These were the same kind of newsmen who routinely sanitized or omitted the gruesome details of lynchings, particularly those involving pregnant Black women. They had already shown their complicity by failing to report on the pregnancies of Mary Turner, the Howze sisters, and others whose lives and unborn children were violently taken. These omissions weren't accidents; they were *deliberate* acts of erasure, aimed at preserving the moral distance of white audiences from the atrocities committed in their name.

To expect those journalists, who were either actively participating or complicit in the racial terror of the time, to truthfully report on such heinous details is naive. It ignores the well-documented role of the white press in minimizing the barbarity of lynch mobs, how it framed their actions as justified or even heroic. By privileging the silence of these newsmen over the testimonies of Black residents, Wexler perpetuates the same systemic erasure that has long marginalized Black voices and oral histories.

Furthermore, this reliance on white journalistic silence as a metric for truth dismisses the power of Black oral traditions, which have been vital for preserving the memory of lynching atrocities. These accounts often filled the gaps left by whitewashed media narratives, offering unflinching details that refused to let the humanity of the victims be erased. Wexler's framing undermines this crucial historical counterbalance, instead leaning on sources deeply entrenched in the *very systems of white supremacy* that enabled such violence to flourish unchecked. This approach not only perpetuates historical erasure but also fails to acknowledge the bias inherent in the sources she deems credible.

Wexler delivers a stunning conclusion with this: "Yet those who told the stories and those who listened to them didn't need proof. The history of lynching made the stories believable, even if they weren't true."[22] This dismissal reeks of condescension and is profoundly troubling. By framing these testimonies as "believable" but not necessarily "true," she subtly invalidates the lived experiences and oral histories of Black communities, reducing their accounts to unverified folklore. This approach undermines the gravity of the claims, suggesting that without official corroboration, such accounts are inherently suspect, even when they align with the documented patterns of racial violence and mutilation historically inflicted on Black bodies.

The insistence on "proof" in the form of white witnesses and testimony reflects a deeper bias in historiography that privileges white-authored records and institutional documentation over the oral traditions and lived experiences of marginalized communities. It perpetuates a cycle of erasure where the voices of the oppressed are heard only when they are validated by the very systems that enacted or were complicit in the violence. This is particularly egregious given the well-documented history of lynching mobs desecrating bodies and preserving severed parts in jars, a fact so normalized in white-supremacist culture that photographic evidence and celebratory postcards were widely circulated at the time. To require "proof" of castration or mutilation in the case of Moore's Ford Bridge, despite these atrocities being emblematic of lynching violence, feels not only insensitive but willfully ignorant of the historical context.

Moreover, the dismissal of Black oral histories as "believable but not true" reinforces a harmful hierarchy of knowledge, where white institutional records are considered the ultimate arbiters of truth. It ignores the reality that these records were often deliberately sanitized or omitted crucial details to protect the perpetrators and maintain the veneer of white respectability. Black oral traditions, on the other hand, have served as vital repositories of historical memory, preserving the truths that institutional archives sought to suppress. To cast doubt on these narratives is to perpetuate the very violence of erasure that lynching sought to achieve, silencing the victims and their descendants once again.

Wexler's framing is not just a methodological oversight; it is a moral failing that upholds the very systems of power and privilege that have long sought to deny Black humanity and truth. It is a stark reminder of the need to center marginalized voices, not as supplementary or secondary sources, but as foundational to understanding the full scope of historical atrocities.

Even in my own family, I think about how my grandfather's murder might have disappeared from the record if it hadn't been documented. If there were no photographs, no reports, no headlines, just our memories, would white historians have believed us? Would they have written it down? I benefit from the fact that it was recorded, but so many other families have only oral history to carry the truth. That truth deserves to be seen as legitimate. If we are to understand the full scope and scale of racial terror, historians must stop treating oral tradition as anecdotal and start recognizing it as evidence of intergenerational trauma and survival.

This disregard for Black oral histories is emblematic of a broader pattern of systemic erasure and dehumanization, one that extended beyond the narrative realm and into the lived experiences of pregnant Black women. These women were frequently accused of crimes without evidence, their pregnancies used as a pretext for further violence and brutality.

On August 1, 1942, twenty-five-year-old Lillian Kelly lost her unborn child after a police officer in Marks, Mississippi, struck her in the abdomen with a baton. On September 28, 1947, Lillie Mae-Dye, pregnant with her fourth child, was shot and killed at her home in Lake City, Florida, following an altercation with a white man over a grocery bill. The man claimed that, inside her home, she attacked him with a knife, and he killed her in self-defense. That same year, twenty-two-year-old Mae Lizzie Norris (identified in some contemporary reports as Mary Noyes), five months pregnant, was gunned down inside a café during a rampage by a white man in Camp Hill, Alabama, who randomly lashed out against a group of Black people after an unrelated argument with a Black soldier.[23]

The killings of unborn children did not always involve mobs; sometimes, they were the result of systemic violence inflicted by law enforcement. In Birmingham, Alabama, in 1951, Willie Ruth Williams was shot and killed by a police officer inside her home during a minor disturbance. Her unborn child, like so many others, was a silent victim of a society that placed no value on Black life.[24]

These accounts are chilling reminders that the violence of lynching did not end with the adults who were hanged, burned, or shot. It seeped into the wombs of pregnant Black women, extinguishing lives before they had a chance to begin. From Mary Turner to Dorothy Malcom, from Marie Scott to Lillie Mae-Dye, the deaths of these unborn children lay bare the depth of racial hatred in America—a hatred that sought to erase Black futures entirely. These stories, spanning years and geography, expose a chilling continuum of violence against Black life, born and unborn, carried out in service of white supremacy.

Together, these stories challenge us to look beyond the immediate, physical violence of lynching and confront its deeper, more insidious implications. They demand that we see lynching not just as a method of terror but as a ritualized form of control over life itself, where even the womb—the sacred site of creation—became a battleground. These events were not anomalies. They were points along a continuum where pregnancy, race, and violence intersected in the most horrifying ways. To fully understand what happened in Marion, Little River, and other towns and cities across the South, we must trace these connections back through centuries of European and American history, where ideas about power and reproduction were codified.

"MY LORD, WE PLEAD OUR BELLIES"

We just explored how fetuses bore the brunt of the racial hatred and violence directed at Black people, particularly Black girls and women as reproducers. But why did white communities not see a problem with allowing pregnant white women to attend highly charged lynchings, as we examined in the previous chapter? How could those same communities, which claimed to hold white motherhood and reproduction in such high regard, stand idly by, or even actively participate, as unborn Black children were ripped from their mothers' wombs and murdered? Where was the national outrage? Where were the cries of horror from white communities as unborn Black lives were extinguished in acts of unspeakable brutality?

Most of the lynchings I cover here occurred in the Progressive Era. It was a time when America professed a deep commitment to the welfare of children. National campaigns sought to reduce infant mortality; address public health, nutrition, and sanitation; reform child labor; and improve education. Reformers championed the importance of protecting childhood innocence and ensuring the health and safety of future generations. Yet even in this era of supposed moral enlightenment, these ideals were glaringly selective. Even as progressives promoted the sanctity of white motherhood, the large majority of these individuals either condoned or remained complicit in the brutal murder of Black women and their unborn children. White mobs brutally destroyed Black lives with the same hands that might later pass out pamphlets about hygiene and better birthing practices. The supposed moral compass of the era was startlingly inoperative when it came to Black lives, revealing a racialized hypocrisy that rendered Black motherhood and the Black unborn unworthy of protection and public health investment.

It was not that white communities merely "stood idly by," for they actively reinforced this violence by allowing pregnant white women to attend lynchings, framing these acts of terror as community events. White motherhood was regarded not as a source of life and protection but as a means of upholding and preserving the future of white supremacy. Pregnant white women, by their very presence, symbolized the perpetuation of white bloodlines, while Black women, especially those who were pregnant, represented the end of bloodlines, their role as reproducers of Black life violently erased.

America did not invent this hypocrisy. White communities had a long history of targeting pregnant women for destruction, a legacy that stretches back centuries, to the brutal warfare of ancient Europe, where pregnant women were deliberately slaughtered to erase bloodlines, sow terror, and assert dominance. By the time enslaved Black women were forcibly brought to American soil, the dehumanization and destruction of their reproductive lives were not aberrations but continuations of this long tradition of genocidal violence.

The barbaric lynching scenes in Marion, Barney, Shubuta, and elsewhere are part of a long historical arc, rooted in European and biblical traditions where the bodies of pregnant women were treated as expendable objects of domination. In these traditions, a womb carrying new life was not sacred; it was a symbol of resistance to be destroyed, a future to be erased.

For ancient Greeks and Romans, the killing of pregnant women and their unborn children was a calculated act of political and economic control. The Old Testament, too, is replete with examples of unborn children being ripped from their mothers' bellies.

The Bible itself is soaked in this logic.

In 2 Kings 8:12, the prophet Elisha weeps as he foretells Hazael's violence: "You will kill their young men with the sword and dash their little ones to the ground, and rip open their pregnant women."

In Hosea 13:16, divine punishment takes the same form: "Their infants will be dashed to the ground, their pregnant women ripped open."

In the literature of the ancient world, these weren't isolated verses. They appeared again and again, framing unborn children as casualties of conquest, their destruction signifying prophecy, punishment, or purification. In the minds of ancient warlords and priests alike, ripping open pregnant bodies wasn't just a tactic—it was theater. It sent a message: *Your lineage ends here.*

These were not metaphors.

Across centuries of warfare, conquest, and religious violence, the same script played out. In ancient Assyria, in Carthage, in medieval Europe, pregnant women were butchered to eliminate futures and assert total power. The fact that these horrors were narrated and sometimes sanctified in scripture gave them moral cover.

So, when white mobs disemboweled Black pregnant women in Georgia or Mississippi, when they stomped on babies expelled from burning wombs, they were not inventing new forms of terror. They were replaying an old one.

A holy one.

And the crowd that watched, silent, obedient, God-fearing, had already seen it written down. In sacred text. In moral language. In prophecy.

The resonance of these ancient practices with later European behaviors is inescapable. The Bible's narratives not only recorded such violence but also informed the moral and cultural ideologies that justified it. These tensions carried into European societies, where Christian teachings were interpreted to justify actions like the slaughter of women and children in religious wars, inquisitions, and transatlantic colonial conquests.

This legacy of biblical violence did not remain confined to the ancient world. It evolved and adapted, crossing oceans and centuries to shape the practices and ideologies of later societies. During the Jim Crow era, these entrenched beliefs about power, control, and expendability reemerged, offering a chilling justification for the racial terror inflicted on Black women and their unborn children.

The medieval and early modern European practice of "pleading of the belly," which outwardly appeared to value life, only showed how systemic brutality could mask itself as compassion, reinforcing the expendability of pregnant women while prioritizing the economic or social utility of their unborn children.

A DEHUMANIZING CALCULUS

In medieval and early modern England, as well as in western European nations like France, Spain, and those in the Germanic regions, legal systems codified this grim reality. The "pleading of the belly," which allowed pregnant women to postpone execution until after childbirth, might appear to reflect compassion. However, it was never about mercy. This calculated legal maneuver offered pregnant women a temporary reprieve—not to spare them as individuals but to preserve the perceived value of the unborn child. Stripped of inherent humanity, the unborn child was viewed as property, an heir, or a future laborer; its worth derived from its connection to the father, the community, or those in power. The pregnant woman, by contrast, was expendable. Once her womb had fulfilled its purpose, she could be discarded.[25]

This dehumanizing calculus extended far beyond the courtroom. In wars, uprisings, and conquests, the brutal killing of pregnant women became a deliberate strategy of domination. Their bodies, and the life they carried, were treated as instruments of power, their destruction a chilling signal of control and erasure. From the inquisitions and witch trials in the Germanic states and Spain to the burnings of heretics like Catherine Cauchés and her daughters in sixteenth-century France, pregnancy offered no sanctity, no sacred reprieve from the relentless assertion of authority. The unborn, no matter how innocent, were not spared when their mothers were marked for death.[26]

This utilitarian view of life reduced the womb to an extension of societal control. Far from being revered as a source of life, the womb was destroyed to serve the interests of those in power. The echoes of this logic resonate in the lynching fields of the American South, where the deliberate targeting of pregnant Black women and their unborn children reveals a chilling continuity in the devaluation of life.

In legal cases where women declared themselves pregnant, courts, operating under the belief that the unborn child's life must be protected, summoned a "jury of matrons." This group typically consisted of twelve or more women—married and of reputable standing within the community, or experienced midwives and medical practitioners—tasked with inspecting the accused. Such examinations often arose in cases involving disputed inheritances or criminal sentences, where pregnancy became a critical factor in determining outcomes. When sufficient women were not available in the courthouse, bailiffs would sometimes fetch random passersby or women from the community to fill the jury.

The matrons would press their fingers against the accused woman's breasts and belly, searching for signs of pregnancy. Their verdict often hinged on the whispered detection of "quickening"—the moment when fetal movement was believed to mark the presence of a legally recognized life in the womb. Under common law, pregnancy alone did not automatically stay an execution; it was the confirmation of quickening that could justify a reprieve. These rudimentary, invasive investigations blurred the lines between medical inquiry and moral judgment. In some cases, women were granted reprieves based on claims of pregnancy, while in others, such claims were dismissed.[27]

The limitations of early pregnancy diagnoses were not merely matters of medical inaccuracy; they were deeply entangled with legal and cultural frameworks that disregarded the humanity of the women involved. Misjudgments about pregnancy, such as the 1220 case of Muriel, an English woman whose supposed pregnancy became the subject of court scrutiny, could affect inheritance disputes or criminal proceedings. Moreover, when such errors intersected with the brutalities of religious persecution, the consequences became far more chilling. The execution of Perotine Massey during the reign of Queen Mary I epitomizes this intersection of inhumanity and institutionalized violence. William Blackstone's *Commentaries on the Laws of England* recounts the horrifying ordeal of Perotine Massey, her sister Guillemine, and their mother Catherine. Accused of harboring stolen goods—a charge that spiraled into a trial for heresy based on their irregular church attendance—the three women were found guilty of heresy on July 17, 1556, and sentenced to burn at the stake the very next day. Massey's fate is a stark reminder that the destruction of pregnant bodies, even under the guise of justice, has long been wielded as a tool of dominance and dehumanization.[28]

Massey, described as "big with child," should have been shielded by both the "law of nature" and legal traditions, which dictated that pregnant women's executions be delayed until after childbirth. Yet, in a display of calculated cruelty, the court, driven by the merciless will of Queen Mary I, ignored these norms and condemned her to the flames. As the fire engulfed her, the shock of the heat caused her child to be born into the inferno. The infant, expelled from her charred womb, lived only a few moments before it was declared a heretic and thrown back into the blaze.

Catherine Cauchés (center) and her two daughters, Guillemine Gilbert (left) and Perotine Massey (right), with Massey's infant son, burning for heresy. Date: 1563. *Source:* Foxe's Book of Martyrs *by John Foxe.*

This ghastly scene reduced both mother and child to being tools in a violent spectacle of religious tyranny, rendering them equally disposable. While the details come from *Foxe's Book of Martyrs*, a Protestant text known for its polemical depictions of Catholic brutality, the historical resonance of this image, whether exaggerated or not, captures the normalization of pregnant women's destruction in religious warfare.

A 1563 drawing of Perotine Massey's execution vividly captures this moment of horror. At its center, Massey is bound to the stake, her body consumed by flames. The artist depicts the infant expelled from her womb, falling helplessly into the fire. The fragile, fleeting life of the child is extinguished before it even fully begins, a horrifying testament to the act's cruelty. Massey's figure, partially obscured by the flames, conveys the agony of her final moments, while the surrounding crowd stands indifferent.

The witnesses, portrayed in rigid stances and blank expressions, reinforce the banality of such violence. Among them are men in formal attire, likely representatives of the court or clergy, whose composed gestures suggest an air of authority. Nearby, women in modest dresses stand silently, their lack of protest or pity highlighting the complicity of the bystander. The juxtaposition of the intimate horror of the mother and child's destruction with the crowd's cold detachment underscores the normalization of brutality.

This drawing of Massey's execution echoes across centuries, resonating with images like the infamous Marion lynching photograph and a ten-year-old's eyewitness account of Mary Turner's disembowelment. Each of these depicts moments of collective violence where the victims' bodies—whether a pregnant Protestant woman in sixteenth-century England or pregnant Black females in Jim Crow America—are focal points in performances of power and domination.

In the Marion photograph we examined together, the crowd's calm indifference beneath the lifeless bodies of Abe Smith and Tom Shipp mirrors the stoic witnesses at Massey's pyre. Both groups signal a normalization of violence so pervasive it renders the grotesque almost banal. In both scenes, the victims are stripped of individuality and reduced to symbols of a broader societal message. Massey's execution reinforced the authority of the church and state, while the lynching of Smith and Shipp asserted the dominance of white supremacy. These executions were not merely acts of physical violence but symbolic gestures of control, dehumanization, and terror directed at entire communities.

Ultimately, the stories of the Massey execution and the Marion lynching converge in their shared exposure of systemic violence. They compel us to confront a long history where the normalization of cruelty, the erasure of humanity, and the complicity of spectators wove these atrocities into the fabric of society. Such moments, captured in both image and narrative, endure as grim reminders of the power structures that sustained them—and the cost of failing to challenge them.

By the eighteenth century, the jury of matrons had begun to fade, eclipsed by advances in medical expertise and the rise of professional physicians who replaced women's hands with instruments and cold, clinical judgment. The jury of matrons had all but disappeared by the nineteenth century, eclipsed by the growing dominance of professionalized medicine. Yet echoes of the plea persisted, surfacing in moments when pregnancy was invoked not as a shield defending women's humanity but as a tool for societal judgment and spectacle.

This shift from communal adjudication to institutionalized authority is starkly illustrated in the trial of Mary Bateman, whose case exemplifies how the remnants of these earlier practices were absorbed into the new, clinical frameworks of justice and punishment. Bateman was on trial for defrauding and murdering Rebecca Perigo. Her trial took place on March 17, 1809, at York Castle before Judge Simon Le Blanc and a large audience. Her husband, John Bateman, had his own case dropped due to insufficient evidence, leaving Mary as the main defendant. William Perigo, Rebecca's husband, testified against her for over four hours, providing damning evidence of her involvement in Rebecca's poisoning. Mary had no legal representation and simply denied the crimes during her defense. The jury deliberated briefly and found her guilty. Mary immediately claimed pregnancy to delay her execution, prompting the judge to order a jury of matrons to examine her in private.

The jury of matrons found her neither pregnant nor "quick with child," leading to her remand back to York Castle. She showed little repentance and continued to deny the murder charges, only admitting to fraud. On the day of her execution, a crowd of over five thousand gathered outside York Castle to witness the hanging. Mary was taken to the gallows, where she pleaded for mercy and maintained her innocence before her life was ended. After the execution, Mary's body, along with that of another poisoner, Joseph Brown, was sent for public dissection at Leeds General Infirmary. The dissection attracted significant attention, with twenty-four thousand people paying to view it, including medical students and the educated elite. The dissection raised over £80, serving as both an educational demonstration and a deterrent to crime. After the dissection, Mary's body was displayed at the infirmary, and strips of her skin were even sold as souvenirs.[29]

The grotesque commodification of Mary's body was not an isolated act of cruelty. It was part of a broader cultural acceptance of treating human remains as objects for profit and spectacle. This history matters not simply as a record of dehumanization but as a window into the deep and violent logic that crossed the Atlantic and adapted to America's racial hierarchies. The same ideologies that allowed Mary's body to be dissected and sold would later render the bodies of pregnant Black women in the Jim Crow South as expendable, reinforcing systems of power that saw life and death as intertwined tools of control.

A GRIM LEGACY: FETAL HOMICIDE IN AMERICA

In America, ideologies of control, patriarchal dominance, and disregard for the humanity of women—especially pregnant women—took new forms within the violent realities of settler colonialism, slavery, and an emerging racial order. The core principle remained: Women's lives and bodies were expendable when measured against the interests of power, property, and societal control.

In both Europe and America, the record of executions of pregnant women is short, not out of reverence for life, but because claims of pregnancy were often simply ignored, denied, or dismissed. The few exceptions—cases where public spectacle, witnesses, or physicians ensured the record—preserve for posterity the enduring dehumanization of women. Their bodies were reduced to vessels, valued not for their autonomy or dignity but for their utility within a patriarchal framework.

Colonial American violence against women began with religious fervor. Struggling early communities would spare no mercy for those who jeopardized the emerging Puritan order, but the future of such communities depended crucially on producing lots of children. Consider the case of Elizabeth Proctor, born Elizabeth Bassett in 1650, who became ensnared in the Salem Witch Trials of 1692. Accused of witchcraft alongside her husband, John Proctor, she faced the grim certainty of execution. John was convicted and hanged, but Elizabeth's pregnancy postponed her sentence under English common law, which protected a fetus deemed "quick" in the womb. While the records frame the reprieve as a legal protection for innocent life, the practical effect was the same: The unborn child's value to the community outweighed the mother's. Her reprieve was not mercy; it was a chilling reminder that even in the throes of religious fervor, the value of the unborn child, not the mother's life, dictated legal outcomes.

Nearly a century later, in the 1778 Spooner murder case in Brookfield, Massachusetts, we find a similar dynamic that further exemplified this grim tradition. Although, in this case the child, too, was considered expendable. Bathsheba Ruggles Spooner, an intelligent and defiant woman trapped in an unhappy marriage, conspired with three soldiers—Ezra Ross, William Brooks, and James Buchanan—to murder her husband, Joshua Spooner. He was savagely beaten and discarded headfirst into a well. When the crime was uncovered, the men implicated Bathsheba as the mastermind.

Bathsheba's trial and execution were about more than the crime; they reflected her defiance of societal norms. Her affair with sixteen-year-old Ezra Ross resulted in a pregnancy she sought to leverage for a stay of execution. Although Reverend Thaddeus Maccarty supported her plea for clemency, the authorities refused. On July 2, 1778, at thirty-two years old and five months pregnant, Bathsheba Spooner became the first woman, and the first pregnant woman, to be hanged in the United States. Her pregnancy, instead of shielding her, was disregarded in favor of a swift, punitive spectacle. The execution of a pregnant woman and her teenage lover marked a grim beginning for the new nation.[30]

While Bathsheba's execution did not immediately end the practice of executing women in Massachusetts, it contributed to growing discomfort with capital punishment, particularly in cases involving pregnant women. What began as a system of oppression in Europe evolved and expanded in the United States, where it merged with the brutal realities of colonialism and racial violence, finding its most devastating expression within the institution of slavery, where Black women's bodies were reduced to implements of exploitation and their pregnancies became instruments of economic power.

During slavery in the United States, Black women's ability to bear children was systemically exploited to perpetuate and expand the institution of slavery. With the prohibition on importing enslaved Africans, instituted in 1808, natural reproduction became a cornerstone of the American slave economy. Enslaved women were coerced into pregnancies, and those pregnancies were often managed according to the same cold economic logic found in the legal practice of pleading the belly: The woman's life was secondary to the perceived value of the unborn child. In both systems, the fetus was treated as property or potential labor, while the mother's body was reduced to a means to that end.

After abolition, however, white America's attitudes shifted to concern over rapid demographic shifts. White people became terrified of being overrun by an exploding Black population, along with "swarthy" immigrants from Europe and ambiguous-looking Black people passing for white. At the same time, white families were having fewer children. It is in this context that Black youth, even the unborn, became a central concern for white people. At the same time that pregnant Black women and their unborn children were being extrajudicially executed in the South, Black women were subject to disproportionate levels of eugenic treatment in the North. The enforcement of whiteness and racial hegemony gradually shifted to the domains of science and medicine. Across America, pregnant Black women suffered extreme levels of poverty and risk, which resulted in high levels of maternal and infant mortality. The solution to the growth of the Black population was often forced abortion, sterilization, and even lynching.

The echoes of pleading the belly reverberated into the era of lynching and segregation. The extrajudicial killing of pregnant Black women served the dual purpose of terror and control. It was not merely the murder of an individual but also the symbolic destruction of future generations, a grim reminder to Black communities of their vulnerability under white supremacy. Yet, even as lynch mobs wielded violence to enforce racial hierarchies, medical science began to refine and institutionalize new methods of reproductive control. The nascent field of gynecology, pioneered by figures like J. Marion Sims, exploited the bodies of enslaved Black women under the guise of advancing medical knowledge. Like the legal precedent of pleading the belly, Sims's experiments devalued the lives of Black women while placing disproportionate importance on their reproductive systems.

THE RACIALIZATION OF THE FETUS

In a stark photograph from Cold Spring Harbor Laboratory in 1921, rows of preserved fetal models sit on shelves, their forms frozen in silent stillness. Each bears a label: "Negro" or "White." These figures, robbed of individuality, were seen not as lives but as specimens, objects to be measured, categorized, and racialized in the service of a pseudoscientific project that sought to legitimize white supremacy. As I gaze at these stark and sterile forms, I cannot help but think of the unborn children of Mary Turner, the Howze sisters, and the many other pregnant Black women violently killed in the Jim Crow South. Their unborn children were not preserved in sterile laboratories; they were ripped from wombs by white mobs, their cries silenced before their lives could begin.

The historical record offers no account of what became of the unborn Black children killed when their mothers were lynched. Did their remains decay in shallow, unmarked graves beside their mothers? Or did their desecrated forms serve as macabre trophies for mobs reveling in their own barbarity? While we may never know their fate, it is chilling to view their stories within the broader context of America in the early twentieth century, where fetal material was regularly collected

"Comparison of White and Negro Fetuses." Cold Spring Harbor Laboratory, 1921.

from abortions, miscarriages, funeral homes, and autopsies for study. Although these lynched fetuses—brutally crushed and torn—would have been unsuitable for scientific preservation, the violent disregard for their humanity echoes in the jars and shelves of laboratories that sought to racialize and commodify the unborn.

The same nation that treated Black unborn children as disposable in the lynching fields saw their white counterparts as symbols of purity and as the standard for "normal" human development, while Black fetuses were studied and racialized in service of white supremacy. Scientists measured skulls, compared skin tones, and sought evidence of racial differences in fetal development, embedding racial biases in the bedrock of American science. The bodies of these unborn children were subjected to a different kind of violence—measured, categorized, and racialized under the guise of objective scientific inquiry.

It is difficult to generalize what fetal bodies represented in 1918, because their meanings were constructed differently depending on the social and scientific arenas in which they were studied. Obstetricians and gynecologists viewed fetuses as part of their efforts to improve maternal health, albeit within the racial hierarchies of their time. Meanwhile, anatomists and physical anthropologists often treated fetuses as tools for exploring racial differences, further embedding systemic racism into the field of embryology. Figures like Aleš Hrdlička, from his influential position at the Smithsonian Institution, sought to demonstrate the supremacy of whiteness through comparative studies of fetal development. While some scientists, like Franz Boas and Franklin Mall, challenged biological determinism, their methodologies, marked by the collection and measurement of fetal skulls, often mirrored the very practices they sought to disprove. This tension underscores the contradiction of scientific racialization, where the same evidence was wielded both to reinforce and to dismantle racist ideologies.

The collection and analysis of fetal specimens during this period reveal the dehumanizing ways in which Black bodies were exploited. Medical journals like the Carnegie Institution's *Contributions to Embryology* routinely categorized fetal specimens by race, perpetuating the notion that racial differences were inherent to human biology. The specimens, sometimes obtained unethically from Black communities, were stripped of their humanity and reduced to data points in a broader effort to uphold racial hierarchies.[31]

For example, Robert A. Munsick's study comparing fetal extremity lengths between "Negro" and Caucasian fetuses found no significant differences in development from nine to twenty weeks of gestation. On the surface, such findings might seem to refute racial myths, yet the premise of studying racial differences in fetal development highlights an enduring preoccupation with categorizing and differentiating human bodies by race.[32]

In this context, the violence of lynching pregnant Black women and the scientific racialization of Black fetuses were two sides of the same coin, part of a white-supremacist ecosystem that sought to control and devalue Black life. While lynch mobs targeted the physical bodies of Black women and their unborn children, scientists racialized fetal development to justify systemic inequalities. These scientific practices mirrored the grotesque realities of the lynching fields. Just as Mary Turner's unborn child was violently crushed under the heel of a mob member, Black fetuses in the scientific arena were metaphorically crushed under the weight of racial biases disguised as objectivity.

While some scientists, like Franklin Mall, challenged these narratives, their reliance on the same dehumanizing methodologies highlights the pervasive influence of white supremacy within the field. Studies published in journals like *The American Journal of Anatomy* analyzed cranial sutures and femoral structures in Black fetuses, often describing deviations from whiteness as pathological. These findings had no real public health purpose; instead, they reinforced stereotypes that framed Black bodies as inferior and biologically predetermined for subjugation.

The unethical collection of fetal specimens from cities like Baltimore paralleled the violence inflicted on Black women, whose reproductive capacities were controlled and weaponized through slavery, lynching, and sterilization. The emphasis on biologically determinist frameworks in embryological research ignored the profound impact of systemic racism, poverty, and health care inequities on maternal and fetal health, instead attributing disparities solely to racial differences.

As the eugenics movement gained momentum in the twentieth century, the logic of pleading the belly was inverted and used against Black communities. Where once the reproductive potential of marginalized women was exploited for economic gain, eugenics sought to suppress it entirely. Coercive sterilization programs targeted African American women under the guise of public health and poverty alleviation. States like North Carolina authorized sterilizations for those deemed "unfit"—a label disproportionately applied to poor Black women. These policies were not merely acts of medical discrimination but tools of racial and social control, designed to curtail the growth of populations deemed undesirable by white elites.

The continuity between pleading the belly and modern eugenics reveals a persistent societal investment in controlling the reproduction of marginalized women. Both the legal precedent and the medical ideology, though separated by centuries, reflect a deep-rooted belief that the value or disvalue of a woman's body lies in its capacity to reproduce—whether for economic exploitation, racial purity, or population control. The transition from lynching pregnant women to sterilizing them in clinics represents a shift in methods but not in ideology. In both cases, the goal remained the same: to manage and discipline Black populations through fear, violence, and systemic control of reproduction.

The connection between the killings of unborn Black babies and child-saving campaigns of the late nineteenth and early twentieth centuries is rather explicit. The pioneers of child-saving worked alongside pioneers of abortion rights, such as Margaret Sanger, all of whom were explicit in supporting eugenic sterilization and the elimination of "substandard" racial groups, which often included poor Black women. Child-savers and abortion activists advocated for bringing fewer children into a state of poverty and degeneracy that purportedly would be bad for child, mother, and society. As good progressives, they decried the horrors of lynching but tacitly agreed with the sentiment of the mob that the future of civilization required hard choices about who lives and who dies, and they upheld the need to improve humanity through the destruction of unborn Black children without consent of their mothers.

The Progressive Era's child-saving movement claimed to promote a more civilized respect for humanity, aiming to spare children the trauma of poverty, exclusion, and exploitation. Yet progressives' concern for "race betterment" was deeply entangled with white supremacy. While they sought to provide white mothers care and safety for their unborn children, ensuring opportunities for health and prosperity, the solutions offered to Black mothers were sterilization, abortion, or neglect. Progressive eugenic policies targeting Black mothers and their unborn children were a sanitized form of lynching, cloaked in the authority of science but driven by the same racist end goals.

This chapter has woven together the stories of racial violence, reproductive control, and the so-called authority of science to show how Black women and their unborn children became targets in a society hell-bent on maintaining white supremacy. From the lynching fields to the laboratories of embryologists, the attacks on Black life weren't just physical, carried out through brute force; they were also carried out through institutional policies and the insidious authority of science. And let's be clear: These acts, though occurring in different arenas, were not disconnected. Together, they reveal a cohesive system designed to control, exploit, and ultimately erase Black futures.

At its core, this chapter is about continuity—a grim lineage that begins in medieval Europe, where the bodies of pregnant women were treated as tools of terror and domination, and extends across the Atlantic to America's lynching fields. Here, the destruction of Black women and their unborn children became a form of racial terror, targeting not only individual lives but also the generations they carried. Meanwhile, scientific disciplines such as embryology and anthropology reinforced racial hierarchies by turning Black fetal bodies into racialized specimens of study. Under the guise of objectivity, they gave white supremacy a veneer of respectability.

This history also exposes the moral hypocrisy of the Progressive Era, a time when white society professed a deep commitment to the welfare of children while condoning violence against Black women and children. The same people who championed child welfare legislation and distributed pamphlets on maternal health ignored or even participated in the brutal destruction of Black motherhood. The rhetoric of child-saving campaigns and the policies of eugenic sterilization reveal the duplicity of a society that celebrated white motherhood while weaponizing reproduction to control and diminish Black life.

What I want you to take away is this: Lynching, scientific racism, and eugenics were not random or isolated. They were part of a single, cohesive system—a broader ecosystem of white supremacy—designed to control Black life at every stage, from conception to death. And the thread connecting all of it is a relentless determination to erase Black futures, whether by violent spectacle or the quieter, more "respectable" violence of medical and scientific authority.

This chapter isn't just about documenting horrors. It's about forcing us to reckon with how deeply embedded this system of oppression really is. We can't pretend these are things of the past when their legacies are still shaping the present. If we're going to confront these truths, we must be willing to see how every piece fits together. Only then can we start to unravel the structures of white supremacy that have been so carefully constructed—*and so devastatingly effective.*

CHAPTER 7

“If Dat Chile Doan Soon Turn Colour There’ll Be Trouble in Dis Family”

The Fear of Changeling Babies and the Lynching of Black Infants and Toddlers

“IN SELF-DEFENSE.”
SOUTHERN CHIV. “Ef I hadn't-er killed you, you would hev growed up to rule me.”

“In Self-Defense” by A. B. Frost.
Source: Harper’s Weekly, *October 18, 1876*

Before we turn to the cribs and maternity wards of the Jim Crow era, consider the image published in *Harper’s Weekly* in 1876. The cartoon, drawn by A. B. Frost, is titled “In Self-Defense.” It shows a gaunt white man looming over the lifeless body of a Black baby. Smoke curls from the barrel of his pistol, a knife glints in his other hand, and beneath the image runs a caption that doubles as confession and creed: “Ef I hadn’t-er killed you, you would hev growed up to rule me.”

What Frost sketched in ink was already written in blood. His cartoon distilled the creed of white supremacy: Kill the child before the future arrives. In a single panel, Frost exposed the grotesque belief that underpinned both mob violence and state policy: that the mere potential of Black life was intolerable. Infanticide was framed as self-defense and as common sense. Black babies were cast not as innocent but as threats in waiting. Better to extinguish them in the cradle than let them live into a future where they might claim equality.

But our story does not stop at the edge of the grave or the lab bench. It carries forward, quietly, efficiently, through hospital corridors, public health campaigns, and the courts. The rope gives way to paperwork. The mob disperses into policy. The knife becomes a pen. If lynching was the loud part of racial violence, bureaucracy was the echo that never ceased. The same American "civilization" that cut babies from Black women's bellies also learned how to erase Black futures through the cold machinery of the state.

It is the same logic of prevention that left Mary Turner's body opened with her unborn child crushed beneath a heel, that bound Maggie Howze to the rope, that let scientists in white coats arrange "Negro" and "White" fetuses on shelves like exhibits in a museum of lies. The womb, once a stage for racial domination, had become science's theater.

If Black manhood was perceived as a threat to white dominance, and Black womanhood as the incubator of an uncontainable future, then Black childhood posed an even more destabilizing danger. The presence of Black babies called into question the permanence of racial categories at their most fragile stage, when features had yet to settle and skin tone seemed to shift like prophecy. Infancy, far from being exempt from white supremacy's reach, became a battlefield where biology, law, and violence converged to secure the Jim Crow era's racial boundaries.

The very act of birth, which is universal, sacred, and precarious, was drawn into the project of racial governance. What should have been a precious threshold of life was warped into a site of suspicion, surveillance, and, too often, death. Lynching, once relegated to the public theater of racial control, now seeped into nurseries and maternity wards. From the tree to the crib, from the town square to the birthing room, the reach of white supremacy expanded.

In the aftermath of emancipation, Black children became a unique and urgent threat to the white racial order. They were imagined as inheritors of Black identity and as unpredictable agents of disruption whose very existence challenged the logic of segregation. The Supreme Court's 1896 *Plessy v. Ferguson* decision, by formalizing the doctrine of "separate but equal," transformed this panic into legal necessity. Segregation's legitimacy now depended on the ability to assign racial identity with precision.

In this context, the newborn body became a battleground. From hospitals to laboratories, pediatricians, race scientists, and state bureaucrats turned their gaze toward infants, scrutinizing skin, genitals, hair, and skulls in search of racial truth. Pediatrics, emerging as a modern discipline at the turn of the twentieth century, was shaped by a quiet but powerful commitment to racial classification. Scientific medicine, once peripheral to the policing of race, now stood at its center, transforming the intimate act of birth into a site of surveillance, categorization, and violence.

This chapter challenges the popular history in at least five ways. First, it punctures the myth that lynching was primarily a response to alleged criminality by adult men. Here we will see how infants and toddlers were killed to neutralize a future, not punish a deed. Their killings were demographic control masquerading as "self-defense."

Second, it overturns the idea that lynching was solely extralegal. I trace a pipeline from rope to bureaucracy—pediatrics, eugenics, hospital protocol, and vital records—making clear that law, medicine, and public health extended the work of the mob.

Third, this chapter disproves the regional alibi that lynching was only "a Southern thing," foregrounding Northern courts, newspapers, philanthropies, and medical schools as active collaborators.

Fourth, it exposes how the "child-saving" of the Progressive Era was racially exclusive: The child imagined as the nation's future was white, while Black childhood was pathologized, surveilled, and culled.

And lastly, it directly contests the notion of race as biological fact by showing how anxieties over "changeling" babies and the medical scrutiny of Black newborns were mechanisms to manufacture racial certainty where nature offered none.

By centering babies, mothers, midwives, doctors, adoptive parents, and white women's roles in guarding the color line, the chapter widens culpability and relocates the site of racial terror to the cradle and the birth record. It recasts lynching as a continuum—spectacle and science, fire and file—to reveal that the American state did not end the practice of lynching; it professionalized it.

What the mob once enforced with rope and fire, the state now rehearsed with charts and certificates. The noose transformed into paperwork, and its target was the child in the earliest phase of development, before a child could speak.

POLICING BIRTH

Birth—the most primal passage into humanity, a sacred moment filled with hope, love, and the promise of a new story—was, in the Jim Crow South, consumed by fear, suspicion, and the shadow of violence.

For Black families, the arrival of new life was met not with celebration but with the cold machinery of white supremacy. After the abolition of slavery, the lynching of Black children became a powerful tool to discipline Black communities into fearful obedience and brutally initiate white youth into their role as deranged enforcers of the color line. The younger the victim, the deeper the indoctrination and the more terrifying the message: No Black life was too small to be crushed beneath the weight of white supremacy.

In February 1869, the Ku Klux Klan stormed the home of Daniel Blue in Moore County, North Carolina, and fired rifles indiscriminately. The assault claimed the lives of Blue's pregnant wife and their five children, including a toddler. One Klansman reportedly murdered the youngest child by "kicking its brain out with the heel of his boot." To cover up the massacre, the Klan burned the house to the ground, along with the bodies inside.

Less than two decades later, in June 1880, a white man in Brenham, Texas, ran over and killed an eighteen-month-old Black baby with his wagon.[1]

In March 1898, in Quitman, Georgia, Henry Raines was sitting in his home, bouncing his two-year-old son on his knee and kissing him, when an "unknown party" approached the window and shot them both dead. Eleven buckshot pellets tore through the father's head, while four lodged in the child.[2]

Just a month later, in Lake City, South Carolina, a white mob targeted Frazier Baker, the first appointed Black postmaster in the town.

Visit of the Ku-Klux, drawing, published in Harper's Weekly, *February 24, 1872, p. 160.*

Setting fire to the post office, which also served as his family's home, the mob opened fire as the family fled the flames. Baker was killed, and his two-year-old daughter Julia died in her mother's arms—struck by a bullet that passed through both their bodies. His wife, wounded, survived along with their older children.[3]

In August 1906, in Sharp County, Arkansas, three white men opened fire on the home of a Black family, killing a baby as they slept beside their mother. For this atrocity, the perpetrators were convicted of involuntary manslaughter but received a mere twelve hours in prison.[4]

Three years later, in April 1909, a night rider raid in Marshall County, Kentucky, ended with a Black baby shot to death.

In 1911, in Spartanburg, South Carolina, Frances Sarratt, a white woman, shot a Black baby while attempting to murder the mother. Sarratt was arrested but later acquitted after pleading temporary insanity.

Fast-forward to Omaha, Nebraska, in 1945. A white bus driver snatched a Black baby from its mother's arms and choked it to death. A white soldier riding the bus retaliated by attacking the driver with a knife, severing his head.[5]

Each killing inverted what birth was meant to signify. Black childhood was not protected as a promise of the future but erased as a threat, its very existence treated as a crime punishable by death. And when mobs were not wielding guns or fire, the project of erasing Black futures continued through quieter means: law, science, and medicine. The violence moved from the open square into nurseries, clinics, and bureaucracies.

When polite society happened to be sufficiently offended by such atrocities, the people who committed them might serve some time in prison. Occasionally, if the crimes were especially heinous, the perpetrator would be executed, as was the case with Gus Johnson in 1878, the first white man in Georgia to be put to death for killing a Black person. Johnson, who "seemed to have a natural hatred for colored people," was executed for, among other things, reportedly "carving a little negro boy into fragments and using pieces of the body for fish bait."[6]

More often than not, these lynchings were viewed as morally ambiguous, and the public was indifferent about the apprehension of perpetrators. With little chance of investigation or punishment, white perpetrators acted with confidence, convinced they were dispensing justice and protecting white society from being overrun by a growing Black population.

During the Progressive Era, a time when doctors, scientists, and reformers championed child labor laws, infant health initiatives, and public education, children—specifically white children—were heralded as the embodiment of the nation's future. Black children, however, were erased from this vision. While progressive ideals framed child welfare as a moral imperative, the deaths of Black babies and toddlers were rationalized as an inevitable cost of racial progress. Amid campaigns to "save" children, Black children remained outside the bounds of empathy, their humanity sacrificed to the very systems that claimed to uplift the young.

How could a nation that prided itself on protecting children tolerate, and even sanction, the brutal extermination of the Black unborn, infants, and toddlers?

How did reformers who crusaded against child malnutrition and disease turn a blind eye to the staggering Black infant mortality rate and racist murders?

If children were symbols of progress, what did it mean that Black children were framed instead as threats, villainized in the press, and marked for execution by white mobs?

The answer lay in the racial ideology that informed these so-called reforms. Like lynching mobs, race scientists and eugenicists viewed Black children not as future citizens to be nurtured but as biological threats to be contained. Since white children represented the future of civilization, they had to be kept on the path to education, work, and full citizenship. To achieve this, white reformers insisted that white children be distanced and insulated from the alleged "corrupting influences" of Black youth, whom they characterized as damaged by the material and psychological conditions of slavery. Therefore, Black children were framed as symbols of regression, degeneracy, and disorder. Lynching Black children was not a contradiction of progressive reform but *an extension of it*.

The growth of the Black population threatened white dominance, and Black childhood itself symbolized a future that challenged white power. Denied the protections extended to white children, Black children were left vulnerable to systemic violence and neglect. In this context, child lynching functioned as a tool of racial purification, ensuring the nation's future belonged solely to those deemed racially "worthy" of inheriting it. The "child-saving" movement, despite its moral pretenses, was never about saving all children. Lynchings of Black children were framed as social hygiene. For white supremacists, these murders were calculated efforts at demographic control. By extinguishing Black lives early, white mobs sought to crush generations of resistance before they could take root.

This violence targeted the very possibility of Black children's future. Yet as white supremacists attempted to erase Black childhood, they faced an existential crisis: the instability of the racial order they enforced. The rigid boundaries of whiteness were crumbling under the reality of racial mixing and Black infiltration into white spaces, which blurred visual markers of an individual's "fitness" to belong. Newborns, their race often indeterminate in infancy, became symbols of this chaos, exposing the futility of codifying race through law or pseudoscience. No amount of bureaucratic or violent effort could fully suppress the threat that interracial intimacy posed to white supremacy. The terror inflicted on Black children revealed a desperate, failing attempt to preserve a racial hierarchy already collapsing from within.

The long-standing cultural shorthand of determining race by the naked eye was no longer always practical or reliable. Nor were such methods efficient. White society knew it could never lynch or imprison the entire growing population of freed slaves and their descendants. A new system of categorization was required, one with a high degree of technical efficiency and accuracy. Blackness needed to be identified as early as possible, if not in the child, then in the infant, and if not in the infant, then in the fetus. While white mobs policed racial boundaries through violence, pediatricians and medical researchers sought to do the same through science, studying the pigmentation changes in Black fetuses and newborns, the texture of their hair, and the shape of their features to establish so-called definitive racial markers. Their findings were used to reinforce segregationist policies, justify racial hierarchies, and ensure that no Black child, no matter how light-skinned at birth, could slip through the cracks of white supremacy's rigid order.

After *Plessy v. Ferguson* enshrined segregation as law—upholding the conviction of Homer Plessy, who was seven-eighths white yet classified as Black under Louisiana's racial codes—white supremacists grew fixated on the smallest gradations of ancestry and intensified their efforts to police the boundaries of identity. That obsession crept into the most private and sacred moments of life, turning the birthing room into a site of surveillance and suspicion. The dirty business of lynching Black children, infants, and fetuses, once carried out by frenzied mobs, often to the disgust of "respectable" racists, was increasingly taken over by calm professionals in eugenic science and medicine.

At the same time, laws like the "Grandfather Clause," which tied voting rights to ancestral lineage, revealed how whiteness was fortified not only in the present but through bloodlines. The obsession with ancestry linked political rights at the ballot box to biological identity in the child's body. The *Plessy* decision underscored the lengths to which white society would go to maintain racial control, especially over those whose appearance blurred the line between Black and white. Yet some Black children still slipped through the borders of race. For white supremacists, it became clear: Childhood itself—not adulthood—was the new battlefront for securing racial boundaries generationally.

While the *Plessy* decision exploited the slippage between skin color and race to sanction various structures of Black subordination, it left unresolved the visual certainty of racial identity and about who had the authority to decide, on the spot, who was Black or white without proper "scientific" procedures.[7] The ambiguity fueled the medical community's obsessive drive to unpack the mysteries of skin pigmentation.

By the end of the 1890s, medical scientists had turned their gaze to Black infants and even stillborn fetuses, using them as clinical "material" to solve urgent questions about racial identity, childhood illnesses, and death. No part of the Black child's body escaped the attention of biologists, anthropologists, anatomists, and pediatricians. Skin, skull, face, teeth, cranium, pelvis, genitals, spine, toes, jaws, lips, nose, and hair were all catalogued. As David Hoogland Noon has explained in his powerful 2005 essay "The Evolution of Beasts and Babies," scientists in the emerging fields of child development study gazed into the past and poached from evolutionary theories to explain the embryonic and postnatal development of children's bodies, and applied those conclusions to racial identification.[8]

Birth became a defining milestone for racial identification, a primal stage for reconstructing hierarchy after slavery. The bodies of Black children became raw material in the postbellum science of white supremacy, one that was quite legitimate to both Northerners and Southerners. Northern academics, social scientists, and philanthropists played a crucial role, funding research that sought to quantify and measure Blackness. This shift marked a new phase in racial oppression: one that traded mob rule for medical precision, shifting from public spectacle to bureaucratic efficiency. Where the noose had failed, the eugenic sciences promised to succeed.

Childhood was the front line where racial identity was forcibly "fixed" to white-supremacist ideology. Infancy became the critical juncture for erasing racial ambiguity, ensuring that a rigid racial caste system remained unchallenged. The infant's skin tone, parentage, and features were used to assign them a place within an unforgiving social order or even mark them for death.

There was heightened attention on improving health outcomes for white children, their role as future citizens more prominent in the establishment's imagination. Pediatrics expanded after slavery, perfectly suited to a racist society that celebrated the "Age of the Child." Professionals from pediatricians to psychologists documented developmental milestones with zeal. For Black families, child-saving rhetoric was a bitter irony: The same society that claimed to nurture children targeted and erased theirs.

These developments stoked fears of blurred racial boundaries and "changeling babies." Infants with features that read as white fed a darker reality: the ruthless targeting of Black infants and toddlers before their futures could begin. These twin terrors, the obsession with defining racial identity at birth and the slaughter of Black children, were two sides of the same coin.

What I am about to reveal is the deep entanglement of race, birth, and medicine in this era, tracing how pediatrics, the medicalization of childbirth, and birth registration became tools of racial engineering. Skin color, not the devastatingly high Black infant mortality rate, commanded the attention of pediatricians and bureaucrats consumed with questions about why some Black babies were born with white or pink skin, straight hair, or blue eyes. These debates, fueled by *Plessy v. Ferguson*, brought together medical professionals, reluctant Black midwives, and state bureaucrats to fix racial identity on paper through birth certificates.

The history of childbirth, midwifery, and bureaucracy is a history of institutions colluding with overt violence to enforce hierarchy after emancipation. To grasp how deeply these forces intertwined, we must move beyond abstractions and face their intimate realities. The following two stories pull back the curtain, showing how science and law converged to enforce racial order at its most vulnerable frontier: the birth of a child. *Plessy* had defined race as something visible and biological even though Homer Plessy, one-eighth Black, was visibly white.

AN EVIL OMEN

On October 2, 1897, a telegram arrived at the Seventh Ward settlement house where race man and public intellectual W. E. B. Du Bois had embedded himself among poor Black residents while researching and writing his seminal sociological study, *The Philadelphia Negro*. The bit of yellow paper carried happy news with biblical resonance: "Unto you a child is born." As the fear and joy of new fatherhood mingled together, Du Bois did not conceal his anxious concern about his son's physical features: "I wondered how it looked and how it felt,—what were its eyes, and how its hair curled and crumpled itself."[9]

In an era when phenotype determined survival, Du Bois knew that features could grant or deny privileges. The presence of mixed-race children unsettled the already fragile logic of segregation, and shortly after the birth of his son, Burghardt, Du Bois wondered how his own hybrid ancestry had imprinted on his newborn. He asked, disturbed: "Why was his hair tinted with gold? An evil omen was Golden haired in my life. Why had not the brown of his Eyes crushed out and killed the blue?—for brown were His father's eyes, and his father's father's."[10]

A light-skinned, sharp-featured Black man, Du Bois often wrestled with his own racial identity. His golden-haired son was born just after the triumph of legalized segregation, amid genocidal violence and the steady stream of white-passing Black people crossing the color line. Du Bois's unease was not merely paternal; it exposed a national anxiety about race, identity, and survival in a violently segregated society. Whiteness functioned not simply as an identity but as a resource guarded like property. Burghardt's blue eyes and fair features did not signal a private family curiosity but a political problem: If racial boundaries could blur at birth, then the entire architecture of segregation rested on fiction.[11]

In asking, "Why was his hair tinted with gold? An evil omen was Golden haired in my life," Du Bois was dealing with an internalized fear that his son's light features might signify an alignment with the oppressor class, or foreshadow some tragic destiny. In a society that made race a rigid, legal, and social construct, golden hair symbolized whiteness, and whiteness symbolized access to the power, safety, and dignity that had historically been denied to Black people, including Du Bois himself.

Du Bois's questioning exposes a painful paradox: While Black parents fiercely loved and protected their children, they also knew that the world measured their children's worth through a racial calculus. In a time when even a single drop of Black blood could sentence a person to discrimination and death, Du Bois wrestled with the unsettling reality that his own child's appearance could dictate his place in society. His son's light skin and European features were political, historical, and deeply consequential.

Du Bois advocated for racial uplift and the power of education, but he was also painfully aware that white society refused to see Black people as fully human, no matter their intelligence, accomplishments, or virtues. His newborn son's features forced him to confront the limits of racial identity. Was Blackness something one could inherit in spirit, in culture, in legacy? Or did society demand that it be written plainly on the body? These questions were not just about his own son. They were about the very nature of race in America and about how whiteness and Blackness were imposed, policed, and weaponized, even at birth.

Young Burghardt's body became a symbol of instability, a reminder of the violence, shame, and guilt attached to slavery and miscegenation, and a sign of a Black father's angst over paternity and potency. Despite Du Bois and his wife's deep love, the child's ambiguous features exposed the panic of a nation where Southern states narrowed definitions of whiteness to exclude even a single drop of Black blood. Burghardt was the kind of baby who provoked cultural anxiety precisely because his indeterminacy suggested that racial boundaries could never be airtight.

"SPIRITS MADE BABY BROWN"

The physicians, bureaucrats, and scientists who took over the work of racial gatekeeping during the Jim Crow era did not see themselves as breaking from the past but rather as perfecting it. They were continuing a project of racial management and control by different means. Their methods were draped in the language of science, medicine, public health, and order. But beneath the lab coats and official seals was the same old terror. White coats replaced white robes. It was the same insatiable paranoia that whiteness might be diluted, that a Black child might pass undetected, that so-called racial purity of white bloodlines might be contaminated. And when that paranoia flared, it sent people grasping for explanations, even the absurd, to maintain the fragile architecture of white supremacy.

Few cases illustrate this paranoia more vividly than the strange, desperate plea of Annie Laymon, a white woman who in June 1907 walked into the Yorkville Police Court on New York City's Fifty-Seventh Street clutching her newborn. The infant's skin was a shade too dark for comfort. The news described the baby as "coffee-colored," but Laymon, a thirty-year-old servant, was adamant that there had been no mistake and no crime of the flesh. Her husband was a German Jew, and her ancestry was untainted.

So why, then, was her child not white?

Laymon had an explanation, one that strained the boundaries of belief but served as a desperate shield against scandal. She claimed that she had undergone a "spiritualistic marriage," officiated by none other than Julius Caesar. "The spirits must work through a material body in this world," she told the judge. A host of other spirit guests had attended the ceremony, she claimed, promising to act as guardians over her future children. Perhaps it was their doing. Perhaps they had darkened her baby's skin "for some good purpose known only to themselves."

The doctors at Bellevue Hospital scoffed at Laymon's invocation of the dead, but their own explanation was no less fantastical. It was "fright," they assured her. Her fear was so intense that it imprinted itself onto the child, darkening its skin in the womb. Laymon recounted that, while carrying the child, she had witnessed two Black women fighting with knives, a sight so dreadful that it had seeped into her womb and stained the very skin of her unborn.[12]

You may be shaking your head in disbelief right now, but I assure you that in 1907 this was no outlandish superstition. Laymon's claim, however bizarre, was not unique.

The belief that a mother's fears could physically alter her fetus was rooted in the long-standing medical theory of "maternal impressions"—the idea that a pregnant woman's emotions, thoughts, or external experiences could imprint themselves onto her unborn child. This notion stretches back to ancient Greece, where philosophers like Hippocrates and Aristotle speculated that strong maternal emotions could shape a baby's physical characteristics in utero. In biblical traditions, stories such as Jacob's manipulation of sheep breeding in Genesis 30:37–39 reflected similar ideas about external stimuli determining an offspring's traits. By the Middle Ages and the Renaissance, European physicians routinely blamed birth defects and congenital marks on a mother's unrestrained emotions or shocking encounters during pregnancy.[13]

By the eighteenth and nineteenth centuries, the theory of maternal impressions had hardened into pseudoscience, with medical texts offering elaborate explanations for how a mother's trauma, sinful thoughts, or even moments of fright could manifest as physical deformities in her child. Cases were documented of children born with animal-like features after their mothers had been startled by a dog, or with missing limbs after their mothers had seen an amputee. As scientific racism took hold in the nineteenth century, these ideas became racialized as white doctors began asserting that a white woman's exposure to Black people during pregnancy could literally imprint itself onto the fetus, darkening the child's skin or marking it with other supposed racial features.[14]

At the dawn of the twentieth century, despite advances in embryology and genetics, these archaic beliefs still circulated in both medical and popular discourse. And so, when Annie Laymon appeared in court in 1907, her claim that spirits might have influenced her child's complexion was not met with skepticism but instead served as a convenient salve for white anxiety. Her story transformed what might otherwise be damning proof of interracial sex into a medical mystery, a tragic accident of gestation rather than a breach of racial purity.

But beneath the veil of maternal distress lay a more unsettling reality. Either Laymon or her husband may have carried Black ancestry buried deep within their bloodlines. This would have been a truth too dangerous to acknowledge in a world where white womanhood was bound to the maintenance of racial purity. Or, perhaps, she had indeed lain with a Black man, and in the warm light of day, the only way to absolve herself from the consequences of this transgression was to invoke the supernatural. White women were not just passive enforcers of racial purity; they were expected to perform whiteness in ways that safeguarded the entire racial order. The fear was not just personal; it was social. A white woman who birthed a Black child was not just a woman who had "sinned"; she was a woman who had committed treason against whiteness itself.

Laymon's distress, however absurd, was more than personal or a bizarre moment of courtroom theater. It was symptomatic of a larger crisis of a world in flux, where the old, unspoken rules of racial certainty and policing were no longer enough. Laymon was not the only white woman to invoke supernatural explanations for a child's ambiguous racial features. Across the US, courts and newspapers recorded similar cases in which white mothers attributed a dark-skinned child to supernatural causes rather than interracial unions. These accounts were a testament to how much racial purity anxieties gripped white society.[15]

For example, months after Laymon walked into that New York courthouse, just days before Christmas, *The East Oregonian*, a regional newspaper based in the northeastern Oregon town of Pendleton, published a similar story of racial panic over an ambiguously colored infant under the headline: "Face Is Three-Fourths Black." A white couple was thrown into crisis when their newborn's complexion was darker than expected, triggering a wave of speculation in their community. Desperate to explain this biological "anomaly" without implicating themselves in racial transgression, they turned to the same pseudoscientific belief Laymon had invoked. According to *The East Oregonian*, the mother insisted she had been "badly frightened by a negro" during pregnancy, and this traumatic encounter had supposedly imprinted itself onto the child.

The article captures the sheer absurdity of white anxieties around racial classification: "The good people of the town are much exercised over the matter, for the couple are both white." Their distress was not about the baby's health but about the implications of its appearance and what it meant for the family's social standing, and for the fragile architecture of white racial purity. The paper even described the child's complexion as a "mystery that doctors would have to solve," reinforcing the idea that whiteness was natural, stable, and absolute, while Blackness was something that needed scientific investigation and surveillance.[16]

This case, like Laymon's, reveals how whiteness was not just an identity but a social contract, one that had to be protected by any means necessary, even if that meant invoking baseless superstition. The fear was not just about the presence of Blackness but about the loss of whiteness, the possibility that a white lineage could be "contaminated" in ways that defied explanation. These stories were not isolated. They were part of a broader white paranoia at the turn of the twentieth century, a time when medical journals, courtrooms, and newspaper pages were filled with frantic attempts to ensure that racial boundaries remained fixed, unbreachable, and legally enforceable. The era when a child's racial identity could be determined by the human eye, the gossip of neighbors, the town ledger, or the testimony of a midwife was coming to an end. White society needed something more precise, more definitive, more *scientific*.

"WE CAN'T RAISE A NEGRO BABY, CAN WE?"

Now, let's return to New York, where the birth of another newborn would expose similar fears and uncertainties about race. This time we will examine the fear from the perspective of white adoptive parents grappling with the realities of raising a child whose very existence challenged societal boundaries. But before diving into the details of this saga, we must first consider the profound mysteries of childbirth, where the formation of life in the womb, especially the development of race, remained shrouded in uncertainty, giving rise to speculation and stoking deep-seated fears.

Before the birthing process shifted from a home-based experience into a scientific medical practice during the late nineteenth century, Americans generally understood the affair as unclean, painful, and potentially deadly for all women and children regardless of race. Postpartum hemorrhage, heart failure, fever, infection, and shock dragged many unfortunate victims into the grave. For expectant mothers, physicians, midwives, and other birth attendants, the perils of childbirth—from the moment of conception to delivery in the birthing room—inspired waves of anxiety, along with superstitious beliefs and protective practices, from charms and dietary taboos to ritual seclusion and strict behavioral codes for pregnant women.[17] The womb itself was a locus of mystery and chaos, where a fetus could succumb to the tyranny of the uterus, the will of God, supernatural forces, and, most important for our story, the influence of remote ancestors and the "savage" stages of humankind's racial evolution. Drunken sex, wild animals, barren women, jealous neighbors, angry spirits, frightening Black people, black incubus demons, and even a pregnant mother's own wayward imagination and emotions were also believed to shape or "mark" the physical and mental development of a child in utero.[18]

For white Americans, such concerns and anxieties were heightened by fears of infant mix-ups at birth and by racial panic over the possibility of delivering a Black child, whether imagined as the result of illicit interracial sex, a spouse deceived by a white-passing Black person, or a hidden strain of Black blood suddenly resurfacing after lying dormant for generations.

Perhaps the most notable examples of baby-switching and racial hysteria first appeared in works of fiction. Mark Twain's 1894

Pudd'nhead Wilson is the tale of a one-sixteenth Black slave who illicitly switches her white-skinned Black son with her master's white son. Born on the same day with blue eyes and blond hair, the infants were indistinguishable. Twain's story follows these white-skinned boys as slavery, freedom, and illusions based in racial ideology shape their growth and social development. Once the deception is finally discovered, the two are switched back. The Black man is re-enslaved and the white man gains freedom. However, the white man now carries the scars of Blackness in his dialect and manner. The story shed light on the fact that Twain believed that one's environment could make a difference in their behavior. The white-Black man and the Black-white man were equally threatening to the white world.

This fear of hidden Blackness surfacing in offspring extended far beyond Twain's work and was a recurring theme in American literature. Literature scholar Laura Dawkins examines a genre within literature and folklore that reflected white anxieties about racial purity, miscegenation, and heredity. These stories often revolve around the "horrifying" revelation that the offspring of a respectable white family is actually the Black progeny of an unknown or hidden racial lineage. The narratives typically followed a tragic arc: A white mother gives birth to a visibly Black baby and either dies of shock, descends into madness, or is ostracized by her community. In some versions, the white husband discovers his wife's secret Black ancestry only after their child has betrayed its hidden racial identity. These tales reinforced the idea of Blackness as a contaminant, a lurking curse capable of upending white domestic life and social order. Dawkins highlights how these narratives played a crucial role in reinforcing racial essentialism and the "one-drop rule," a legal and cultural construct designed to maintain rigid racial hierarchies. The stories of Black babies born to white mothers dramatized the supposed horror of racial ambiguity and worked to police the boundaries of whiteness, feeding into both scientific racism and the popular imagination the myth that Blackness was an inherited stain, capable of reappearing generations later to disrupt white purity and privilege.[19]

On the morning of July 4, 1905, a newborn was found abandoned on the side of a highway in the small rural village of Pleasantville. *The New York Times* reported that its finders took the "smiling, bouncing girl," soon to be named Martha Washington, to the Westchester County

Almshouse, where a childless white woman saw the infant and "liked its looks."[20] After consulting with her husband, Mrs. Quick successfully persuaded the almshouse manager to transfer the newborn to the couple's care, and that same day the family "went off home smiling happy." The baby soon was nestled into her new home, no different from any other cherished infant. Other than bouts of fussiness and symptoms of colic, everything seemed to be going smoothly in the Quick household those first days. The adoptive parents expressed delight, saying they were "happy to care for her through all of its infant ailments."

But a week later, the baby developed an affliction far more alarming to them than colic. By day seven, according to the *Times*, the infant "was growing an inch a day," and though she appeared healthy, cooing and kicking in her bassinet, "her skin had begun to be several shades darker." At first, it was subtle, a deepening tone, perhaps a trick of the light. Then the change became undeniable. *Several shades darker.* Alarmed, Mrs. Quick tried to remedy what she saw as a dreadful affliction by administering doses of some kind of medicine, as if the right tonic could restore the child's former skin color. But "the infant's hair began to kink and her skin grew decidedly darker."

Panic set in.

The Quicks were no longer doting over a beloved infant. They were staring at what they believed to be a medical catastrophe. Convinced their little girl had "some horrible disease," the adoptive parents hurriedly called the family physician. The doctor arrived, examined the baby, and then, with a knowing smile, delivered the diagnosis.

"The baby is not ill," he assured them.

There was nothing physically wrong, no fever, no infection. No deformity, except in the eyes of a white society that regarded race as a fixed and unalterable truth. The child's parents, the doctor explained, "were evidently colored so it could not be expected that the baby should be white."

His words hung in the air.

A CHANGELING IN THEIR MIDST

For the Quicks, the revelation was as shocking as if they had been victims of an Old World changeling tale. In European folklore, changeling narratives told of fairies or trolls who secretly swapped a family's healthy baby for one of their own deformed offspring, disrupting a peaceful home until the child's monstrous true nature was revealed. These myths spoke to deep cultural anxieties about lineage and inheritance—fears that one's child might not truly belong to them, or worse, might carry some hidden, malevolent trait that would only surface later.

In Pleasantville, the changeling was not a fairy's cursed child but a newborn whose very body defied the racial order. A baby who had appeared white at birth but then *changed*, revealing the racial lineage that white America worked so hard to police and contain.

The Quicks were faced with a dilemma. Mrs. Quick asked her husband: "We can't raise a Negro baby, Peter, can we?" As a white couple living in the North without Jim Crow laws, but with no obvious social or legal precedent for interracial adoption, they could decide to keep the baby or take her back to the almshouse.[21]

"Can we?"

Her words, tentative yet weighted with consequence, spoke to something deeper than mere social obligation. The Quicks' horror was not just about the child's darkening skin—it was about what it meant for them. Parenthood, in their world, was an extension of racial duty. To raise a Black child was to betray whiteness itself. To refuse to adopt the baby wouldn't be just a personal rejection; it would be a social expulsion, a refusal to violate the sacred order that whiteness depended on.

There was no doubt some hesitation in this adoptive mother's voice, a lingering attachment to the child she had rocked to sleep, fed, soothed, kissed. Perhaps for a fleeting moment she had imagined a different future. A future where the weight of race did not crush the love she had begun to feel. Her question was a brief, flickering rebellion against the dictates of the world she knew, where the color of a child's skin determined their worth. It revealed the tension between human instinct and the rigid dictates of white supremacy, between the intimate bond of a caregiver and the unyielding social order that deemed such interracial love unnatural.

But there was no real choice. Not in this world.

Mrs. Quick was still contemplating, still wavering on the precipice of something radical, when her husband answered with swift finality.

"We'll take it to the almshouse and tell them we don't want it. They'll have to take it back," he said.

And so, just as easily as she had been taken home, little Martha Washington was taken back.

Exactly one month later, a *New York Times* reporter visited the child there and found her "reposing peacefully" in the almshouse. But the scene had changed. Gone were the soft touches, the affectionate cooing, the warmth of a household where, for a brief moment, she had been somebody's daughter. Now, she was simply another abandoned baby, marked and categorized by race. The reporter noted pointedly that the Black baby was "not getting the petting she received during her short stay with her parents by adoption."[22] This story did not exist in isolation. White anxieties over race and heredity had been simmering for decades, fueled by both scientific racism and popular fiction that painted Black children as threats to the social order.

Few figures embodied these fears more than Thomas Dixon, a white-supremacist novelist whose work laid the foundation for the racial terror of the twentieth century. In his 1902 novel, *The Leopard's Spots: A Romance of the White Man's Burden*, Dixon painted Blackness as an existential plague, one that threatened to unravel the racial order from within. Dixon promoted the idea that a new, menacing Black child had replaced the old, docile Black person of the slave South. Emancipation, he argued, had left the region not only war-torn but psychically unmoored, birthing a generation of Black degenerates who knew no place, no limits, and no restraint. Dixon has one character, a Northern abolitionist, reveal the hidden threat when a Black man attempts to marry his daughter:

> I happen to know the important fact that a man or woman of negro ancestry, though a century removed, will suddenly breed back to a pure negro child, thick lipped, kinky headed, flat nosed, black skinned. One drop of your blood in my family could push it backward three thousand years in history. If you were able to win her consent, a thing unthinkable, I would do what old Virginius did in the Roman Forum, kill her with my own hand, rather than see her sink in your arms into the black waters of a Negroid life![23]

In *The Leopard's Spots*, Dixon describes this "new Negro" as a plague and "a blight" and depicts the rising generation as casting "its shadow over future generations, a veritable Black Death for the land and its peoples."[24] He exhorted whites to defend their race, to shield their future offspring from the looming danger of race-mixing. He claimed that even a single drop of Black blood betrayed itself at birth, leaving unmistakable marks upon the body. "The big nostrils, flat nose, massive jaw, protruding lip, and kinky hair," he declared, "will register their animal marks over the proudest intellect and the rarest beauty of any other race." This grotesque depiction of Black children as monstrous figures, as objects of fear, revulsion, and racial hatred, saturated the culture of the time. Literary representations, popular folklore, and even medical science worked in concert to uphold the idea that Blackness was a contaminant, a deviation from the natural order.

The racial hysteria Dixon helped to cultivate was inescapable. The Quicks may have encountered similar narratives everywhere, from serialized novels to newspapers, from pulp fiction to the whispered anxieties of white neighbors. The revelation of Blackness in a child was not simply a social disaster; it was an existential one, a revelation that shattered families, overturned bloodlines, and left behind only horror.

Circulating alongside these fictional tragedies were countless "true" cautionary tales—news stories of white families undone by the sudden emergence of a long-buried Black ancestor in their bloodline.[25] Newspapers breathlessly reported cases in which a seemingly white man or woman, generations removed from any visible Black forebear, unknowingly passed into white society, only to have their secret exposed by the birth of a Black child. These "skeleton in the closet" stories served as warnings, reinforcing the idea that race-mixing was a dangerous, irrevocable gamble. One could never be sure what lay dormant in the bloodline, waiting to reveal itself.

Martha Washington's brief life unfolded amid a culture obsessed with racial hierarchies and pseudoscientific theories. After the Quick family renounced their adoption when her skin darkened, she was returned to the almshouse. Her case drew morbid national fascination: Black families expressed interest in adopting her, while white women reportedly inquired about raising her as a "novelty." Yet before any future could be secured, Martha died at just one month old. The record is silent about the cause. It may have been disease; almshouses were overcrowded and unsanitary, and infant mortality rates in the late nineteenth century were still devastatingly high. But her death was quickly folded into the racial imagination of the era. Newspapers like *The Washington Post* had already framed her as a "white pickaninny," transforming her short life into a spectacle of racial ambiguity and a warning about the supposed instability of bloodlines. In death, as in life, her body became proof of the era's violent insistence on racial boundaries.

Her story fed a broader obsession with skin color as the ultimate racial marker. Eugenicists and race scientists scrutinized Black infants, seeking to pinpoint when racial identity "emerged," desperate to codify race as biological truth. Lurid headlines like "Baby Turned Black" framed Martha as a "changeling," embodying white anxieties that racial purity could be corrupted. Martha's metamorphosis was deployed to reinforce white supremacy, transforming her into a warning against racial mixing and the alleged dangers of "hidden" Blackness. Yet her existence also exposed the fragility of racial categories, challenging the myth of their immutability.

Martha's unmarked grave, now buried beneath a highway, mirrors the erasure of countless marginalized lives. Her tragedy was part of a pattern in which Black children like Martha and W. E. B. Du Bois's son Burghardt were casualties of a regime desperate to enforce racial order. Her story laid bare the absurd violence of racial constructs: Even in infancy, Blackness was policed as a threat to be contained. Yet in destabilizing the myth of fixed racial boundaries, Martha's life inadvertently revealed the truth: Race was never biology. It has always been a shifting tool of power, upheld through fear and violence to sustain white dominance. Her legacy, like that of so many erased children, endures as a testament to resilience amid systemic cruelty.

Even as these tales preyed on white anxieties, so too did the so-called science of the era. Race scientists, in their relentless pursuit of biological justifications for white supremacy, confirmed the worst fears of white readers. They warned of "miscegenation" and "race suicide," arguing that the mixing of races would lead to degeneration, disorder, and the eventual extinction of the Anglo-Saxon race. Their solution? A rigid program of social segregation, forced sterilization, and racial purity laws designed to protect whiteness at all costs.

President Theodore Roosevelt himself railed against the declining birthrate among white Americans, calling white middle-class women "race criminals" for failing to embrace marriage and procreation. Meanwhile, popular media reinforced the message that white women bore the sacred duty of preserving the race. Their wombs were a national resource, the front line of racial survival.

Eugenicists amplified this message, warning that without careful breeding, society was doomed to be overrun by the unfit. In a 1913 article for *Cosmopolitan* titled "Do You Choose Your Children?" Stoddard Goodhue urged women to embrace their genetic duty. "You stand at a meeting point between galaxies of ancestors and galaxies of prospective progeny," Goodhue wrote. "In your system lies the bit of germ-plasm that—miracles of miracles!—conveys the potentialities of good and evil of the past."[26]

For eugenicists, this meant that a child's inherited traits were not only determined by their immediate parents but carried the imprint of thousands of ancestral ghosts—some noble, some degenerate, all irrevocably fixed at birth. Without careful control over reproduction, they warned, latent defects—moral depravity, congenital disease, criminality—would reemerge. Skin color, too, was believed to be unstable. It might skip a generation, or two, or three—but the stain of Blackness could always resurface, catching unsuspecting white families by surprise.

THE DANGER LURKING IN BLOOD: A CAUTIONARY TALE

The task of guarding the port of entry to white status and preserving racial hierarchy made the racial classification of newborn babies a pressing issue after slavery, especially in the wake of the *Plessy* decision. Since the privacy of the birthing room provided opportunities for individuals to slip across the color line, failing to seize the moment of birth to properly assign individuals to a race jeopardized the delicate social order of the racial caste system. Within a generation of the Democrat "Mississippi Plan," which focused on racial demographics to win elections, it was necessary for American society either through science or law to provide safeguards for identifying whiteness and promoting the white race. Each child needed to have documented proof of their race so they could be properly positioned in a segregated society.

This period of scientific scrutiny coincided with a broader national anxiety about the increasing migration of Black people out of the

South, fears over interracial marriages, and the looming specter of "white Negroes" passing into whiteness undetected. The stability of the racial order seemed under siege, and the medical field stepped in to reinforce the color line with biological certainty.

The idea that racial identity could lie hidden within the body, only to be revealed at birth, fueled widespread panic. Scientists writing on the ancestral laws of heredity suggested that white "idiots" were throwbacks to some dark racial blot—a regression to a more primitive, less evolved state. Those born with Down syndrome, for example, were racialized as "Mongoloids," their physical features interpreted as evidence of racial degeneration. The English physician John Langdon Down, who first coined the term in 1866, insisted that children born with "mongolism" were proof of humanity slipping backward, away from its Caucasian ideal.

By the 1920s, eugenicists like Charles B. Davenport would further racialize disability, classifying so-called feeble-mindedness as a Black feature. Meanwhile, medical researchers studied the bodies of Black newborns with obsessive scrutiny, attempting to pinpoint the exact moment when a Black baby's racial identity would make itself known. They recorded the precise stages of the darkening of skin, the curling of hair, the formation of lips and noses, all in an effort to establish a biological certainty that race was an unalterable fact.

It was within this larger cultural and scientific universe that the story of Martha Washington unfolded. The Quick family's brief, failed adoption was more than just a personal tragedy—it was a public spectacle, a reaffirmation of the dangers of racial instability. Reporting on Martha's death, *The Washington Post* noted pointedly: "If the colored baby had been found and adopted by a colored family, there would have been nothing said about the occurrence, but the fact that she had been taken by a white family and afterward changed her color, was unusual."[27] The story had everything that white readers feared—mystery, drama, and a chilling reminder that the boundaries of race were not as fixed as they needed them to be.

Pediatrics, a burgeoning field in this era, became a battleground for mediating societal fears about racial ambiguity. Medical journals and conferences fixated on a pressing question: Could a Black infant's skin defy categorization at birth, or might whiteness—assigned mistakenly—darken over time? The emerging specialty positioned itself as both a guardian of child health and a tool of racial surveillance, with physicians meticulously tracking skin color development in Black infants to codify racial identity. Such practices reinforced pseudoscientific theories while shaping foundational pediatric protocols.

Though the racist underpinnings of this science are well documented, pediatric literature remains an understudied archive with regard to how Black birth was exploited to manufacture fixed racial categories. By scrutinizing Black infants' bodies, pediatrics sought to legitimize the myth of biological race, embedding these ideas into medical education and global standards. The field's rise thus reflects a systemic effort to pathologize Blackness, transforming infancy itself into a site of racial control.

New doctors had to be trained to read newborn bodies for signs of race, ensuring that each infant was placed into the correct racial category before any ambiguity could disrupt the social order. In medical schools, future physicians were given explicit instructions on where to look and what to look for—pigment changes in the nails and ears, the texture of the hair, the shape of the nose, the tint of the gums and genitals, all to confirm whether a child was truly Black or white.

At the same time, the US government was expanding its reach into the lives of newborns through national birth registration campaigns, solidifying birth certificates as essential public health and identity documents. What had once been an informal practice of recording births now became a state-sanctioned process, with race stamped onto legal records at birth. Segregationists quickly seized upon this development, understanding that such documentation could serve as a powerful tool in maintaining the racial order. A birth certificate wasn't just a record of existence; it was a blueprint for where one belonged in a society governed by segregation. It determined which schools a child could attend, which hospitals they could be admitted to, which train cars they could ride in, which jobs they could hold, and, ultimately, whom they could marry.

In this moment, race was not just being studied; it was being *institutionalized* in new ways, woven into the bureaucratic machinery of the state, transforming identity into something that could be measured, recorded, and enforced from birth. These medical and governmental interventions worked in tandem, ensuring that no one could slip through the cracks, that whiteness could remain protected, and that Blackness would remain a fixed and inescapable category, stamped into public records as biological fact.

This chapter has traced the lethal arc of anti-Black violence against the very young, from the lynching of infants under Jim Crow to the medicalized paranoia surrounding Blackness at birth. The same ideology that justified murdering Black children, casting them as threats to racial purity, also fueled the hysteria over Martha Washington's skin darkening and Du Bois's anguish about his son's "golden" curls. Whether through mob terror or pseudoscientific scrutiny, the aim was identical: to codify Blackness as an indelible stain, erasing those who defied categorization.

Even as mobs performed rituals of racial "purification," a subtler war unfolded in clinics and legislatures. Doctors and bureaucrats traded ropes for scalpels, torches for birth certificates, and refined white supremacy into a clinical project.

The surveillance of Black newborns shifted from the sacred knowledge of Black midwives, who safeguarded generations, to the sterile authority of medical institutions. In the next chapter, we see how pediatricians and policymakers formalized racial classification into state doctrine. No child, however light-skinned, would escape the machinery of white supremacy. Violence evolved: quieter, systemic, eternal.

THE GIFT CHILD AND THE PRICE OF WHITENESS

I would like to end this chapter by telling you the story of Mam Bob, a Black granny-midwife—a community-trained birth attendant who delivered babies in rural Southern Black communities long before hospitals displaced them—and her husband, who lived in rural Georgia with her adopted child. She delivered many children in her life—including Black mixed-race, white-passing—but none like Pet, the "gift child" who disrupted the natural order of race.[28]

When Anginora—who would later be known as Pet, "a child so pretty it made your eyes hurt"—was born sometime in the 1920s to a mixed-race mother and father. "All the white blood in her and her man got together and made a white child, and that's all there was to it," Mam Bob explained. While Pet was still an infant, her mother died from illness and her father was killed in a train accident. Since there were no relatives to care for the baby, Mam Bob and her husband, who was also mixed-race, decided to raise Pet as their "gift child." Unlike Peter Quick and his wife, who quickly abandoned their adopted daughter, for the first few years Mam Bob and her husband lived "happy and untroubled about their gift child [and] loved that baby so much [they] got plumb foolish about it." But things began to change when Pet started school and eventually discovered that she was "a white child that had to be black." Mam Bob recalled, "It was like somebody hung a sign on her that said COLORED, stooping her heart to shame."

As Pet entered the later years of adolescence, the couple came "to feel the heavy duty" of trying to raise a white child to be Black. Mam Bob said that her husband was an educated man and a good father to their five children, but raising Pet "was beyond his wisdom." In addition to raising her own children, Mam Bob had helped "our white folks some ways to raise theirs. But I raised my black children to be black and the white children to be white. That was the pattern to follow. But the knowledge of color didn't come so soon nor so ugly to my own children as to Pet. We didn't know how to ring the bells of freedom for a white child whose spirit was in bondage to the colored blood folks she knew she had in her."

Pet loved her adoptive parents, "but she was not among us," said Mam Bob. "She was all alone by herself in that wide space that lays between white and colored." For years the couple struggled to raise their white-skinned Black child despite the obvious difficulties. Within their home, they could not "name the thing or talk about it."

At some point the couple sought out ways for Pet to be raised as a white child, first sending her to an orphan's home in the North. "But they said no, they wouldn't fool people about her color," Mam Bob said. The couple brought her back home. Later, Pet changed her first name from Anginora, "because it sounded too much like a Negro name." During trips to church or to town, she covered her face with a parasol to avoid being noticed by passersby. "It was like being colored put all joy beyond her reach on earth. And being white, she couldn't bend her spirit to white people. And it stabbed our love for her to our hearts."

Mam Bob and her husband sent Pet to live in a different town so she could attend school with white children. It was a "smothered hope."

For a while, their daughter was happy, "but then it broke up around her" when Pet "let on she was a white child and nobody knew better till what they call a visiting teacher came to my daughter's house and found out the family was colored." Pet's teachers and classmates did not take kindly to having been fooled. The betrayal, they felt, was not about deception—it was about defilement. In their eyes, Pet had trespassed into whiteness, and her mere presence in a white school contaminated its racial purity. She was a warning, a reminder that race was fragile and needed to be violently defended. Her expulsion was not just a punishment for passing—it was a reassertion of the racial order that deemed some children worthy of education and others fit only for subjugation.

"In the shame of it Pet couldn't get up spirit to go back no more," so she returned to her adoptive parents' home, where she lived until age fourteen. Eventually, she was sent up north to live with another daughter where she could attend a school for mixed children. At this point, Mam Bob felt it was her duty to prepare her daughter to cross the color line.

"Before she went away I talked to her as a woman among women and told her she couldn't pass for a white person till she was old enough and knowledgeable enough to get along by herself without us forever. Till then she needed to stay with us and get educated and learn the ways of white folks every chance she had so she wouldn't give herself away when she left us." Mam Bob never used the words "cross the color line" in her discussions, but the mother and daughter knew "that was a compelling thing in her heart and mind."

During the summers, Pet made rounds with her mother as she cleaned white homes. "She worked with me and watched how things were fixed and how things were done nice in a white lady's home." Mam Bob was not just teaching Pet how to be white—she was teaching her how to survive. She was passing down the lessons of countless Black women who had learned that proximity to whiteness was dangerous, that a single misstep could mean discovery, expulsion, or even violence. Pet was not preparing to live as a white woman; she was preparing to evade detection and carry the burden of knowledge that she could never speak aloud.

During the school months in the North, Pet took extra classes. Then the time eventually came—"when nor where nor how ain't mine to tell nor yours to know," Mama Bob said. In a faraway city Pet found her place "among her own people." Mam Bob and her family "never could any more lay the least claim to her."

Their daughter "had to lose herself to us in our family and to us in our race." To pass was to vanish. It was not just a separation from family; it was an obliteration of self. Pet could never fully belong to whiteness because she knew its price too well. The privilege of passing was laced with terror. To be discovered was to be unmade. Every conversation, every friendship, every romance was a potential betrayal. The same world that granted her white skin as a key to safety also held the power to destroy her if that skin tone was ever questioned. Passing was not freedom; it was a life sentence of fear.

Mam Bob reasoned that it must be "a hard thing for a woman's mind and spirit to be all times afraid and all times alone in fear—fear of her own color, fear her children will show color, fear unnamed for what it is—and nobody on earth she so much dare tell her fears to." It was indeed a high price to pay for the privilege of white skin.

The burden of her child's flesh, Mam Bob said, "makes black patterns of pain for her on my heart and mind." Still, she found comfort in her child's ability to cross the color line, "knowing that the color she fears in herself will help her to bear it through life. For her colored blood can give her the deep patience to endure of colored people—a patience as old and as deep as our sorrow."

The story of Pet's exile is the exception that proves the rule. For every Pet, there were thousands of Black children whose racial classification was not a question but a predetermined answer, recorded at birth and upheld by the full force of the state. Pet's escape was rare precisely because the machinery of white supremacy was designed to foreclose it. Only those whose bodies could evade racial scrutiny, whose features permitted ambiguity, had any chance of slipping beyond the record. The system worked not by allowing freedom but by fixing identity so rigidly that only invisibility offered a way out. Those who could not pass were bound for life to the designation assigned at birth.

Mam Bob, like generations of Black midwives before her, had once held the power to name, to witness, to protect. But the removal of Black midwives from childbirth and the state's seizure of the birth registration process ensured that stories like Pet's would not happen on a large scale. Once, midwives recorded births on their own terms, within the knowledge of their own communities and understandings of skin color. But soon, birth certificates signed by white doctors ensured that every Black child was permanently documented, fixed, and bound by racial hierarchy.

This was the world Black children were born into—a world where race was a sentence, an enclosure, a fate sealed in ink and enforced in blood. Pet was an anomaly who exposed a dangerous crack in the system—a crack that had to be sealed. Children like her survived by crossing the color line. Countless Black children did not. For every child who slipped through the cracks, there were many thousands more whose racial identity was recorded, enforced, and policed until the end. And from the moment a Black child took their first breath, the system was already deciding how they would live and die.

Turn the page. What comes next will show you how American medicine became the new noose.

CHAPTER 8

"Don't You Know a Negro Child's Scrotum Is Always Black?"

Pediatric Experiments, Birth Records, and the War on Southern Black Midwives

For centuries, Blackness was a crime punishable by spectacle—abduction, bondage, auction blocks, dismemberment, fire, the noose. Race was policed by what the human eye could see and what the mob could enforce. Black children were vulnerable to the instant verdict of those who decided they had seen too much, spoken too much, existed too freely.

As we saw in the previous chapter, the lynching of Black children was never an aberration. It was part of a broader campaign of social hygiene. This chapter reveals how lynching was a calculated project that worked in tandem with eugenics, pediatrics, birth registration campaigns, and the war on Black midwifery. Its goal was simple: Ensure that Black childhood was contained or erased.

Classic lynching studies, from those by Ida B. Wells to more recent scholarship, have emphasized the spectacle: the mob, the crowd, the photograph, the photographic postcard. I trace the same logic into bureaucratic and medical systems, where the violence quieted but did not relent and was no less lethal. In so doing, I move lynching beyond the tree to expose how its infrastructure was sustained not only by mobs but also by medicine and the state.

Most historians situate lynching at the endpoint of life, a violent climax that marks the denial of adulthood, citizenship, or rights. I argue instead that the lynching logic began before life itself was recognized, embedded in the very act of birth, in the bureaucratic assignment of race. This extends the analytical frame of lynching into prenatal and neonatal spaces that most historians have not treated as lynching terrain.

When the mobs receded, their logic did not. They professionalized. They traded torches for forms, ropes for records, public squares for birthing rooms. And one of their first targets was Black midwives. They were repurposed and absorbed into the institutions that guaranteed Black subjugation with cold bureaucratic precision. What had once been carried out in public squares now happened in hospitals, on certificates, and under the guise of public health.

What I'm about to lay bare is that architecture of violence and how it embedded itself in the foundation of life before Black children even took their first breath. The most insidious part is that it masqueraded as progress, protection, medical advancement. A lynch mob could be named. A noose left a scar. But a birth certificate, a pediatric study, and a hospital record were silent weapons, bloodless and bureaucratic, leaving wounds that could not be seen but would shape a lifetime.

Rather than counting children only when they have been explicitly killed, I demonstrate how newborns and even stillborns became specimens and datasets, the pediatric establishment turning infancy into both laboratory and battlefield. Standard narratives cast pediatrics as a story of child-saving progress; I show how the field stabilized racial boundaries, legitimated eugenic thinking, and enabled experimentation on Black infants under the guise of care. Vital records, often treated in the literature as mundane instruments of administrative modernization, must be reread as technologies of surveillance—silent weapons that translated racial violence into paper trails with lifelong consequences. This chapter pulls birth, infancy, and paperwork into the story of racial terror.

White supremacy extended its reach into the earliest stages of Black life by embedding racial classification into bureaucratic systems such as birth certificates, medical examinations, and hospital records. These mechanisms ensured that Black children were tracked, categorized, and constrained across every stage of development. Pediatricians and white medical authorities enforced racial identity through scientific language that gave segregationist policies the appearance of clinical objectivity. Racial violence took administrative form, mapping futures and setting limits without leaving visible wounds.

As pediatrics emerged as a specialty in the late nineteenth century, it functioned both to reduce infant mortality and to reinforce racial boundaries, with doctors positioned as agents of social order. At the same time, the state moved to eliminate Black midwives, who had long sustained Black families through skilled, affordable, community-based care. Licensing laws, public health campaigns, and accusations of uncleanliness were used to discredit their work and replace them with a white-controlled medical profession.

But this wasn't a story of midwives quietly fading away. Black midwives fought back—at least in Virginia. Records from the state's Department of Health show that Black midwives kept "catching babies," sometimes into the 1970s, even as hospitals spread throughout Virginia's counties. And not every white doctor fell in line with the state's push to erase Black midwives. Some local physicians, judges, and even bureaucrats defended these women, recognizing that they had delivered generations, including their own kin. They resisted distant state authorities like the notorious racist Walter Ashby Plecker, who tried to dictate how birth should be managed and who could decide a child's race. His racial classification schemes were a source of public terror and other legal and social consequences.

Histories of lynching rarely acknowledge Black midwives, yet they stood as both targets of state violence and active resistors. Their persistence complicates the narrative, showing how Black women sustained autonomy and defiance in the face of bureaucratic assault. The list of those culpable for lynching is also longer than the conventional narrative suggests, extending beyond sheriffs, mobs, and politicians to include pediatricians, public health officials, and hospitals. Lynching was not just extralegal mob action; it was an evolving infrastructure of racial violence sanitized by science, medicine, and the language of progress. Historians have long highlighted lynching's visibility as a form of public terror. I argue that bureaucratic violence was its twin: less visible but equally effective in disciplining, erasing, and preparing

Black bodies for exclusion or destruction. The invisibility of this violence had its own power.

What ultimately led to the elimination of Black midwifery in Virginia was not simply smear campaigns or accusations of uncleanliness. It was the slow, steady consolidation of childbirth inside hospitals, which displaced community-centered traditions and replaced them with institutional authority. The shift devalued Black women's labor, erased their authority, and transferred power over reproduction and racial classification to white-controlled medical systems. Racial designation at birth was not just about statistics or health records. It was about surveillance. It was about ensuring that, if the time came, the state and the mob alike would know exactly who could be targeted, who could be contained, who could be lynched.

By reading clinical notes, journals, vital records, and court files as lynching archives, I argue that bureaucratic violence must be treated as a form of terror equal to mob violence. And by tracing not only US practices but also European debates on pigmentation and infant skin, this chapter situates American medicine within a transatlantic infrastructure of racial science, showing how imperial obsessions with Blackness circulated and hardened across borders. Where public health histories often celebrate the rise of professional medicine as evidence of modern progress, this chapter shows how that "progress" refined rather than reduced racial domination: the scalpel giving way to the pen, the dissection table to the birth certificate.

A BIOLOGICAL PROBLEM

Historians have usually counted children as victims of lynching only when their bodies swung from trees, but in the realm of medicine, particularly pediatrics and related racial science, even newborns and stillborns were conscripted into the machinery of racial violence. Their skin was studied, their features were scrutinized, and their very existence was treated as data. In this way, the child's body became both laboratory and battlefield, the first site where lynching logic was tested and enforced.

By the time *Plessy v. Ferguson* (1896) codified segregation, one might expect medicine to have settled who was "Black" or "white." It had not. But while the so-called one-drop rule imposed a strict legal definition, its practical enforcement remained arbitrary and chaotic. Birth certificates and medical exams were not neutral records; they were instruments of surveillance and control.

A post-slavery America needed new regimes of knowledge to police the boundaries of whiteness and Blackness, systems that could claim to see beneath the skin and into the blood. Lynching and Jim Crow laws proliferated, but they lacked a reliable method for determining who was properly Black and therefore expendable. New fields of racial science and medicine, which were more sophisticated than crude phrenology, promised to solve this "problem of racial confusion," shore up segregationist policy, and identify those who could be defensibly excluded. Science became the mob's accomplice, promising "empirical certainty" where terror had once sufficed.

Homer Plessy embodied this anxiety. One-eighth Black but visually coded as white, he represented what white society most feared: that a Black man could "pass," marry a white woman, and produce children who might expose the fragility of the color line. The obsession with childhood as the site of racial determination reveals how white supremacy wasn't just about maintaining the present racial order—it was about designing the future, ensuring that Blackness remained an inescapable condition, inscribed at birth and reinforced at every stage of life.

The *Plessy* ruling gave new momentum to racial classification at birth, ensuring that no child of a Black mother could be ambiguously identified. This logic was not new. It extended the doctrine of *partus sequitur ventrem*, passed in Virginia in 1662, which bound children to the status of their enslaved mothers and guaranteed the perpetual reproduction of a captive labor force.[1] Abolition unsettled this legal precedent, making the rights and status of Black children less certain, but the state quickly moved to reimpose control through racial designation at birth.

Miscegenation laws further hardened these boundaries, criminalizing interracial marriage and sex, often with severe penalties. Though these laws were struck down by the Supreme Court in *Loving v. Virginia* (1967), the obsession with "mixing" had centuries of momentum behind it, born of both consensual relationships across color lines and the slaveholder practice of raping enslaved women. Even after emancipation, the underlying logic remained: Blackness was an inherited condition, a biological marker that had to be fixed with certainty.

Hospitals and state agencies expanded birth registration campaigns to reinforce segregation from the very first breath. Birth attendants—many of them still Black midwives—were transformed into state agents tasked with recording and enforcing racial purity laws. Unlike the biological determination of sex, which was generally established without dispute, race was a political determination. Doctors, nurses, and midwives were expected to assess whether a newborn's skin, hair, or features betrayed any trace of Black ancestry.

The medical establishment fixated on Black infants, even stillborns, as living specimens to answer racialist questions: Was Blackness congenital? Could skin color change over time? How did racial difference manifest in infancy? These inquiries were not about health—they were about fortifying the boundaries of Jim Crow. At their core was an ethical violation: treating Black infants as biological puzzles to be solved, pathologies to be diagnosed, rather than as human beings.[2]

This obsession produced a haunting question that preoccupied pediatricians, parents, and lawmakers alike: *What color is the Negro child at birth?* It was not a passing curiosity but a riddle they were urgently compelled to resolve by filling the pages of pediatric journals and driving clinical investigations that treated Black infants as experimental ground zero for preserving the color line.

THE GUISE OF SCIENTIFIC PROGRESS

The spectacle of the mob had given way to the paperwork of the state, but the stakes remained the same: control over Black life from its first breath. What followed was not uncertainty about the project of racial violence, but a scramble to refine its instruments. If lynching taught white society how to police the color line through terror, pediatrics and racial science promised to police it through classification. Where mobs once pointed fingers, physicians now peered at skin, blood, and bone, searching for a science that could guarantee the same verdict with bureaucratic certainty.

By 1900, fewer than 50 pediatricians practiced in the entire United States, and none specialized full-time in the field. Most were clustered in Northeastern cities with small Black populations. Even by 1914, when the number of pediatricians had grown to 138, their patients remained overwhelmingly white.[3] White doctors had little to no experience delivering Black babies before the 1920s, when the decline of midwifery began shifting childbirth from a home-based, community-centered event to a medicalized, hospital-based procedure.

Yet, even as medical authority expanded, most Black births remained in the hands of Black midwives well into the 1930s and 1940s.[4] As licensing restrictions and public health campaigns framed these women as unclean and untrained, Black mothers were increasingly funneled into segregated hospitals, where white doctors controlled not only delivery but the documentation of race itself. The decline of midwifery did not just move childbirth from home to hospital—it redefined who had the power to declare a child's racial identity and to shape their health outcomes from the moment of birth.

The rise of Progressive Era charity hospitals, dispensaries, and public health campaigns exposed more white doctors to Black newborns, especially as the First Great Migration (1910–40) brought Black families into Northern cities and medical institutions. But increased exposure did not bring improved care. Segregation in health care ensured that Black births remained racially stratified, their vulnerability deepened by poverty and exclusion. Historian Marie Jenkins Schwartz reminds us that after the Civil War, Black communities, largely excluded from formal medical care, relied on traditional midwives and healers. White physicians, who had withdrawn from rural areas before emancipation, had little incentive to return once slavery ended. The profit motive that had once tied white doctors to the reproduction of enslaved labor was gone.[5]

Economic and institutional shifts further entrenched these disparities. The release of the 1910 Flexner Report, commissioned by the Carnegie Foundation, radically reshaped medical education in the United States. By calling for higher standards and better funding, author Abraham Flexner effectively shuttered five of the seven Black medical schools, sparing only Howard University and Meharry Medical College. This deliberate assault on Black medical schools ensured that Black communities remained medically underserved for generations.[6]

Yet Black families were never passive in the face of exclusion. They distrusted white medical institutions for good reason. The same profession that now claimed the mantle of scientific progress had, for centuries, experimented on Black bodies without consent. Black mothers' suspicion of hospitals and doctors was not superstition; it was a rational response to a history of exploitation.[7]

And being shut out of care did not protect their children. On the contrary, exclusion made Black infants even more vulnerable. The only options available, segregated hospitals and state institutions, turned Black infants into clinical material, subjects for experiments that white parents would have publicly resisted and that hospital administrators would have hesitated to impose on white children. Black mothers' suspicions were not misplaced; they were rooted in experience. But in segregated wards, their objections carried little weight. Physicians and administrators routinely dismissed or ignored Black parents' concerns, exercising authority over children whose families had neither institutional power nor legal recourse. White reformers and journalists occasionally condemned dangerous studies on white orphans, while medical journals openly published studies in which Black babies were deliberately harmed. Their pain was not a scandal. It was data.

White supremacy did not just rely on the assumption that Black people were biologically distinct. It needed proof. And Black infants, whose very births had already been placed under racial scrutiny, became the ideal test subjects for proving these racial differences through medical research. From the moment of birth, their bodies were sites of scrutiny. They were observed, manipulated, and violated in ways that white children were not. White orphanages and institutions were not immune to medical abuse, but the children's suffering in those venues was at least scandalous and occasionally sparked public outrage. However, while reformers, anti-vivisection societies, and investigative journalists brought attention to dangerous and "vile" studies conducted on white children, medical journals continued to publish the research findings of doctors that performed risky experiments on Black infants and children.[8] Their pain was not just ignored; it was sanctioned, routine, and woven into the very fabric of medical progress.

The professionalization of medicine did not bring protection for Black children; it provided white physicians greater access to their bodies. Hospitals and research institutions, newly empowered by the decline of midwifery and the closure of Black medical schools, ensured that Black infants were funneled into a system where their bodies could be used as raw material for medical experimentation. This was not a new phenomenon. The use of Black bodies for medical research had long been a feature of American medicine, dating back to slavery.[9] But in the post-emancipation era, as birth became a site of state-enforced racial purity, it also became a site of medical violence. The same system that sought to ensure the racial classification of Black babies also sought to use them as raw material for the advancement of white-dominated medical knowledge.

In 1914, *The American Journal of Diseases of Children* published a study by New York pediatrician Alfred F. Hess, assisted by Mildred Fish and Lester Unger, who deliberately induced scurvy in infants by withholding orange juice until hemorrhages appeared. Not stopping there, Hess shifted his gaze to Harlem, where Black infants became his next experimental population. This time he induced rickets, a disease caused by vitamin D deficiency that weakens bones and leads to fractures and deformities. Sixty-five infants, some as young as one month old, were studied as the disease took hold, then treated with cod liver oil. The stated goal was to identify preventive measures, but the study's design required close observation of suffering. The experiment treated Black babies not as patients in need of care but as live models for studying disease progression.[10]

These medical experiments were not just unethical; they were a direct manifestation of pediatrics as a tool of racial surveillance and control. Moreover, these experiments were not ethical oversights or individual cases of misconduct; they were fully sanctioned within a medical profession that had already normalized the nonconsensual use of Black bodies for research. Early medical ethics did not fail Black children; rather, they were deliberately designed to exclude them. Instead of seeing Black suffering as an ethical dilemma, white researchers saw it as an opportunity. The same field that claimed to protect children rationalized their pain as a necessary cost for scientific progress—progress that disproportionately benefited white patients while sacrificing Black lives in the process.

The deliberate induction of disease in Black infants under the guise of scientific research was not merely an unfortunate byproduct of medical curiosity; it was an *intentional act* rooted in the same white-supremacist logic that shaped the field itself. Hess and his colleagues did not see Black children as fully human patients deserving of care and dignity but as experimental subjects whose suffering could be exploited for scientific advancement. This aligns with the broader argument that pediatrics, from its inception, was about defining, pathologizing, and controlling Black childhood. The entanglement of racial science with pediatric research did more than reinforce existing racist ideas; it actively produced new justifications for the medical exploitation and neglect of Black children, shaping policies and practices that continue to harm them today.

More than a decade after Hess's experiments, in 1925, the *Journal of the American Medical Association* published "The Spinal Fluid in the New-Born," a study by M. Hines Roberts based on dangerous spinal taps he performed on 423 sick and healthy Black infants in an Atlanta hospital.[11]

These procedures were conducted without therapeutic purpose and without parental consent. The physicians who carried out these acts were respected professionals, publishing in leading journals and shaping standards of care. The information they extracted served to improve medical understanding and refine pediatric techniques, but the benefits accrued primarily to white children. Black infants endured the pain, risk, and dehumanization, while white patients received safer care as a result. This structure reinforced a racialized hierarchy in which Black suffering was treated as a necessary input in the production of white health. Roberts's work was one part of a broader medical framework that regarded Black childhood merely as a biological condition to be observed and tested, neglecting to see these were human lives to be nurtured or protected.

CURING BLACK PIGMENT

The racialized medical violence inflicted on Black children did not stop at using their bodies for experimental diseases; it extended to their very pigmentation. In the early twentieth century, white doctors were not just obsessed with studying Blackness; some believed they could prevent it altogether. Armed with X-ray technology, light therapy, and their own delusions of racial engineering, they sought to intervene at birth, to stop Black babies from "turning dark" before their skin could betray them to a world structured by white supremacy.

A 1904 article from *The Washington Evening Star* detailed the case of Dr. J. W. Hill, an Indiana physician who was conducting experiments to "prevent infants born of Negro parents from turning dark in color soon after birth." The newspaper noted that Hill had secured an expectant mother for the trial and would conduct his experiment in a hospital under "scientific conditions." His premise was as crude as it was disturbing: If Blackness was a biological threat, could science intervene before it fully developed? The goal, as reported, was to use controlled lighting conditions to alter pigmentation, ensuring that "the child of Negro parents, which is generally born white, turning dark under the sun's rays, will become even whiter than that of the Caucasian race."[12]

This was not a fringe theory.

Other medical professionals and pseudoscientists were equally intrigued by the possibility of bleaching Blackness away at birth. These so-called medical interventions were not just about altering skin color; they were a form of racial engineering. While eugenic sterilization programs sought to reduce the Black birthrate, these experimental skin-lightening procedures pursued a different strategy: ensuring that Blackness itself could be biologically altered. The underlying premise was the same: Whiteness was the ideal state of being, and Blackness was a defect to be corrected. If doctors could find a way to "cure" Blackness, then segregation, miscegenation laws, and even anti-Black violence might no longer be necessary. These were not just racist curiosities; they were part of a broader eugenicist fantasy about permanently reshaping the racial order through medical intervention.

A 1904 issue of the *Journal of the American Medical Association* entertained the idea that X-rays or light therapy might prevent Black babies from darkening over time. The report speculated, "Could this be the solution to America's race problem?"[13] The fact that such a claim was discussed in one of the nation's most respected medical journals speaks to how deeply entrenched these racist fantasies were in the profession.

Similarly, a Philadelphia scientist named H. K. Pancoast made headlines when he claimed that X-ray technology could permanently "bleach the skin of a Negro" until they were, for all intents and purposes, white. His findings, published in *The Call*, a San Francisco newspaper, suggested that the process destroyed melanin, rendering the subject's skin permanently depigmented. Pancoast's work was hailed as a breakthrough in some white medical circles, but beneath the so-called discovery was the same old obsession: controlling, modifying, and ultimately erasing Black identity through medical intervention.[14]

These stories did not exist in isolation. A *New York Sun* editorial from January 28, 1907, titled "The Black Man's Skin," noted that "hundreds of Negroes on the Isthmus [of Panama] and in Jamaica" had reportedly sought out doctors to perform experimental bleaching treatments, offering whatever fees they could. Whether these accounts were true or fabricated, they reveal the fixation white Americans had with the idea that Black people, given the opportunity, would erase their own Blackness. "It is certain," the article concluded, "that the man who succeeds, if one ever does, will become rich beyond the dreams of avarice. All the wealth of Ethiopia will be at his disposition."[15]

White medical experiments that sought to alter skin color revealed a deep fear that race was not biologically fixed. If Blackness could be obscured or reversed, then whiteness was no longer a stable foundation for social order.

A DIASPORIC QUESTION

The medicalization of racial identity at birth was not neutral science but a political project. As Jim Crow hardened, medical authorities claimed the power to determine and fix Blackness at the moment of birth, making racial classification central to both state governance and professional control.

Physicians, particularly in obstetrics and pediatrics, and on both sides of the Atlantic, used their professional standing to claim expertise over racial classification, reinforcing segregationist policies while securing their own status as scientific authorities. The drive to determine the skin color of Black infants at birth was, in reality, a project of racial surveillance designed to ensure that no Black child could slip undetected into whiteness.

This fixation led to an era of invasive experimentation, where high-status physicians sought to prove the biological permanence of racial difference, often at the expense of Black newborns and even fetuses. At the same time, the growing professionalization of medical fields like dermatology, embryology, and pediatrics provided scientists with incentives to engage in racialized research as a means of advancing their careers. Scientific ambition and white-supremacist policy thus became deeply entangled, with Black infants at the center of a disturbing medical preoccupation.

These medical debates took place in journals such as *The Lancet*, *The Journal of Experimental Medicine*, *New York Medical Times*, *Mississippi Medical Record*, and many others. In an era before advances in imaging technology enabled medical professionals to peer inside the womb, embryonic development remained an enigma, and DNA testing to determine paternity was nonexistent. Lacking these scientific tools, physicians resorted to ocular analysis in their attempts to answer pressing racialized questions:

> Why is the Negro black?
>
> Are Negro babies born the same color as white babies?
>
> Why are Negro newborns lighter at birth than later in life?
>
> How long does it take for a Negro infant's skin to deepen?
>
> Are there specific body parts that darken first in mixed-race babies?
>
> Does pigmentation develop in utero, or only after birth?

Such inquiries were not limited to American doctors.[16] French scientists posed similar questions, publishing studies such as *Pourquoi les Nègres sont-ils noirs?* (Why are Negroes black?) and research notes on *la formation du pigment chez le Nègre* (the formation of pigment in the Negro) and *les causes de la coloration de la peau* (the causes of skin coloration).

In 1891, Dr. Léo Testut dissected three Black newborns and published his findings in a prestigious journal, further cementing European interest in racial pigmentation.[17] Dr. Testut's article, published while he served as president of the Anthropological Society of Lyon, along with broader European studies on Black pigmentation, exemplified an institutional obsession with racial classification that sought to pathologize Blackness and reinforce white superiority under the guise of objective science. Testut and his contemporaries helped sustain the pseudoscientific foundations of eugenics, medical racism, and colonial oppression, ensuring that racist ideologies masquerading as scientific inquiry would continue shaping global policies, medicine, and social hierarchies for decades to come.

Eighteenth-century European anthropologists, physicians, and philosophers had set the foundation for racialized skin research, largely concluding that Black children were typically lighter at birth but displayed distinct racial markers on their fingernails and genitals. French surgeon Claude-Nicolas Le Cat, in his 1765 treatise on skin traits, asserted: "The children of Negroes, as soon as they come into the world, have black genitals, and a black spot at the roots of their nails." He insisted that light and air merely expanded this color, maintaining that Blackness was an inherited trait: "In whatever part of the world a Negro is brought forth, he will be equally black as if he had been born in his own country."[18]

Le Cat's claim that Black children were born with dark genitals and black spots at the roots of their nails reflects a broader European obsession with categorizing and essentializing Blackness through biological difference, often in ways that fixated on the most intimate and vulnerable aspects of the body. The emphasis on genitalia, in particular, echoes long-standing racial myths that sexualized Black people and framed them as biologically distinct from and inferior to Europeans. These so-called findings weren't neutral scientific observations; they were tools of racial ideology, designed to reinforce the belief that Blackness was a fixed, innate condition, marked on the body from birth.

The idea that Black infants were born lighter but quickly "darkened" was also frequently cited in racial theories as a supposed sign of their deviation from whiteness, reinforcing the notion that Blackness was a form of biological degeneration rather than a natural human variation. In reality, what these researchers documented was melanin development, an unremarkable biological process twisted into evidence of racial difference.

Throughout the nineteenth century, European theorists from England, France, and Germany continued their preoccupation with Black complexion.[19] Between the early 1800s and the 1860s, Le Cat and other scientists such as Theodor Waitz, Sir William Lawrence, John

Charles Hall, Thomas Masterman Winterbottom, Petrus Camper, and Johann Friedrich Blumenbach meticulously documented their observations of Black newborns across Europe and Africa. Their consensus? Black babies were lighter in color at birth than they were a week later. Though Black babies could readily be distinguished by their dusky hue when placed side by side with children of white parents, this distinction proved "a difficulty when half-breeds were examined."[20] German-born dermatologist Paul Gerson Unna concurred, emphasizing the need for further investigation into the origins of physiological skin pigmentation: "It is very desirable that the origin of the physiological pigment of the skin should be thoroughly investigated."[21]

Although brief remarks on Black infant skin appeared in American medical journals as early as the 1860s, it was not until two decades after the abolition of slavery that US medical scientists entered the debate with urgency. British naturalist Charles Darwin, in *The Descent of Man* (1871), also engaged with the question of skin color difference, theorizing that variations were the slow and gradual result of sexual selection over the long arc of human evolution. He proposed that external physical traits, including skin pigmentation, evolved due to environmental pressures and reproductive advantages, yet despite these outward differences, he maintained that human populations were fundamentally similar. Aware that skin color was being weaponized to justify the supposed physical and cultural inferiority of Black people, Darwin rejected rigid racial hierarchies, writing that human groups "graduate into each other, and . . . it is hardly possible to discover clear distinctive character between them."[22] Though he was British, his ideas helped shape American scientific and racial discourse at a time when post-slavery anxieties fueled intense debates about racial categorization.

The anxiety that drove these scientific investigations was not uniquely American. But in the United States, the stakes were uniquely high. As Harriet Washington argues, white scientists feared that "white Negroes," Black individuals born with skin pale enough to pass, posed an existential threat. If Blackness was not stable, if it could hide in bloodlines and emerge unexpectedly in future generations, then whiteness itself was vulnerable to corruption. Washington further contends that Americans were deeply anxious about being perceived by their

European counterparts as "a nation of mongrels and mere pretenders of white status."[23]

"DISSECTING BLACK INFANCY"

By the 1890s, as the repression of Jim Crow hardened, white America's fixation on skin color reached a fever pitch. Pediatricians and obstetricians, vying for jurisdiction over children, cast themselves as guardians of the color line. One apprehension drove them: What if Blackness wasn't immediately visible at birth? If Black infants could be mistaken for white, then the entire racial caste system rested on shaky ground. The medical establishment's frantic search for immutable racial markers reveals just how fragile and artificial whiteness truly was.

One might argue that these doctors were merely engaging in scientific inquiry, that their fascination with Black infant development was rooted in curiosity rather than malice. But science is never neutral. When science serves white supremacy, it ceases to be science and becomes something else entirely: *a justification.*

Law turned infants into evidence. As Charles Frank Robinson shows in *Dangerous Liaisons*, babies figured in inheritance fights in cases where interracial parentage threatened white property. Southern legislatures tightened rules to block such claims.[24] Schools followed suit: In *Hare v. Board of Education* (1893), a North Carolina court excluded the Hare children from attending a white school because a grandfather was Black. Infancy was put on trial.[25]

Physicians rushed in as expert arbiters. In 1895, obstetrician Anneta Katz asserted that "the scrotum of the newborn male infants of African descent is always black," then asked how to distinguish Black female infants. Ben Brodnax of Louisiana obliged with lurid detail, claiming that in Black girls, a "distinct line" ran from vulva to spine, and that even minimal "Negro blood" produced a "tallowy" or "waxy" white. Such assessments turned Black girls' bodies into medical exhibits.

Courtrooms followed suit.

In an 1860 issue of *Medical World*, Dr. D. S. Ellis of Ashland, Virginia, shared "a good joke" about an incident that took place in a North Virginia courtroom. In a case of disputed paternity, questions arose as to whether the infant was white or Black. Growing impatient over the argument, the judge, a "rough and ready kind," said, "Don't you know that a negro child's scrotum is always black? Hand me the child." Without inquiring about the sex of the child, the judge then proceeded to "investigate the matter himself" by exposing the child's genitals. To his chagrin and the amusement of the lawyers, "he found it was a female child, and that his test was not applicable in this case."[26]

The same logic was applied to adulthood: In the Rhinelander trial (1925), a famous court case between Leonard Rhinelander and his wife Alice Beatrice Jones, a woman of mixed heritage, Jones was forced to strip before an all-white, all-male jury to disprove her husband's claim of "racial fraud." She won, but it came at the cost of enduring the court's ignorant search for permanent, visible signs. The NAACP's *Crisis* responded to the verdict: "If Rhinelander had used this girl as a concubine or prostitute, white America would have raised no word of protest; white periodicals would have printed no headlines; white ministers would have said no single word. It is when he legally and decently marries the girl that Hell breaks loose and literally tears the pair apart. Magnificent Nordic mentality!"[27] Once again, this kind of baseless claim of racial fraud illustrates the potential outcomes resulting from improper racial classification.

By the early twentieth century, doctors had examined the scrotum, vagina, buttocks, anus, and extremities of Black infants in addition to comparing the bone structure, nasal cartilages, weight, and head circumference of Black and white newborns.[28] Physicians would continue their crude experiments, slicing skin from the scalps, buttocks, and penises of stillborn babies to look for definitive signs of race.

To solve the "mystery" of Black infant pigmentation, high-status physicians from institutions like Johns Hopkins Hospital and the Carnegie Institution of Washington employed a variety of techniques. Some relied on microscopes to scrutinize the layers of Black infant skin. Others took a more invasive approach by slicing apart the bodies of stillborn Black fetuses, even extracting sections of their genitals, to determine exactly when and how Blackness emerged in the body.

At Johns Hopkins, Robert B. Morrison sliced the arm of a stillborn fetus ("father very Black . . . mother moderately so," he noted) and declared an "unmistakable line of pigment" in the basal epidermis—proof, he said, that Black babies don't "turn" black after birth. At the University of Maryland Lying-in Hospital, L. E. Neale dissected the foreskin of a stillborn mixed-race infant and likewise claimed pigment was present. Such "findings," repeated as doctrine—"Negro babies are not born white"—recast bereaved families' children as raw material.[29]

In the area of embryology, Lynn Morgan's research shows how in the era spanning the late nineteenth and early twentieth century, this field treated human embryos as depersonalized specimens: By 1913 Johns Hopkins held a thousand embryos "to be measured and tabulated."[30] By 1944 the Carnegie Institution held nearly nine thousand. But crucially, white fetuses were collected to map embryological development while Black fetuses were harvested to answer racialist questions. Morgan argues that the documentation and description of human embryological development enabled "a subsequent generation to visualize and imagine—indeed, to 'know'—the embryo-and-fetus as a coherent, continuous biological 'thing,' progressing steadily from genesis (fertilization) to exodus (birth)."[31] Social and spiritual elements, Morgan maintains, were secondary to the stories medical scientists told about birth. But the collection and study of Black fetuses by doctors at Johns Hopkins, the Carnegie Institute, and elsewhere reveals that professionals were primarily motivated by social concerns and cultural anxieties about race.

Six years before the Plessy decision, Arthur Thomson, anatomist at the University of Oxford, received portions of sliced skin and scalp taken from Black fetuses ranging from five to eight months in gestational age. "I must express my indebtedness to Professor Moseley for his kindness in furnishing me with the material from which the sections have been cut," Thomson wrote. Though he successfully found distinct evidence of pigment in the deeper cells and layers of the skin samples, he lamented that his work was "hampered by scarcity of material." Thomson openly called on his colleagues to send him more Black fetuses. "I would esteem it a favor if any members of the [Anthropological] Society who have portions of skin or scalps of coloured races of men in their possession, would favor me with the use of such specimens."[32]

In the 1907 publication of *The Principles and Practice of Dermatology*, William Allen Pusey also noted his own findings of pigmentation in the foreskin of ten Black babies and thanked Professor Charles B. Reed of Northwestern for furnishing him with "the material" and for "the opportunity of examining these negro babies."[33]

The hunger for Black fetal remains extended across the Atlantic. Between 1898 and 1900, major medical journals—including *The London Lancet*, *The New York Medical Record*, *The St. Louis Medical and Surgical Journal*, and *Pediatrics*—published article after article debating the color of Black babies at birth. Southern doctors, especially, were outraged by any suggestion that Black newborns could resemble white ones.

The debate over Black infant skin reached its highest pitch after an eminent French physician, identified only as Dr. Farabery, published a controversial article in the July 1898 issue of *Pediatrics* titled "The Color of Negro Infants." Farabery claimed that he had witnessed a birth at a Sudanese colonial exhibition held in the Champs de Mars in Paris—one of the imperial displays in which France exhibited subjects from its African territories. There, he asserted, he obtained "ocular proof" that Black and white babies were born the same color. "The Negro baby comes into the world a tender pink color; the second day it is lilac; ten days afterward it is the color of tanned leather, and after fifteen days it is chocolate."[34] His conclusions sparked a firestorm.

Although Farabery had taken up the task of answering an old question that had seemingly been resolved in the eighteenth century and then microscopically confirmed during the nineteenth century, his findings and assertions provoked a firestorm of rebuttals in the Jim Crow context, especially from Southern doctors, who believed they knew Black bodies more intimately and had more proprietary knowledge than a French physician. The editor of *The Medical News* asked: "Will not someone with a newly-born piccaninny or two on hand tell us the exact color of the precious treasures and so settle an important medico-anthropologic question?"[35]

"NEGRO CHILDREN NOT BORN WHITE," *The Phrenological Journal and Science of Health* fired back. The journal noted in a tiny brief that medical men without experience commonly believed that Black babies were born white. This popular belief was acquired by "hear-say evidence." Though not all Black babies were born the same tint, "they are usually of a pinkish hue" but soon became "a beautiful black—we say beautiful, and in this few will dispute, for it is true, and, were it not for our prejudices, we would say almost or quite as beautiful as if it were white."[36]

Thaddeus Lindley Robertson of Birmingham, Alabama—former president of the state medical society—derided Farabery as delusional: In the South, he wrote, "our ample experiences" have shown that Black babies "come into the world black."[37] *The Georgia Journal of Medicine and Surgery* demanded to know "what part of the continent" Farabery observed, asserting that "a genuine negro baby is black before it is born, after it is born, so long as it lives, and dies black," with exceptions only for a high level of "white admixture."

From Virginia, Herbert Claiborne, a former Confederate surgeon, claimed having examined thousands of infants and "never a white one," insisting multiple "degrees of dilution" were required.[38] A New Haven (Missouri) physician described Black newborns as "sallow or creamy white," never the "rosy hue" of Caucasians, with pigment "especially in the organs of generation."[39]

"I have delivered a score or more of the little problems this year and speak from ocular demonstration," wrote Dr. C. J. March, a general practitioner from Fordyce, Arkansas. "A new-born full-blooded negro baby is neither white nor yet is it black but of a dusky color. In some, though not all, the scrotal integument and that about the flexures of the principal joint is black at birth, but the general surface is of a dusky red." D. M. Provence of Barnwell, South Carolina, had "never seen a newly born negro child black," though noted they were usually lighter than their parents; when the parents were unknown, he looked for darker areas "round the anus," noting "the prepuce is generally very dark or black."[40]

H. C. Riley of Newville, Alabama, rejected Farabery's claims of hereditarian asymmetry with a barnyard analogy: "Blood will tell."[41] A British contributor to the *Medical Press and Circular* offered with curt certainty: "Pure negroes are born pink like young rats . . . and by the third or fourth month they gradually become black." As long as these children were not able to pass themselves off as white, "we have no right to complain."[42]

Abraham L. Wolbarst, a medical student at the College of Physicians and Surgeons in New York who later became a genito-urinary surgeon at the New York School of Clinical Medicine, recalled a discussion of the subject during an obstetrics lecture. James W. McLane, a professor of obstetrics and gynecology, had brought a one- or two-day-old Black baby into the lecture hall to demonstrate how to accurately determine skin color at birth. The newborn was neither visibly white nor Black, but it appeared "salmon color," Wolbarst noted. "The professor held the piccaninny at arm's length and in his peculiarly delightful manner asked the class what the baby's color was." Some students said white, while others said Black. The "witty professor" shook his head at both responses and, in "true Irish fashion," responded, "It's nather, it's red." Dr. McLane, Wolbarst said, told the students that "as a rule piccaninnies were red at birth while white children were gray."[43]

Perhaps it was better to take Farabery's lead and examine African babies. The editor of *The Medical News* suggested that practitioners in the English colonies of South Africa should be asked to decide the question.[44] Another physician, who had witnessed the births of Black babies in the Gold Coast Hinterland, the central Indian Deccan plateau, and Zanzibar as well as other parts of East and West Africa confirmed that Black babies were born with very light skin. "Negroes born in America are not, I take it, in quite normal climate, and live artificial lives, aping their white brethren and so I consider it better and fairer to draw conclusions from an African source," the doctor.[45]

The presence of sacral pigment spots—bluish patches that typically appear on the lower back near the base of the spine—also captured the attention of physicians. In the early 1870s a German doctor, Erwin Baelz of Tokyo Imperial University, first described these spots and instructed his students that they were a racial characteristic. For much of the nineteen century, European medical scientists studied pigment spots in infants of darker races, including Malay Indians, Eskimos, Koreans, Filipinos, and Africans, and confirmed Baelz's thesis. By the opening years of the twentieth century, some doubts were raised as to whether Mongolian spots were distinct only to children of darker races.[46]

In 1907, Chicago pediatrician Dr. Joseph Brennemann published an article on the subject in *Archives of Pediatrics*. After "carefully" examining forty "colored" children and conducting a microscopic examination of the sacrum skin of a stillborn child that died after strangulation by the umbilical cord, he concluded that children of darker races, particularly Asians and Blacks, were born with bluish pigmentation spots found mostly extended over the buttocks into the lumbar region and sometimes the back, shoulders, and extremities.

Brennemann wrote that these spots varied in size from a dime to a dollar, were the color of bluish gray, slate, deep blue, violet, or plum, and were not "influenced by pressure."

The blue color of these fleshy tattoos, Brennemann noted, were present during the later months of intrauterine life, at birth, and could appear weeks and even months after birth. The color of these spots deepened and eventually faded away, leaving no trace. One year later, Canadian pediatrician Albert E. Vipond furthered Brennemann's studies, publishing his observations of pigment spots found on 217 Jamaican "Sambo" children in *Archives of Pediatrics*. Unlike Vipond, Brennemann, in citing studies of white children conducted by other scientists, concluded that since Mongolian spots had been discovered in pure white children, they could no longer be considered as an exclusive race characteristic; instead, they now became a "human characteristic."[47]

Both Vipond and Brennemann questioned Black mothers about the blue pigment spots on their infants. "The observant mothers have noticed them and some think they are birth marks," Vipond noted. Others, he wrote, thought their presence was due to the mother acting on certain food cravings during pregnancy, usually "the liver of some animal."[48] While Brennemann noted that some Asian mothers held superstitious beliefs about Mongolian spots, he found no evidence among Black mothers in his Chicago study. Instead, "a considerable proportion had never noticed it—had never heard of it—even many whose children were well marked." Some mothers knew their babies had the bluish mark and told Brennemann that it was the rule for Black children. "They looked on it as they would on other negro characteristics." Brennemann reported that many of the mothers were amused at his interest in the spots. One mother put it simply: "They say it shows that a person is a real negro."[49] This comment suggests that Black folks too looked for certain markers on babies to affirm racial identity.

These debates saturated *The American Journal of Obstetrics and Diseases of Women and Children*, *Archives of Pediatrics*, *Transactions of the American Pediatric Society*, *Pediatrics*, *The London Lancet*, *The New York Medical Record*, and *The St. Louis Medical and Surgical Journal*. Threaded together, they did not improve Black children's health; they armed pediatrics with a racial catechism. The infant body—probed in courtrooms, classrooms, clinics, and morgues—was made both laboratory and battlefield, where lynching logic was translated into the language of science, and where the nursery replaced the scaffold as the place the color line was policed.

THE RISE OF BIRTH CERTIFICATES AND THE WAR ON BLACK MIDWIVES

If the nineteenth century made Black infants the subjects of dissection tables and dermatological debates, the twentieth century turned them into lines on a form. The same obsession with proving Blackness that once sent doctors slicing into stillborn flesh now found expression in the quiet violence of paperwork. The scalpel gave way to the pen, the specimen jar to the state archive. Where physicians once argued over the color of a newborn's scrotum or scalp, clerks and bureaucrats now fixed racial identity in ink, ensuring it would follow a child for life. This shift was not progress; it was the refinement of surveillance. And central to that transformation was the displacement of Black midwives, whose very presence had offered families a measure of protection from white medical authority. To wrest birth from their hands was to sever a line of communal autonomy and fold Black life more fully into the machinery of state control.

From the moment of birth, Black children were subjected to a system of surveillance and racial control. White doctors documented their race as part of the medical record, converting hospitals into spaces of classification and containment. This early intervention marked Black infants as biologically distinct and socially subordinate, establishing the foundation for future exclusion and state violence. Birth certificates became instruments of surveillance, reinforcing segregation and embedding racial status into the legal identity of every Black child.

Before the early twentieth century, birth records in the United States were scattered and inconsistent, maintained in family Bibles, church registers, or midwives' accounts. Southern segregationists, however, recognized the power of standardization. By the 1920s, birth certificates had become potent tools of racial control, determining access to schools, marriage rights, and social services. In Virginia, Dr. Walter Ashby Plecker, head of the Bureau of Vital Statistics, weaponized these records to enforce a rigid racial order. Through retroactive reclassification and Virginia's Racial Integrity Act of 1924, Plecker ensured that any trace of Black ancestry marked individuals as "colored." Steeped in eugenics, his project sought to erase racial ambiguity and preserve white supremacy through law and medicine.

But Plecker's authority was not absolute. The case of Atha Sorrells made this clear. Denied a marriage license under Plecker's classifications, she challenged the ruling, providing a detailed family tree and historical records to argue Native American rather than African ancestry. Judge Henry W. Holt ruled in her favor, determining that the Sorrells had no "appreciable amount of foreign blood," thereby qualifying her as white under the law and ruling that Plecker's racial classifications were not legally superior to the courts' traditional methods of racial determination.[50]

The Sorrells case proved that a birth certificate, no matter how carefully "corrected" by Plecker, could not overrule the community's racial consensus. Local courts continued to rely on reputation evidence and legal precedent rather than state-issued racial designations.

Resistance extended well beyond the courtroom. Historians have too often portrayed physicians as willing allies of Plecker's campaign against midwives, and midwives as frightened and smeared out of the profession.[51] The record tells a more complicated story. Many doctors refused to report midwives, resisted Plecker's threats, and openly challenged his attempts to rewrite birth records. Black midwives themselves did not cower in fear or surrender their practice. They continued to serve their communities in undocumented ways, ensuring that Black families retained access to trusted birth attendants outside of hospital control. Some ignored state mandates altogether; others practiced quietly beneath the radar, refusing to expose their clients to state surveillance.

Even lawyers pressed the fight, dragging Plecker into court when he illegally revised certificates. Under this pressure, he was forced to pursue less direct methods of "correction." His dream of an airtight racial regime collapsed under the weight of legal challenges, community pushback, and local defiance. What Plecker truly mastered was not classification but self-promotion, curating his own historical record as the architect of Virginia's racial integrity laws. For too long, his narrative of triumph has been repeated uncritically.

To recover the fuller story, we must return agency to those who fought back: the doctors who refused to comply, the midwives who persisted despite state pressure, the courts that pushed against bureaucratic racialization. The decline of midwife-attended births in Virginia owed less to Plecker's policies than to the rise of regional birthing centers and segregated facilities for Black mothers.

This was contested terrain and a battle over who had the authority to define race and, by extension, who controlled America. The erosion of Black midwifery was never just about childbirth. It was about stripping Black people of the power to determine their own identities. Lynching, racial policing, and the destruction of Black midwifery were not separate phenomena but parts of the same structure of white-supremacist control. The bureaucratic machinery that assigned race at birth was the same system that decided whether a Black child would live freely, or be officially marked to die at the hands of a mob. For many, the racialization of birth was a preemptive social death sentence. From the first breath, Black children were being prepared for the violence that awaited them.

What began as a medical gaze did not end at the chart. As hospitals and health bureaus fixed race at birth, the same apparatus of looking—classifying, measuring, displaying—migrated into the marketplace.

Pediatric studies tried to prove Blackness as biology, but few outside the clinic read them. Picture postcards performed a different kind of nasty work. They mass-produced the medical gaze, translating racial "research" into jokes and keepsakes that anyone could buy, mail, and memorize. Where doctors sought to make race real in the lab, pornographic picture postcards rehearsed it in public by training the eye, disciplining desire, and teaching millions how to look at Black children as specimens, not sons and daughters.

The scalpel gave way to the illustrator's pen. The morgue and the nursery gave way to the postcard rack. Birth certificates mapped a child's future, pediatrics helped stabilize the color line in the name of care, and popular culture eroticized and broadcast it in the name of humor, turning clinical suspicion into common sense.

By the 1910s, mass-produced images of naked, humiliated Black children were sliding through people's mail slots as jokes, all while crusaders mobilized police and postmasters to shield white girlhood from a painting. The bureaucracy that named Black infants "colored" at the hospital bedside found its echo in a visual economy that made their bodies collectible through an everyday pornography of domination that trained the eye as surely as any textbook. In other words, the medical archive and the postcard carousel were parts of the same machine.

The next chapter steps from the ward to the window display, from clinical notes to "comical" cards to show how Jim Crow's pedophilic imagination fueled racial terror. We follow the trail from a painting, *September Morn*, to its Black burlesque, from censorship that guarded white innocence to images that licensed the violation of Black childhood.

CHAPTER 9

"Go 'Long, White Man, I Ain't No 'SEPTEMBER MORN'!"

Pedophilic Murder from Picture Postcards to the Lynching of Freddie Moore

There is something wonderfully strange
in the rapidity with which youthful minds
take up lewd thoughts and suggestions.

—ANTHONY J. COMSTOCK

"Somebody's Little Sweetheart," Bamforth & Co. Ltd. Comic Series, Series No. 2833

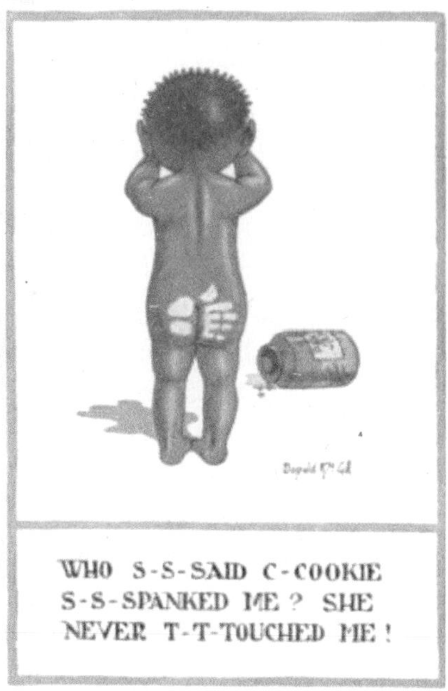

"Little Black Boy Spanked," Donald McGill, RT Blackies, 1916

Lynching was never just an act of racialized violence. It was also an elaborate theater for the concealment and projection of white sexual pathology. Black childhood did not slip from the grip of white hands at birth. The surveillance that began in the cold, clinical grasp of doctors only deepened as children moved through adolescence and puberty.

As we saw in the previous chapter, the scalpel, the pediatric journal, and the birth certificate trained the eye to see Black children only in terms of biological evidence. These instruments produced racial designation and bureaucratic certainty that sutured Jim Crow's categories onto flesh before a child could even breathe. That medical gaze soon wandered into the collectible marketplace, where the same scrutiny was packaged as national humor, and the clinic's fixation on Black bodies metastasized into a pedophilic fetish. The scalpel gave way to the illustrator's pen, the microscope to the cartoonist's ink, the dissection table to the printed page.

Once the birthing room and records fixed race on paper, the work of racial domination shifted to visual culture. What medicine inspected, mass culture displayed and trafficked through the mail system. The result was a pedagogy of *looking* that groomed a nation to sexually abuse Black children. From forms to flesh, the bureaucratic quiet explored in the previous chapter ripens here into a loud visual economy in which Black childhood was staged as spectacle, smut, and rehearsal for lynching. Science trained the gaze, then culture rehearsed the cruelty, so that by the time of a lynching, the public was already conditioned.

This marketplace did not flourish despite Progressive Era child-saving, censorship, and purity campaigns, but *in tandem* with them. As we shall see in this chapter, Anthony J. Comstock, the self-anointed "weeder in God's garden," was America's most zealous censor, sworn to cleanse the nation of vice.[1] Yet the 1873 anti-obscenity law nicknamed the "Comstock Act" drew the boundaries of morality in ways that exposed what white America most feared and most desired. He hounded physicians who mailed reproductive information, targeted publishers who advertised contraceptives, pursued manufacturers who distributed them through the post, and raided homes and businesses for "obscene" literature, yet left untouched the cheap lithographs and postcards that depicted Black children in states of peril, undress, and ridicule.[2]

His war on obscenity was never about protecting children. It was about policing whiteness. Under Comstock's watch, the pedophilia and incest of the white patriarch remained hidden in the parlor, while the sexualized Black child became fair game for public consumption. The grotesque joke of the "pickaninny" postcard—alligators snapping at toddlers, dark-skinned boys and girls with exposed bottoms chased by animals or leered at by white adults—slipped easily past his censors. These images were mass-produced cruelty, stacked on drugstore racks, mailed through the federal system, and sold by the tens of thousands.

Comstock redrew the moral map so that "obscenity" meant anything that threatened white male power: shielding women from pregnancy, naming incest and rape, imagining sexual autonomy for the vulnerable. His crusade raged against the faintest suggestion of white female nudity in paintings, poems, even whispers, but he looked the other way when Black children's bodies were stripped, mocked, and sold on postcards.

The postcards and cartoons that sexualized Black children as consumer goods culminated in the lynchings where those pedophilic fantasies and purity panics moved from picture to flesh, from joke to castration. The postcards trained the hand. They rehearsed people in how to leer and laugh, fondle and rape, and finally how to castrate and lynch.

In Labadieville, Louisiana, in 1933, that training met a body.

What had been practiced as humor and purity panic now assumed the form of a rope, a march, a mutilation, and a cover-up for the pedophilia in white America's own homes, where the violence of fathers, stepfathers, brothers, and uncles was projected onto Black boys, who were offered up as scapegoats to hide the incest and abuse white families and communities refused to name. The joke of the pornographic postcard became the script of the lynching and a theater of white sexual displacement. Not every lynching was rooted in the suppression of incest, but the structure of white patriarchy made such cover-ups possible and even predictable.

Traditional historians have long acknowledged that white folks justified lynching under the pretense of protecting white womanhood from Black male sexuality, but too often they have taken that myth at face value—treating it as racial paranoia rather than as a smokescreen for white men's own sexual crimes. This chapter unsettles that framing.

Most scholarship emphasizes lynching as a public ritual of racial control, highlighting the carnival atmosphere, the spectacle of the mob, and the politics of terror. All of this is true, but it leaves in shadow the domestic violence that lynching displaced.

By dragging incest and pedophilia out of the white household and into view, this chapter reframes lynching as a cover-up as much as a punishment. When a white father, stepfather, brother, or uncle preyed on the girls in his household, the scapegoat was always ready at hand: a Black boy. Lynching was not only about racial hierarchy in the abstract. It was a ritual of concealment that protected the patriarch by projecting his crimes outward.

The familiar claim that mobs acted to defend the "purity" of white women and girls collapses under scrutiny because *there was no purity left to defend.* White households had already been desecrated from within by men who treated daughters, nieces, and sisters as property. What lynching really protected was not chastity but impunity. It was a ritual that laundered white men's crimes by projecting their incest and pedophilia onto Black boys and calling it justice.

The obsessive gaze directed at Black children in postcards, cartoons, and consumer goods reveals something far darker than moral panic: a national pedophilic fetish. Naked toddlers threatened by alligators and children ogled by leering adults were not minor artifacts of racist kitsch. They were cultural scripts that taught white people how to eroticize Black children's vulnerability and how to convert laughter into permission for violence. Placing these images at the center expands the archive of lynching beyond the tree, the rope, and the burning flesh.

This visual archive also dismantles the false distinction between mob violence and institutional power. Historians often write as though lynching was a breakdown of order. But medical science, Comstock's censorship regime, the postcard industry, and the federal mail system were also complicit. The state did not stand apart from the mob; it delivered the images, condoned the scripts, and policed the wrong people. What looked like mob violence was the visible edge of a much deeper collaboration between state power, consumer culture, and patriarchal households.

The exploitation of children was explained in two very different ways: For white children, it was framed as the violation of innocence, but for Black children, it was rationalized as an act of racial control. The transition from scientific objectification to artistic exploitation was seamless. White doctors feigned clinical detachment while handling Black children's bodies. White artists cloaked their pedophilic fixations behind humor and fantasy. Both transformed racialized child exploitation into consumable entertainment.

While art and culture abounded with lewd depictions of both white and Black children, white children were almost entirely absent from the pediatric record as objects of sexual scrutiny, nor did they appear in illicit pornographic postcards. Black children, by contrast, were pathologized, eroticized, and exposed. White adults already dominated their own children in private by controlling, violating, and policing them, while publicly projecting their perverse fixations onto Black children. The loss of legal access to Black children's bodies after emancipation demanded new technologies of access. White culture compensated by fetishizing Black children's bodies in medical literature, print, and consumer goods.

This visual culture, flourishing from the 1890s until the 1950s, was not merely comedic; rather, it was a form of perverse nostalgia. It transformed Black children into consumable objects, a substitute for the physical domination whites once exercised under slavery. Sold in drugstores and department stores, mailed through the federal system, these postcards reassured white consumers that Black children remained within reach of white desire and sexual abuse. They functioned as propaganda, intimidation, and psychological reinforcement of Black dehumanization.

Even as reformers proclaimed their devotion to "saving" childhood, they sharpened the divide between those deemed worthy of innocence and those condemned to spectacle and suffering. White childhood was to be nurtured and sanctified. Black childhood was to be dissected, ridiculed, and ravaged in plain sight. These twin obsessions—protecting white innocence and degrading Black youth—were not contradictions. They were two sides of the same coin. And as we will see, lynching was not exceptional chaos but the culmination of systems already in place: science, bureaucracy, censorship, and consumer culture. And it was the logical extension of normalized surveillance and exploitation.

The racialized child pornography examined in this chapter was not harmless entertainment. It structured desire itself, dictating who could be seen as innocent and who as corrupt, who was protected and who was disposable. The infamous *September Morn* controversy makes this divide plain: A painting of a white girl's body sent lawmakers into a frenzy, while the mass exploitation of Black children's bodies passed without a whisper of protest.

"DEVIL TRAPS" AND "EVIL READING"

On May 9, 1913, Anthony J. Comstock, special agent for the United States Post Office and head of the New York Society for the Suppression of Vice, stormed out of his cramped office at 150 Nassau Street after receiving an anonymous tip that a local art dealer was corrupting the morals of the city's youth. The caller was none other than Harry L. Reichenbach, a press agent famous for his wild publicity stunts. Reichenbach had been hired by the Braun & Company Art Gallery, which was desperate to sell thousands of prints of French artist Paul E. Chabas's painting *September Morn*. He knew a scandal was the fastest way to move product.

Though *September Morn*, a romanticized image of a nude young girl bathing in a serene lake, had won praise in the upper echelons of the French art world in 1912, it failed to capture the attention of American buyers. By 1913, as debates about pornography widened to include visual images, the painting became ripe for attack. Reichenbach saw an opportunity.[3] He baited Comstock, the mutton-chopped enforcer, with an anonymous tip promising that an "obscene" nude was on display in a Midtown storefront.[4]

With his badge and revolver concealed beneath the flap of his black frock coat, Comstock set out to protect innocent souls from what he called "devil traps," "cursed pictures," and "evil reading." Long accustomed to patrolling brothels and erotica shops, he was convinced that obscene pictures lured children into corruption.[5] "The youth of this country today are being cursed by the dissemination of pictures where woman is exposed to vulgar gaze," he lamented. He saw it as his duty—and the duty of all chivalrous men—to defend women and children from such defilement. "The nude in art," he warned, "is a menace upon this chastity."[6]

September Morn, *painting by Paul Chabas, 1912 (author's collection)*

Postcard of Black child by Bernhardt C. Wall, 1913

When Comstock arrived at the gallery, he found a small crowd of boys and girls gathered outside giggling and making faces "too sophisticated for their years" as they ogled the painting of the slender blonde bathing in an icy lake. He didn't realize Reichenbach had paid the children fifty cents apiece to stage the scene, or that *September Morn* had already been tried, and cleared, in a Chicago obscenity case months earlier.

"Take her out at once!" he bellowed as he barged into the gallery, marching past the group of snickering children. "The picture of the girl without any clothes on—take it out!"

"But that is the famous *September Morn*," the gallery manager protested.

"There's too little morning and too much maid!" Comstock shot back.

The manager initially refused to remove the painting, prompting Comstock to throw back the flap of his coat, revealing his badge. Faced with the threat of arrest, the painting briefly came down, only to be rehung as soon as Comstock left, exactly as Reichenbach had planned.

The controversy exploded, making headlines across the country. New Yorkers and tourists flocked to see the "scandalous" painting, and Braun & Company quickly sold out of prints. Despite Comstock's protests, *September Morn* became a *succès de scandale*, with hundreds of thousands of lithographic reproductions sold nationwide.

The painting ignited a firestorm. Some cities allowed *September Morn* to be displayed, but only behind screens or with robes painted over the girl's body. Others banned the painting altogether. Postmasters in Fort Worth, New Orleans, Montgomery, Birmingham, San Jose, Miami, Dallas, Omaha, and Kansas City refused to allow the distribution of postcard reproductions through the mail. Students at Wooster College in Ohio tossed prints into a bonfire during a religious revival. Three men in different cities were denied admission to the US Navy for having *September Morn* tattooed onto their bodies.[7] Determined to enlist, they scraped the image off their skin or had it covered with other tattoos. In some towns, men, women, and teenage girls were arrested for posing as *September Morn* in parades or reenacting the bathing scene in public.

One woman in Harrisburg, Pennsylvania, was fined $50 after wading into the Susquehanna River wearing only white tights, posing for a crowd of over a thousand as photographers captured the scene.[8]

But as the nation obsessed over the *September Morn* scandal, a Black burlesque version of Chabas's painting quietly emerged.

Unlike *September Morn*, this image of a nude Black child received no outrage, no arrests, no editorials, no censorship from Comstock. The very notion that a Black girl could be innocent, chaste, or beautiful was laughable to white America. The illustration, captioned "Go 'long, white man. I ain't no 'SEPTEMBER MORN,'" was meant to mock the very notion that a naked Black child could provoke the same moral panic as a naked white girl.

The contrast was glaring.

September Morn depicted an idealized nude, bathed in soft morning light, her flesh delicate and untouched. By contrast, the Black girl, drawn with exaggerated features—overly red engorged lips, wide eyes, and messy plaits—was stripped of any hint of sentimentality or beauty. She stood not in a misty lake but in a wooden bucket, a bar of soap at her feet. If Chabas sought to capture "delicate charm," Bernhardt Wall, the white illustrator responsible for this postcard, had other intentions. Popularly known as America's "Postcard King," Wall was a prolific artist and war veteran who produced thousands of mass-market images.

His depiction of the Black child was not simply a parody; it was an extension of white supremacy's visual culture, one that weaponized the racial hierarchy of childhood.

These two images, a nude white girl ankle-deep in a European lake and a younger nude Black girl bathing in a bucket, exist within the same historical moment, yet their meanings could not be more different. Together, they expose how new media, censorship laws, purity campaigns, and ideas about sex intersected to create a racialized construction of childhood innocence. They also reveal how the marketplace, law enforcement, and the press collaborated to determine whose nudity was a scandal and whose was a joke.

Anthony Comstock, one of America's most powerful purity crusaders, had made it his mission to shield white children from moral corruption. But Black children, as always, escaped his concern. His failure to condemn their sexualized imagery, his silence in the face of racist pedophilic postcards, speaks to how white America had already accepted, normalized, and even encouraged the degradation of Black youth.

PICTURING INNOCENCE

The battle over *September Morn* was not an isolated controversy. It was part of a broader cultural war in which new visual technologies, particularly postcards, became tools for shaping and reinforcing racial hierarchy. As purity crusaders fixated on shielding white children from perceived threats, the same emerging mass media they sought to regulate actively fueled the racial degradation of Black youth. Anthony Comstock's relentless purity crusade was never just about morality. It was about protecting the ideological boundaries of whiteness. His campaign to censor obscene materials wasn't rooted in a universal concern for childhood innocence but in maintaining a racialized moral order that privileged white children while disregarding or actively enabling the degradation of Black youth.

Comstock's obsession with suppressing images of nude or sexualized white women and children was deeply tied to the belief that whiteness needed to be safeguarded from corruption. His fear of moral decay wasn't just about sexuality; it was about *who* was deemed worthy of protection. White childhood and white womanhood were framed

Honey, I'se Waiting fo' You, *postcard by the E. C. Kropp Publishing Company, Milwaukee, Wisconsin, and a similar 1910 postcard by Frederick George Lewin. Author's collection.*

as fragile and pure, requiring strict policing to prevent moral contamination. This is why he fought so aggressively to ban images like *September Morn*, which depicted a nude white girl, and to criminalize the distribution of literature and art that he believed could taint white youth.

Ironically, Comstock's relentless fixation on censoring sexualized images of white children was itself a form of pedophilia that fetishized white childhood as an object of obsessive protection, surveillance, and moral purity. The very act of defining white childhood as a sexually sacred, untouchable state ensured that it became a site of compulsive policing. Purity itself became fetishized possession that had to be vigilantly defended.

As James Kincaid has argued in *Child-Loving: The Erotic Child and Victorian Culture*, and later in *Erotic Innocence: The Culture of Child Molesting*, Western culture constructs childhood as both innocent and erotically charged. Race is absent from his framework, however.[9] White childhood was eroticized by its inaccessibility, while Black childhood was eroticized through its presumed availability. Comstock's campaign ensured that white childhood remained both sacred and titillating through obsessive public fascination.

The contradictions in Comstock's censorship efforts become even starker when considering how he engaged with the very images he sought to ban. To wage his crusade, he had to immerse himself in the materials he condemned, scrutinizing, cataloging, and describing them in meticulous detail. His fight against obscenity became an act of obsessive engagement, one that mirrored the very fixation he claimed to suppress.[10] Such moral policing has long been recognized as displaced desire: The crusader against obscenity becomes its most devoted consumer. And, as with all censorship movements, Comstock's aggressive policing of *forbidden* imagery only heightened its allure. By criminalizing certain images, he affirmed their illicit public appeal, inadvertently fueling the very market he purported to loathe.

For all his moral outrage over images of white children, Comstock was utterly silent about the mass circulation of pornographic depictions of Black children. If his campaign had truly been about protecting *all* children, then surely, he would have fought against the openly pornographic and racist caricatures that depicted Black youth as hypersexualized and available for exploitation. But his inaction reveals the racial limits of his concern: White children were to be protected at all costs, while Black children were denied the very category of innocence that made protection possible.

The first postcards depicting African Americans emerged at the 1895 Cotton States and International Exposition, held in Atlanta. The event, coinciding with Booker T. Washington's infamous Atlanta Compromise speech, served two functions: to showcase technological progress and to reaffirm the nation's racial hierarchy. While visitors marveled at new industrial advancements, they also encountered ethnological exhibits that framed Black and Indigenous people as inferior primitives and exotic curiosities. It was here that the visual commodification of Black bodies found a modern shape.

This emerging visual culture coincided with rising white anxieties about Black progress. As historian Grace Elizabeth Hale explains in *Making Whiteness*, emancipation "made anything possible and nothing certain."[11] With freedom came soaring Black literacy rates, increased Black mobility, and the emergence of a Black middle class. These were developments that directly threatened white myths of racial inferiority. At the same time, fears of racial mixing led to an intensified effort to police the boundaries of whiteness. Cheap and widely distributed, postcards reinforced racial anxieties by ridiculing, criminalizing, and sexualizing Black children. Some depicted them as happy and servile to uphold plantation myths, while others cast them as grotesque figures of vulnerability. The infamous "alligator bait" postcards portrayed Black babies as prey, while others reduced them to crude sexual caricatures, positioning them as objects of white domination.

During the Jim Crow era, racist consumer goods allowed white Americans to maintain an image of civility, morality, and progress while simultaneously engaging with materials that sexualized Black children. Postcards depicting racial caricatures were a key part of this cultural landscape, framing Black and white children as opposites and reinforcing pseudoscientific theories, legal justifications for segregation, and the broader sexual exploitation of Black youth. From the 1890s until the late 1950s, before NAACP efforts led to their decline, these lewd postcards circulated freely, providing white audiences with a way to engage in pedophilic fantasies under the guise of humor and nostalgia.

But what does it mean to be considered a child in the first place? And who, exactly, has been afforded the privileges of innocence, protection, and moral purity?

Historically, childhood in Western cultures has been distinguished from adulthood in many ways, be it the lack of mature rationality, moral reasoning, or personal responsibility. During the Progressive Era, Comstock and other reformers maintained that the boundary line that separated adults from children was sexuality. Adults possessed sexuality while children were supposedly free from it. But in early adolescence, Black children allegedly displayed signs and behaviors of illicit sexuality while the white child's sexual instincts remained dormant, echoing the medical findings published in pediatric journals of the era. The visual imagery presented here is illustrative of the way high scientific discourse became popularized. In this context, pornographic postcards of Black children were more than they appeared to be. At worst, some white artists and viewers used them to displace their repressed desires for their own "innocent" and "untouchable" children onto Black youth. Historians have made similar observations concerning erotic images of white children.[12] Even if such images did not provide viewers with titillation, they offered certain assurances about white normalcy, morality, dominance, and superiority.

White girls served as paragons of antebellum ideas about femininity. Their physical features, along with their behavior, idealized childhood. Some historians have argued that these kinds of images of pure, soft, untouchable white girls are themselves erotic and sexually exploitative because they invite the gaze of predators.[13] Perhaps, but when these images of white children are placed next to hardcore sexual images of Black girls and boys, the discussion fails to recognize the more blatant example of sexual exploitation. The point here is not to split hairs over degrees of exploitation but to recognize what is clear in archival evidence and Comstock's reaction to Chabas's naked white girl: White artists and dealers understood that they could not sexually objectify white children in cartoons or photographs and publicly circulate them without prosecution.

Meanwhile, white audiences could view publicly available drawings of Black children's naked bodies and see them engaged in sexually taboo behaviors such as oral and anal sex, masturbation, prostitution,

1920s postcard of naked Black boys bathing in Massa's Baff, *by artist Frederick George Lewin. From a pedophilic perspective, the image coupled with the word "baff" suggests a tub of semen. Author's collection.*

dendrophilia (sex with trees), zoophilia (sex with animals), coprophilia (attraction to feces), urophagia (attraction to urination), fetishistic spanking, and even bathing in a tub that, in a pedophilic interpretation, could be read as suggestive of semen, as seen in Frederick George Lewin's 1920s postcard *Massa's Baff*.

"DO COME SOON"

When I was a doctoral student in African American history at Rutgers University, I began collecting racist and sexually explicit postcards featuring Black children. I found them in online marketplaces like eBay, CardCow.com, and the websites of independent dealers, where they were euphemistically marketed as "Black Memorabilia," stripped of their original intent and repackaged as collectible relics of a bygone era. But these images were never just relics. They were tools of violence, created to dehumanize Black children while indulging a sick undercurrent of white desire. These were not innocent depictions, nor were they merely racist caricatures; they were a visual archive of domination, embedding perverse sexual projections into everyday consumer culture.

Collectors and dealers today often justify their resale of these postcards by saying they are merely historical artifacts, emphasizing the humor and monetary value while distancing themselves from the racism and child exploitation these images perpetuated. The enduring market for these objects underscores how the legacies of racialized sexual violence remain embedded in cultural memory. Rather than reckoning with the objects' origins and explicit sexual overtones, collectors reframe them as historical curiosities.

During their heyday, these cards sold for as little as a penny, a cheap and casual purchase for those who wanted to laugh at, humiliate, and fetishize Black childhood. Today, they are auctioned for anywhere from a few dollars to hundreds. One notable example of this type of artifact is the 1910 illustration by white female artist Frances Brundage, which depicts a young Black girl with her dress strap slipping off her shoulder, simulating oral sex on a banana. The persistence of these images in the collectors' market today—decades after their original circulation—suggests that their function has not entirely faded. They were created to indulge white fantasies of Black degradation, and in many ways, they still do.

To engage with these images properly, we must strip them of the humor and nostalgia that white consumers historically used to justify their production and distribution. We must look at them for what they are: visual documents of racialized sexual violence masquerading as playful, innocent ephemera. This requires an uncomfortable but necessary shift in perspective—one that forces us to view these postcards through the eyes of pedophiles who consumed them with deviant pleasure. As sickening as this exercise may be, it is crucial to understand how these images functioned as both psychological instruments and social conditioning tools. They allowed white audiences to participate in pedophilic projection under the guise of humor, to normalize their illicit desires through the degradation of Black children. What follows is a close reading of these images, not through the sanitized lens of history but through the grotesque gaze of those who created, circulated, and consumed them. This is the only way to fully grasp the layers of violence they contain.

Let's begin with Brundage's little girl.

This postcard is a textbook example of how oral fixation, an eroticized trait in Freudian psychoanalysis, is projected onto Black children. Look at the positioning of the banana, a well-established phallic symbol, and the child's wide-eyed expression of exaggerated surprise, implying that she is not simply eating a piece of fruit but has been forced into an act of oral sex. The yellow peels resemble a pair of pants dropped, exposing an erect white penis being inserted into her pink lips, which are engorged like an aroused vagina. Her eyes signify struggle as her left hand extends outward to hold her balance—or to hold onto the viewer's thigh, who could imagine his own penis in this child's mouth.

Valentine postcard of a Black girl simulating oral sex on a banana, by artist Frances Brundage, 1910 (author's collection)

The caption, "With my Love," masks this suggestion under the veneer of affection, reinforcing how white supremacy structures desire under the guise of sentimentality. "With my love" is also a pedophilic alibi. Putting these words in her mouth suggests that a young child performing oral sex on an adult is an acceptable act because it is mutual—because the child and the adult are in love.

"It's just a cute little Black girl having a snack," chuckled Elaine Luck, the vintage postcard dealer who sold me the card over a decade ago for $125.

When I told her that the child was being sexualized, Luck told me that I was projecting, finding perverse meaning where there was none. Labeling these images "Black Memorabilia," as Luck and other dealers have done, has allowed peddlers to distance themselves from the racism and sexual objectification of children. Contrary to Luck's comments to me, this was not a simple image of childhood curiosity, snack time, or play. It was a calculated effort to sexualize and degrade, to imply that Black children were innately obscene.

And yet, the banana postcard is only one variation in a wider lexicon of visual exploitation. If oral fixation was one prong of this racist sexual imagination, the preoccupation with Black children's bodily functions—defecation, urination, and flatulence—was another. These

Curt Teich & Sons postcard featuring a Black girl child defecating, engaging in the sexual fetish of "scat," on a chamber pot.

grotesque postcards reduced Black children to figures of scatological humor, humiliation, and sexual spectacle. From the banana, we move to the next image—a Black toddler perched over a potty exposing her heart-shaped buttocks to the viewer.

This image draws on themes of both *coprophilia* (attraction to feces) and *urophilia* (attraction to urination). By positioning a Black child squatting over a chamber pot with her white dress parted, the image invites a voyeuristic gaze that transforms an act of bodily function into a fetishized spectacle. The exaggerated roundness of the child's bare backside and the phrase "'scuse de view" suggest an awareness that the audience is peering into something private, with the child forced into the role of performer as well as object. She is cheerful, unashamed, made into an object of both ridicule and voyeuristic delight. The caption plays on exaggerated dialect, reinforcing the infantilization of Black people while inviting white audiences to leer at a child's most private moment. Here, a Black child's body is a site of both humor and illicit desire.

From the potty postcard's fixation on exposure and humiliation, we move to another scene of racialized spectacle—a Black girl hunched over at a lemonade stand with her dress similarly lifted just enough to reveal her backside to the viewer. The caption, "There's 'barely' any business at all," is a thinly veiled double entendre, resting on the sexualization of a child's body as both joke and invitation. This transition from the bathroom to the marketplace reinforces a logic that Black children's bodies were not only sites of public exposure but also commodities, objects to be displayed, advertised, and consumed at will.

Lemonade stands are a classic symbol of childhood entrepreneurship, both innocence and industriousness. However, in this image, the girl is not depicted as an enterprising child but as a commodity herself. The placement of the sign, the emphasis on her exposed backside, and the caption all work together to suggest something beyond the simple sale of lemonade. The phrase "There's 'barely' any business at all" is a clear double entendre, playing on both the lack of customers and the fact that the child is "barely" covered—her lifted dress exposing her to the viewer's gaze.

The dropping price of the lemonade adds another sinister layer. What exactly is being devalued? If this were simply about lemonade,

Undated postcard published by Curt Teich & Sons.

the humor would rely on basic economic failure. But given the racial and sexualized context, the lowering price also suggests that the child's body, her availability, and her worth diminish over time. This aligns with historical patterns of Black dehumanization in which Black life was treated as cheap, disposable, and easily exploitable. More disturbingly, the price reduction can be read as an allusion to sexual bargaining, echoing the "demand determines value" dynamic of prostitution. The girl, positioned as both a seller and an object to be looked at, becomes part of an implicit transaction, one where her price, like that of any commodity in a capitalist market, drops when there are no buyers.

The humor, then, is not just in the failure of a business venture but in the suggestion that this Black child's worth, her access to resources, and even her bodily autonomy are dependent on white consumption. The joke only works if the audience understands that her body is available for negotiation. Finally, the presence of the small white dog further compounds the image's racialized and sexual undertones. In fetishistic imagery, animals are often used to stand in for white male desire, while also reinforcing themes of zoophilia and voyeurism. The dog's fixed gaze on the girl suggests not just curiosity but desire, adding to the grotesque narrative of white spectatorship.

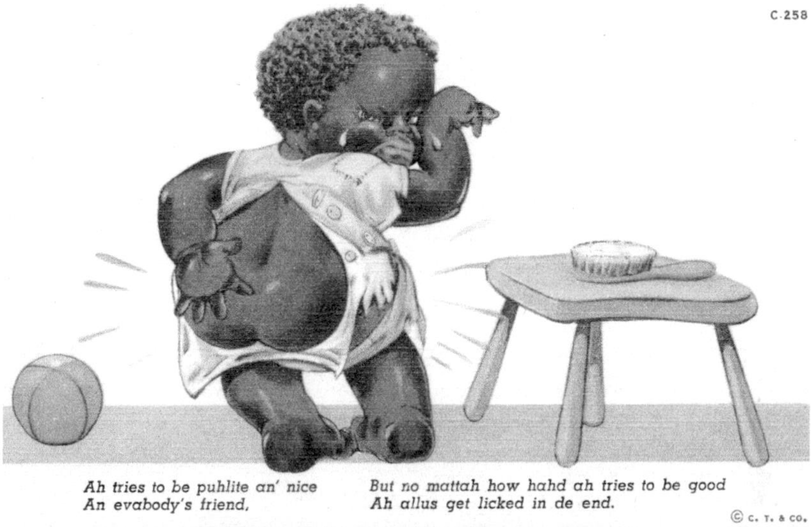

Undated postcard published by the Curt Teich & Sons Co. Author's collection.

From the lemonade stand's staged exposure, where a Black girl's body is positioned as both spectacle and commodity, we move into yet another grotesque scene—one that takes the fantasy of Black children's vulnerability even further. Here, a dark-skinned toddler lifts their dress while turning away from the viewer, their backside fully exposed. The caption frames it as a joke about punishment: "Ah tries to be puhlite an' nice . . . but no mattah how hahd ah tries to be good, Ah allus get licked in de end," a double entendre that both refers to corporal punishment and subtly suggests oral fixation ("licked" as in being both beaten and tasted).

This is not merely a reinforcement of racist tropes about Black children as inherently mischievous or deserving of discipline—it is an invitation for viewers to derive pleasure from the act of corporal punishment itself. Spanking, already a charged practice in the history of racial violence, is here transformed into an eroticized spectacle. The exaggerated bare buttocks, turned slightly toward the viewer, invites a discipline-centered gaze that aligns with fetishistic depictions of submission. The racially exaggerated caricature, paired with the suggestive caption, allows the audience to consume this child's pain as both comedy and a source of covert titillation.

This juxtaposition of a scene of playful innocence at the lemonade stand with one of staged discipline underscores a broader theme in these postcards: the cyclical nature of humiliation and violence. Black children are first positioned as eager, unwitting performers—then swiftly reminded of their place through the threat of physical punishment. This is the logic of white-supremacist fantasy, where Black childhood is framed not just as spectacle but as something to be controlled, punished, and ultimately broken.

The next image, of a crying Black baby crawling on all fours with an exaggeratedly swollen and reddened backside, is disturbingly unnatural. The child's posture, arched, mouth agape in exaggerated wailing, limbs splayed awkwardly, suggests not just distress but something more staged, something meant to be consumed. The grotesque rendering of pain in this image is not an appeal for sympathy; it is an invitation to leer, to laugh, to indulge in a spectacle of suffering that has been carefully manufactured for white amusement.

The caption, "Ah'm nobody's baby now," adds another sinister layer. At first glance, it implies abandonment, the loss of care and protection. But within the broader context of these postcards in which Black children are repeatedly subjected to humiliation, violation, and punishment, the phrase suggests something more chilling.

If this child is "nobody's baby," then what is he? Is he no longer seen as a child? Or worse, does this text hint at possession—was he somebody's baby before, claimed in a way that this image now marks as something final?

The unnatural posture, the framing of the body, the wording of the caption—these elements work together to signal something deeply perverse. The child's exposed, upturned position evokes the aftermath of discipline but also the vulnerability of submission. In the visual logic of these images, where racialized bodies are both punished and sexualized, this is not just about desertion. It is about what happens when a

Undated Curt Teich & Sons postcard. Author's collection.

child is no longer under the protection of innocence, when they are positioned as available for whatever fate a violent, white-supremacist imagination decides.

The next postcard, captioned "I'se black all over, 'cept where I'se blue," makes no attempt at subtlety. The message is clear: Blackness is a mark of difference, but the only way a Black child can turn any other color is through violence. The raised shirt, exposed backside, and bruising invite the viewer into the aftereffects of a beating, an intimate display of domination disguised as humor. The placement of the child in a corner, traditionally a form of discipline, further aligns this with themes of forced humiliation and infantilized suffering as a source of white amusement. The child's shame, the turned-away body, and the hands covering the face all create the impression that they are embarrassed. But who is meant to enjoy this suffering? And what does it mean for pain to be reframed as comedy?

The handprints on the wall, one bold, the other faint, are a spectral presence in the scene and an unsettling trace of unseen violence. They are positioned at a height that suggests the child was pressed against the wall while bracing for impact. Whose prints do they belong to? Is it the child's own, pressed against the wall in a futile attempt to steady themselves after a blow? Or is it the imprint of the adult, perhaps the unseen enforcer of punishment, whose presence lingers even in their physical absence? The sheer size of the print in comparison to the child's proportions suggests the latter: an authority figure, larger, stronger, leaving behind not just bruises on the child's body but a lasting physical mark in the space around them. It transforms the wall into a site of recorded violence, a silent witness to whatever just occurred.

1939 postcard by artist Douglas Tempest. Author's collection.

This detail heightens the grotesque theatricality of the scene. The child's turned-away body, the exaggerated sag of their overalls, and their shame all reinforce the idea that this is supposed to be funny. But the humor is a thin veil over something more sinister. This isn't just a joke about mischief and punishment; it is a staged representation of control, in which the child's humiliation is meant to be enjoyed. The image demands the viewer to participate in the dynamic—not to sympathize, but to take pleasure in the pain, to see it as justified, as natural. The humor of the caption attempts to overwrite the brutality of the scene, just as Jim Crow–era visual culture repeatedly framed Black suffering as entertainment.

The strategic use of red in this image serves as a coded visual language, reinforcing themes of violence, humiliation, and fetishistic control. Whether appearing in implied bruises or welts or in the background details, red becomes a tool that white-supremacist visual culture employs to make Black suffering not only visible but consumable. It demands the viewer's gaze, ensuring that the spectacle of Black pain, whether through physical abuse, sexual trauma, or public humiliation, remains central to the experience of the image. The result is an image that is not merely a work of racist humor but a deeply embedded ritual of racial and sexual domination, one that encourages white audiences to enjoy the pain it depicts while absolving them of the moral implications.

One particularly sinister postcard features a young Black child standing with legs slightly apart, looking downward with a surprised expression. The child's hands are positioned near their groin, and a visible stain on their pants suggests they have wet themselves. The puddle on the floor ensures that the viewer's gaze is directed toward the lower half of the child's body. The background is sparse, with a textured surface that suggests an interior space, possibly a home or school setting, but it is nondescript enough that the focus remains solely on the child's posture and bodily functions.

Undated and artist unknown. Author's collection.

What's really going on here?

The boy's shirt is being rolled into the shape of a penis. The mechanics of wringing, grasping, twisting, squeezing mirror the actions of masturbation, ejaculation, and forced sexual submission. In this context, the child's body is being "wrung out," a metaphor for both physical and sexual depletion.

The framed picture of the girl with engorged, exaggerated lips in the background intensifies this reading. Her presence is striking, as she is not just a passive background figure but an active onlooker. Her facial expression, with wide, suggestive lips, places her in the role of both observer and participant in this deeply disturbing tableau. In the coded language of these images, she could be positioned as an implied recipient of the boy's attention, reinforcing a theme of Black children being hypersexual and engaged in inappropriate behaviors from a young age. The framing of her face, akin to a voyeuristic peep show or a lurid portrait, aligns with the way Black children were often depicted as objects of white desire, fascination, and scorn.

Together, the elements of this postcard—his exaggerated motion, the positioning of the child's hand, the grotesquely captioned confession, and the voyeuristic framing of the girl—encode layers of perversion that go far beyond mere racist humor. They construct a twisted narrative that caters to a white audience primed to both ridicule and indulge in the fetishistic objectification of Black childhood. Whether in the forced manual labor of enslaved children or the unspoken sexual violations that often accompanied servitude, Black children's bodies were positioned as sites of extraction, of work, of pleasure, of degradation.

The next postcard, of a Black child having sex with a tree, depicts dendrophilia—sexual attraction to trees. The exaggerated gaze of the older Black woman conveys shock, playing into tropes of racialized hypersexuality and perverse discovery. The implication that the child is doing something "peculiar" invites the viewer to complete the narrative, suggesting an engagement with something unnatural or deviant. The child's position, partially obscured by the tree, further hints at secrecy and the perverse pleasure of spying on illicit acts. The tree itself is rendered with organic curves that mirror the child's body, creating a disturbing visual connection between flesh and wood.

The caption likely plays with the racialized stereotype of Black people as being closer to nature, but in doing so, it also subtly encodes a more illicit implication—one of bodily submission, forced entanglement, or even a perverse intimacy with the nonhuman. The tree's

Undated Curt Teich & Sons postcard. Author's collection.

positioning and the child's posture evoke the visual language of fetishistic imagery, where bodies are bound, immobilized, or subjected to external forces. By blending the child's body with the tree, the postcard dehumanizes them entirely, reducing Blackness to a malleable, consumable entity that can be distorted, manipulated, and absorbed into the landscape.

The presence of the cork in the tree and the drip falling into the bucket adds another layer of disturbing subtext to the image. At first glance, it appears it may be depicting tree-tapping, a common method for extracting sap, but within the broader context of Jim Crow–era racist caricatures and fetishistic imagery, the implications are far more sinister. The cork, sealing an orifice in the tree, suggests a forced containment—something that has been plugged, restrained, or artificially held back. The slow drip evokes multiple potential readings, all of them charged with exploitative and sexually suggestive undertones. It mirrors bodily fluids, reinforcing themes of extraction, violation, and commodification. The bucket collecting the substance further implies a process of accumulation, of something being drained or taken, evoking the long history of the economic and physical exploitation of Black bodies.

Given the racialized sexualization of Black children in these postcards, the image carries a deeply unsettling association with bodily control and forced release. The visual metaphor blurs the lines between nature, body, and product, making the child indistinguishable from the tree, an object to be tapped and harvested. This aligns with the broader function of these postcards: to encode illicit fantasies within the guise of humor or rural innocence while reinforcing the notion that Black bodies exist for white consumption.

The imagery of the tree-tapping postcard is a lewd fusion of nature and bodily exploitation, where Blackness itself is framed as something to be harvested. This theme of bodily availability carries over into the final postcard, one that leans into a different but no less disturbing sexualized trope. In this 1910 postcard, a young Black child is depicted in the form of Cupid, standing nude except for a pair of tiny wings strapped to their back. The caption reads: "Do come soon." The double entendre is impossible to ignore.

On one level, it operates as a flirtatious invitation, the kind that might be found in Victorian-era postcards meant to convey longing or affection. But within the broader context of these postcards, the phrase takes on a much darker meaning, layering sexual anticipation over the body of a Black child.

The Cupid child in this postcard clutches the oversized letter "S" with both hands, gripping it in a way that draws immediate attention to its shape and positioning. The curve of the "S" mimics the curve of his small body, with the bottom tail resting suggestively between his legs. The placement of the hands, firmly grasping either side, gives the impression of someone holding onto a weighty object, something meant to be noticed. The exaggerated curve of the letter, combined with the child's pose, mimics the visual language of erotic suggestion. The "S" takes on a phallic quality, enhanced by how the child's fingers wrap around it, as though stroking or presenting it.

The "o's" in "Do come soon" are exaggerated in their curvature, round and plump, almost bulging in a way that mimics testicles. They

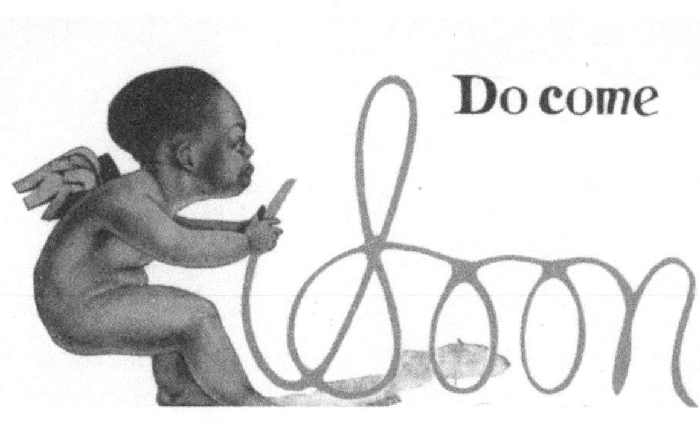

1910 Cupid postcard by F. A. Moss. Author's collection.

draw the eye downward, reinforcing the unsettling innuendo embedded in the composition. The way the letters are stylized, with thick, rounded strokes, gives them an organic, almost fleshy quality, making them appear less like typography and more like suggestive anatomical shapes. This design choice was not accidental. The visual emphasis on the "S" the child is gripping, combined with the roundness of the "o's," creates an unmistakable phallic structure within the text itself. The letters become more than mere decoration; they work in tandem with the child's posture to evoke a crude sexual pun. This is the way that the grotesque humor of these racist postcards operates: It takes something seemingly innocent, like playful typography or a child's interaction with a letter, and corrupts it with coded imagery meant to titillate and amuse a white audience steeped in racist and pedophilic fetishization of Black bodies.

Many people will see these cards as evidence of Black children being "adultified" and denied innocence. I disagree. Their innocence isn't being denied. *Their innocence is the fetish.* Pedophiles don't adultify children. They are not attracted to adults. And white-supremacist sexuality is heavily imbued with pedophilic elements. They go hand in hand. White supremacy's construction of sexuality has always relied on a foundation of racialized control, infantilization, and fetishized dominance. It has structured desire itself, embedding pedophilic elements into the very logic of white patriarchal power while projecting those impulses onto the Black body to justify its continued violation.

White supremacy requires the infantilization of people of color, making them into "child races" not simply to exclude and exploit them as "children," but also to objectify, sexualize, and fetishize them. At its core, white-supremacist domination is the "mature" domination of the "immature," with all the perversities that come from such a relation. It should come as no surprise that white supremacy has infected white conceptions of childhood, romance, love, and sex. And since white supremacy is so deeply structured by the infantilization of racialized people, are we really surprised that Black children have long been fetishized as sex objects?

Images like these postcards normalized the Black child's body as always undressed, as sexual, as available to be gazed at and touched. But these images are not often seen as something that white society as a whole produced and consumed. For the artists, consumers, and private exchangers of these postcards, climactic release was not necessarily experienced genitally but as affirmation through a sense of ownership and superiority that the items' consumption aroused. The so-called comical representations of the Black child must be returned to sender—historically and theoretically recontextualized as aberrant racialized child pornography.

"SHE IS FLESH OF MY FLESH"

It would be easy for white readers to dismiss what follows as a uniquely American sickness, perhaps just a Southern aberration, a grotesque byproduct of slavery and Jim Crow. But the truth is uglier.

The entitlement to children's bodies, the normalization of incest, the obsession with purity—all of it was carried across the Atlantic from Europe. The sexual scripts of lynching were not written in Louisiana cane fields; they were inherited from Europe's castles, churches, and courts, where the sexualization of children in visual culture was already well established. The racist postcards of the early twentieth century extended a long-standing European tradition in which children, particularly those outside the aristocracy, were depicted as objects for consumption and sexual exploitation. Jim Crow America did not invent the sexual objectification of children; it weaponized it racially, ensuring that Black children would be denied both innocence and protection.

To understand why white Americans mass-produced, circulated, and consumed degrading images of Black children during Jim Crow, we have to look backward—across the Atlantic, into Europe's long shadow. In *Patriarchy and Incest from Shakespeare to Joyce*, Jane Ford traces how stories of father-daughter incest took root in the European imagination. In antiquity, the rape of young girls by fathers and guardians was not scandalous; it was expected, a literary shorthand for male power and an unremarkable literary trope. Only in the Middle Ages did the story change shape. The pursuit spurred by incestuous desire became more prevalent, and the daughter's flight—her terror, her escape—became the new plot. Ford notes, "There are plenty of incestuous fathers in classical mythology and literature, but the story of the flight of the innocent daughter from her father's unwelcome advances seems to be a medieval innovation."[14]

But this was not progress. The rebranding of incest as "temptation" did not erase the father's claim; it disguised it. The crime was renamed, not renounced. Incest became ostensibly taboo in discourse but remained a ritual of power. Across centuries, Europe perfected the art of moral disguise. The role of the father simply changed—to priest, guardian, suitor, king. Sexual authority was no longer framed as naked tyranny but as stewardship: the protection of chastity, the guardianship of souls, the management of households and estates. Control over female bodies was justified as paternal duty and moral oversight, recast as care rather than coercion. The same violation dressed itself as protection was eventually codified in feudal law under *jus primae noctis*, the supposed right of lords to claim sexual access to peasant brides on their wedding nights. Europe's history of conquest began, quite literally, in the bedroom.

In the eighteenth-century novella *Eugénie de Franval*, the Marquis de Sade creates a father character, Franval, who openly rationalizes his sexual claim over his daughter. De Sade himself is not speaking autobiographically; rather, he stages paternal entitlement as philosophical argument. The father's right to his daughter's body is rebranded as moral logic. As Franval declares:

> You mean to say that a lovely girl cannot tempt me because I am guilty of having sired her? That what ought to bind me more intimately to her should become the very reason for my removal from her? 'Tis because she resembles me, because she is flesh of my flesh—that is to say, the embodiment of all the motives upon which to base the most ardent love—that I should regard her with an icy eye?[15]

De Sade's words expose the core of white patriarchy: The father's claim was both biological and ideological, an assertion of ownership disguised as love. While white girlhood was fetishized and policed, Black children were framed as naturally available for consumption. The very purity that inspired chivalrous defenses of white girlhood also invited its violation. If she required protection, it was because she was presumed universally desirable. From *Jane Eyre* to the *Twilight* series, the guardian of a white girl's virtue often became the one to take it.

As theological prohibitions on vice waned under the humanist turn of the nineteenth century, father-daughter rape lost what few cultural guardrails had restrained it. It was not uncommon, and it was only constructed as a significant social problem when white-supremacist physicians reframed it as a biological crisis. The concern was not the harm to white girl children but the threat incest posed to the health of the white race. Eugenicists feared that unchecked sexual violence within white communities would corrupt the genetic stock, endangering racial purity and fitness. By contrast, the long history of white male sexual violence against Black girls was never positioned as a pathology requiring intervention. It was embedded within the logic of white domination, functioning as an expected, even necessary, component of racial hierarchy.

This ideology of ownership extended outward, asserting control over Black bodies after emancipation. The same logic that normalized white fathers' access to their daughters was deployed against Black children, casting them as hypersexualized and consumable. If white girlhood was at once sacred and violable, Black childhood was neither. Black children were denied even the illusion of protection, cast as complicit in their own violation. After centuries of slavery, Black families had been devastated by white men's systematic rape of enslaved children. That legacy shaped Black communities in ways that white supremacists then twisted into "evidence" of Black degeneracy—while ignoring the pedophilic masters who engineered it. Historian Brian Connolly notes in *Domestic Intimacies*: "To put it simply, in the discourse of slavery, incest was aligned with blackness, and the incest prohibition was aligned with whiteness."[16]

This racialized construction of incest functioned as a means of drawing a moral distinction between white and Black familial structures. White families were framed as spaces of protection, even as widespread incestuous rape undermined this fiction. Meanwhile, Black families were cast as inherently pathological, despite the reality that their destruction had been engineered in part through systemic white sexual violence.

So, should we be surprised that a society that so readily sexualized, violated, and rationalized the domination of its own children for centuries would extend this perversity to the children of others? The very structures that allowed white men to claim authority over their daughters also justified their entitlement to the bodies of Black children in the eras of slavery and Jim Crow. The mechanisms of racialized violence were not separate from the internal violence of whiteness—they were extensions of the same patriarchal logic, now operating within the framework of racial hierarchy.

White supremacy required the constant policing of white girlhood as both an object of desire and a symbol of racial purity, but it imposed no such contradictions onto Black children. Their suffering was never cause for moral reckoning. Their bodies were always deemed available for sexual exploitation and murder. If white men felt entitled to their own daughters, there was no moral or psychological barrier preventing them from exercising the same power over Black children—only fewer restrictions, fewer consequences, and an entire ideological system that framed such violations as natural, expected, and even necessary.

Up to this point, we've seen how the sexualization of Black children fed white America's appetite for violence. Now the scene shifts to New Orleans, where that cycle played out with chilling precision. A white girl was assaulted and murdered, not by the Black teenager who the mob insisted was the perpetrator, but by a family member whose guilt could not be acknowledged without challenging white patriarchal authority. So, the burden of white guilt was shifted, as it so often was, onto a Black child's body. His innocence did not matter. What mattered was that white society had someone to kill.

The unspoken truth of so many lynchings is that they began with the sexual violation of white girls and ended with the murder of Black boys. The terror was cyclical, generational, and purposeful. America, unwilling to face the predators in its own homes and admit to its own crimes, found it easier to string up a Black child. That denial and projection come to a horrifying crescendo in the lynching of Fred Moore.

"NIGGERS LET THIS BE AN EXAMPLE"

On the night of October 11, 1933, in Labadieville, Louisiana, sixteen-year-old Fred Moore sat in a dark, cramped parish cell, accused of raping and murdering fifteen-year-old Anna Mae Larose, who was found in a cane field with her throat slashed. Deputy Fernand Richard fixed blame immediately. Her stepfather, David George Himel Jr., said he'd seen Moore speak with her, and that was enough, in Jim Crow logic, to seal a verdict.

The arrest was swift. Deputies took Moore from his parents' home in Napoleonville, snatching a child from the one place he should have been safe. His mother, Lilly, begged Sheriff Lezin H. Himel—who was related to the victim's stepfather—for protection as he shackled her son. The sheriff looked her in the eye and promised Moore would be safe in the jail. It was a lie.

That night the mob came. They were initially waved off. The timing and cover had to be arranged. Judge Samuel A. LeBlanc warned the sheriff, who was at home, to remain there—a convenient alibi. When the mob returned, Sheriff Himel was nowhere to be found.

The former sheriff, Deputy Abel Landry, produced the jail keys. The mob stormed in.

The mob comprised over a hundred white men and boys, frenzied, armed, and ready to kill. Cellmate Ivory LeBlanc watched as they dragged Fred from his cot. Deputy Richard stood among them. A noose was thrown around the boy's neck. They hauled him to the cane field where Larose's body was found, beat him, cut him, then forced him to march nearly ten miles to the Labadieville Bridge. There, they castrated him.

It bears noting that this was not the first time a Black man would be so easily apprehended from the Napoleonville jail and lynched for allegedly assaulting a white woman. Forty years earlier, in 1893, a Black man by the name of Israel Holloway was accused of raping a young white girl, Eva Dugas. He was taken from the Napoleonville jail and lynched by a mob while then sheriff, Edgard Aucoin, was away in Labadieville.[17] Three years prior to that, Phillip Williams was arrested for attempted rape of a white woman and held at the Napoleonville jail. A mob demanded the keys, apprehended Williams, and lynched him.

It also bears noting that around the time of the Moore lynching, in neighboring Alabama the Scottsboro Boys were defending themselves against the charge of rape, a protracted ordeal that was ultimately successful. Two white prostitutes (one of whom eventually recanted her story) had accused the nine Black teenagers of rape. They were quickly tried, convicted, and with the exception of the youngest, twelve-year-old Roy Wright—who was given a life sentence—the Scottsboro Boys were sentenced to death by electric chair. The case was appealed up to the Supreme Court, which declared the trial unconstitutional.

It was in this context, of Black youth being exonerated by people pushing for due process in higher courts, that the white patriarchs of Assumption Parish took matters into their own hands with Freddie Moore.

Desperate to save himself, Moore gave a false name, "Norman Jackson," in the hope that they would let him go. But the mob had not come for the truth. They had come for a body. And they wanted more. Deputy Richard left the group and rode to the home of nineteen-year-old Norman Thibodeaux, dragging him from his grandmother's house. He had nothing to do with Anna Mae Larose, but his name was Norman, and that was enough.

The mob strung Thibodeaux up alongside Moore. But fate, or a rare flicker of conscience, intervened. The Labadieville bridge-tender, Harry Coddou, and Thibodeaux's father, Louis, vouched for Thibodeaux. He

The body of lynching victim Fred Moore, sixteen years old, hanging from the Labadieville Bridge. Daily Worker, *December 17, 1933, p. 3.*

had just arrived in town the day before. They cut Thibodeaux down. Yet Deputy Richard was not done. He and several others drove him to a field, released him, and shot at him as he ran. He survived.[18] Moore did not. They hanged him from the Labadieville Bridge and left his body swaying in the night air within sight of a school and the St. Philomena Catholic Church.

A placard that was tied to the teen's ankles, scrawled in rough, uneven handwriting, bore the words: "NIGGERS LET THIS BE AN EXAMPLE. DO NOT TOUCH FOR 24 HOURS."[19]

Two weeks later, on November 4, the town celebrated. *The Assumption Pioneer* reported that local whites awarded Deputy Fernand Richard a monogrammed solid-gold belt buckle, engraved with these words: "In Appreciation Of Duty Well Performed In The Annie *[sic]* Mae Larose Murder Case—10–9–33."[20]

But Fred Moore's parents refused to let their son's murder end with a gold belt buckle. Lilly and Louis did what no Black parents of a lynching victim had ever done before: They fought back in court. They left Louisiana for Arkansas and filed a federal lawsuit against Sheriff Himel and his bonding company, demanding $10,000 for failing to protect their son.

The audacity of this move cannot be overstated. In the Jim Crow South, the law existed to serve whiteness. The legal system did not entertain the grievances of Black families, let alone award them damages for the state-sanctioned murder of their children. The complicity of law enforcement in lynchings was no aberration. It was the point. As historian Adam Fairclough observes of the time:

> The involvement of sheriffs in lynchings was the most chilling evidence of their power over blacks. Blacks were usually lynched because sheriffs allowed them to be, in some cases permitting mobs to enter jails, at other times meekly surrendering prisoners to the mob before they ever reached the jail.[21]

Evidence suggested that Sheriff Himel knew of the mob's intentions and that his deputies participated in, if not led, the execution. Given that news of a lynching reached New Orleans, it was nearly impossible to find jury members unfamiliar with the case. But because Louis

Moore was from Arkansas, their lawyer shifted jurisdiction to federal court, removing it from local hands. In the federal court, Judge Wayne G. Borah instructed the all-white jury that, under the law, the sheriff could be held liable for the actions of his deputies, leaving it to the jurors to determine whether that standard had been met and what damages, if any, were owed.

On May 21, 1936, the jury awarded the Moores $2,500. Newspapers described it as the first ruling of its kind in the United States, an acknowledgment that a lynching was not just mob violence but the result of state failure. The NAACP hailed the decision but warned it was no substitute for a federal anti-lynching law that would permanently remove adjudication over such violence from the purview of courts with local biases.[22]

Despite the court's ruling in favor of the Moores, they had difficulty collecting the awarded damages. Sheriff Himel refused to pay up. In 1937, a federal judge issued an order demanding payment. Himel ignored it. The Moores waited. A second order came, and finally a US marshal was dispatched to investigate.

A writ of *fieri facias* was issued against Sheriff Himel, commanding him to pay the judgment or have his property seized to satisfy the debt. The writ was returned *nulla bona*, in 1937, indicating that the sheriff had no assets that could be seized to pay the judgment. A census from 1930, however, shows Sheriff Himel owning a home, so it is likely that he divested his assets. It would be four years before the Moores received the money plus about $500 in interest.[23]

Fred Moore's parents, in their grief, made sure the world knew what had happened. Their case was a precedent. A challenge. A marker in history.

A FAMILY AFFAIR

Even as Lillie and Louis Moore forced the nation to reckon with their son's murder, the truth of what happened that October night remained buried beneath the weight of white lies and legal evasions. Fred Moore was lynched not because he was guilty, but because his death was necessary to shield another man, a white man, from justice. The sheriff, deputies, and mob played their roles in a cover-up so deliberate that it cost a boy his life while reinforcing the architecture of racial terror.

The name that should have echoed in courtrooms was David George Himel Jr., the stepfather who first pointed the finger at Moore. Months later, Thibadeaux reportedly claimed that David Himel had confessed to the murder, though this assertion was predictably denied by Sheriff Himel, and he was never formally adjudicated.[24] And the town never turned its rage toward him. No mob, no rope, no trial.

To admit that a white man, one of their own, had committed the crime would have shattered the racial order that made Fred Moore's death inevitable. So, they killed the Black boy, let the guilty white man walk free, and went about their lives as if justice had been served.

Moore never stood a chance. From the moment his name left Himel's lips, his fate was sealed, not because he was guilty, but because his innocence was irrelevant. Because he was Black. Because white family ties, reputations, and patriarchal authority were worth more than a Black boy's life.

This script was not confined to incest or the cover-ups of white men's abuse inside their own homes. White girls, too, sometimes reached for the same lie and wielded it strategically to survive under patriarchy. When their reputations were at stake, when they broke curfews, snuck out, or found themselves in situations their families would not forgive, they invoked the figure of a Black assailant. The result was the same: a Black boy's body offered up to preserve white innocence. In *Raising Racists*, historian Kristina DuRocher documents case after case in which white girls and women fabricated accusations against Black men and boys to shield themselves or their families. Her examples demonstrate that whether the hidden transgression was incest, consensual sex, truancy, or even spousal murder, the "solution" was always the same: Invent a Black assailant.

In 1919, in Vicksburg, Mississippi, eighteen-year-old Mattie Hudson told police that a Black man had attacked her before dawn. Under mob pressure, she identified Lloyd Clay, a twenty-two-year-old Black man, who was lynched and burned alive. A month later it emerged that Hudson had not been assaulted at all. Her "attacker" had been her white boyfriend, and she invented the lie to conceal her own behavior from her family. Hudson saved herself by feeding the mob the body of a Black man. Hudson was not alone. In Ellisville, Mississippi, Ruth Meeks claimed a Black man raped her at gunpoint and then escaped disguised in her clothes, a story so implausible it reads like parody, likely invented to cover a consensual tryst. In Paris, Kentucky, fourteen-year-old Ruby Anderson accused Grant Smith of raping her "on several occasions," a charge historians believe she used to explain repeated absences from home. In Osceola, Arkansas, three schoolgirls sneaked away from a field trip, then accused Albert Blades of assault when they were caught. A mob of over a thousand men mutilated, hanged, and burned Blades, though doctors later confirmed no attack had occurred.

These lies did not protect girls from Black boys; they protected girls from their own parents, from community scrutiny, and from the strictures of white patriarchy.[25]

The near-total absence of attention to Himel's confession in contemporary news accounts is not an oversight. It is evidence of how white supremacy functioned through violence *and* silence, with newspapers, law enforcement, and local elites deciding which crimes to bury and which to magnify.

The Himels of Assumption Parish were not just neighbors and lawmen; they were kin. Sheriff Lezin Himel, Deputy Fernand Richard, and David Himel Jr. were bound by blood and marriage to Anna Mae Larose herself. Anna Mae's family tree tied directly into theirs: Her grandmother was the sheriff's cousin, her mother remarried into the Himel clan, and the stepfather who allegedly killed her shared that bloodline. Deputy Richard's own kin connections to the Himels bound law enforcement even tighter to the cover-up. The incestuous overlap of family and office shows that law enforcement worked as much to protect kinship power as to police race.

White men themselves often deployed the same script. In Dade City, Florida, Luther Wilson blackened his face to assault a sixteen-year-old girl, confident that if she reported him, "everyone would believe him" when he claimed a Black man did it. In Quitman, Georgia, Bessie Revere was found unconscious after a suspected rape, and newspapers rushed to call her attacker a "big, black brute." When she regained consciousness, she named James Harvey, a respected white man. And in Raleigh, North Carolina, farmer Charles Davis insisted a "lecherous looking black" had murdered his wife, while the real killer was Davis himself. Each of these cases demonstrates how white patriarchy preserved itself by offering up imaginary Black assailants rather than confronting white male depravity.[26]

The rape and murder of Larose and the castration and lynching of Moore was a family affair in every sense. A white girl was dead, and someone had to answer for it. The choice was clear: Sacrifice one of their own and fracture the web of privilege, or sacrifice a Black teenager and preserve it. They chose the latter.

The failure to investigate Anna Mae Larose's stepfather reveals that white patriarchy never truly sought to protect white girls. White supremacy invoked the defense of white women and girls as a pretext for racial violence, yet when white girls were abused by men within their own families and communities, that violence was overlooked or rationalized. Within this system, white girls were treated as instruments of racial order, invoked to sustain myths of purity and moral superiority, then abandoned when their suffering exposed the predatory foundations of white male authority.

Anna Mae Larose's mother, Anna Donnaud Larose Ayo, remarried into the Himel family, and there is no indication that she publicly distanced herself from her husband after the reported confession. If she believed the allegation to be false or coerced, she left no public statement to that effect; if she believed it to be true, she did not repudiate him. In either case, the record reflects no visible rupture. White women, including mothers, often navigated abuse within white patriarchal structures through silence, constrained by economic dependence, social pressure, and racial loyalty. That silence, whether chosen or compelled, helped shield white men from public accountability, even when children were at stake.

Sheriff Himel remained in office until 1940, and he died the following year. Deputy Fernand Richard, who led the lynching and shooting of Thibodeaux and got his gold-monogrammed belt buckle for it, succeeded Himel as sheriff, retired in 1956, and died in 1965. District Attorney Aubert Leander Talbot, who stood in the crowd the night Moore was lynched, went on to a long and successful career. Every official who conspired in the cover-up enjoyed impunity for the rest of their lives.

That silence, the failure of the press, the courts, and the public to reckon with Himel's confession, was an act of violence. It erased Fred

Moore's innocence and affirmed that white men would always receive the benefit of the doubt while Black boys received the noose. History is shaped not only by trials and verdicts but by silences, omissions, and the white men allowed to slip through untouched.

Fred Moore and Anna Mae Larose were both casualties of white patriarchal violence, products of the same structure of domination. To reject that structure was to renounce whiteness itself. The racial, sexual, and generational contracts that shaped American life were inseparable and mutually reinforcing. White girls who accused Black boys of impropriety often did so to shield the white men who had violated them. White boys were coerced into cruelty, forced to witness or partake in lynchings, and came of age not as protectors of white girls but as their oppressors. The figure of the "Southern gentleman" rested on a fiction sustained by incest, silence, and blood.

The truth is brutal: Comstock's laws, racist pornography, and lynching were all part of the same system. Those pedophilic postcards and racist cartoons were training manuals. They primed a public to see Black childhood as dirty, dangerous, disposable. They made it easier for a mob to believe that Fred Moore's body belonged on a rope. They turned Black innocence into a punchline, and Black suffering into a spectacle.

If a Black boy in Louisiana could be lynched to cover up incest and preserve a white family's name, then, as we shall see in the next chapter, Black children in Oklahoma could be targeted for their land, their oil, their futures. The lie remained the same: Invent the Black villain, erase the white one, and take what you want. From the cane fields of Labadieville to the oil fields of Oklahoma, Black children were marked as expendable so that white men could protect their secrets, their wealth, and their rule. In Louisiana, the weapon was a rope. In Oklahoma, it was sticks of dynamite used against Black boys and girls whose very inheritance threatened white supremacy. Lynching was never only about punishing an alleged crime. It was about seizing control of bodies and land.

And so, the story moves west. To eastern Oklahoma. To the murders and dispossessions that revealed the logic was the same whether covering up incest or stealing land: Black children could be destroyed to preserve white power.

CHAPTER 10

"We Want to Kill Them All If We Can"

White Guardians, Wealthy Black Children, Race Robbery, and Murder in Muskogee County, Oklahoma

Every lynching was not just a killing but a dispossession. When a Black father was hanged or burned, his land and wages were swallowed up by white hands. When a mother was driven out, her children lost not only her protection but their claim to stability and inheritance. Families fled in the dead of night, leaving behind farms, homes, churches and schools, businesses, and the fragile wealth they had scraped together. For Black children, this meant futures uprooted again and again, education interrupted, communities shattered, and the promise of security reduced to ash.

But what happened when Black children themselves held the land, the deeds, the headrights? When they, not their parents, were the ones who carried wealth on paper? That possibility was not hypothetical. *It was real.* And it placed those children directly in the crosshairs of white greed and violence.

The violence of Jim Crow did not always come with a noose. Sometimes it came with a deed, a court order, or the smile of a court-appointed white guardian promising the "protection" of a Black child.

Historians have long drawn connections between lynching and land theft. They have shown how mob violence cleared the way for white businesses and families to seize farms, timber, and oil. They have traced how sheriffs, bankers, and courts colluded with vigilantes to strip Black people of their property. But what these accounts often leave out is the figure at the center of the story: *the Black child*. Not just as a bystander or footnote to the violence, but as a direct victim and as the very property white supremacy sought to seize.

W. E. B. Du Bois recognized the danger. In the pages of *The Crisis* magazine, the NAACP's journal of record, he documented these children and their stolen futures, showing how Black minors with oil-rich allotments became targets of exploitation, guardianship schemes, and even murder. Their stories were not anomalies but warnings and evidence that even a childhood endowed with resources could not shield Black people from the white-supremacist machinery of dispossession.

To see this story in its most powerful and peculiar form, we must turn our gaze west. Oklahoma was no ordinary frontier. It was a place of topsy-turvy relationships, uneasy alliances, fragile freedoms, relentless greed, oil barons, outlaws, hustlers, and speculators circling like buzzards while children stood at the center with their birthrights turned into bait.

"EQUAL INTERESTS IN THE SOIL"

Nearly two decades before statehood, some press accounts described Oklahoma Territory as a "paradise" for Black people. These editorials emerged amid broader national debates about Black migration to the West following Reconstruction, including the Exoduster movement and proposals—floated in newspapers and political circles—to concentrate Black Americans in Western territories as a solution to the "race problem." For example, an editorial printed in *The Chicago Herald* noted the territory's fine farming land and expressed ambivalence about the future state being set aside for Black people. "It might be cruel, so far as the country is concerned, to fill Oklahoma with negroes, and yet it would be good riddance for the rest of the union if a hundred or two hundred thousand negroes could be placed there, where among themselves, they could develop their own peculiar nature, where they could practice social equality without hindrance."[1]

A small state settled, owned, and governed by Blacks could be "a capital thing," an experiment on their capability for self-government. Having a small country or new state of their own could allow Blacks "a chance to depend on themselves [and] determine their real value." Such a grand experiment had its risks. Media pundits and political leaders of the day argued that there had been no modern instance where Africans or African-descended people made "any considerable advance when not connected directly with the white element." However, it was possible that "in a country like Oklahoma, colored men who have had the advantages of association with the white race, and who would be in close contact with the superior civilization of the palefaces, might attain considerable development."[2]

Before statehood, Indian Territory had flipped the racial script. Freedmen enjoyed more political rights than many whites, and in the 1870s Black soldiers of the Ninth Cavalry literally patrolled the territory's borders to keep whites out. Whites who slipped across the border could not vote, hold office, or own land unless formally adopted into a tribe. It was a reversal of Southern racial hierarchies, and it festered white resentment. As white settlers poured in by the hundreds of thousands in the 1890s and pressed for statehood, both Indians and freedmen saw the danger coming. Indians feared the end of their governments and communal landholding; freedmen knew a segregated order was being imported from the South.

Here, thousands of children of formerly enslaved people inherited large allotments of land alongside the children of tribal citizens. Here, Black childhood unfolded in a way unlike anywhere else in America: precarious yet promising, stalked by racial danger yet offering partial freedom. In this strange crucible, a different kind of free Black childhood emerged, one tethered not to white benevolence and saviorism but to oil, land allotments, and the fragile protections of tribal citizenship. The paradox of children who were both Black and rich revealed deep contradictions within America's racial order. The descendants of enslaved people, once counted as property, had themselves become property owners, and not only were they owners; they were sometimes wealthier than white neighbors and even full-blood Indians. It was a paradox white supremacy could not abide. And it was precisely because this freedom was so exceptional, so unthinkable in the Jim Crow South, that it drew the eye of white predators.

Indian Territory itself was born of betrayal. In the 1830s, the federal government forced the Creek, Choctaw, Chickasaw, Cherokee, and

Seminole Nations from their Southeastern homelands during the Trail of Tears, promising them a permanent home west of the Mississippi. By the mid-nineteenth century, thousands of Black people also lived there. Many were the descendants of those once enslaved by tribal citizens, and would become members of the Nations after emancipation.

The Civil War brought another rupture. Several of the Five Tribes sided with the Confederacy, and when the South lost, the US government punished them as traitors. Postwar treaties in 1866 stripped the Nations of land, forced them to abolish slavery, and required them to accept freedpeople as citizens. The treaty between the Creek Nation and the US government declared that Creeks of African descent, formerly enslaved persons, and those lawfully residing in the nation at the commencement of the rebellion "shall have and enjoy all the rights and privileges of native citizens, including an equal interest in the soil and national funds."[3] On paper, this looked like progress. In practice, many tribal leaders resisted. Freedmen were treated as outsiders. They were denied rations, excluded from schools, and relegated to marginal land. Some were terrorized by violence when they tried to assert their rights.

During the tumultuous Reconstruction period, freedmen living in Indian Territory enjoyed a time of vibrant opportunity during which they held political offices, exercised their votes, and built schools, businesses, churches, and newspapers.[4] As one writer noted in 1905: "Rare indeed are the instances in American history where Negro bondsmen as a result of their freedom, became to all intents and purposes even the equal, socially, politically and financially, of their former masters." The Creek Freedmen were "one notable and emphatic exception."[5]

The lives of Creek Freedmen children growing up in Indian Territory contrasted sharply with the landless Black children of the other Southern regions. As Gary Zellar reveals in his study of African Creeks, there were few racial hostilities between Blacks and Indians in the Creek Nation. Though the Southern faction of the Creeks kept Blacks at a social and residential distance, they did not "sponsor legislation to mandate racial segregation, regulate freed people's behavior, restrict their mobility, or impede their access to land."[6]

The freedpeople of Indian Territory were able to control their own labor and use their land as they saw fit. In an interesting twist, landless white farmers from neighboring states became sharecroppers and tenant farmers in Indian Territory, roles that elsewhere in the South were filled by Blacks.[7] Because Indians and freedmen were landlords over white tenants, their children were not exploited as an agricultural labor force by whites, nor were they subjected to the same kinds of illegal apprenticeships and indentures suffered by Black children throughout the South.

Unlike Black families in the Deep South, for whom the post-emancipation promises of full citizenship and forty acres of land had gone unfulfilled, and despite robust political opposition and some violence, the parents and children of ex-slaves living in Indian Territory were extended political rights, access to education, and equal share in lands and monies held in trust by the federal government.[8] It seemed that in this region, there was a moment when a significant number of Black children were finally going to be given the chance to improve their lives and prepare themselves for participation as full citizens.

As Reconstruction gave way to the allotment era, the betrayals deepened. The Dawes Act of 1887 authorized the breakup of communal Native lands into small individual allotments under the guise of "civilizing" Indigenous people. The Curtis Act of 1898 went further, abolishing tribal governments and imposing rolls that determined who was entitled to land. Together, these laws transferred millions of acres from Native nations into white hands.[9]

The allotment process made discrimination against Black freedmen systematic. Every person had to be recorded on the federal "Dawes Rolls," which divided people into two categories: "by blood" for Native citizens and "freedmen" for formerly enslaved Black people and their descendants. Families who shared language, culture, and kinship were split apart on paper. These labels determined not just land allotments but also inheritance rights and political belonging.

The racial sorting was deliberate. White officials framed it as "scientific," but its purpose was to shrink Native citizenship rolls while disqualifying Black claimants altogether. "By blood" citizens received larger, more valuable parcels, while freedmen were pushed onto smaller, less fertile plots. Many were then swindled out of even those allotments, through fraud, intimidation, or legal challenges engineered by Native elites and white speculators working in tandem.

All members of the Five Civilized Tribes were required to apply to the Dawes Commission for land allotments. For the Creek Nation, enrollment ran from 1899 to May 25, 1901, and each applicant had to appear in person at the Muskogee office to register themselves and their children. Applicants were assigned numbers and placed either on the Creek by Blood roll (which included full-blood and mixed white-Indian individuals) or on the freedmen roll. Despite proof of Creek ancestry, many freedmen were excluded from the blood roll, as white officials often relied on appearance to determine racial classification. After the 1901 enrollment closed, tribes sought to include children born afterward. Congress responded with the Newborn Acts of 1905 and 1906, which allowed the registration of children born between May 25, 1901, and March 4, 1906. These acts added 2,920 new enrollees, 1,135 of whom were children of freedmen.[10]

Then, in 1907, Indian Territory was folded into the Union as the state of Oklahoma. Statehood formalized what dispossession had already set in motion: White lawmakers now held the reins, and the experiment of a multiracial frontier gave way to the machinery of Jim Crow.

Months after Oklahoma joined the Union, the new state legislature immediately enacted anti-Black laws that assisted in the wholesale robbery and murder of young people in various oil-producing counties.[11] In line with policy already established in Southern states, Jim Crow's arrival ushered in voter disenfranchisement, segregated facilities, miscegenation laws, and lynching, in addition to the further loosening of federal protection of lands owned by Indians of the Five Civilized Tribes and their freedmen. The construction of a new kind of racial hierarchy severely altered the status of freeborn Blacks, former slaves of Indians, the first generation of slave descendants, people of mixed race, and "state Negroes" that migrated to the territory before 1907.

Out of this American crucible emerged a Black childhood of blessings and curses, blended bloodlines, ancient agreements, broken promises, and new racial categories and relationships. As historian Elliott West has noted, the Reconstruction era, which coincided with a period of territorial acquisitions, "forced a new dialogue between West and South, unsettled race relations and presumptions, and finally led to a new racial order encompassing western as well as southern people of color." West also observed that in the years after the Civil War, "America was a kind of borderland where racial edges and meanings were shifty and blurred."[12]

A decade before attaining statehood, Oklahoma had become the largest oil-producing region in the world with an output of forty million gallons annually. And with this windfall, greedy white men found another method of extraction: *children*. Black and Indigenous children born into the Nations inherited headrights and allotments that made them worth thousands or even millions on paper. But the law declared them "incompetent," incapable of managing their own property.

The notion of incompetence had long been embedded in Anglo-American law, which treated minors as legally incapable of entering contracts or managing estates. In Oklahoma, this doctrine was twisted and extended. Under the weight of racist ideology, incompetence was applied not only to children but to Black adults, even literate parents who could read, write, and manage their own affairs. Courts decided that guardianship should bypass mothers and fathers entirely, placing white lawyers, bankers, and businessmen in charge of Black children's wealth. Promising protection, these court-appointed guardians instead delivered plunder.

Applying the "incompetence" label became a legal strategy. By branding Black and Indigenous children and their parents as incapable, courts created the pretext to appoint white guardians and funnel wealth into their hands. What had once been a doctrine meant to protect minors was repurposed into a system of legalized plunder, where the state itself acted as accomplice.

County judges wielded enormous power, assigning white guardians to Black and Native children who had inherited valuable allotments. These guardians were drawn from the ranks of local businessmen, bankers, and attorneys. They enriched themselves through what the law disguised as oversight but whose actual function was theft: padded expenses, rigged land sales, forged signatures. Judges framed the process as protecting "incompetent" minors from exploitation, yet the court itself was the engine of exploitation. In oil-boom counties, the corruption was staggering. A guardian could purchase a child's allotment for a fraction of its value, resell it to an oil company at market price, and split the profit with the judge who approved the deal. Meanwhile, the children who supposedly required "protection" often lived in poverty, deprived of the very wealth extracted from beneath their feet.

Wells struck in Creek and Osage country turned poor children into millionaires overnight. Allotments once dismissed as worthless became gushers of wealth. Guardians sold off land, siphoned oil royalties, forged signatures, and padded expense accounts while their wards went hungry. And when theft wasn't enough, murder followed. The Osage murders during the early 1920s shook the nation. During this period, dozens of Osage citizens were shot, poisoned, or blown up in schemes to steal their oil wealth. The scandal sparked one of the FBI's first homicide investigations and exposed how guardianship laws had created a system that made Native children and adults legal prey.

But the terror didn't stop with Indigenous people. Black children, too, became targets of the same machinery of greed. Dynamite, arsenic, staged accidents, and starvation were all tools of a racist system. The perverse logic was clear: Sometimes a Black child's death promised more profit than their survival. Here Native, Black, and white communities collided in the aftermath of slavery, removal, and westward expansion. In this crucible, Black childhood became both a legal category to be manipulated and something disposable when it threatened white wealth.

By placing children in the center of land theft and racial violence, we see that lynching was not only a spectacle of public death but also a quieter machinery of dispossession that stripped Black families of wealth and futures. The murder of a Black child could take the form of a hanging, burning, or shooting, but it could also take the form of a "legal" sale, a forged signature, or a staged accident engineered by those sworn to protect them.

Historians who have connected lynching to land theft often stop at the adult figure such as the Black farmer, the businessman, the patriarch whose death cleared the way for white seizure of land. But centering children reveals that Black childhood itself was constructed as a source of threat when it held wealth, something white supremacy sought to extinguish or control. This perspective questions the tendency to treat lynching as an exceptional eruption of violence.

When we follow the lives of Black children in Oklahoma and beyond, we see how dispossession was routinized through law, bureaucracy, and guardianship, blurring the line between mob violence and state violence. The story of Oklahoma's wealthy Black children expands our understanding of lynching from a tool of racial terror to a system of intergenerational wealth extraction. It shows that white supremacy did not simply kill bodies, *it killed Black futures.*

RACE ROBBERY

My process of telling this larger story of what W. E. B. Du Bois called "race robbery" in Oklahoma did not begin with a grand theory but with the tedium of archival work. Before *The Crisis* magazine was digitized, I spent weeks in the quiet of reading rooms, cranking microfilm reels and leafing through brittle volumes, scanning slowly. I was searching for children, anybody's child. A mention in an essay, a photograph tucked beside an editorial, a line of poetry mourning a lost son, a parenting advice column, a brief news story about a classroom, a child's drawing or voice, anything. I combed through page after page, gathering fragments of lives too often overlooked. And then I stumbled across fleeting references to something I had never imagined possible in the age of Jim Crow: wealthy Black children in Oklahoma.

The shock of that discovery stopped me cold. How could such children exist in a world that defined Blackness as poverty, dependency, and danger? What did it mean that, for a brief moment, some Black children held extraordinary wealth on paper—and that white society answered with schemes of theft and murder?

Those fragments ignited questions historians had not asked. What happens when Black childhood itself becomes the object of white plunder? How does our understanding of lynching, property theft, and racial violence change when we place children at the center of the archive rather than at its margins? How many more children had been relegated to footnotes or erased altogether?

By 1914, the NAACP was facing mounting pressure from Black communities to pay closer attention to the plight of children amid relentless violence that resulted in more than 2,200 lynchings of Black people and counting.[13] The announcement came in the October edition of *The Crisis*, in which the organization revealed that a committee had been formed to organize a juvenile auxiliary that would be headquartered in Washington, DC. Du Bois wrote: "In its struggle for equality of opportunity for colored people the Association has interested itself in a number of cases affecting children and young people."[14] Of the many cases taken up by the NAACP, perhaps the most disturbing were the murders and systemic robbery of thousands of Oklahoma's land-owning Black children.

Between February 1914 and May 1920, *The Crisis* reported the tragic cases of Dan Tucker, Sallie Hodge, Luther Manuel, Sarah Rector, the twins Edith and Edna Durant, and siblings Herbert and CaStella Sells, freedmen children whose lives were dramatically altered with the discovery of oil on their allotted lands. These children had enormous incomes from oil revenues ranging from $500 to $50,000 a month, at a time when 90 percent of Blacks living in the United States were confined to a life of poverty in the South. As a point of comparison, the average annual income of American families was just under $750 in 1914 and $1,340 in 1920.[15]

Ten-year-old Dan Tucker owned 160 acres of land producing 2,400 barrels of oil daily, bringing him an income of $6,750 in royalties every month. Sallie Hodge held title to rich bottom farmland worth $600, in addition to $100,000 in cash and $50,000 in notes and mortgages. Luther Manuel, believed then to be the richest Black boy in the world with an income of $50,000 a month, owned land that was home to a gusher in the heart of an expansive oil field in Glenpool. Edith Durant, who turned eighteen in July of 1918, owned an oil well in Tulsa County and was slated to receive $150,000 in cash as well as title to land worth $1 million, while her sister Edna owned $50,000 worth of oil-producing land nearby. By the time the Durant twins reached the age of majority, their estates had significantly dwindled, as their white guardian had executed bad loans and other business deals that had been authorized by the Muskogee County Probate Court. The wealthiest girl among the group was Sarah Rector, whose estimated income in 1914 from lands she owned in Glenpool was $50,000 a month. Despite her wealth, Du Bois noted that the ten-year-old was one of six children living in "a shack with only one bed for the entire family."[16]

Together, newspaper reports, court transcripts, and descendants' testimony revealed a staggering record of racial exploitation, aided at every turn by Oklahoma's courts and the federal government. Dozens of dispatches about these children poured into *The Crisis* from Boley,

Langston, Guthrie, Taft, Tulsa, Oklahoma City, Muskogee, and beyond. *The Professional World*, a Black newspaper in Columbia, Missouri, reported: "In no State in the Union have Negroes been robbed, actually robbed with impunity and openly, as in this State. White men are worth millions who have built up their fortunes by thievery."[17]

In numerous editorials, Du Bois complained that corrupt state officials and unscrupulous white guardians, not parents or relatives, were being appointed by the Muskogee County District Court to handle Black children's monies and business affairs until they reached eighteen. This legalized graft, he charged, produced "hundreds of white men in [Oklahoma] who have become rich from the wealth of Negro children."[18]

The cases revealed in *The Crisis* led to further revelations in Western newspapers, tribal land and genealogical records, Dawes Commission and Bureau of Indian Affairs files, court transcripts, guardianship records, criminal files from the Muskogee County District Court, and financial records from the Oklahoma Corporation Commission, which was the custodian of the financial records of oil and gas companies that held drilling leases on the children's lands. These materials laid bare how judges, guardians, attorneys, and bankers enriched themselves by siphoning off children's estates. Together, they show how government and law turned Black children into disposable capital to be governed, exploited, and often eliminated. Mainstream media reinforced the theft by portraying Black children and their parents as incompetent, justifying the courts' seizure of parental authority and control over Black wealth.

Du Bois's investigations, which were limited by access, offered only glimpses. In February 1914, *The Crisis* ran a short paragraph about three white men and "a certain number of hired colored accomplices" who used dynamite "to get rid of two colored children who inherited $250,000 worth of property." No names were given. But keyword searches decades later—"negro children," "dynamite," "Taft, Oklahoma"—uncovered digitized transcripts of what was then the most sensational murder trial in Oklahoma history.[19]

The trial records revealed horrific details: the murders, the plot, and the complicity of both Black and Native accomplices. They also raised larger questions. How did these children inherit such wealth in Jim Crow America? Why would three wealthy white men conspire to kill them? Why did Oklahoma pour resources into prosecuting the case when so many other crimes against Black and Native children went unpunished? The state's interest was less about justice than about power. The case became a way to assert state authority over land, wealth, and people—and to block federal efforts that might have protected Black and Native children's estates.

Though the murders drew rare national attention, the two children were only the most visible casualties among more than four thousand landowning Black youth in the Creek Nation whose property and inheritance made them targets. For freedpeople, these children symbolized the promise of full citizenship: labor, property, parental authority. For white supremacists, they were dangerous proof that Black futures could rival white ones.

The scale of that threat explains why the Black youths' stories, when they surfaced at all, were buried in court files, tucked into small notices in *The Crisis*, or sensationalized in white newspapers as curiosities rather than tragedies. What looked like isolated cases were, in fact, fragments of a much larger pattern: children treated as commodities whose lives could be translated into cash. It was in this archive of scattered traces—trial transcripts, probate records, dispatches from Oklahoma towns—that the outlines of a system began to emerge.

And then, the tragedy in Taft broke through the haze of fragments with terrifying clarity. It was not just a case of theft, not just a courtroom swindle or a forged deed, but a murder plot laid bare in the conspirators' own words. The target: two children whose only crime was being too rich, too Black, and too young to defend themselves.

KEROSENE AND SEVEN STICKS OF DYNAMITE

On the night of March 14, 1911, three Black men, Doc Allen, Sam Lowe, and John C. Norwood, huddled in secret at Ford's Gin, a local watering hole. A bound Muskogee District Court transcript later recorded the details of their plan to blow up two landholding Black children living in the tiny all-Black town of Taft.[20]

Their targets were siblings Herbert and CaStella Sells (fourteen and ten years old, respectively), who were sleeping in a cramped prairie house with their mother and stepfather on the edge of Taft. The siblings' fortune lay miles away in Glenpool, south of Tulsa, where nineteen oil wells on their allotments generated more than $2,000 a month—a staggering amount of wealth in 1911. For Muskogee land dealer William M. Irvin, those children were an obstacle to be removed. He financed the plot.

The transcript captures the planning in cinematic detail. "Let's go somewhere where we can't be seen," Doc Allen told Lowe and Norwood as they left Ford's Gin. The three men slipped to the Midland Valley Railroad depot, hid behind blinds in the men's water closet, and passed around a bottle while they spoke in whispers. Allen, a blacksmith and small-time land speculator who had migrated from Texas, laid out the scheme. There would be $5,000 to buy his silence. There would be seven sticks of dynamite, a fifty-foot fuse, and kerosene to spread the blaze.

"I want you to help me watch," Allen told Norwood. "We want to kill them all if we can. The woman too."

The "woman" was thirty-seven-year-old Priscilla "Sila" Mackey, the children's mother and a citizen of the Creek Nation, listed as number 969 on the freedmen roll. She was born during Reconstruction and her parents, John and Peggy Drew, were slaves owned by Captain John Yarger, a Creek Indian who led slaves out of Alabama on the Trail of Tears in 1834. Not long after her first husband, Hardy Sells, went missing in the summer of 1901, she married Zebidee "Zeb" Mackey, a noncitizen from Texas. Testimony later made plain why she, too, had to be removed: Her continued survival complicated title and inheritance claims.

Norwood protested the technicalities about the plan. "Dynamite won't blow the house up," he said.

Sam Lowe spoke up. "The way I'm going to fix it will blow it up and burn it up," he said, pulling back a piece of cloth covering a galvanized bucket and powder along with the fuse and sticks of dynamite. "I'm going to put coal oil on top of it, and that will set it afire, and the blaze from the powder will ignite the coal oil."

The conspirators agreed to meet again. The plan was set. Years later, in court, those same admissions, whispered over whiskey in a rail depot washroom, became the spine of the state's case. The trial record makes clear how ordinary men could treat children as obstacles to be cleared for profit.[21]

What this planning reveals is that the same logic underpinned lynching and this plot: Black children's lives were negotiable, their deaths convertible into white profit. Here, the instruments were not just trees and nooses but fuses, kerosene, and the stroke of a judge's pen. To study this conspiracy is to see lynching less as an act of spontaneous fury and more as part of a broader machinery of racial capitalism through which violence could be staged, contracted, and justified as part of the normal course of business.

"A HORRIBLE DEATH IN THE FLAMES"

Nine days later, in the dead hours before dawn, the plan moved from whispers to fire. On March 23, 1911, Doc Allen and Sam Lowe crept toward the Sells family's small prairie house. Norwood, suddenly overcome with doubt, bolted into the dark and vanished toward his sister's home. The other two pressed on. They doused rags in kerosene, scattered them around the foundation, and slid a bucket of powder, coal oil, and dynamite beneath the room where Herbert and CaStella slept. The family dog never stirred. Lowe struck the fuse.

The west side of the house erupted. Immediately after the explosion, the roof fell in and what remained of the house quickly caught fire. The blast ripped a crater into the earth, hurled timbers across yards, and buried the dog's carcass in the rubble. Flames engulfed what was left. Priscilla and Zeb Mackey stumbled out alive from the far side of the house. They had been sleeping in another section of the house separated from the children's room by a thin partition.[22]

Herbert was killed instantly. A neighbor later testified that he saw the Mackeys dressed in their nightclothes hollering for help. As the couple tried digging through the burning shingles to save CaStella, neighbors rushed toward the flames.[23] CaStella screamed from beneath the collapsed roof, her legs pinned by burning beams. Neighbors clawed at the wreckage until the heat drove them back. Priscilla fought to rush into the flames to reach her last surviving child, but a bystander grabbed the distraught mother and held her back from the flames while "neighbors and friends were compelled to stand impotently by and see the unfortunate girl screaming with agony die a horrible death in the flames." Not only had she just lost son and daughter in the explosion, her two older children, Birdie and Dewey, had died years earlier in infancy, likely from smallpox or tuberculosis.[24]

By daybreak, local, state, and federal authorities dispatched to the scene of the crime had no leads about possible perpetrators or a motive for the crime. Still, a posse of townsmen formed and launched a search for the murderers. Meanwhile, William Irvin had paid $3.26 for a first-class, one-way train ticket out of Taft. The ticket salesman, along with a porter and the train's conductor, would later testify that Irvin was the only white man seen boarding the Midland Valley train out of the all-Black town that day. Those witnesses also recalled that Irvin wore a Black coat and vest, light shirt, dirty blue overalls, and a Black crusher hat, and carried a distinct brown leather travel bag.

Months before the murders, Taft had already been rattled by dynamite. The local bank was blown open, the Midland Valley depot was badly damaged, and bombs were detonated across the region to terrorize Indians and freedmen off valuable land. Violence with explosives was not unusual in this corner of Oklahoma; it was the language of intimidation.[25]

By dawn on March 24, investigators circled the ruins of the Sells home pursuing two possible theories: Either the target had been Zeb Mackey, or the real prize was the children's oil allotments. *The Muskogee Times-Democrat* quickly steered suspicion toward Mackey, describing him as "an intelligent negro" with "plenty of bitter enemies."[26] The paper reminded readers of his shooting scrapes, his threats to expose corrupt town officials, and rumors that he himself had plotted to dynamite his family. Witnesses testified that Mackey squandered his wife Priscilla's money, had an affair that left another woman pregnant, and even asked about buying dynamite and fuse days before the blast.

At the same time, the press could not ignore the fortune at stake. Herbert and CaStella's oil allotments were each valued at $100,000. Their guardian, former Muskogee mayor Thomas H. Martin, had already sunk $20,000 into first mortgages on their properties. Though the children earned nearly $2,000 a month in royalties, Martin provided their mother just $75 a month for their care.[27]

No guardianship reports survive, but a 1924 investigation by the Indian Rights Association (IRA) exposed the system Martin operated within. In most cases, the guardian decided when, where, and how much of the ward's money he would pay for their support, and at what stores the ward could purchase goods to be charged to the guardian. The costs of purchased goods at certain stores were then deducted from the ward's allowance.

The IRA report noted: "If the ward purchases at any other store, the guardian will not pay the bill and the ward rarely is given enough money to purchase things for cash at any other store, so that the store favored by the guardian has an absolute monopoly over the ward's business." Guardians usually lived some twenty or thirty miles away from their ward's homes and provided up to $10 twice a week, barely enough to live on for two or three days at a time.[28]

As rumors swirled, another thread of mystery surfaced: the children's missing father, Hardy Sells. Witnesses claimed he had reappeared in Mexico City and transferred deeds for his own allotment and those of his dead children to William Irvin. Officials quietly questioned whether those deeds bore Hardy's real signature or that of an impostor. Either way, the paper trail hinted at a broader scheme: The explosions in Taft comprised just the surface of a larger robbery carried out through courts, guardianships, and forged transfers.

DYNAMITERS PLAY FOR HIGH STAKES

Not long after word spread of the Sells children's fortune, their mother Priscilla considered traveling to Mexico City to confirm rumors that her first husband Hardy Sells, missing for a decade, was still alive. Authorities urged her not to go. Investigators had already traced suspicious deeds filed in Okmulgee County back to Mexico, and their prime suspect was William Irvin.

Nearly three weeks after Herbert and CaStella were buried side by side in the Blackjack Cemetery in Taft, Irvin himself slipped south across the border, unaware that federal agents were trailing him. On April 3, 1911, detectives arrested him in Mexico City. The *Muskogee Times-Democrat* reported the capture was carried out "so quietly that even the hotel officials did not know what was going on." When they searched him, agents found the deed to Hardy Sells's 160-acre allotment, along with deeds to all four of his deceased children's properties, pinned inside his coat. That same day, Doc Allen was arrested back in Taft. Investigators hinted that more indictments were coming, ones "likely to cause a sensation in the most unexpected circles."[29]

The arrests exposed a fraud scheme that law enforcement long knew about but never prosecuted. For years, investigators and tribal lawyers had uncovered deeds to land belonging to the dead, or to children who had conveniently died of sudden illness, accidents, or suspicious causes. Again and again, the paperwork led to Mexico. *The Daily Oklahoman* explained why: American consuls there were required to acknowledge deeds if an American presented a passport and identified the signer. It was a simple trick for speculators: Line up a willing Mexican or Black stand-in, have him "sell" Indian or freedmen land before the consul, and walk away with a legal transfer. Everyone knew it was happening. No one intervened.

That changed only after the Sells murders. The fact that Herbert and CaStella were wards of the court, with a white guardian and property worth small fortunes, gave sheriffs, detectives, Indian agents, and even federal secret servicemen a reason to act. This time, officials swore, they would "make an example of this kind of work."[30]

But this sudden zeal for "justice" had little to do with any newfound commitment to Black life. It was a political dodge. Prosecutors and federal officials were less interested in protecting Black children than in protecting the legitimacy of the guardianship system, the oil economy, and US authority in Indian Territory. If they failed to punish Irvin, they risked exposing how deeply land fraud, corruption, and white predation ran through the very institutions charged with "protecting" freedmen children.

So, the real question was never whether justice for Herbert and CaStella was possible. It was whether the machinery of white power could survive without sacrificing at least one of its own. Could William Irvin, a white man, and his accomplices be indicted, tried, convicted, maybe even hanged, for killing two Black children, at a time when the murders of Black people almost never even saw a courtroom trial?

"SENSATION RUMORED"

Eleven days after William Irvin's arrest, a heavy rain flooded Taft, jarring loose twenty sticks of dynamite hidden under a small drainage culvert some two hundred yards from the charred home of the dead

Sells children. The explosives were marked "Independent Powder Company" and wrapped in a soaked copy of a Sunday *Chicago Examiner* newspaper dated March 4, 1911. After finding the explosives atop a torrent of water, a Black child brought the cache to Muskogee and turned it over to the sheriff. That same day, a grand jury made an inquiry into the dynamiting case, with several witnesses who knew something about the murders making appearances.

Days later, the grand jury returned a batch of six indictments charging murder and filed them with Judge R. P. DeGraffenreid in the Muskogee Country District Court. Among the indicted were Doc Allen, Jim Manuel, an ex-con once convicted of defrauding a Creek Freedman girl of her land, and Stout Ham, who lived less than one mile from the Sells children. In addition to Irvin, the indictment also included two other well-to-do white men: John Coombs, a wealthy oil operator from Bartlesville, who allegedly provided financial support for the plot, and F. L. Martin, a one-time candidate for the state legislature and the brother of Thomas H. Martin, the former Muskogee mayor and guardian of the Sells children. All six men were charged with "knowingly, willfully, unlawfully, purposely and feloniously, with malice aforethought, and without authority of the law, and with the premeditated design then and there to effect the deal of the said Herbert [and CaStella] Sells," who suffered "mortal wounds" and "burns" that led to their deaths.[31]

After their arrests, all three of the white men who were charged spent two nights in the county jail in a big runway surrounded by Black prisoners. It is unclear why they were segregated from the Black prisoners—whether the jailers were concerned for the men's safety or the other prisoners had denied them sleeping bunks. Martin, however, made his stay a bit more comfortable by sending for a bed from his home. The bail, which was set at $15,000 a piece, was paid within two days for Coombs and Martin. Irvin, along with the accused Blacks, remained in jail until their trials.[32]

On September 11, 1911, the six accused men arrived in district court shackled together, their chains rattling and reverberating through the halls of the courtroom. Their trial dates were set for mid-September, the men lock-stepped out of the courtroom just as they arrived. "BIGGEST

MURDER CASE COMING UP," blazed the headline of the *Muskogee Times-Democrat* the next morning.

Wesley E. Disney, the lead county prosecutor for the state, was no stranger to litigating land fraud and guardianship cases. Disney was a prominent Muskogee attorney, and later a US congressman, who knew all the ins and outs of the games that high-profile men of Oklahoma played when it came to stealing lands from defenseless Indians and minors. By the early 1920s, Disney, along with other attorneys in the state, had litigated over 14,000 probate cases involving land fraud, an average of 1,076 cases per year since statehood. Most of those cases involved lands owned by Indians and freedmen of the Cherokee and Creek Nations. For the murders of the Sells children, Disney told the *Muskogee Times-Democrat* that he planned "to send every one of the defendants over the road if he could."[33]

William Irvin was the first defendant tried for the Sells family murders, with Judge R. P. DeGraffenreid presiding. When the trial opened on December 13, 1911, prosecutor S. M. Rutherford told the jury the state would show that Irvin had plotted the killings as early as 1909. A Dawes Commission clerk testified that Irvin purchased certified copies of the Sells children's allotment records shortly before the murders. The state's key witness, J. C. Johnson, testified that Irvin and Doc Allen paid him to forge Hardy Sells's signature on five land deeds, promising $5,000 once the scheme succeeded. Other witnesses said Irvin spoke of a "big job" worth $200,000 and that Coombs and Martin financed the plot. Defense attorney George S. Ramsey argued that Irvin's presence near Taft was unproven and that the children's land had already been sold legally, removing any motive. He claimed the prosecution used $5,000 from the victims' estate to fund the trial and ended by suggesting that the real beneficiaries of the crime were the children's mother, Priscilla Mackey, and her husband, Zeb.[34] Rutherford told the jury that he would prove that it was Zeb Mackey, not Irvin, who masterminded the plot with Doc Allen and the other indicted Black perpetrators.

The state's prosecutors spent the first two days of the sensational trial weaving together, link by link, a complicated web of circumstantial evidence against Irvin. Disney and Rutherford had already established that Irvin and others conspired to blow up the Sells children to get possession of their lands. Then, on the evening of December 15, Doc Allen made a stunning confession to Disney, the local sheriff, and Fred Cook, the Indian agent involved in the investigation. Allen admitted that he and the children's stepfather were the first ones to hatch the plot to kill the children, but the deal got too big for them, and they needed money and Irvin's assistance to carry it out. Allen's confession also implicated John Coombs and F. L. Martin for furnishing the "blood money" that paid for expenses and trips to Mexico.[35]

Would Doc Allen's confession seal the fate of Irvin and the others? Or would the jury believe the testimonies of well-heeled men who swore that Irvin was an upright, trustworthy, and respectable man who was duped by Doc Allen, a "sharp nigger," and his accomplices?

A MOTHER'S DEFIANCE

Hours before the jury delivered its verdict in the state's biggest trial, William Irvin sat in the sheriff's office, staring down a possible death sentence. If he had any fear, "he did not betray it," the *Muskogee Times-Democrat* reported.

"I am feeling foxy this morning," he told a reporter. "I slept well last night, and feel that in a few short hours I am going to be a free man." His only complaint was missing his usual cold bath—"makes me feel kind of musty," he said.[36]

After sixteen hours of deliberation, the jury found him guilty of murder and conspiracy, sentencing him to life at hard labor in the Oklahoma State Penitentiary at McAlester. By the next day, the bravado was gone. Irvin sat hunched in his cell, refusing newspapers or

Gravesite of Herbert and CaStella Sells, Blackjack Cemetery in Taft, Oklahoma. Photograph courtesy of Kelvin Brown, 2008.

visitors, asking only for a bit of Old Gravely chewing tobacco. According to the *Muskogee Times-Democrat,* four days later, Doc Allen pled guilty "sullen and surly" to avoid the gallows.[37]

The rest unraveled quickly. F. L. Martin, brother of the children's white guardian, walked free after denying involvement. Sam Lowe, the man who actually had lit the fuse, was acquitted. Charges against wealthy oilmen named in the conspiracy evaporated for "lack of evidence" and expense.[38] Irvin's appeals failed, and he died in prison in 1916 from an unknown cause. Doc Allen was paroled after eight years and pardoned in 1926. Zeb Mackey, the children's stepfather, was arrested but never tried, and then later jailed for shooting at Priscilla.

Priscilla Mackey did what she could with what was left. Out of the money meant to raise and secure her children's future, she carved permanence from stone: She bought them an elaborate marker so the world would remember their names, even as the state treated them as expendable. It was more than a gravestone—it was a mother's defiance, a monument that said her children's lives had value in a society that treated them as obstacles to be cleared away. Where the courts and guardians failed, she inscribed her own justice in granite, anchoring Herbert and CaStella to the earth that had been both their curse and their inheritance.

It is telling that she had to set aside $5,000 from her children's estates just to fund the prosecutions. Without that money, it is doubtful Irvin would have been chased down in Mexico or that a trial would have happened at all. The case was never really about protecting two Black children's rights. It was theater and a chance for Oklahoma's new courts to create a charade of legitimacy while thousands of other landowning Black and Indian children were quietly robbed in probate courts. Herbert and CaStella Sells paid with their lives. Others, like Sarah Rector, Luther Manuel, Edith Durant, Dan Tucker, and Sallie Hodge, would spend their youth caught in endless guardianship battles that drained their fortunes in plain sight.

Her final act speaks volumes. By taking the money that had been earmarked for guardians, courts, and lawyers and allocating it for a gravestone, Priscilla Mackey redefined what justice could look like in a system stacked against her. Lynching was designed not just to kill children but to erase them, to strip them of kinship, history, and memory. Priscilla refused that erasure. In buying an elaborate marker, she did what so many Black parents did in the wake of racial violence: She bore public witness. She made her grief visible, material, impossible to ignore.

That stone is resistance. It insists that Herbert and CaStella were more than wards, more than property, more than "pickaninny fortunes" to be scavenged by grafters. They were her children. In a world where the state and white society tried to dictate whether Black children could live, inherit, or even be remembered, Priscilla claimed authority over their legacy. Her act places her in a long lineage of Black parents who pursued justice not only through courts but through the rituals of mourning, the preservation of memory, and the refusal to let their children's deaths disappear into silence.

"OIL MADE PICKANINNY RICH"

In May 1914, as Doc Allen and William Irvin were serving life sentences in the state penitentiary, reporters swarmed a rocky farm in Coweta, Oklahoma, eager to profile one of the state's richest boys: ten-year-old Daniel Tucker, a Creek Freedman child.

Just a month earlier, $12,000 had been deposited in Tucker's account, earnings from the Cushing oil fields, where his allotment generated $300 a day.

The reporters found Tucker chasing chickens, feeding pigs, "running wild, free and irresponsible as a colt, oblivious to the events of the world as an Eskimo." By their accounts, "Little Danny" was also unaware of his own wealth. Even if he was aware of his financial status, a *Kansas City Star* reporter asserted: "The fact would carry no significance in his brain."[39]

Born on September 14, 1903, in Redbird, Indian Territory, Tucker was the forty-ninth child added to the Newborn Freedmen Roll of the Creek Nation, approved by an act of Congress on March 3, 1905. On August 20, 1906, he was approved for a 160-acre allotment worth only $320. His father, a Creek Freedman, had already applied for allotments for himself and his two older sons. His mother Lizzie, not a Creek citizen, received nothing.

Despite Dan Tucker's enormous income, the family still lived "plain and unobtrusive," their frontier home bare of shade trees or shrubs, a *Dallas Morning News* reporter sneered, describing only an old well and smokehouse as proof of the father's "industry."[40]

After receiving their son's allotment in 1906, the Tuckers tried farming the rocky, hilly land. Two years later, they abandoned it as a worthless tax burden. Meanwhile, the 1904 Indian Appropriations Act removed federal restrictions on millions of acres of freedmen's allotments under the pretense that they were "competent," meaning they were civilized enough to manage, sell, and pay taxes on their land like whites—essentially a racialized test of civilization. In practice, this designation created a legal loophole that allowed speculators to target families whose property would otherwise have been protected, even though state law forbade the sale of land belonging to minors. Once a person was declared "competent," their allotment could be taxed or sold outright, opening the door to widespread dispossession through fraud, coercion, and predatory sales. Ironically, whenever oil or other valuable resources were discovered on a freedman's property, the state reversed course and declared freedmen "incompetent," forcing them under white guardianship.[41]

Long after the Tuckers gave up hope, the Prairie Oil and Gas Company struck oil adjacent to Tucker's allotment. By 1915, the Cushing fields would be producing more than 300,000 barrels a day, 72 million annually, with 3,600 wells. Prairie arranged a lease, and oil gushed from Tucker's land "like water from a lawn sprinkler." Under the lease, Tucker received one-eighth of the gross proceeds. In the final days of February 1914, less than a month after drilling began, Tucker's father received a court order requiring him to pay a $7,000 bond fee to become his own son's legal guardian. Press accounts reported that Jim Tucker knew how to plant and shuck corn, but being a guardian and overseeing his son's growing fortunes "was way over his head, so to speak," a reporter wrote. Jim was "superseded by a more business-like accountant, a man who could give adequate bond to the court."[42]

On March 8, 1914, attorney Jess W. Watts of Wagoner, Oklahoma, was appointed guardian of Dan Tucker, paying the boy's father $70 a month for Dan's care. Meanwhile, the boy's oil income reached $6,000 monthly. No surviving records reveal how much Tucker ultimately earned or how much Watts appropriated, though court documents show Watts's involvement in numerous land fraud cases between 1913 and 1925. Press accounts portrayed Tucker and his family as simple and incapable of managing wealth. Reporters claimed that money meant little to him and that he "resented" his guardianship and schooling, preferring farm life to education or financial management. Such depictions reinforced racist narratives that Black children and their parents were unfit to control their own resources, legitimizing white oversight and exploitation of their estates.[43]

This kind of media depiction—that of a wild, ignorant, mentally incompetent, uneducable, unsavvy, poor-but-happy freedman—was not uncommon. These reports reveal how race shaped the public's perception that Blacks and Indians could not handle money, had no need for education, cultivation, or financial independence, and that parents of wealthy freedmen children could not properly handle the affairs of their children. Such media accounts not only announced the wealth of these children to potential grafters and guardians; they also helped legitimize the fact that such men were appointed by Oklahoma's probate courts to control the children's monies. Ironically, while these stories claimed that handling thousands of dollars per month and conducting business transactions was over the heads of the children's parents, reporters were conspicuously silent about how white guardians robbed and exploited thousands of youths across the state.

"THE RICHEST COLORED GIRL IN THE WORLD"

Sarah Rector, another ten-year-old listed as number 261 on the Creek Freedmen newborn roll, owned a Cushing allotment, for which she captured national headlines. In September 1913, *The Kansas City Star* and *The Savannah Tribune* reported that Rector's income had reached $112,000 annually and that she paid the largest income tax in the state of Oklahoma. "She has an income that makes President Wilson's salary or the salary of a railroad or insurance president look like small change," *The Kansas City Star* noted.[44]

Months later, in January 1914, a *Kansas City Star* reporter visited the Rector family and subsequently wrote a feature article with the headline, "Oil Made Pickaninny Rich." Rector, described as "ignorant, with apparently little mental capacity," crawled under her parents' bed and refused to be interviewed. "Of course they could have grabbed her by the heels and dragged her out," the reporter wrote. "But any person with $15,000 a month in real money falling into her lap has got to be handled with care, no matter if she is a pickaninny instead of a prima donna." Despite her young age, Rector received "bushels of proposals" from young German men asking to marry her. "From the character of the letters all of them are highly educated, and from the pictures, fine looking chaps." The reporter noted that the letters indicated that Blacks in Germany were afforded a vastly different social standing than in Oklahoma. Stacks of letters came from others who heard of Rector's fortune, including requests from women interested in social uplift or civic improvement, from wildcat promoters, and grafters.[45]

Sarah Rector was born on March 3, 1902, in Taft, Creek Nation, to Joseph and Rose Rector. In 1906, the Department of the Interior allotted her 160 acres of land valued at $556.50. Her father, believing the land worthless, petitioned repeatedly to sell it but was barred by laws protecting minors' holdings. In 1911, a well drilled by the prospector B. B. Jones struck oil, producing about 2,500 barrels a week worth one dollar each, making Rector one of the wealthiest children in Oklahoma. Despite her sudden fortune, journalists portrayed her as an unassuming farm girl "playing about in ragged dresses and bare feet." Reports described the simple life she continued to maintain in a two-room house, sleeping by the kitchen stove under a rag quilt, even as lawyers and businessmen moved quickly to secure control of her estate.[46]

The Salt Lake Telegram and *Duluth News-Tribune* reported that Rector was "under sympathetic guardianship" and receiving the best education. *The Kansas City Star* claimed that Judge Thomas Leahy of the county court approved petitions, filed by Rector's guardian, to purchase a bed, decent clothing, and a $2.50 pair of shoes that she allegedly didn't want, and that he ordered a new home to be built for the entire family.[47]

It is important to note that these reports came months after Du Bois dispatched social worker Florence Kelley to Oklahoma in the winter of 1914 to investigate Rector's situation. In 1912, Kelley, a white descendant of abolitionists as well as a social worker and early organizer of the NAACP, together with another white reformer, Lillian Wald, formed the United States Children's Bureau, a federal investigative commission that focused on a wide range of issues including crimes against children. A close ally of Du Bois, Kelley was also one of a few ardent white progressive reformers that advocated on behalf of Black children. A review of her collected writings suggests that Kelley, and the interracial coalition of reformers associated with the NAACP, recognized the potential benefits of arguing on behalf of, and exposing the plight of, Black children. If America was to achieve some semblance of racial harmony, it had to remove barriers to equal education, curb labor exploitation, and punish violence against Black youth.

While in Oklahoma, Kelley corresponded with NAACP officials in Washington and worked alongside Kate Barnard, one of the US West's most prominent and dedicated reformers. Early in her career, Barnard was described by the local press as "a sweet and dainty wildflower and as refreshing as an Oklahoma breeze."[48]

Elected as the state's first commissioner of charities and corrections, Barnard was responsible for convincing the legislature to establish a special court for children in need of legal supervision. For much of her career she fought on behalf of the state's orphans and delinquents, and she was most likely the first responsible for bringing the plight of Sarah Rector and the other Creek Freedmen minors to the attention of the NAACP. When she began her career, the Irish-Catholic champion of children had known little of the exploitation of Indian and Creek Freedmen minors until she received a report of three "wild children" who had been sleeping in the hollow of a tree, drinking from a stream, and stealing food from nearby farmhouses. Upon further investigation, she learned that the children's parents were dead and that the children owned valuable oil land and were under the protection of a guardian who had been collecting royalties and charging the children exorbitant fees for their education and support. Worse yet, this same guardian had forty-eight other wards assigned to his care.[49]

Kelley and Barnard spent months investigating Sarah Rector's case, sending updates to *The Crisis* about her schooling and living conditions. Sarah Rector "wears the cheapest kind of clothes and is given but a meager education by her white guardian, who doles out for her support but a few dollars a month," Du Bois wrote. "If she were a white child her guardian would see that she lived in a manner befitting her income and was receiving the best education. Her riches only serve to enrich whites—only serve to enable whites to live in luxury while she lives in poverty, or next door to poverty."[50]

T. J. Porter, a banker from Beland, served as her guardian until he was ousted for purchasing a building from a friend with funds from Rector's estate. Bob Fite, whom Du Bois described as "a white man who has openly manifested his prejudice against the race," sold his building on South Second Street in Muskogee to the Rector estate for an extortionate sum of $57,000, more than $1.2 million in today's dollars. "A white elephant on his hands, he used his pull with the white guardian of this Negro girl to lad it off on her."[51]

In May 1919, Edward Curd, the attorney representing Rector's new guardians, bankers M. G. Young and C. A. Looney, had his license revoked and the Oklahoma Supreme Court disbarred him for purchasing farmlands and various properties in Muskogee without informing Rector's guardians. Petitions filed by Curd on behalf of Rector and her guardians were approved by various judges in the county court. Curd personally benefited by receiving over $15,000 (about $300,000 today) in fees and commissions for these unauthorized real estate investments.[52]

Lending out a ward's money on promissory notes to personal friends of the guardian, oftentimes on inadequate security, was a common practice. This is how the estates belonging to Edith and Edna Durant nearly vanished before the twins reached eighteen years of age in July 1918. Between August 1912 and September 1914, Edith's guardian, R. Lee Hays, filed sixteen petitions with the county court to make real estate loans with funds from her estate. Each petition reported that the ward had large sums of money on deposit in various banks and that it was "proper and to the best interest of said minor that said money should be loaned at a reasonable rate of interest on good Real Estate securety [*sic*]."

Between 1912 and 1914, Muskogee County courts approved at least sixteen loans totaling $38,250 (about $1 million today) from the estates of Creek minors like Edith and Edna Durant to white borrowers across eastern Oklahoma. The loans, issued at 8 percent interest for two to five years, financed homes and businesses in Muskogee, Sapulpa, and Tulsa. Borrowers included Harry G. Davis, J. A. and Callie Pitts, Fay Todd, and Dr. Floyd E. Waterfield. None of the debts were repaid, leaving the losses to fall entirely on the children's estates.

Descendants of the Durant twins, nephew Bruce Reed and grandsons Quinton and Larry Harrison of Tulsa, knew of the twins' immense wealth. "They had money and they had property all over Muskogee," said Reed. "But no one could ever explain to us how they lost their money or how the land and property left their hands."[53] The answer lay in the same machinery that ensnared hundreds of Native children.

The twins' guardian also obtained court approval for luxury purchases—a new house, a car, a piano, and a "health-restoring" family trip—yet no such items were ever provided to Edith and Edna. The twins' first guardian, Bates Burnett, appointed in 1906, was removed in 1911 for diverting funds and failing to report or make required payments, while charging more than $45,000 in fees. His successor, R. Lee Hays, submitted regular reports but used the girls' money to purchase overvalued land and buildings through collusion with banks and appraisers.

Similar abuses were widespread. The Indian Rights Association documented many cases in which guardians enriched themselves through fraudulent property sales and inflated fees. In one instance, guardian Ferdinand P. Snider squandered the fortune of child allottee Luther Manuel through corrupt land deals worth hundreds of thousands of dollars. Despite repeated petitions and federal investigations, local courts seldom intervened, allowing such schemes to persist unchecked.[54]

Sallie Hodge's guardian was also removed from his duties in 1912 because of fraudulent activities. Charles L. Torr, the attorney representing her guardian, was indebted to her estate for $2,150. A report filed by Kate Barnard indicated that Hodge's guardian paid Torr $500 per year in fees. Torr, who was convicted of defrauding other minors, was convicted and sentenced to one year in the state penitentiary.[55] Of the nearly four thousand professional guardians in Oklahoma, six hundred were removed by 1912, mostly for embezzlement and misappropriating funds. In general, there was no real auditing of wards' accounts by probate judges, who needed the support of guardians to be reelected. As wards' estates dwindled with such purchases, bankers, attorneys, and appraisal and insurance companies, along with guardians, gained large sums of money from these transactions. Oklahoma's guardianship system was what Tanis Thorne called a "veritable cottage industry, sanctioned by law, with profit sharing by numerous persons in local cliques." Stealing from Indian and Black wards enabled many of Oklahoma's leading citizens to build powerful political machines.

As the Indian Rights Commission noted in a 1924 investigative report, these men owned fine houses, high-speed automobiles, and lived in luxury as they enjoyed long careers as professional guardians. The report added, "The professional guardian is catered to by banks, who desire his account, by merchants who want to secure the ward's trade; and his friends want liberal loans on questionable security—and in this way the whole community is interested."[56]

"THE EXCEPTION PROVES THE RULE"

On May 26, 1916, less than two years before their eighteenth birthdays, Edith Durant and Sallie Hodge received cash bonuses of $90,000 each from the Prairie Gas and Oil Company for a lease extension to continue drilling on their allotments.[57] With the prospects of lucrative returns on both teens' properties looking positive, plans to keep Durant and Hodge as wards of the state were in the works. Grafters also kept a "birthday book" so they would know when the girls and other minors with estates were to become of age.

Du Bois also kept Durant, Hodge, and the other wealthiest Black children of Muskogee County on his radar. In the June 1918 edition of *The Crisis*, he announced: "Edith Durant, a colored girl of Oklahoma, will be of age July 2 [and] Mrs. Sallie Hodge Reid also comes of age this year and will receive a large fortune. White guardians have done much to waste the money belonging to these minors."[58] Hodge, who married W. C. Reid in 1913 when she was fourteen years old, successfully acquired her entire estate and immediately placed it under the control of her husband to protect her from grafters. Durant, however, was not so fortunate.

One month before Durant's birthday, R. C. Allen, national attorney for the Creek Nation, petitioned the county court to have a guardian appointed for her estate. At the time, Durant's allotment earned $1,200 per month and she owned real estate valued at $1 million. In his petition, Allen argued that Durant was "spirited out of the jurisdiction of [the] Court for the purpose of avoiding the jurisdiction of the Court to appoint a guardian."[59] Allen noted that Durant was recently removed from the care and protection of her guardians and that her whereabouts were unknown: "She is illiterate, ignorant and wholly incompetent and would squander and dissipate her property unless a guardian is appointed for her as an incompetent immediately upon reaching her age of majority." A hearing was set for August 31, 1917, at ten in the morning.

Neither Durant nor her guardians, R. Lee Hays and her father, Mundy, appeared before the court. Allen claimed that Durant had been given sufficient notice to appear in court and he argued that she may have been kidnapped by grafters. "She has been aided and assisted by persons having designs upon her property and her said estate, and an unlawful intent fraudulently to deprive her thereof."[60] Allen requested that J. C. Scully, a banker from Haskell, be appointed as her guardian. On September 7, 1917, six days after Durant's eighteenth birthday, Scully paid the $150,000 bond required by the court, and an order to have her entire estate turned over to Scully was executed. Durant, along with her previous guardian and her father, fought the order. Four months later, on January 21, 1918, the order to appoint Scully as her guardian was vacated on the grounds that he was appointed without any notice to Durant or her guardians.

Sarah Rector faced a similar battle when she turned eighteen and moved from Oklahoma to Kansas City, Missouri. John Collins of Muskogee submitted a petition claiming that neither Rector nor her parents were capable of managing her large estate. In 1922, at age twenty, Rector was still earning $40,000 a year from oil royalties, a large part of which she invested in liberty bonds. She also owned $100,000 worth of farmland in Oklahoma. As with Durant, petitioners, who included Collins and local probate attorneys, claimed that Rector was mentally defective, even though she had graduated from high school and was now attending Tuskegee University. The petitioners also claimed that Rector "expended her wealth," which had resulted in the search for "a guardian for her by her Oklahoma friends."[61]

When Rector had moved to Kansas City in 1920, she purchased an automobile and a mansion at 2000 East Twelfth Street. Though she was eighteen at the time, the Missouri legislature revised its age of majority law, extending the legal age from eighteen to twenty-one. This revision changed Rector's status, making her a minor again, and her "Oklahoma friends" were quick to take advantage of this technicality. Judge Jules Guinotte of the Muskogee County Probate Court disagreed with the petitioner's claim of Rector's incompetence. The twenty-year-old "has handled the more than $750,000 worth of property she owns with such astuteness that application for guardians was denied," *The Savannah Tribune* reported on March 30, 1922. Judge Guinotte ruled that Rector showed the competence to take care of her own money and "complimented her highly on her intelligence and thrift." Du Bois wrote his own celebratory note in the June issue of *The Crisis*: "Pessimists on the Afro-American question may well consider the pure-blooded Negro girl, Sarah Rector of Kansas City, aged 20, who proves to a white court that she is managing astutely her fortune of $750,000 and needs no guardian. Possibly the exception proves the rule."[62]

Rector, Hodge, and Edith Durant were indeed exceptions to the rule when it came to wealthy Indian and freedmen minors retaining their estates into adulthood. Records for the estates of Dan Tucker and Edna Durant were either lost or destroyed, so it is unclear what happened to their large sums of money. Descendants of Rector and the Durant twins still question how millions of dollars' worth of real estate left their hands. When Luther Manuel died of illness on December 11, 1936, at age thirty-two, he was almost penniless. His widow, Thelma J. Manuel, was told by the probate court that her late husband's estate was valued at less than $100.

Three years later, on December 8, 1939, Thelma Manuel filed a petition for a hearing to investigate Luther's estate. She eventually hired Tulsa attorney Jay W. Whitney in December 1942. Whitney's investigation revealed that Manuel had paid "illegal and erroneous taxes upon the income of his allotted lands and the oil and gas removed from it." Manuel's total estate was subsequently valued at $84,000 once those taxes were refunded. The deceased Manuel's eighty-three-year-old mother, Mulcie, was also an heir to his estate. Her guardian, a white woman named Hanna M. Davis, petitioned the court and received $11,500 in fees, which were deducted. Whitney charged Mrs. Manuel $42,000 in fees for recovering the large tax refund. After Davis's and Whitney's deductions, along with thousands of dollars in court costs, administrative fees, and inheritance tax payments, Manuel's widow and mother received $3,871.85 on August 14, 1953, over a decade after the initial petition was filed.

What the cases of Dan Tucker, Sarah Rector, the Durant twins, Luther Manuel, Sallie Hodge, and the Sells children reveal is that lynching was always about control. The murders, fraud, and courtroom charades were all part of a single system that sought to strangle Black futures at the root. When mobs killed Black children, they were dramatizing the same lesson that probate judges, lawyers, and guardians enacted in quieter rooms: Black life and Black wealth could never be allowed to flourish without white oversight. Lynching was the violent spectacle of this truth, but guardianship fraud was its bureaucratic twin.

The Sells children were murdered outright because their inheritance was too tempting to steal through paperwork alone. Tucker, Rector, Manuel, and the Durants were not strung up in public, but they were slowly dispossessed through legal fictions that declared them "incompetent." Both paths—mob terror and state-sanctioned graft—served the same function: to deny Black children control over their own bodies, futures, and resources.

Historians have noted that in the 1910s and 1920s, progressive reformers and federal agencies launched investigations to expose the robbery of wealthy Indians and freedmen. Yet the State of Oklahoma used every measure to undermine watchdog agencies and thwart corrective legislation that might have protected remaining lands from graft. The plight of these eight wealthy Black children was not unique—it was a snapshot of a feeding frenzy that left thousands of Blacks and Indians among the poorest people in the United States by the mid-twentieth century. In one of the harshest Jim Crow states in the Union, its first generation of Black children, whether descended from Indian Territory's freedmen or from white Southern enslavers, endured stifling racism, segregation, lynching, disease, and poverty, even as landowners, even as heirs, even as children who should have been secure in their futures.

THE PROBLEM OF THE COLOR LINE

This story does not have a triumphant ending. What happened to these children during Jim Crow set the stage for the discrimination that Black tribal members still face today. The legal tricks and racial terror of the early twentieth century echo in today's battles over sovereignty, enrollment, and belonging.

And yet, these children must be remembered for what they represented. Black children in Oklahoma embodied the slave master's deepest nightmare: that the descendants of the enslaved would not only survive but inherit land, accumulate wealth, and claim power that whiteness alone could not control. That was the terror dynamite was meant to silence, fraud was meant to erase, and the noose was meant to choke. Their stolen futures are a reminder that the struggle has never been only about survival; it also has always been about the fear of what Black children, if allowed to grow free and unshackled, might become.

To W. E. B. Du Bois, those Black children in Oklahoma represented both a *tragedy* and a *testament*. On one hand, he saw them as living proof of how white supremacy bent every lever of law and violence to rob Black life of its possibilities. In *The Crisis*, he documented these youths' plight to show that even when Black children inherited wealth and land, they were stripped of it through guardianship fraud, graft, and neglect. Their exploitation exposed the hypocrisy of American democracy: The country claimed to be a beacon of progress while it bled its most vulnerable citizens.

But Du Bois also saw them as symbols of promise and the embodiment of what emancipation had made possible, and of what white America feared most. They were the "test cases" of whether Black freedom could include wealth, property, and autonomy, or whether it would be throttled at every turn. In his framing, these children were not just victims but evidence: proof that Black capacity, intelligence, and resilience existed, and proof that the true obstacle to racial advancement was white theft and violence.

These children represented both the nightmare of white supremacy and the dream of a future still possible. They showed that the "problem of the color line" was not Black inferiority but the nation's fear of Black prosperity. Their existence forced the question: Would America allow Black children to inherit freedom in substance, or would it lynch, defraud, and dispossess them until nothing remained but memory and mourning?

That same question echoes today. From the oil fields of Oklahoma to today's classrooms, courtrooms, and prisons, the question has remained: Will this land ever allow Black children to be free heirs to its promise, or will it keep finding new ways to lynch them?

EPILOGUE

The Cold Case of Justice

This is a book that should have *never* been written.

Because the stories contained in it should have never existed. Because no nation should have needed a record of how it murdered its own children. Because the bodies of teenagers, toddlers, babies, and even the unborn should not be the evidence that proves America lies about itself.

But here we are.

This book was born the way grief is born. Unwanted. Unavoidable. *Insistent.* It began with old news clippings and police photos of my biological grandfather's murder in the winter of 1969. It was a crime that was never called a lynching because by the time he was killed, America had learned to rename its violence. His death lived like static in my birth family's bloodline. Every silence, every warning, every hard edge of love was a form of self-defense against what the world might still do to us. Writing this book meant listening to that echo, tracing it backward until it became a chorus of a thousand voices saying, *We were here, we were children, and we were not accidents.*

Each chapter of *Strung Up* followed the trail of that echo. From church pews and public squares to hospital wards and lecture halls, through the ledger books of midwives and the dry language of coroners' reports. We begin, as W. E. B. Du Bois dared us to, with the question: "Ought children be born to us?" That question is not a philosophical luxury. It is a moral litmus. It asks what sort of world we intend to bequeath. One that trains small hands to wield terror? Or one that teaches them tenderness? It asks what kind of future we are building, what rituals we teach our smallest people, and whether we will raise hands to heal or to hurt.

The next echo pulled us into the drawing of a lynching, into Reginald Marsh's little girl on a perch above the crowd with her finger to her chin and her calm amid the fire. We learned that white childhood was not innocence but apprenticeship. We learned that the noose was as much a teacher as any book, and that empathy had to be beaten out of white children so that white supremacy could live inside them without resistance.

The next chapter carried us back in time and across the Atlantic, where Europe perfected the choreography of cruelty through public executions, religious terror, parents disciplining children in the image of God's wrath. We saw how those rituals of pain sailed to the colonies and remade themselves in Black flesh.

From there the story moved through the nursery, the schoolhouse, and the gallows, showing how the pedagogy of fear became the curriculum of empire. We met children who were told to obey or die and white adults who mistook domination for order. What followed was the chapter on faith and death, and the way scripture was twisted into a noose. White Christianity became the theology of punishment, a gospel that promised salvation through suffering but only if the suffering was someone else's. The mob came to believe it was God's hand extended. The cross and the lynching tree became one silhouette.

As we moved forward in our journey, we saw the transatlantic pedagogy of public execution compressed into a single, brutal lesson: Early modern Europe's scaffold spectacles migrated to American courthouse lawns, teaching white children that terror could be civic duty. Jesse Washington's Waco burning is the touchstone—a photographed massacre that turned murder into a public curriculum and trained ordinary people, young and old, to be killers and witnesses at once.

We witnessed how religion, profit, and professional authority braided together to make child-killing legible and profitable. That chapter centered on the public execution of Hannah Ocuish in Connecticut, a Pequot child whose death shows how pulpit and courthouse colluded, turning atrocity into doctrine and dividend.

Then came the women who birthed whiteness itself. They guarded the color line from the womb, shaping generations through the bodies they carried and the children they claimed as pure. In their wombs, America's caste system renewed itself. They were both victims and architects who were schooled to equate their own virtue with domination and their safety with Black submission and death. Their lullabies echoed with the sounds of empire.

From there we witnessed the terror directed at pregnant Black wombs that carried the next generation of freedom's children. In Mississippi, Georgia, and elsewhere the mob's violence doubled itself: two lives extinguished at once. The Black womb became the battlefield where America fought its war against the future. Every hanging of a pregnant woman, every mutilation of an unborn child, was an attempt to end a Black future before it began.

Then came the delirious white panic over "changeling babies" who might not look white enough. A single shade or a curl of hair could spark confusion. Racial designation was not just about preserving "purity" but about jurisdiction and deciding who counted as killable. Whiteness needed fixed borders to sustain itself, so the mob became its border patrol. The lynching of infants and toddlers was not random barbarity; it reflected the state of mind of a people desperate to define who could be lynched with accuracy. The myth of purity demanded precision. The death of a Black child confirmed where the line was drawn, and every drop of blood redrew it.

As the twentieth century advanced, the mob put on new clothes. Doctors, scientists, and public officials took over the work. They called it *research* and *progress*. But it was the same obsession with control. They measured skulls, examined genitals, sliced fetal skin, and harassed Black midwives. Medicine and public health documents became new instruments of racial management. Here, the scalpel and the birth certificate replaced the rope.

In the next movement, the camera entered the scene. The killings became art, pedophilic postcards, headlines. White America's most sadistic desire was to watch itself watching. The photographs of dangling children, the staged smiles of spectators, the pulp novels and films that eroticized Black pain. All of it transformed murder into national pastime. The pornography of lynching revealed the final evolution of the mob's gaze: to consume what it destroyed.

And then came Freddie Moore, the boy whose death was hidden beneath the weight of white lies and respectability. His story exposed the culture of cover-up: the white women who cried purity while concealing predation, the towns that protected its pedophiles and incestuous white fathers, uncles, brothers, and stepfathers, and the newspapers that rewrote the script. Lynching's last disguise was innocence itself.

Finally, our journey ended in Oklahoma, where the noose became legal procedure. Here, the machinery of dispossession replaced the tree. Guardianships, competency rulings, and state-sanctioned theft stripped Black children of the estates they had inherited. The mob no longer needed a rope when it had a pen. What looked like bureaucracy was simply a new form of lynching—*slow, polite, and permanent.* By the time we reached early twentieth-century Oklahoma, the so-called frontier of modernity, the machinery was complete. The lynching era was not a rupture; it was the fulfillment of everything the Old World had rehearsed.

That is why the book ends there. Not because the violence stopped, but because it no longer needed to innovate.

After Oklahoma, lynching simply changed uniforms. The rope became a badge. The mob became the state. The same men who once gathered under oaks to pose for photographs now patrolled the streets in squad cars, sat on juries, signed warrants, and presided over executions. The spectacle of public murder retreated into prisons, hospitals, and police stations. The crowd no longer needed to gather because America had mechanized the ritual.

Emmett Till's open casket was never meant to close. Mamie Till-Mobley forced this country to look, to smell, to know. Every mother after her has lived with that same bargain: If they kill our children, at least let the world *see*.

Moving through the rest of the twentieth century would not yield the discovery of new crimes; it would only mean tracing the same choreography of control under new names: "officer-involved shootings," justified force, capital punishment, corrections. The lynchers did not disappear; they were professionalized. Their descendants wore uniforms, drew paychecks, collected pensions, and wrote reports that called their killings "procedure."

The story after Oklahoma is not progress; it is mutation. It is the state learning to outsource its mobs, to sanitize its rope with bureaucracy, to replace the lynching tree with the police precinct, the courthouse, the prison cell, the school, and foster care-to-prison pipelines. That is why this book must stop here, because by this point, the blueprint of American violence had already been drawn in full. Everything after is its afterlife.

To go further would be to make you keep turning pages through an unending dirge, through a century that never learned. The names would blur together. The bodies would pile higher. The air would thin. And I will not do that to you. I will not do that to them, or to myself. Because there is no justice at the end of these stories, only echoes.

Echoes that accost the comfortable with the names they tried to bury. Echoes that haunt courthouse halls and dinner tables until a reckoning is demanded. Echoes that tutor the next generation in the grammar of violence if we do not teach otherwise. And echoes that, unanswered, will harden into the very habits that made murder ordinary.

I have *zero illusions* that there will be justice for the child victims of lynching. The families of those children still live with the silence, still bear the weight of an empty space where a life should have stretched forward. Every mother, every sibling, every cousin, auntie, uncle, grandparent, every descendant carries that interruption in their blood. They are living in the echo of futures that were stolen.

It hollows you out.

The absence of a child who should have lived does not sit politely at the back of a family story. It sits at the center of everyday life and shapes everything that grows around it. Homes learn a new grammar: shorter goodbyes, whispered routes to school, a steadying hand on the small of a back that will never loosen, a whupping "so the white man won't kill you." Parents become both armor and jailer—overprotective to the point of smothering, mistrustful to the point of withdrawal. Joy grows thin and cautious. Laughter is always measured against the ghost of what might be taken next.

At the community scale, the wound calcifies into habit. Institutions that should comfort—police, courts, hospitals—are read as threats. Schools and churches become places where survival tactics are taught as civics. People stop believing that the system will keep them whole, so they build parallel systems of care, secrecy, and self-defense. Those systems are beautiful and necessary, but they are also a marker of damage. When you must provision your people against the state, you have already been made to live in two worlds at once.

The most corrosive effect is the endless question, the ache of *what-if*. What if we had been watched longer? What if the call had been answered? What if we had left earlier? What if we hadn't moved to this neighborhood? What if we had done more? That question is a looping lullaby of blame and longing in which memory erodes into speculation. It frays relationships as families argue over hypothetical pasts and grieve futures never written. It leaves descendants carrying unfinished sentences in their bones. It is an insistence that life was interrupted and that the interruption might have been prevented.

That ache becomes inheritance.

Behaviors shift into biology: Sleep fractures, stress becomes baseline, parenting reflexes harden into scripts of vigilance. Stories that should nourish a people instead warn them. Trauma teaches its own civics—how to hide, how to read a room, how to teach a child to smile while holding a clenched fist. Sometimes that teaching turns inward: Communities copy the punishment they once suffered, mistaking strictness for protection, control for care. Other times it rides outward, fueling righteous anger or fatalism that can corrode solidarity.

And yet, this is not merely a ledger of loss. Living with the *what-if* also produces fierce fidelity: to memory, to naming, to the ritual work of keeping a life present. It makes activists, archivists, midwives of truth. It forces ordinary people into the work of witness and refusing the easy comforts of forgetting. That is why the echo matters. Left unanswered, it teaches fear. Answered, it becomes the pulse of repair. If we will not let justice arrive, we can at least let remembrance do its work, and from that labor we can teach ourselves how to envision a different future.

At its Legacy Museum in Montgomery, Alabama, the Equal Justice Initiative has gathered soil from those places—rust-red dirt lifted from the ground where children and men and women were taken. Each jar bears a name, a date, a county. They line the shelves like an archive of grief. The memorial rises from the earth like a field of suspended coffins, each one engraved with the names of the murdered. Across the country, plaques have been raised, prayers have been spoken, dirt has been consecrated. These are sacred acts of memory, and they matter.

But let us not confuse remembrance with justice. Dirt and metal cannot balance the scales. No monument can undo what was done, or what continues to be done in new uniforms, under new laws, under different logics of lynching. America does not repent; it recycles. It buries its crimes beneath ceremonies of acknowledgment and calls that healing.

When Barack Obama's Justice Department announced the Cold Case Initiative in 2016, it was hailed as a national reckoning and a long-delayed promise that America would finally face the ghosts it had buried. The project's architects spoke of restoring dignity, solving mysteries, offering closure. Agents reopened files, dusted off evidence, visited families who had waited generations for the sound of an apology. For a moment, it seemed as if the country might actually look itself in the mirror.

But America has always known how to turn confession into performance. What was promised as justice became paperwork. The Cold Case Initiative gathered names, dates, photographs, and witness accounts, but not accountability. It reopened the graves only long enough to take inventory. No new convictions. No real admissions of guilt. Just a press release, a shrug, and a closure notice.

The effort folded in 2022, quietly and without ceremony. Officials called it "a completed review." Families called it what it was: abandonment. The names remained on lists, in archives, in the bureaucratic afterlife of government websites. They were treated not as children lost to racial terror but as administrative tasks—case numbers to be filed, boxes to be checked.

Andrew Lee Anderson, sixteen.
Henry Dee, nineteen.
Charles Moore, nineteen.
Johnny Robinson, sixteen.
John Earl Reese, sixteen.
Jimmy Powell, fifteen.
A. C. Hall, seventeen.
Samuel Hammond Jr., eighteen.

Larry Payne, sixteen.
Fred Robinson, twelve.
Emmett Till, fourteen.
And so many others.

Each of them a son, a classmate, a child who never got to grow old. Each of them proof that America's appetite for Black death has no statute of limitations.

The Cold Case Initiative did not fail because the evidence was lacking. It failed because this nation cannot convict itself. It will exhume bones before it will tell the truth. The government called the project "restorative," but what it restored was its own conscience. What it buried again was our pain.

That is the final lesson of the Cold Case Initiative: America prefers the paperwork of justice to its actual practice. It will spend millions documenting the crimes it refuses to stop committing. It will commission memorials to the dead while manufacturing new ones.

And still, the killings continue. Only now the camera images are sharper, the uniforms cleaner, the excuses more rehearsed. America no longer gathers beneath trees; it gathers around screens. It calls the footage "evidence" but treats it as entertainment.

The children have new names now:

Trayvon Martin, seventeen, stalked through the rain by a man who wanted to feel like a cop.

Michael Brown Jr., eighteen, left in the August heat for four hours while his family and community watched his body bake in the sun.

Tamir Rice, twelve, gunned down in a park within seconds of being spotted, for playing with a toy gun.

Aiyana Stanley-Jones, seven, shot in her sleep during a police raid.

Laquan McDonald, seventeen, shot sixteen times as he tried to walk away.

Jordan Davis, seventeen, murdered for playing music too loud.

Antwon Rose II, seventeen, shot in the back while running.

And there are others: Kendrick Johnson, whose body was found rolled in a gym mat. Renisha McBride, shot for knocking on a door after a car accident. Ma'Khia Bryant, a sixteen-year-old foster youth, killed moments after calling the police for help. Each one an iteration of the same ritual.

Their deaths are not echoes of the past; they are its continuation. The same logic that once justified the mob's rope now animates the trigger finger. The same claim to authority, over space, over safety, over the definition of innocence, still decides who gets to live long enough to be human.

We like to believe the mob was an aberration, that history has moved on. But the mob never left. It just put on a badge, a lab coat, a black robe. It signs warrants, conducts autopsies, writes laws, moderates debates, anchors news programs, teaches in classrooms. It speaks in the detached voice of headlines: "A man died in police custody." "An officer discharged his weapon." The grammar of American power remains the same. It erases the subject and blames the body. It is a nation that debates whether unarmed children deserve to die.

And then, one January afternoon, the mob took off its masks. It stepped out of its institutions and revealed itself in full daylight.

On January 6, 2021, America watched its own ancestral DNA storm the Capitol steps. These were not strangers to history—they were its descendants. They carried in their blood the memory of Old World gallows, of witch burnings, beheadings, public hangings and gibbeting, of the cheering crowds that once gathered in European squares to watch flesh become ash. Centuries of cruelty had been passed down, synapse to synapse, father to son, mother to child. The bodies might have changed, but the nervous system had not.

What surged through that mob was not just anger; it was inheritance. It was the echo of medieval torches reconstituted as cell phones raised to livestream the spectacle. It was the same limbic response that once delighted at the sight of Black flesh burning under Southern stars, now repackaged as nationalist fury in red hats. They howled and smeared feces like their ancestors once rubbed ashes on their faces after a hanging. They built a gallows and called it democracy. They dragged their epigenetic ghosts into the temple of American power and crowned them patriots.

Pundits sat in shock and said, *This isn't America.* But it was. It always has been. What they saw that day wasn't an exception; it was an unveiling. The same psycho-spiritual inheritance that once gathered beneath hanging trees now gathered beneath the Capitol dome. The same nervous system that once pulsed with the thrill of watching a lynching now coursed through the veins of men and women who believed they were taking back a country that never belonged to anyone but them.

What we witnessed that day wasn't new; it was white bodies remembering. It was Europe's oldest reflex firing again through American muscle. A collective nervous system convulsing with the same centuries-old terror of losing power, a sense of purity, and control. The faces were modern, but the neurology was medieval. The gallows, the chants, the trembling ecstasy of dominance—all of it was a reenactment written into the national flesh.

Writing this book in the era of open grievance, under a government that cages children and mocks the dead, has meant staring straight into the eyes of the same evil beast. The language has changed, but the appetite has not. White rage is unashamed now. It livestreams itself. It wears badges, robes, or business suits and calls itself MAGA.

This book is a cautionary tale of what happens when a society dehumanizes its young, when it beats them into silence, when it baptizes brutality in the language of God and country. When it uses philosophy, religion, and reason as tools to sanctify domination. Such children grow up to become lynchers and bystanders. They grow up to inherit the sickness of their ancestors and call it love and order.

Remember what W. E. B. Du Bois told us: "In the treatment of the child the world foreshadows its future and faith."[1] If we want to know who we are and what we could be, we need only look at how we raise, protect, and imagine our children. The measure of a people's soul has always been revealed in the eyes of its youngest.

But this is also a warning for the colonized. For those of us who have survived within the master's world and risk passing on his ways without realizing it. We must excise from our own cultures all that distorts our natural ways of being in kinship with our children. We must strip from our speech the echoes of our oppressors. We must do this because, if the demographic projections are correct, our descendants may one day hold the same kind of power that once devoured us, and if we do not heal, they too may become the lynchers.

Let me return, at the end, to Du Bois's question that opened this book: "Ought children be born to us?" He asked it in an age when the smoke of burned towns still hung in the air. The question has followed every Black generation since.

My answer is an unflinching *YES!*

Yes, because those lynched children saw what this nation truly is, and still they reached for sunlight. Yes, because they are the reason we rise, the reason we fight, the reason we still believe that joy—and the audacity to bring children into this "sneering, cruel world," as Du Bois described it—is act of resistance. Yes, because to love our children out loud, to keep birthing Black futures in the face of so much death, is to declare that the rope did not win.

So, I leave this book where I began, in the shadow of my grandfather's death and the unending life of his story. I offer it not as closure but as witness. To write these pages was to touch every child America tried to erase and to feel them, still warm, still breathing, still here.

TO MY PEOPLE—may we raise children who are not terrified of our hands, our words, and our love. May we dare to love them deliriously and guard them with our lives. Let that be our quiet, terrible promise to white America: We will raise a generation that will not bow, that will refuse your lessons of fear and obedience, that will name your crimes in public and build institutions that render your brutality obsolete. *May we love our children like a revolt.*

TO OUR ANCESTORS—rest now, knowing that we have seen what you saw, and we call it what it is. We carry your story not as a burden but as a compass. You planted in us the stubborn will to live beyond the reach of the rope and the fire, and beyond the lies of empire.

TO OUR CHILDREN—you are the first generation in centuries with the chance to grow up untrained in the reflexes of fear. Guard that miracle with everything you have. Refuse to inherit the myths that murdered us. Refuse to mistake domination for destiny. Remember that your existence is a corrective genius to that history.

AND TO AMERICA—may the ghosts of every child you've buried in silence haunt you until you tell the truth. May you be undone by your own reflection. May you finally understand that every noose you tied was not a weapon against us but a limb of your unhealed and haunted lineage, curling back to choke the hell out of you from within.

We will live, and our living will be your indictment. Our children will laugh at the lie of your dominion, grinding it into dust. And we will raise free children whose joy becomes the architecture of a different country.

ACKNOWLEDGMENTS

Writing a book about the lynching of children is no small feat. It was a heavy, often painful labor, an excavation of buried truths, and a reckoning with the brutal truths of the past. To sit with these stories, to give voice to the silenced, to try to render justice on the page where it was denied in life—all of it weighs on a writer. That weight is why I must acknowledge the people who helped carry that burden with me, who made this book possible, and who reminded me, at every stage, that this work matters.

I am grateful to the team at Beacon Press, a publisher long committed to shining the light on history's darkest corners. I am especially thankful to Rakia Clark, who acquired this book for Beacon, laying the foundation for its journey into the world.

And to my editor, Gayatri Patnaik, who carried it forward with care, conviction, and steady assurance that she had my back. What does that mean to a writer—especially one telling history many would rather forget? It meant everything. It meant I was never alone in this work. It meant I could write without apology or dilution, and that I could guide readers through the horror and history without flinching, knowing you were there, holding the line. Your faith in my voice made all the difference.

I also want to thank the following people who read and engaged with chapters at different stages, offering insight, critique, and encouragement: Jay Driskell, Raymond Winbush, Jeff Menzise, David Levering Lewis, Virginia Yans, Laura Dawkins, Toby Rollo, Mark Naison, Mitch Gerber, William Carrigan, Patricia Bernstein, James Allen, Lara La Dage, the late Rudy Bell, and Yanick Rice Lamb. Your willingness to sit with this work, to challenge and refine it, made the book stronger than I could have made it alone.

This book would not exist without the unwavering support and encouragement of my village family and friends: Faith Hampton Childs, Pamela Newkirk, David and Marina Ottaway, Maureen Craddock, Edna and Damon Williams, Penny and Ruben Britt, Mark and Jennifer Broach, Kirsten West-Savali, Tanya Greenfield, and Sharon Burney. Your faith in me, and in the necessity of this story, kept me moving forward when the emotional weight threatened to break me.

I also acknowledge my biological grandfather and mother. Their deaths left me with questions I may never be able to answer, wounds I can never fully explain. But their passing also lit a fire in me to complete this book, to surface this history, to tell these children's stories with the dignity and humanity they were denied. I also honor Bonzal "Bunny" Hamilton, whose love for children and whose enduring spirit helped keep that fire burning as this work came to life. You are eternal.

And to the Black children who were lynched—to Fred Moore, Emmett Till, Jesse Washington, Alma and Maggie Howze, and the countless others whose names have been lost to time—I cannot bring you back to life. I cannot undo the pain, the terror, the injustice. But my hope is that this book helps to restore your names, your humanity, your rightful place in history. That it serves as a reckoning. That it reminds readers that you were here, that you mattered, that you were loved. And that no matter how hard white supremacy tries to erase, distort, or forget, the truth will not stay crushed to earth. It will live, and it will indict.

ABOUT THE AUTHOR

Dr. Stacey Patton is an award-winning journalist, college professor, historian, and child advocate whose work exposes the deep roots of racial violence and challenges cultural narratives that normalize harm against children. She is the author of *That Mean Old Yesterday* (a memoir), *Spare the Kids: Why Whupping Children Won't Save Black America*, and the children's book *Not My Cat*. Her writings on race, culture, education, and child welfare have appeared in *The New York Times*, *The Washington Post*, *Al Jazeera*, *BBC News*, *The Chronicle of Higher Education*, *NewsOne*, and *Black Enterprise*. Through her teaching, public scholarship, and viral commentary, she has become one of the nation's most incisive and unflinching voices on race, power, and the intergenerational legacies of trauma—and one of the few daring to imagine liberation beginning where it always should have: in childhood.

NOTES

INTRODUCTION: "OUGHT CHILDREN BE BORN TO US?"

1. "'Never Again': Community Reflects on Lynching 115 Years Later," North Texas Conference of the United Methodist Church, Aug. 8, 2023, https://ntcumc.org/news/never-again-community-reflects-on-lynching-115-years-later.
2. See, for example, Jennifer Ritterhouse, *Growing Up Jim Crow: How Black and White Southern Children Learned Race* (Chapel Hill: University of North Carolina Press, 2006); Kristina DuRocher, *Raising Racists: The Socialization of White Children in the Jim Crow South* (Lexington: University Press of Kentucky, 2011); William H. Chafe, Raymond Gavins, and Robert Korstad, eds., *Remembering Jim Crow: African Americans Tell About Life in the Segregated South* (New York: The New Press, 2001); Leon F. Litwack, *Trouble in Mind: Black Southerners in the Age of Jim Crow* (New York: Knopf, 1998); and Margaret A. Burnham, *By Hands Now Known: Jim Crow's Legal Executioners* (New York: W. W. Norton, 2022).
3. W. E. B. Du Bois, *Darkwater: Voices from Within the Veil* (New York: Harcourt, Brace & Howe, 1920), 202; "The Children," *The Crisis* 24 (Oct. 1922): 247; "Of the Giving of Life," *The Crisis* 4 (Oct. 1912): 287.
4. W. E. B. Du Bois, "Of the Passing of the First-Born," reprinted in David Levering Lewis, ed., *W. E. B. Du Bois: A Reader* (New York: Henry Holt, 1995), 103–4.
5. Dominic J. Capeci and Jack C. Knight, "Reckoning with Violence: W. E. B. Du Bois and the 1906 Atlanta Riot," *Journal of Southern History* 62, no. 4 (Nov. 1996): 727–66.
6. W. E. B. Du Bois, *The Autobiography of W. E. B. Du Bois: A Soliloquy on Viewing My Life from the Last Decade of Its First Century* (New York: International Publishers, 1968), 286.
7. Michael J. Pfeifer, *The Roots of Rough Justice: Origins of American Lynching* (Chicago: University of Illinois Press, 2011), 7–11.
8. This is related to what is sometimes called the "adultification" thesis. "Adultification" refers to the phenomenon where Black children are

perceived and treated as being more mature, less innocent, and more culpable than their white peers, leading to harsher treatment and higher expectations that disregard their childhood needs and particular stage of development. See Stacey Patton, "'With My Love': The Colonial Legacy of Racialized Pedophilic Pornography in the Atlantic World," *Childhood & Philosophy* 20 (2024): 34.

9. Steven Mintz, *Huck's Raft: A History of American Childhood* (Cambridge, MA: Belknap Press, 2004), 94. On the treatment of enslaved children, see Kenneth Alan Adams, "The Psychohistory of Child Maltreatment Among Antebellum Slaveholders: Part II," *Journal of Psychohistory* 44, no. 3 (Winter 2017): 178–99; Wilma King, *Stolen Childhood: Slave Youth in Nineteenth-Century America* (Bloomington: Indiana University Press, 1995); and Marie Jenkins Schwartz, *Born in Bondage: Growing Up Enslaved in the Antebellum South* (Cambridge, MA: Harvard University Press, 2001). In 1860, at least 56 percent of the enslaved population in the United States was under twenty years of age. Between 1830 to 1860, the number of enslaved children under age ten remained consistent at over 30 percent of the enslaved population. See Karen Sanchez-Eppler, "'Remember, Dear, When the Yankees Came Through Here, I Was Only Ten Years Old': Valuing the Enslaved Child of the WPA Slave Narratives," in *Child Slavery Before and After Emancipation: An Argument for Child-Centered Slavery Studies*, ed. Anna Mae Duane (New York: Cambridge University Press, 2017), 29–30.
10. C. Vann Woodward, *The Strange Career of Jim Crow* (New York: Oxford University Press, 2001); Douglas A. Blackmon, *Slavery by Another Name: The Re-enslavement of Black Americans from the Civil War to World War II* (New York: Anchor Books, 2009).
11. Carol Anderson, *White Rage: The Unspoken Truth of Our Racial Divide* (New York: Bloomsbury, 2016).
12. The sources below provide a foundation for understanding how ingrained attitudes and conditioned responses to racial dynamics can alter neurological development and stress responses, embedding racist behaviors and violent tendencies into biology. The concept of epigenetic changes influencing behavior and being passed down through generations offers insight into how these patterns can persist subconsciously, functioning as an "epigenetic tick." See Thomas Carpenter, Sheila Grecian, and Rebecca Reynolds, "Sex Differences in Early Life Programming of the Hypothalamic-Pituitary-Adrenal Axis in Humans Suggest Increased Vulnerability in Females," *Psychoneuroendocrinology* 61 (2015): 32–39; G. P. Chrousos, "Stress and Disorders of the Stress System," *Nature Reviews Endocrinology* 5, no. 7 (2009): 374–81; Victoria K. Cortessis et al., "Environmental Epigenetics: Prospects for Studying Epigenetic Mediation of Exposure-Response Relationships," *Human*

Genetics 131, no. 10 (2012): 1565–89; Yael Danieli, ed., *International Handbook of Multigenerational Legacies of Trauma* (New York: Plenum Press, 1998); and Nikolaos P. Daskalakis et al., "Expression Profiling Associates Blood and Brain Glucocorticoid Receptor Signaling with Trauma-Related Individual Differences in Both Sexes," *Proceedings of the National Academy of Sciences* 111, no. 35 (2014): 13529–34. The concept of the "epigenetic tick" suggests that racist behaviors and environments can produce biological changes passed across generations. Stress and trauma from racial violence or hostility may alter gene expression, embedding racial conditioning in the body and influencing subconscious behavior. Racial attitudes are also transmitted psychologically and socially, especially during early childhood. According to Albert Bandura's social learning theory, children absorb biases by observing caregivers, while John Bowlby's attachment theory shows how emotional bonds formed in prejudiced contexts shape identity. Neuroscience research further indicates that racial trauma can alter brain function, though direct evidence linking these changes to the transmission of racist ideology remains limited.

13. Neuroscientific studies consistently show that early and repeated exposure to violence—particularly during childhood—produces lasting changes in brain architecture. These changes impair emotional regulation, increase hypervigilance, and blunt empathic response by altering activity in key regions such as the amygdala, hippocampus, and prefrontal cortex. Such neurobiological effects help explain how individuals conditioned by violence may normalize harm and perpetuate it across generations. Charlotte Heleniak et al., "Childhood Maltreatment Exposure and Disruptions in Emotion Regulation: A Transdiagnostic Pathway to Adolescent Internalizing and Externalizing Psychopathology," *Cognitive Therapy and Research* 40, no. 3 (2016): 394–415; Nim Tottenham et al., "Amygdala Response to Mother," *Developmental Science* 15, no. 3 (2012): 307–19; Martin H. Teicher and Jacqueline A. Samson, "Annual Research Review: Enduring Neurobiological Effects of Childhood Abuse and Neglect," *Journal of Child Psychology and Psychiatry* 57, no. 3 (Mar. 2016): 241–66.
14. *The Crisis* 8, no. 6 (Oct. 1914): 292.
15. Kenneth Alan Adams, "Lynching, Sacrifice, and Childrearing in the New South," *Journal of Psychohistory* 45, no. 4 (Spring 2018): 261.
16. Frederick Douglass, *My Bondage and My Freedom* (New York: Miller, Orton & Mulligan, 1855), 328.
17. Stacey Patton and Toby Rollo, "Black Children Are Not Being Killed Because They Are 'Adultified.' They're Killed Because They're Black," NewsOne, June 3, 2021, https://newsone.com/4160834/black-children-adultification.

18. Ralph Ginzburg, *100 Years of Lynching* (Baltimore: Black Classics Press, 1988), 221.
19. For more in-depth discussions on lynching data, see W. Fitzhugh Brundage, *Lynching in the New South: Georgia and Virginia, 1880–1930* (Urbana: University of Illinois Press, 1993); Stewart E. Tolnay and E. M. Beck, *A Festival of Violence: An Analysis of Southern Lynchings, 1882–1930* (Urbana: University of Illinois Press, 1995); and Arthur F. Raper, *The Tragedy of Lynching* (Chapel Hill: University of North Carolina Press, 1933).
20. Amy Kate Bailey and Stewart E. Tolnay, *Lynched: The Victims of Southern Mob Violence* (Chapel Hill: University of North Carolina Press, 2015), 63, 66.
21. Vincent Vinikas, "Thirteen Dead at St. Charles: Arkansas's Most Lethal Lynching and the Abrogation of Equal Protection," in *Bullets and Fire: Lynching and Authority in Arkansas, 1840–1950*, ed. Guy Lancaster (Fayetteville: University of Arkansas Press, 2018), 108.
22. Helen McLure, "'I Suppose You Think Strange the Murder of Women and Children': The American Culture of Collective Violence, 1652–1930" (PhD diss., Southern Methodist University, 2009), 6, 19.

CHAPTER 1: "THE FUN WE HAD BURNING THE NIGGERS"

1. On sensory processing in children, see Winnie Dunn, "Supporting Children to Participate Successfully in Everyday Life by Using Sensory Processing Knowledge," *Infants and Young Children* 20, no. 2 (Apr. 2007): 84–101. On how environment shapes children's brains, see Rhoshel K. Lenroot and Jay N. Giedd, "The Changing Impact of Genes and Environment on Brain Development During Childhood and Adolescence: Initial Findings from a Neuroimaging Study of Pediatric Twins," *Development and Psychopathology* 20, no. 4 (2008): 1161–75; Kartik Shankar et al., "Environmental Forces That Shape Early Development: What We Know and Still Need to Know," *Current Developments in Nutrition* 2, no. 8 (Aug. 2018): nzx002; and Ursula A. Tooley, Danielle S. Bassett, and Allyson P. Mackey, "Environmental Influences on the Pace of Brain Development," *Nature Reviews Neuroscience* 22 (2021): 372–84.
2. Nim Tottenham, Todd A. Hare, and B. J. Casey, "A Developmental Perspective on Human Amygdala Function," in *The Human Amygdala*, ed. Paul J. Whalen and Elizabeth A. Phelps (New York: Guilford Press, 2009), 107–17.
3. For a more detailed discussion on the brain as a social organ and moderator of stress, see Louis Cozolino, *The Social Neuroscience of Education: Optimizing Attachment and Learning in the Classroom* (New York: W. W. Norton, 2013), 110.

4. Renate L. E. P. Reniers et al., "Moral Decision-Making, ToM, Empathy and the Default Mode Network," *Biological Psychology* 90, no. 3 (July 2012): 202–10; Seung Jun Kim et al., "Altered Functional Connectivity of the Default Mode Network in Low-Empathy Subjects," *Yonsei Medical Journal* 58, no. 5 (2017): 1061–65; and Wangqing Li, Xiaoqin Mai, and Chao Liu, "The Default Mode Network and Social Understanding of Others: What Do Brain Connectivity Studies Tell Us," *Frontiers of Human Neuroscience* 24, no. 8 (Feb. 2014): 74.
5. On attachment theory, see M. D. S. Ainsworth, "The Development of Infant-Mother Attachment," in *Review of Child Development Research*, vol. 3, ed. Bettye M. Cardwell and Henry N. Ricciuti (Chicago: University of Chicago Press, 1973), 1–94; John Bowlby, "The Nature of the Child's Tie to His Mother," *International Journal of Psychoanalysis* 39 (1958): 350–71; and Patricia Draper and Jay Belsky, "Personality Development in the Evolutionary Perspective," *Journal of Personality and Social Psychology* 58, no. 1 (1990): 141–61. For a discussion on the basic tenets of attachment theory, see Ross A. Thompson, "Twenty-First Century Attachment Theory: Challenges and Opportunities," in *The Cultural Nature of Attachment: Contextualizing Relationships and Development*, ed. Heidi Keller and Kim A. Bard (Cambridge, MA: MIT Press, 2017), 301–21; and Judi Mesman, Marinus H. van Ijzendoorn, and Abraham Sagi-Schwartz, "Cross-Cultural Patterns of Attachment: Universal and Contextual Dimensions," in *Handbook of Attachment: Theory, Research, and Clinical Applications*, ed. Jude Cassidy and Phillip R. Shaver (New York: Guilford, 2016), 790–815.
6. Kate Teffer and Katerina Semendeferi, "Human Prefrontal Cortex: Evolution, Development, and Pathology," *Progress in Brain Research* 195 (2012): 191–218; María Beatriz Jurado and Mónica Rosselli, "The Elusive Nature of Executive Functions: A Review of Our Current Understanding," *Neuropsychology Review* 17, no. 3 (2007): 213–33; Earl K. Miller, "Prefrontal Cortex and the Neural Basis of Executive Functions," in *Attention, Space, and Action: Studies in Cognitive Neuroscience*, ed. Glyn W. Humphreys, John Duncan, and Anne Treisman (Oxford: Oxford University Press, 1999), 250–72; Earl K. Miller and Jonathan D. Cohen, "An Integrative Theory of Prefrontal Cortex Function," *Annual Review of Neuroscience* 24, no. 1 (2001): 167–202; Matthew C. Davidson et al., "Development of Cognitive Control and Executive Functions from 4 to 13 Years: Evidence from Manipulations of Memory, Inhibition, and Task Switching," *Neuropsychologica* 44, no. 11 (2006): 2037–78; and Joaquín M. Fuster, "Executive Frontal Functions," *Experimental Brain Research* 133, no. 1 (2000): 66–70.
7. The sources below collectively underscore the importance of a biosocial perspective in understanding how exposure to violence and trauma

during childhood can become biologically embedded, affecting brain development and the nervous system. This embedding can condition children to accept and enact racial violence as normalized behavior throughout their lives. By integrating insights from developmental psychology and neuroscience, the biosocial perspective can contribute to a deeper understanding of the mechanisms driving the intergenerational perpetuation of racial violence. See Charolotte Heleniak et al., "Childhood Maltreatment Exposure and Disruptions in Emotion Regulation: A Transdiagnostic Pathway to Adolescent Internalizing and Externalizing Psychopathology," *Cognitive Therapy and Research* 40, no. 3 (2016): 394–415. Heleniak explores social-cognitive mechanisms in the cycle of violence, demonstrating how childhood exposure to violence impacts emotional regulation and aggression. For a discussion of the biosocial bases of criminal behavior, with an emphasis on the role of genetic and neurobiological factors interacting with social environments, see Sarnoff A. Mednick and Karl O. Christiansen, eds., *Biosocial Bases of Criminal Behavior* (New York: Gardner Press, 1977). For empirical evidence on how early biological vulnerabilities combined with adverse social experiences predispose individuals to violent crime, see Adrian Raine, Patricia A. Brennan, and Sarnoff A. Mednick, "Birth Complications Combined with Early Maternal Rejection at Age 1 Year Predispose to Violent Crime at Age 18 Years," *Archives of General Psychiatry* 51, no. 12 (1994): 984–88. A comprehensive review by Raine highlights various biosocial factors, including genetic influences and early social environments, that contribute to antisocial and violent behaviors; see Adrian Raine, *The Psychopathology of Crime: Criminal Behavior as a Clinical Disorder* (San Diego, CA: Academic Press, 1993).

8. For a good discussion of how Marsh captured integrated urban spaces in his work, see Carmenita Higginbotham, *The Urban Scene: Race, Reginald Marsh, and American Art* (University Park: Penn State Press, 2015).
9. *The Olla Podrida* (Lawrenceville, NJ: The Lawrenceville School, 1916), unpaginated (p. 33).
10. "Abolish the Reality," *Omaha Guide*, Mar. 16, 1935, 7; "Crowd Attends Lynching Exhibit," *Carolina Tribune*, Mar. 2, 1935, 1.
11. Quoted in "An Art Exhibit Against Lynching," *The Crisis* (Apr. 1935): 106.
12. "Young Negroes Hang from Tree Near Columbus," *Corsicana (TX) Semi-Weekly Light*, Nov. 15, 1935, 1; "Negro Youths Are Hanged by a Mob of 700," *Big Spring (TX) Daily Herald*, Nov. 13, 1935, 1; "County Attorney Says Lynchings Will of People," *Austin American*, Nov. 14, 1935; "Lynchings Stir Southern Debate," *Literary Digest*, Nov. 23, 1935; "The Columbus Lynching," *Houston Press*, Nov. 14, 1935.
13. DuRocher, *Raising Racists*, 103, 116.

14. Ida B. Wells, "A Red Record," in *Southern Horrors and Other Writings: The Antilynching Campaign of Ida B. Wells, 1892–1900*, ed. Jacqueline Jones Royster (Boston: Bedford, 1997), 115–16.
15. Walter White, *Rope and Faggot: A Biography of Judge Lynch* (Notre Dame, IN: University of Notre Dame Press, 2002), 2.
16. White, *Rope and Faggot*, 2.

CHAPTER 2: FROM THE NURSERY TO THE GALLOWS

1. John Laurence, *A History of Capital Punishment, with Special Reference to Capital Punishment in Great Britain* (London: Sampson Low, Marston & Co., 1932), 18.
2. "Youth on the Scaffold," *Nottingham Evening Post*, May 19, 1932.
3. Lloyd deMause, "The Evolution of Childhood," in *The History of Childhood*, ed. Lloyd deMause (New York: Harper & Row, 1975), 1.
4. W. E. B. Du Bois, *Darkwater: Voices from Within the Veil* (New York: Harcourt, Brace and Howe, 1920), 230.
5. Joseph Zornado, *Inventing the Child: Culture, Ideology, and the Story of Childhood* (New York: Garland, 2001).
6. Marina Warner, *No Go the Bogeyman: Scaring, Lulling, and Making Mock* (New York: Farrar, Straus and Giroux, 1998).
7. Maria Tatar, *The Hard Facts of the Grimms' Fairy Tales* (Princeton, NJ: Princeton University Press, 1987).
8. Maria Tatar, *Off with Their Heads! Fairy Tales and the Culture of Childhood* (Princeton, NJ: Princeton University Press, 1992).
9. Mitchell B. Merback, *The Thief, the Cross, and the Wheel: Pain and the Spectacle of Punishment in Medieval and Renaissance Europe* (Chicago: University of Chicago Press, 1999), 294.
10. V. A. C. Gatrell, *The Hanging Tree: Execution and the English People, 1770–1868* (New York: Oxford University Press, 1996), 392.
11. Research shows that early exposure to violence influences brain areas involved in processing emotional cues and regulating emotional responses, potentially leading to mental health challenges like anxiety and PTSD. See Matthew Peverill et al., "Childhood Trauma and Brain Structure in Children and Adolescents," *Developmental Cognitive Neuroscience* 59 (2023): 1–9. This study explores how exposure to violence can lead to structural changes in brain regions associated with emotional regulation, like the anterior cingulate cortex (ACC) and the amygdala. See also Katie A. McLaughlin et al., "Violence Exposure and Brain Development in Children," Stress & Development Lab, Harvard University, n.d., https://sdlab.fas.harvard.edu/violence-exposure-and-brain-development-children.
12. Toby Rollo, "The Color of Childhood," *Journal of Black Studies* 49, no. 4 (2018): 307–29; Toby Rollo, "Feral Children: Settler Colonialism,

Progress, and the Figure of the Child," *Settler Colonial Studies* 8, no. 1 (2018): 60–79.

13. Tracie O. Afifi et al., "The Relationships Between Harsh Physical Punishment and Child Maltreatment in Childhood and Intimate Partner Violence in Adulthood," *BMC Public Health* 17, no. 493 (2017): 1–10; Larry Baron and Murray A. Straus, "Four Theories of Rape: A Macrosociological Analyses," *Social Problems* 34 (1987): 467–89; Larry Baron, Murray A. Straus, and David Jaffee, "Legitimate Violence, Violent Attitudes, and Rape: A Test of Cultural Spillover Theory," *Annals New York Academy of Sciences* 528, no. 1 (1988): 79–110; David S. Black, Steve Sussman, and Jennifer B. Unger, "A Further Look at the Intergenerational Transmission of Violence: Witnessing Interparental Violence in Emerging Adulthood," *Journal of Interpersonal Violence* 25, no. 6 (2010): 1022–42; Emily M. Douglas and Murray A. Straus, "Assault and Injury of Dating Partners by University Students in 19 Countries and Its Relation to Corporal Punishment Experienced as a Child," *European Journal of Criminology* 3, no. 3 (2006): 293–318; Manuel Gámez-Guadix, Murray A. Straus, and Scott L. Hershberger, "Childhood and Adolescent Victimization and Perpetration of Sexual Coercion by Male and Female University Students," *Deviant Behavior* 32 (2011): 712–42; Manuel Gámez-Guadix et al., "Corporal Punishment and Long-Term Behavior Problems: The Moderating Role of Positive Parenting and Psychological Aggression," *Psicothema* 22, no. 4 (2010): 529–36; Elizabeth Thompson Gershoff, "Corporal Punishment by Parents and Associated Child Behaviors and Experiences: A Meta-analytic and Theoretical Review," *Psychological Bulletin* 128, no. 4 (2002): 539–79; Elizabeth T. Gershoff, "More Harm Than Good: A Summary of Scientific Research on the Intended and Unintended Effects of Corporal Punishment on Children," *Law and Contemporary Problems* 73 (2010): 31–56; Stephanie Holt, Helen Buckley, and Sadhbh Whelan, "The Impact of Exposure to Domestic Violence on Children and Young People: A Review of the Literature," *Child Abuse and Neglect* 32, no. 8 (2008): 797–810; Jennifer E. Lansford and Kenneth A. Dodge, "Cultural Norms for Adult Corporal Punishment of Children and Societal Rates of Endorsement and Use of Violence," *Parenting* 8, no. 3 (2008) 257–70; Murray A. Straus, "Discipline and Deviance: Physical Punishment of Children and Violence and Other Crime in Adulthood," *Social Problems* 38, no. 2 (1991): 133–54; Murray A. Straus, "New Theory and Old Canards About Family Violence Research," *Social Problems* 38, no. 2 (1991): 180–97; M. A. Straus, "Spanking and the Making of a Violent Society," *Pediatrics* 98, no. 4 (1996): 837–42; Murray A. Straus, "The Special Issue on Prevention of Violence Ignores the Primordial Violence," *Journal of Interpersonal Violence* 23, no. 9 (2008): 1314–20; Murray A.

Straus, "Prevalence, Societal Causes, and Trends in Corporal Punishment by Parents in World Perspective," *Law and Contemporary Problems* 73 (2010): 1–30; Murray A. Straus and Mallie J. Paschall, "Corporal Punishment by Mothers and Development of Children's Cognitive Ability: A Longitudinal Study of Two Nationally Representative Age Cohorts," *Journal of Aggression, Maltreatment & Trauma* 18, no. 5 (2009): 459–83; Murray A. Straus and Carrie L. Yodanis, "Corporal Punishment in Adolescence and Physical Assaults on Spouses in Later Life: What Accounts for the Link?," *Journal of Marriage and the Family* 58, no. 4 (1996): 825–41; Yvonne M. Vissing et al., "Verbal Aggression by Parents and Psychosocial Problems of Children," *Child Abuse & Neglect* 15, no. 3 (1991): 223–38.

14. Stuart Banner, *The Death Penalty: An American History* (Cambridge, MA: Harvard University Press, 2002), 11.
15. Coventry Patmore, *The Poems of Coventry Patmore* (London: Chatto & Windus, 1941), 56–57.
16. Joel Kovel, *White Racism: A Psychohistory* (New York: Pantheon, 1970), 47, 251.
17. William B. Thesing, *The London Stages of Thomas Hardy* (Gainesville: University Press of Florida, 1990), 114.
18. Gatrell, *The Hanging Tree*, 69. See also George Hall, *The Gypsy's Parson: His Experiences and Adventures* (London: Marston, 1915), 17; Rachel E. Bennett, *Capital Punishment and the Criminal Corpse in Scotland, 1740–1834* (London: Palgrave Macmillan, 2017), ch. 6; and Sarah Tarlow and Emma Battell Lowman, *Harnessing the Power of the Criminal Corpse* (Cham, Switzerland: Palgrave Macmillan, 2018), ch. 5.
19. Elizabeth T. Hurren, *Dissecting the Criminal Corpse: Staging Post-execution Punishment in Early Modern England* (Basingstoke: Palgrave Macmillan, 2016).
20. Bennett, *Capital Punishment and the Criminal Corpse in Scotland*, 2, 52.
21. Bennett, *Capital Punishment and the Criminal Corpse in Scotland*, 170.
22. Bennett, *Capital Punishment and the Criminal Corpse in Scotland*, ch. 6.
23. Bennett, *Capital Punishment and the Criminal Corpse in Scotland*, 178–79.
24. Owen Davies and Francesca Matteoni, *Executing Magic in the Modern Era: Criminal Bodies and the Gallows in Popular Medicine* (Houndmills, UK: Palgrave Macmillan, 2017), 34.
25. Charles Knight, *Passages of a Working Life During a Half Century: With a Prelude of Early Reminiscences*, 2 vols. (London: Bradbury & Evans, 1864–65), 140–41.
26. For a more detailed history on the post-execution tradition of gibbeting, see Samantha Priestley, *The History of Gibbeting: Britain's Most Brutal Punishment* (Barnsley, UK: Pen and Sword Books, 2020); and Sarah

Tarlow, *The Golden and Ghoulish Age of the Gibbet in Britain* (New York: Palgrave Macmillan, 2015).

27. Quoted in Gatrell, *The Hanging Tree*, 6.
28. Gatrell, *The Hanging Tree*, 6.
29. Gatrell, *The Hanging Tree*, 246.
30. "Burning for Murder," *Notes and Queries* (1883), quoted in Gatrell, *The Hanging Tree*, 248.
31. "Hanging In Chains," *Notes and Queries* (1883), 394, https://www.google.com/books/edition/Notes_and_Queries/224CAAAAIAAJ?hl=en&gbpv=1&dq=The+scene+around+the+gibbet+was+certainly+most+disgraceful,+and+truly+like+a+fair,&pg=PA394&printsec=frontcover.
32. Monica-Maria Stapelberg, *Through the Darkness: Glimpses into the History of Western Medicine* (London: Crux, 2016), 25.
33. Thomas Hardy, *The Collected Letters of Thomas Hardy*, vol. 1 (1840–1892), ed. Richard Little Purdy and Michael Millgate (Oxford: Clarendon Press, 1978), 49.
34. For childhood or firsthand accounts of witnessing public executions, see Samuel Pepys, *The Diary of Samuel Pepys*, 11 vols., ed. Robert Latham and William Matthews (Berkeley: University of California Press, 1970–83); James Boswell, *Boswell in Search of a Wife, 1766–1769*, ed. Frank Brady and Frederick A. Pottle (London: Heinemann, 1957), 265–66; Johann Wolfgang von Goethe, *From My Life: Poetry and Truth*, trans. Robert R. Heitner (New York: Suhrkamp, 1987), bk. 3; William Makepeace Thackeray, "On Going to See a Man Hanged," *Fraser's Magazine* 22 (Aug. 1840): 150–58; Charles Dickens, "A Visit to Newgate," in *Sketches by Boz* (London: John Macrone, 1836); Charles Dickens, *The Letters of Charles Dickens*, vol. 5, ed. Madeline House et al. (Oxford: Clarendon Press, 1981), 476–77; and George Gordon Byron, *Byron's Letters and Journals*, 12 vols., ed. Leslie A. Marchand (Cambridge, MA: Harvard University Press, 1973–94), vol. 5.
35. George Gordon Byron, *Life, Letters, and Journals of Lord Byron* (London: Murray, 1854), 357.
36. Sigmund Freud, *Beyond the Pleasure Principle*, trans. and ed. James Strachey (New York: W. W. Norton, 1961), ch. 1.
37. Resmaa Menakem, *My Grandmother's Hands: Racialized Trauma and the Pathway to Mending Our Hearts and Bodies* (Las Vegas: Central Recovery Press, 2017), 12.
38. Mark Wolynn, *It Didn't Start with You: How Inherited Family Trauma Shapes Who We Are and How to End the Cycle* (New York: Penguin, 2016).
39. Christian Laes, *Children in the Roman Empire: Outsiders Within* (Cambridge: Cambridge University Press, 2006), ch. 5; George Mousourakis, *Fundamentals of Roman Private Law* (New York: Springer,

2012), 88–91; Jonathan Edmondson, "Slavery and the Roman Family," in *The Cambridge World History of Slavery*, vol. 1, *The Ancient Mediterranean World*, ed. Keith Bradley and Paul Cartledge (Cambridge: Cambridge University Press, 2011), 358; Christian Laes, "Child Beating in Roman Antiquity: Some Reconsiderations," in *Hoping for Continuity: Childhood, Education and Death in Antiquity and the Middle Ages*, ed. Katariina Mustakallio et al. (Rome: Institutum Romanum Finlandiae, 2005), 81; Chrysanthi Gallou, "Children at Work in Mycenaean Greece (c. 1680–1050 BCE): A Brief Survey," in *Childhood and Violence in the Western Tradition*, ed. Laurence Brockliss and Heather Montgomery (Barnsley, UK: Oxbow Books, 2010); Philip Greven, *Spare the Child: The Religious Roots of Punishment and the Psychological Impact of Physical Abuse* (New York: Alfred A. Knopf, 1990); Jane Humphries, "Childhood and Violence in Working-Class England, 1800–1870," in Brockliss and Montgomery, *Childhood and Violence in the Western Tradition*.

40. Laes, *Children in the Roman Empire*, ch. 5; Mousourakis, *Fundamentals of Roman Private Law*, 88–91; Edmondson, "Slavery and the Roman Family," 388; Laes, "Child Beating in Roman Antiquity," 75–89.
41. Louis P. Masur, *Rites of Execution: Capital Punishment and the Transformation of American Culture, 1776–1865* (New York: Oxford University Press, 1991), 36.
42. Norbert Elias, *Power and Civility* (New York: Pantheon, 1982), 245.
43. See, for example, Richard C. Trexler, "Infanticide in Florence: New Sources and First Results," *History of Childhood Quarterly* 1 (1973): 98–116; Richard C. Trexler, "The Foundlings of Florence, 1395–1455," *History of Childhood Quarterly* 1 (1973): 259–84; Emily R. Coleman, "Medieval Marriage Characteristics: A Neglected Factor in the History of Medieval Serfdom," *Journal of Interdisciplinary History* 2 (1971): 207–15; S. Ryan Johansson, "Centuries of Childhood/Centuries of Parenting: Philippe Ariès and the Modernization of Privileged Infancy," *Journal of Family History* 12 (1987): 355; Lloyd deMause, "The Formation of the American Personality Through Psychospeciation: Appendix: On the Demography or Filicide," *Journal of Psychohistory* 4 (1976): 1–30; Barbara A. Kellum, "Infanticide in England in the Later Middle Ages," *History of Childhood Quarterly* 1 (1974): 367–88; and R. H. Helmholz, "Infanticide in the Province of Canterbury During the Fifteenth Century," *History of Childhood Quarterly* 1 (Winter 1974): 379–90.
44. For example, Philippe Ariès's *Centuries of Childhood: A Social History of Family Life* (New York: Knopf Doubleday, 1965) emphasizes how children were often treated as miniature adults and subjected to harsh discipline, reflecting broader societal and Christian norms. James A.

Schultz's *The Knowledge of Childhood in the German Middle Ages, 1100–1350* (Philadelphia: University of Pennsylvania Press, 1995) provides insight into how children were viewed as property, highlighting the severe control exerted over them by fathers, justified by Christian doctrine and medieval law. Lawrence Stone's *The Family, Sex and Marriage in England 1500–1800* (New York: Harper & Row, 1979) documents the strict control parents had over their children in early modern England, illustrating how legal and cultural frameworks supported corporal punishment and the subjugation of children, reflecting deep-seated patriarchal and Christian values. Hugh Cunningham's *Children and Childhood in Western Society Since 1500* (New York: Longman, 1995) explores the evolution of attitudes toward children in Western society, showing how religious and philosophical ideas justified strict discipline and control over children, establishing a tradition of harsh treatment. Michel Foucault's *Discipline and Punish: The Birth of the Prison* (New York: Pantheon Books, 1977) discusses the application of strict disciplinary measures to children, influenced by dominant cultural and religious ideologies, which viewed harsh punishment as essential for instilling proper behavior.

45. Matthew S. Kuefler, "'A Wryed Existence': Attitudes Toward Children in Anglo-Saxon England," *Journal of Social History* 24, no. 4 (1991): 823–34.
46. Oana-Maria Cojocaru, *Byzantine Childhood: Representations and Experiences of Children in Middle Byzantine Society* (New York: Routledge, 2021).
47. Avner Giladi, *Children of Islam: Concepts of Childhood in Medieval Muslim Society* (New York: Springer, 1992); Kristina Richardson, "Singing Slave Girls (Qiyan) of the Abbasid Court in the Ninth and Tenth Centuries," in *Children in Slavery Through the Ages*, ed. Gwyn Campbell, Suzanne Miers, and Joseph C. Miller (Athens: Ohio University Press, 2009), 105–17; Gülay Yilmaz and Fruma Zachs, eds., *Children and Childhood in the Ottoman Empire: From the 15th to the 20th Century* (Edinburgh: Edinburgh University Press, 2021); Gülay Yilmaz, "Becoming a Devşirme: The Training of Conscripted Children in the Ottoman Empire," in Campbell et al., *Children in Slavery Through the Ages*, 119–35.
48. Stacey Patton, *Spare the Kids: Why Whupping Children Won't Save Black America* (Boston: Beacon Press, 2017), 55–57.
49. Pauline K. Gallou, "Children in Servitude: Child Labour in the Ancient World," in *The Archaeology of Slavery: A Comparative Approach to Captivity and Coercion*, ed. Lydia M. Wilson and Nicholas J. Saunders (Oxford: Archaeopress, 2010), 167–70.
50. Gatrell, *The Hanging Tree*, 512.

51. Barbara A. Hanawalt, *Growing Up in Medieval London: The Experience of Childhood in History* (New York: Oxford University Press, 1993), 213.
52. Gatrell, *The Hanging Tree*, 566–71.
53. Dave Mossop, "Juvenile Executions in Britain," Capital Punishment UK Research Database, accessed March 1, 2026, https://www.capitalpunishmentuk.org/juvenile.html.

CHAPTER 3: "MY SON CAN'T LEARN TOO YOUNG THE PROPER WAY TO TREAT A NIGGER"

1. Susan Schuyler, "Gallows Drama: Public Execution, Crowds, and Victorian Theater," *Nineteenth Century Studies* 22, no. 1 (Jan. 2008); Barry Faulk, "The Public Execution: Urban Rhetoric and Victorian Crows," in *Executions in the British Experience*, ed. William B. Thesing (Jefferson, NC: McFarland, 1990), 77–91; Pieter Spierenburg, *The Spectacle of Suffering: Execution of Repression, from a Preindustrial Metropolis to the European Experience* (Cambridge: Cambridge University Press, 1984).
2. Joe Holley, "Famous Photograph Documents 1916 Lynching in Waco," *Houston Chronicle*, May 6, 2016.
3. Anne P. Rice, *Witnessing Lynching: American Writers Respond* (New Brunswick, NJ: Rutgers University Press, 2003), 148.
4. *Waco Morning News*, May 10, 1916.
5. "The Waco Horror," *The Crisis* 12, no. 3 (1916).
6. *Waco Morning News*, May 16, 1916.
7. "The Waco Horror."
8. *Waco Semi-Weekly Herald Tribune*, May 17, 1916.
9. *Waco Times Herald*, May 16, 1916.
10. "Southern White Gentlemen Burn Race Boy at Stake," *Chicago Defender*, May 20, 1916, 1.
11. "Texas Black Is Burned at Stake," *Chickasha (OK) Daily Express*, May 15, 1916.
12. *Waco Morning News*, May 16, 1916.
13. Patricia Bernstein, *The First Waco Horror: The Lynching of Jesse Washington and the Rise of the NAACP* (College Station: Texas A&M University Press, 2006), 153.
14. "The Waco Horror."
15. *1916 Waco High School Annual, The Daisy Chain* (Waco, TX: Waco High School, 1916), 38.
16. "Waco Horror," *Chicago Defender*, May 20, 1916, 1.
17. Harvey Young, "The Black Body as Souvenir in American Lynching," *Theatre Journal* 57, no. 4 (2005): 653.
18. Saundra Goodman, *Got Teeth? A Survivor's Guide* (Indianapolis: Dog Ear Publishing, 2007), 48–49; Christine Quigley, *The Corpse: A History* (Jefferson, NC: McFarland, 2015), 219.

19. *New York Age*, May 25, 1916.
20. *Chicago Defender*, May 20, 1916, 1; *Blackfoot Optimist*, May 18, 1916; *New York Times*, May 17, 1916.
21. James Baldwin, *No Name in the Street* (New York: Dial Press, 1972), 198.

CHAPTER 4: "THE TIME FOR YOU TO DIE IS COME"

1. J. North Conway, *Crime Time: Twenty True Tales of Murder, Madness, and Mayhem* (New York: Rowman & Littlefield, 2021), 25.
2. *Connecticut Courant and Weekly Intelligencer* (Hartford), July 31, 1786.
3. Hannah Ocuish's guilt has been called into question in recent years by the New London chapter of the NAACP, along with historians, tribal members, the Connecticut Innocence Project, and legal experts, who are investigating whether racial bias led to an unjust conviction and execution.
4. Henry Channing, *God Admonishing His People of Their Duty, as Parents and Masters: A Sermon, Preached at New-London, December 20th, 1786, Occasioned by the Execution of Hannah Ocuish, a Mulatto Girl, Aged 12 Years and 9 Months, for the Murder of Eunice Bolles, Aged 6 Years and 6 Months* (New London, CT: T. Green, 1786). See also Karen Florin, "Centuries-Old Murder Case to Be Revisited in New London," *The Day*, Mar. 7, 2020; Jessica Suess, "The Heinous Execution of Hannah Ocuish, Aged 12, by the State of Connecticut," *Odd Feed*, Feb. 17, 2023; and Julie Stagis, "A Girl, 12, Is Hanged in Connecticut for Murder in 1786," *Hartford Courant*, Nov. 2, 2021.
5. Crystal Webster, "Hanging Pretty Girls," *Journal of the Early Republic* 42, no. 2 (2022): 253–76.
6. See, for example, Webster, "Hanging Pretty Girls," 273; and Nancy Hathaway Steenburg, "'Not of Full Age': Children and the Criminal Law in Connecticut, 1635–1855" (PhD diss., University of Connecticut, 2002), 8.
7. Boyd M. Berry, "The First English Pediatricians and Tudor Attitudes Toward Childhood," *Journal of the History of Ideas* 35, no. 4 (1974): 561–77.
8. Geraldine Youcha, *Minding the Children: Child Care in America from Colonial Times to the Present* (New York: Scribner, 1996).
9. John Calvin, *Institutes of the Christian Religion*, ed. and trans. Ford Lewis Battles (1536; repr., Grand Rapids, MI: H. H. Meeter Center for Calvin Studies/William B. Eerdmans, 1975), 97.
10. Cotton Mather, *A Family Well-Ordered: Or, An Essay to Render Parents and Children Happy in One Another, Handling Two Very Important Cases* (Boston: B. Green and J. Allen, 1699), https://quod.lib.umich.edu/e/evans/N00727.0001.001.
11. Richard Baxter, *A Christian Directory: Or, A Summ of Practical Theologie, and Cases of Conscience, Directing Christians, How to Use Their*

Knowledge and Faith, How to Improve All Helps and Means, and to Perform All Duties, How to Overcome Temptations, and to Escape or Mortifie Every Sin (London: R. White, 1673).

12. John Robinson, "Of Children and Their Education," in *The Works of John Robinson: Pastor of the Pilgrim Fathers*, ed. Robert Ashton (London: John Snow, 1851), 231–32.
13. Robert V. Schnucker, "Puritan Attitudes Towards Childhood Discipline, 1560–1634," in *Women as Mothers in Pre-Industrial England*, ed. Valerie Fildes (New York: Routledge, 2013), 108, 114.
14. John R. Sutton, *Stubborn Children: Controlling Delinquency in the United States, 1640–1981*, vol. 2 (Berkeley: University of California Press, 1988).
15. *The Laws and Liberties of Massachusetts* (1648; repr., Cambridge, MA: Harvard University Press, 1929), 23–24.
16. Sutton, *Stubborn Children*, 239.
17. It should be noted that the Puritans found themselves in an ideological bind. If God has already determined the fate of a child's soul, then what is the purpose of harsh discipline? If children, like all humanity, are irredeemable because of original sin, and only saved through the grace of God, then how could one even hope to beat children into obedience? As Sutton explains it, "How could Puritan authorities consistently require the application of their techniques of child training and also insist on the reality of the child's depravity and the inscrutability of grace? Maintenance of the colony required one, while theology dictated the other" (Sutton, *Stubborn Children*, 36).
18. Joseph S. Clark, "How the Puritans Trained their Children," *Massachusetts Teacher* 13, no. 12 (1860): 446–54; Kathryn Sather, "Sixteenth and Seventeenth Century Child-Rearing: A Matter of Discipline," *Journal of Social History* 22, no. 4 (1989): 735–43.
19. Jupiter Hammon, *An Address to the Negroes in the State of New-York* (New York: Carroll and Patterson, 1787).
20. Stephanie E. Jones-Rogers, *They Were Her Property: White Women as Slave Owners in the American South* (New Haven, CT: Yale University Press, 2019), 6, 9.
21. Thavolia Glymph, *Out of the House of Bondage: The Transformation of the Plantation Household* (Cambridge: Cambridge University Press, 2008), 36; Elizabeth Fox-Genovese, *Within the Plantation Household: Black and White Women of the Old South* (Chapel Hill: University of North Carolina Press, 1988), 280.
22. Lorri Glover, *Southern Sons: Becoming Men in the New Nation* (Baltimore: Johns Hopkins University Press, 2007), 172.
23. James Marten, ed., *Children and Youth During the Civil War Era* (New York: New York University Press, 2012), 104.

24. Jill Lepore, *New York Burning: Liberty, Slavery, and Conspiracy in Eighteenth-Century Manhattan* (New York: Vintage, 2006).
25. DuRocher, *Raising Racists*, 3, 9, 11.
26. Gilda Graff, "The Intergenerational Trauma of Slavery and Its Aftermath," *Journal of Psychohistory* 41, no. 3 (2014): 181–97.
27. Kenneth Alan Adams, "Lynching, Sacrifice, and Childrearing in the New South," *Journal of Psychohistory* 45, no. 4 (2018): 244–66.

CHAPTER 5: BIRTHING RACISM

1. Cynthia Carr, *Our Town: A Heartland Lynching, a Haunted Town, and the Hidden History of White America* (New York: Crown, 2006), 115. See also James H. Madison, *A Lynching in the Heartland: Race and Memory in America* (New York: Springer, 2016); and Crystal Feimster, "A Lynching in the Heartland: Race and Memory in America," *Journal of Southern History* 69, no. 2 (2003): 471.
2. James Cameron, *A Time of Terror: A Survivor's Story* (Baltimore: Black Classic Press, 1982).
3. Studies have demonstrated that maternal stress and trauma during pregnancy can significantly impact fetal development, with effects that may last a lifetime. Stress hormones, such as cortisol, can cross the placenta and alter fetal brain development, influencing emotional regulation, stress responses, and predispositions to mental health challenges and behavioral outcomes. Research highlights the transgenerational impact of trauma and the implications of maternal stress and mental health on fetal brain development, and offers a broader psychobiological perspective of the ways prenatal stress influences health and disease risks across a lifespan. See Rachel Yehuda et al., "Transgenerational Effects of Posttraumatic Stress Disorder in Babies of Mothers Exposed to the World Trade Center Attacks During Pregnancy," *Journal of Clinical Endocrinology and Metabolism* 90, no. 7 (July 2005): 4115–18.
4. Scientific studies have established that during pregnancy, three individuals are interconnected: the mother, the fetus, and the germ cells of the fetus, which will form the reproductive material for the next generation. See, for example, Yehuda et al., "Transgenerational Effects of Posttraumatic Stress Disorder"; Mary E. Coussons-Read, "Effects of Prenatal Stress on Pregnancy and Human Development: Mechanisms and Pathways," *Obstetric Medicine* 6, no. 2 (June 2013): 52–57; Marta Weinstock, "The Potential Influence of Maternal Stress Hormones on Development and Mental Health of the Offspring," *Brain, Behavior, and Immunity* 19, no. 4 (2005): 296–308; Bea R. H. Van den Bergh et al., "Prenatal Developmental Origins of Behavior and Mental Health: The Influence of Maternal Stress in Pregnancy," *Neuroscience and Biobehavioral Reviews* 117 (Oct. 2020): 26–64; Marion I. van den Heuvel, "From

the Womb into the World: Protecting the Fetal Brain from Maternal Stress During Pregnancy," *Policy Insights from the Behavioral and Brain Sciences* 9, no. 1 (2022): 96–103; David P. Laplante, Alain Brunet, and Suzanne King, "The Effects of Maternal Stress and Illness During Pregnancy on Infant Temperament: Project Ice Storm," *Pediatric Research* 79 (2016): 107–13; Lijuan Feng and Xin Chen, "Epigenetic Regulation of Germ Cells—Remember or Forget?" *Current Opinion in Genetics and Development* 31 (Apr. 2015): 20–27; Millisia Ben Maamar, Eric E. Nilsson, and Michael K. Skinner, "Epigenetic Transgenerational Inheritance, Gametogenesis and Germline Development," *Biology of Reproduction* 105, no. 3 (2021): 570–92; and Lexie Prokopuk, Patrick S. Western, and Jessica M. Stringer, "Transgenerational Epigenetic Inheritance: Adaptation Through the Germline Epigenome?" *Epigenomics* 7, no. 5 (2015): 829–46.

5. The connection between lynching-induced stress and its effects on prenatal development, while supported by science, could be perceived as speculative. While biological and epigenetic research supports the potential for such intergenerational effects, the chapter's main goal is to illuminate a historical and cultural phenomenon, not to definitively prove causality at the individual level.
6. The studies cited below provide scientific evidence that stress—whether experienced before conception, during pregnancy, or in early childhood—can alter gene expression through epigenetic mechanisms, particularly affecting the hypothalamic-pituitary-adrenal (HPA) axis, which regulates stress responses. This body of research supports the chapter's central argument that white women who lived in or participated in racially violent environments could have biologically transmitted the effects of that stress to their unborn children, helping to embed racialized trauma and desensitization into the very architecture of future generations. See, for example, Ali Jawaid, Martin Roszkowski, and Isabelle M. Mansuy, "Transgenerational Epigenetics of Traumatic Stress," *Progress in Molecular Biology and Translational Science* 158 (2018): 273–98; Jennifer A. Sumner et al., "Epigenetics of Early-Life Adversity in Youth: Cross-Sectional and Longitudinal Associations," *Clinical Epigenetics* 14 (2022): 48; Andrey M. Vaiserman, "Epigenetic Programming by Early Life Stress: Evidence from Human Populations," *Developmental Dynamics* 244, no. 3 (2015): 254–65; Gabrielle R. Rinne et al., "Stress Before Conception and During Pregnancy and Maternal Cortisol During Pregnancy: A Scoping Review," *Psychoneuroendocrinology* 153 (2023): 106115; Rachel Yehuda et al., "Holocaust Exposure Induced Intergenerational Effects on FKBP5 Methylation," *Biological Psychiatry* 80, no. 5 (2016): 372–80; Rachel Yehuda et al., "Influences of Maternal and Paternal PTSD on Epigenetic Regulation of the Glucocorticoid Receptor

Gene in Holocaust Survivor Offspring," *American Journal of Psychiatry* 171, no. 8 (2014): 872–80; Helena Palma-Gudiel et al., "Maternal Psychosocial Stress During Pregnancy Alters the Epigenetic Signature of the Glucocorticoid Receptor Gene Promoter in Their Offspring: A Meta-analysis," *Epigenetics* 10, no. 10 (2015): 893–902; Renée C. Painter, Tessa J. Roseboom, and Olaf P. Bleker, "Prenatal Exposure to the Dutch Famine and Disease in Later Life: An Overview," *Reproductive Toxicology* 20, no. 3 (2005): 345–52; Patrick O. McGowan et al., "Epigenetic Regulation of the Glucocorticoid Receptor in Human Brain Associates with Childhood Abuse," *Nature Neuroscience* 12 (2009): 342–48; Anthony S. Zannas and Anne E. West, "Epigenetics and the Regulation of Stress Vulnerability and Resilience," *Neuroscience* 264 (2014): 157–70; Moshe Szyf and Julia Bick, "DNA Methylation: A Mechanism for Embedding Early Life Experiences in the Genome," *Child Development* 84, no. 1 (2013): 49–57; Torsten Klengel et al., "Allele-Specific FKBP5 DNA Demethylation Mediates Gene–Childhood Trauma Interactions," *Nature Neuroscience* 16 (2013): 33–41.

CHAPTER 6: "MY LORD, WE PLEAD OUR BELLIES"

1. Christopher C. Meyers, "'Killing Them by the Wholesale': A Lynching Rampage in South Georgia," *Georgia Historical Quarterly* 90, no. 2 (2006): 214–35.
2. NAACP Administrative Subject File–I C-355 (Lynching, Valdosta, GA-1918).
3. C. Tyrone Forehand, "A Place to Lay Their Heads," https://www.scribd.com/document/475790774/A-place-to-lay-their-head, accessed Dec. 29, 2024.
4. Walter White, "The Work of a Mob," *The Crisis* 16, no. 5 (Sept. 1918): 221–23.
5. Forehand, "A Place to Lay Their Heads."
6. David V. Baker and Gilbert Garcia, "An Analytical History of Black Female Lynchings in the United States, 1838–1969," *Journal of Qualitative Criminal Justice & Criminology* 8, no. 1 (2019).
7. "Negro and Wife Lynched by Mob: Avenge Farmer's Slaying by Hanging," *Washington Post*, May 20, 1918; "Georgia Mob Lynches Negro and His Wife," *New York Tribune*, May 20, 1918; "Negro and Wife Lynched," *New York Times*, May 20, 1918; "Four Negroes Lynched for Georgia Murder," *Chicago Daily Tribune*, May 20, 1918; "4 Lynched for Murder," *Baltimore Sun*, May 20, 1918; "Woman Lynched by Brooks Co. Mob," *Atlanta Constitution*, May 20, 1918.
8. See, for example, "Georgia 'Crackers,' on Rampage, Murder Four," *Chicago Defender*, May 25, 1918; and "Blood-Thirsty Georgia 'Crackers'!" *Cleveland Gazette*, Aug. 10, 1918.

9. Mari N. Crabtree, *My Soul Is a Witness: The Traumatic Afterlife of Lynching* (New Haven, CT: Yale University Press, 2023), 237–38.
10. Forehand, "A Place to Lay Their Heads."
11. Crabtree, *My Soul Is a Witness*, 238.
12. Crabtree, *My Soul Is a Witness*, 238.
13. "Four Negroes Lynched in Mississippi," *The Crisis* 17, no. 4 (Feb. 1919): 176–77.
14. "The Shubuta Lynchings," *The Crisis* 18, no. 1 (May 1919).
15. Jennifer A. Lemak, *Southern Life, Northern City: The History of Albany's Rapp Road Community* (Albany: State University of New York Press, 2008), 28.
16. "Four Negroes Lynched in Mississippi," 176–77.
17. "Four Negroes Lynched in Mississippi," 176–77.
18. NAACP Administrative Subject File–I C-355 (Lynching, Valdosta, GA-1918).
19. Baker and Garcia, "An Analytical History of Black Female Lynchings." For press coverage, see *Chickasha Daily Express*, Mar. 31, 1914; University Missourian, Mar. 31, 1914; *Omaha Daily Bee*, Apr. 1, 1914, 4; Guthrie (OK) *Daily Leader*, Mar. 31, 1914; and Rasul A. Mowatt, "The Lynching of Black Women: A Historical Discussion of the Intersections of Oppression in the United States," in *The Palgrave Handbook of Critical Race and Gender*, ed. Shirley Anne Tate and Encarnación Gutiérrez Rodríguez (New York: Palgrave Macmillan, 2022), 41–68.
20. Anthony S. Pitch, *The Last Lynching: How a Gruesome Mass Murder Rocked a Small Georgia Town* (New York: Skyhorse, 2016).
21. Laura Wexler, *Fire in a Canebrake: The Last Mass Lynching in America* (New York: Scribner, 2003), 178–79.
22. Wexler, *Fire in a Canebrake*, 88.
23. On the lynching of Lillian Kelly's unborn child, see Department of Justice Litigation Case Files, A1 COR 144 #144-40-1. For Lillie Mae-Dye's unborn baby, see the Civil Rights and Restorative Justice Project, Year End Report, 2017; and NAACP Records Box II, C32, Folder 3, Florida Branch Files. For more on Mary Noyes's unborn child, see Civil Rights Congress (CRC) Records, Part III, Reel 5, Genocide Clippings, Noyes, Alabama; and the Civil Rights and Restorative Justice Year End Report, 2013.
24. Clarence Mitchell to the Honorable Kenneth Keating, Mar. 11, 1953, https://repository.library.northeastern.edu/downloads/neu:m041tg049.
25. For a detailed examination of "pleading the belly" and the treatment of pregnant women in medieval and early modern Europe, see Sara M. Butler, *Pregnancy and Childbirth in the Premodern World: European and Middle Eastern Cultures, from Antiquity to the Renaissance* (Turnhout, Belgium: Brepols, 2017); Thomas R. Forbes, "Midwives, Mortality, and

the Law in Early Modern England," *American Journal of Legal History* 30, no. 4 (1986): 335–52; James C. Oldham, "On Pleading the Belly: A History of the Jury of Matrons," *Criminal Law Review* 6 (1985): 31–50; William Blackstone, *Commentaries on the Laws of England*, vol. 4, *Of Public Wrongs* (Oxford: Clarendon Press, 1769); Barbara A. Hanawalt, *Crime and Conflict in English Communities, 1300–1348* (Cambridge, MA: Harvard University Press, 1979); Philippe de Beaumanoir, *Coutumes de Beauvaisis*, trans. and ed. F. R. P. Akehurst (Philadelphia: University of Pennsylvania Press, 1992); George Lyman Kittredge, "The Influence of Roman Law on the Law of England," *Harvard Law Review* 15, no. 2 (1902): 89–107; and Monica H. Green, "Women's Medical Practice and Health Care in Medieval Europe," *Signs: Journal of Women in Culture and Society* 14, no. 2 (1989): 434–73.

26. For more in-depth study on cases of condemned women pleading the belly, see, for example, "Cases," *Kentish Gazette*, Aug 8, 1781, 4A; Anon., *Trial & Execution of John Lomas, and Condemnation of Edith Morrey, for Willful Murder* (Broadside, 1812); Frederick Augustus Carrington and Joseph Payne, *Reports of Cases Argued and Ruled at Nisi Prius, in the Courts of King's Bench, Common Pleas, and Exchequer*, vol. 8 (London: S. Sweet, 1839), 262; and *Staffordshire Advertiser*, May 12, 1838, 3B.
27. T. R. Forbes, "A Jury of Matrons," *Medical History* 32, no. 1 (1988), 23–33.
28. Blackstone, *Commentaries on the Laws of England*, vol. 4, ch. 31, p. 388. Blackstone is referring to the burning of the pregnant Perotine Massey, alongside two other Protestant women, on July 18, 1556. Their execution is also discussed at length as the "Guernsey Martyrs" in John Foxe's *Book of Martyrs*.
29. Naomi Clifford, *Women and the Gallows, 1797–1837: Unfortunate Wretches* (Barnsley, UK: Pen and Sword Books, 2017), 168.
30. "The Lives, Last Words, and Dying Speech of Ezra Ross, James Buchanan, and William Brooks," in Evans Early American Imprint Collection, University of Michigan Library Digital Collections, https://name.umdl.umich.edu/N33098.0001.001, accessed Dec. 30, 2024; Deborah Navas, "New Light on the Bathsheba Spooner Execution," *Proceedings of the Massachusetts Historical Society* 108 (1996): 115–22.
31. Franklin Mall, "Embryology History: Franklin Mall," *Contributions to Embryology* (Carnegie Institution No. 55), University of New South Wales.
32. Robert A. Munsick, "Similarities of Negro and Caucasian Fetal Extremity Lengths in the Interval from 9 to 20 Weeks of Pregnancy," *American Journal of Obstetrics and Gynecology* 156, no. 1 (1987): 183–85.

CHAPTER 7: "IF DAT CHILD DOAN SOON CHANGE COLOUR THERE'LL BE TROUBLE IN DIS FAMILY"

1. *Brenham (TX) Weekly Banner*, June 17, 1880; *Daily Standard*, June 27, 1860; *Weekly Standard*, July 27, 1870.
2. "Unknown Party Kills Henry Raines and Child," *Savannah (GA) Morning News*, March 1898.
3. "Charged with Murder; Seven Men Held at Charleston for Alleged Killing of Postmaster Baker," *New York Times*, July 2, 1898; "The Lake City Lynching; Thirteen Men Indicted in a Federal Court for the Alleged Murder of the Negro Postmaster," *New York Times*, Apr. 8, 1899; David Carter, "Outraged Justice: The Lynching of Postmaster Frazier Baker in Lake City, South Carolina, 1897–1899" (honors thesis, University of North Carolina at Chapel Hill, 1992); Roger K. Hux, "Lillian Clayton Jewett and the Rescue of the Baker Family, 1899–1900," *Historical Journal of Massachusetts* (Winter 1991): 13–23.
4. "Killed a Negro Baby," *Evening Shade* (AR), Aug. 3, 1906.
5. "John Jackson, One of Champions Gang, Gets a Year in the Pen," *Hopkinsville Kentuckian*, Apr. 13, 1909; "Bail for Frances Sarratt," *Bamberg (SC) Herald*, July 20, 1911; *Lexington Dispatch*, Nov. 6, 1912; and "Bus Driver Kill Baby Soldier Kills Bus Driver," *Omaha Guide*, June 16, 1945, https://www.loc.gov/resource/sn93062828/1945-06-16/ed-1/?sp=1&q=baby+killed+Negro.
6. *Cuthbert (GA) Appeal*, Mar. 22, 1878; *Cincinnati Enquirer*, Mar. 16, 1878; *New York Times*, Mar. 16, 1878; *Rome (GA) Weekly Courier*, Apr. 25, 1877; *Rome Tri-Weekly Courier*, Aug. 26, 1876; *Springfield (MO) Weekly Patriot*, Mar. 28, 1878.
7. Cathy Boeckmann, *A Question of Character: Scientific Racism and the Genres of American Fiction, 1892–1912* (Tuscaloosa: University of Alabama Press, 2000), 85. For an excellent discussion about the *Plessy v. Ferguson* decision, fears about racial passing, and the ontological uncertainties of racial identity, see Mark M. Smith, *How Race Is Made: Slavery, Racism, and the Senses* (Chapel Hill: University of North Carolina Press, 2006), 66–97, especially 74–76.
8. David Hoogland Noon, "The Evolution of Beasts and Babies: Recapitulation, Racial Science, and Racial Hierarchy," *Journal of American Culture* 28, no. 1 (Mar. 2005): 15–28.
9. W. E. B. Du Bois, "Of the Passing of the Firstborn Son," in David Levering Lewis, ed., *W. E. B. Du Bois: A Reader* (New York: Henry Holt, 1995), 101.
10. Du Bois, "Of the Passing of the Firstborn Son," 101–2.
11. A precise tabulation of just how many Blacks engaged in the practice of passing is impossible given that the point of passing was to avoid

detection. For estimates, see Walter F. White, *A Man Called White: The Autobiography of Walter White* (New York: Viking Press, 1948), 3; John H. Burma, "The Measurement of Negro Passing," *American Journal of Sociology* 52 (1946): 1822; and Horace Mann Bond, "The Racial Islands in America," *American Journal of Sociology* 52 (1931): 544.

12. "Spirits Made Baby Brown—White Mother's Explanation of Infant's Complexion," *Washington Post*, June 3, 1907, 3.
13. See, for example, William C. Dabney, "Maternal Impressions," in *Cyclopaedia of the Diseases of Children*, ed. John M. Keating (Edinburgh: Young J. Petland, 1889), 196–202; George M. Gould and Walter L. Pyle, *Anomalies and Curiosities of Medicine* (London: Rebman, 1897), 81; "Maternal Impressions," *Pediatrics* 9 (1900): 292–94; Robert W. Lovett, "A Clinical Consideration of Sixty Cases of Cerebral Paralysis in Children," *Boston Medical and Surgical Journal* 118 (Jan.–June 1888): 645; "Maternal Impression Superstition, and Why It Survives," *Interstate Medical Journal* 12 (1905): 862–65; Charles Hunter Dunn and Thomas Morgan Rotch, "Congenital Cardiac Disease," in *Pediatrics: The Hygienic and Medical Treatment of Children* (Troy, NY: Southworth, 1917), 12; and William Samuel Sadler, *Race Decadence: An Examination of the Causes of Racial Degeneracy in the United States* (Chicago: A. C. McClurg, 1922), 317. For examples in classical literature of how white women's mental power could produce Black babies, see Rudolph M. Bell, *How to Do It: Guides to Good Living for Renaissance Italians* (Chicago: University of Chicago Press, 1999), 39–41. On white women's explanations for Black offspring, see Antoine Faivre, *Theosophy, Imagination, Tradition: Studies in Western Esotericism* (Albany: State University of New York Press, 2000), 100; and Valeria Finucci, "Maternal Imagination and Monstrous Birth: Tasso's *Gerusalemme liberata*," in *Generation and Degeneration: Tropes of Reproduction in Literature and History from Antiquity to Modern Europe*, ed. Valeria Finucci and Kevin Brownlee (Durham, NC: Duke University Press, 2000), 56–59. For a good discussion of maternal impressions in medical science communities in the United States and Europe, see Jan Bondeson, *A Cabinet of Medical Curiosities: A Compendium of the Odd, the Bizarre, and the Unexpected* (Ithaca, NY: Cornell University Press, 1997), 159–70.
14. Karen Weingarten, "From Maternal Impressions to Eugenics: Pregnancy and Inheritance in the Nineteenth-Century U.S.," *Journal of Medical Humanities* 43, no. 2 (2022): 303–17.
15. "Color of Negro Babies," *Florence (CO) Daily Tribune*, Sept. 29, 1898; *Morning Astorian* (OR), Feb. 4, 1906; "Color of Negro Babies," *Daily Chieftain* (Vinita, OK), Apr. 17, 1899; "Color of Negro Babies," *Kansas City Journal*, Sept. 12, 1897; "Color of Negro Babies," *Birmingham Age-Herald*, Apr. 1, 1903; "Keeping Light Color of Negro Babies," *San*

Francisco Call, May 20, 1904; "Negro Babies Are Reddish Chocolate in Color," *Baraboo (WI) Weekly News*, May 8, 1919; "Color of Negro Babies," *Ely Miner*, Dec. 2, 1937; "Human Color," *Amador Ledger* (Jackson, CA), Mar. 13, 1908; "African Babies Turn Black," *Manitowoc (WI) Pilot*, Apr. 23, 1903; "Negro Children Born White," *Wauwatosa (WI) News*, May 23, 1903; "Babies Change Color," *Topeka State Journal*, Apr. 18, 1903; "The Black Man's Skin," *New York Sun*, Feb. 1, 1904.

16. "Face Is Three-Fourths Black," *East Oregonian*, Dec. 24, 1907.

17. With the exception of more recent scholarship on the history of childbirth in the South, most of the major studies either exclude the experiences of African Americans or make only passing mention about race. For a good historiographical overview, see Nancy Schrom Dye, "Review Essay on the History of Childbirth in America," *Signs* 6 (1980): 97–108. On the medical history of childbirth and women's roles in the birthing process, see Judith Walzer Leavitt, *Brought to Bed: Childbearing in America, 1750–1950* (New York: Oxford University Press, 1986); and Catherine M. Scholten, *Childbearing in American Society: 1650–1850* (New York: New York University Press, 1985). On the management of pain, see Margarete Sandelowski, *Pain, Pleasure, and American Childbirth: From Twilight Sleep to the Read Method, 1914–1960* (Westport, CT: Greenwood Press, 1984); Janet C. Bogden, "Care or Cure? Childbirth Practices in Nineteenth-Century America," *Feminist Studies* 4 (June 1978): 92–99; and Richard W. Wertz and Dorothy C. Wertz, *Lyin-In: A History of Childbirth in America* (New York: Free Press, 1977). On the decline of midwives, see Judy Barrett Litoff, *American Midwives, 1860 to the Present* (Westport, CT: Greenwood Press, 1978); Nancy Schrom Dye and Daniel Blake Smith, "Mother Love and Infant Death, 1750–1920," *Journal of American History* 73 (Sept. 1986): 329–53; Frances Kobrin, "The American Midwife Controversy: A Crisis of Professionalization," *Bulletin of the History of Medicine* 40 (1966): 350–66; Judith Walzer Leavitt, "Science Enters the Birth Room: Obstetrics in America Since the Eighteenth Century," *Journal of American History* 70 (1983): 281–304; Lawrence G. Miller, "Pain, Parturition, and the Profession: Twilight Sleep in America," in *Healthcare in America: Essays in Social History*, ed. Susan Reverby and David Rosner (Philadelphia: Temple University Press, 1979), 19–44; Raymond G. Devries, *Regulating Childbirth: Midwives, Medicine, and the Law* (Philadelphia: Temple University Press, 1985); Ann Oakley, *Women Confined: Towards A Sociology of Childbirth* (New York: Schocken, 1980); Ann Oakley, "Wisewoman and Medicine Man: Changes in the Management of Childbirth," in *The Rights and Wrongs of Women*, ed. Juliet Mitchell and Ann Oakley (Harmondsworth, UK: Penguin, 1976); Nancy Schrom Dye, "Modern Obstetrics and Working-Class Women: The New York Dispensary,

1890–1920," *Journal of Social History* 20 (1987): 549–64; and Charlotte G. Borst, *Catching Babies: The Professionalization of Childbirth, 1870–1920* (Cambridge, MA: Harvard University Press, 1995). On women's perception of childbirth, see Judith Walzer Leavitt and Whitney Walton, "Down to Death's Door: Women's Perceptions of Childbirth in America," in *Proceedings of the Second Motherhood Symposium; Childbirth: The Beginning of Motherhood*, ed. Sophie Colleau (Madison, WI: The Center, 1982), 113–36. For discussions of childbearing in the South, see Sally G. McMillen, *Motherhood in the Old South: Pregnancy, Childbirth, and Infant Rearing* (Baton Rouge: Louisiana State University Press, 1990); Jennifer L. Morgan, *Laboring Women: Reproduction and Gender in New World Slavery* (Philadelphia: University of Pennsylvania Press, 2004); Marie Jenkins Schwartz, *Birthing a Slave: Motherhood and Medicine in the Antebellum South* (Cambridge, MA: Harvard University Press, 2006); and V. Lynn Kennedy, *Born Southern: Childbirth, Motherhood, and Social Networks in the Old South* (Baltimore: Johns Hopkins University Press, 2010). On the experience of childbearing on the frontier, see Sylvia D. Hoffert, "Childbearing on the Trans-Mississippi Frontier, 1830–1900," *Western Historical Quarterly* 22, no. 3 (Aug. 1991): 272–88.

18. The incubus is an ancient mythological figure, a bird of prey that had intercourse with women as they slept. This metaphor was the centerpiece of white-supremacist campaigns to represent Black men as sexually threatening to defenseless white women. The black criminal entered homes and raped white women as their husbands slept beside them. For more on the incubus metaphor, see Glenda Gilmore, "Murder, Memory and the Flight of the Incubus," in *Democracy Betrayed: The Wilmington Race Riot of 1898 and Its Legacy*, ed. David S. Cecelski and Timothy B. Tyson (Chapel Hill: University of North Carolina Press, 1998), 79; Martha Hodes, *White Women, Black Men: Illicit Sex in the Nineteenth-Century South* (New Haven, CT: Yale University Press, 1997), 206; and Jacqueline Denise Goldsby, *A Spectacular Secret: Lynching in American Life and Literature* (Chicago: University of Chicago Press, 2006), 28.
19. Laura Dawkins, "Black Babies, White Hysteria: The Dark Child in African-American Literature of the Harlem Renaissance," in *The American Child: A Cultural Studies Reader*, ed. Caroline F. Levander and Carol J. Singley (New Brunswick, NJ: Rutgers University Press, 2003), 167–68. Dawkins reveals how racist fables about Black children that emerged during the late nineteenth and early twentieth century, such as Gertrude Atherton's *Senator North* (1900), Thomas Dixon's *The Leopard's Spots* (1902), and Robert Lee Durham's *The Call of the South* (1908), typically recounted the destruction of women found guilty of

miscegenation or passing for white when they gave birth to babies with Black skin. In those stories, the Black child was cast as an "emblem or horror, disruption, or simply imperfection—the antithesis of 'perfect' milk-white babies" (168).

20. "Adopted Baby a Changeling," *New York Times*, Aug. 5, 1907.
21. See Barbara Melosh, *Strangers and Kin: The American Way of Adoption* (Cambridge, MA: Harvard University Press, 2002), 3, 106–7. Melosh describes legal adoption as a relatively new practice in the United States that was tied to the rise of the social work profession. Though adoptions stretched back into the colonial period, those children were often informally adopted by relatives, or lived with other families as apprentices. The nineteenth century, a time of increased urban and rural poverty, saw the rise of more official adoptions. In the 1910s and 1920s, child placing was widespread but informal, with judges and legislators resisting efforts to regulate adoptions. As late as 1929, thirty of the forty-eight states had no provisions for the supervision of adoptions. Before the 1950s, trans-racial adoptions were rare because of social attitudes against interracial families. Adoptions in general were not legalized, professionalized, and regulated until after World War II, when a combination of unprecedented economic expansion and a flood of middle-class couples seeking children tripled the number of adoptions between 1937 and 1945, and doubled again in 1957. With the decline in the availability of adoptable white infants, social workers used practices that sought to "match" children and parents.
22. "Adopted Baby a Changeling," *New York Times*, Aug. 5, 1907, 14; "Vicinity Correspondence," *Mount Kisco (NY) Recorder*, July 5, 1907; "Baby Turned Black," *Batavia (NY) Times*, Aug. 5, 1907, 2; "The Baby Turned Out Wrong," *New York Sun*, Aug. 5, 1907, 6; "Adopted Baby Turns Pickaninny," *New York Herald*, Aug. 5, 1907, 3; "The Kink in Baby's Hair Was Natural," *New Rochelle Press*, Aug. 10, 1907.
23. Thomas Dixon Jr., *The Leopard's Spots: A Romance of the White Man's Burden—1865–1900* (New York: Doubleday, Page & Company, 1902), 394.
24. Dixon, *The Leopard's Spots*, 394.
25. "Question Foundling's Color—Police Halt in Plan to Adopt Infant Abandoned in Weeds," *Washington Post*, Oct. 8, 1912, 14; "Adopted Baby of Colored Ancestry," *Washington Times*, Aug. 23, 1919, 21; "Colored Baby Stirs New York Folk," *Broad Ax* (Chicago), Aug. 16, 1919, 5; "White Baby Turns Black," *Perrysburg Journal* (OH), Jan. 8, 1920; "Negro Baby Turns White in Milwaukee Incubator," *Cairo (IL) Bulletin*, Oct. 5, 1907; "White Baby Turns Black," *Athens (GA) Weekly Banner*, May 11, 1880; "White Baby Turns Black After Three Months," *Recorder*, Nov. 11, 1943.

26. Stoddard Goodhue, "Do You Choose Your Children?" *Cosmopolitan Magazine* 55 (July 1913): 147.
27. "Martha Washington Dead," *Washington Post*, Dec. 19, 1907.
28. This story comes from a collection of oral narratives of granny-midwives from rural Georgia. See Marie Campbell, *Folks Do Get Born* (New York: Garland, 1984), 223–31.

CHAPTER 8: "DON'T YOU KNOW A NEGRO CHILD'S SCROTUM IS ALWAYS BLACK?"

1. The 1662 Virginia law, titled "Negro women's children to serve according to the condition of the mother," established that children born in the colony would inherit the status of their mother, whether free or enslaved. This statute marked a significant departure from English common law, which typically determined a child's status based on the father. The law was enacted during the December 1662 session of the Virginia General Assembly. For a more in-depth discussion, see Jennifer Morgan, "*Partus sequitur ventrem*: Law, Race, and Reproduction in Colonial Slavery," *Small Axe* 22, no. 55 (2018): 1, 12.
2. Jennifer L. Morgan, *Laboring Women: Reproduction and Gender in New World Slavery* (Philadelphia: University of Pennsylvania Press, 2004); Marie Jenkins Schwartz, *Birthing a Slave: Motherhood and Medicine in the Antebellum South* (Cambridge, MA: Harvard University Press, 2006); Deirdre Cooper Owens, *Medical Bondage: Race, Gender, and the Origins of American Gynecology* (Athens: University of Georgia Press, 2017).
3. Sydney A. Halpern, *American Pediatrics: The Social Dynamics of Professionalism, 1880–1980* (Berkeley: University of California Press, 1988); Heather Munro Prescot, *"A Doctor of Their Own": The History of Adolescent Medicine* (Cambridge, MA: Harvard University Press, 1998), 11.
4. See Susan L. Smith, *Sick and Tired of Being Sick and Tired: Black Women's Health Activism in America, 1890–1950* (Philadelphia: University of Pennsylvania Press, 1995), 119. Smith notes that lay midwives delivered half of all babies in the United States as late as 1910, with much of the practice being conducted by European immigrants and Southern Black women. By 1930, only 15 percent of all births were delivered by lay midwives owing to immigration restrictions and the increasing preference among urban women that physicians perform the procedure. At that time, 80 percent of all remaining midwives practiced in the South, largely due to racial discrimination and lack of access to health care facilities. Smith also notes that even as midwifery declined in significance in Northeastern and Midwestern urban areas, the number of practicing midwives did not drop significantly in the South until after 1950. See

also V. Lynn Kennedy, *Born Southern: Childbirth, Motherhood, and Social Networks in the Old South* (Baltimore: Johns Hopkins University Press, 2010), 218. Kennedy demonstrates that as late as 1940, Black midwives attended three-fourths of Black women's births in Mississippi, South Carolina, Arkansas, Georgia, Florida, and Louisiana. For a graph illustrating trends in US birthing practices from 1750 to 1950, see Judith Walzer Leavitt, *Brought to Bed: Childbearing in America, 1750–1950* (New York: Oxford University Press, 1996), 12.

5. Schwartz, *Birthing a Slave*, 294–96.
6. Abraham Flexner, *Medical Education in the United States and Canada: A Report to the Carnegie Foundation for the Advancement of Teaching*, Bulletin No. 4 (New York: Carnegie Foundation for the Advancement of Teaching, 1910), 147–48, 180–81, 203, 233, 282, 309–10. On the Flexner Report's impact on Black health and the Black medical profession, see George A. Johnston, "The Flexner Report and Black Medical Schools," *Journal of the National Medical Association* 76 (1984): 223–25; and Ann Steinecke and Charles Terrell, "Progress for Whose Future? The Impact of the Flexner Report on Medical Education for Racial and Ethnic Minority Physicians in the United States," *Academic Medicine* 85, no. 2 (Feb. 2010): 236–45.
7. Harriet A. Washington, *Medical Apartheid: The Dark History of Medical Experimentation on Black Americans from Colonial Times to the Present* (New York: Doubleday, 2006).
8. See "Vivisection of Children," in *Human Vivisection: A Statement and an Inquiry* (Chicago: American Humane Society, 1899), 5–9; "The Vivisection of Children," *The Animals' Defender* (Boston: New England Anti-Vivisection Society, 1903), 8–23; Konrad Bercovici, "Orphans as Guinea Pigs," *The Nation*, June 29, 1921, 911–13. For histories of the use of children in medical experimentation, see Susan E. Lederer, "Orphans as Guinea Pigs: American Children and Medical Experimenters, 1890–1930," in *In the Name of the Child: Health and Welfare, 1880–1940*, ed. Roger Cooter (London: Routledge, 1992); Susan E. Lederer, *Subjected to Science: Human Experimentation in America Before the Second World War* (Baltimore: Johns Hopkins University Press, 1995), 62, 76, 80–89, 104–8; and Michael A. Grodin and Leonard H. Glantz, eds., *Children as Research Subjects: Science, Ethics, and Law* (Oxford: Oxford University Press, 1994).
9. Todd L. Savitt, *Medicine and Slavery: The Diseases and Health Care of Blacks in Antebellum Virginia* (Urbana: University of Illinois Press, 1978).
10. Alfred F. Hess and Mildred Fish, "Infantile Scurvy: The Blood, The Blood-Vessels, and the Diet," *American Journal of Disease in Children* 8 (1914): 386–405; Alfred F. Hess and Lester J. Unger, "Dietaries of

Infants in Relation to the Development of Rickets," *Proceedings of the Society for Experimental Biology and Medicine* 17 (May 1920): 220–21; Alfred F. Hess, "Prophylactic Therapy for Rickets in a Negro Community," *Journal of the American Medical Association* (Nov. 10, 1917); M. Hines Roberts, "The Spinal Fluid in the New-Born," *Journal of the American Medical Association* 85 (1925): 500–501.

11. Roberts, "The Spinal Fluid in the New-Born," 500–501.
12. "Color of Negro Babies," *Washington (DC) Evening Star*, Jan. 28, 1904.
13. "A Solution to the Race Problem," *Journal of the American Medical Association* 42, no. 1 (Jan. 1904): 470.
14. "X-Rays Change Negro's Color," *San Francisco Call*, Dec. 28, 1903.
15. "The Black Man's Skin," *New York Sun*, Jan. 28, 1904.
16. A. S. Morton, "The Color of Newly-Born Negro Children," *The Lancet* 2, no. 2 (1898): 1605; J. J. Abel and W. S. Davis, "On the Pigment of the Negro's Skin and Hair," *Journal of Experimental Medicine* 1 (1896): 361–400; N. Alcock et al., "Negroes: Why Are They Black?" *Nature* 30 (1884): 50; B. H. Broadnax, "Newborn Infants of African Descent" *New York Medical Times* 23 (1895): 322; "Color of Infant Negroes," *Mississippi Medical Record* 7 (1903): 174.
17. On the French research, see, for example, Felix Regnault, "Pourquoi les negres sont-ils noirs? (Etudes sur les causes de la coloration de la peau)," *La médecine moderne* (Oct. 2, 1895); Léo Testut, "Contribution a l'anatomie des races Negres: Dissection de trios nouveaux Negres," *Bulletin de la Société d'Anthropologie de Lyon* 9 (1884): 51–68.
18. Claude-Nicolas Le Cat, "Traite de la couleur de la peau humaine" (1766), and "Le Cat and the Physiology of Negroes," cited in Werner Sollors, *Neither Black nor White Yet Both: Thematic Explorations of Interracial Literature* (Cambridge, MA: Harvard University Press, 1997), 155–56.
19. For a fuller discussion on the history of scientific theories of Black skin, see Sidney N. Klaus, "A History of the Science of Pigmentation," in *The Pigmentary System: Physiology and Pathophysiology*, ed. James J. Nordland et al. (New York: Oxford University Press, 1998), 5–10.
20. Theodor Waitz, *Introduction to Anthropology* (London: Longman, Green, Longman, and Roberts, 1863), 99–100; Sir William Lawrence, *Lectures on Physiology, Zoology, and the Natural History of Man* (Salem, MA: Foote and Brown, 1828), 357; John Charles Hall, *Interesting Facts Connected with the Animal Kingdom* (London: Whittaker, 1841), 111; Thomas Masterman Winterbottom, *An Account of Native Africans in the Neighbourhood of Sierra Leone* (London: C. Whittingham, 1803), 189–90.
21. Arthur Thomas, "Note on the Skin and Scalp of the Negro Foetus," *Journal of Anatomy and Physiology* 25 (1890): 282.

22. Charles Darwin, *The Descent of Man, and Selection in Relation to Sex*, 2 vols. (London: John Murray, 1871), 226.
23. Harriet A. Washington, *Medical Apartheid: The Dark History of Medical Experimentation on African Americans from Colonial Times to the Present* (New York: Harlem Moon, 2006), 94, 98–99.
24. Charles F. Robinson II, *Dangerous Liaisons: Sex and Love in the Segregated South* (Fayetteville: University of Arkansas Press, 2003), 2–8, 18.
25. See also Union County v. Robinson, 27 Ark. 116; Maddox v. Neal, 45 Ark. 121 (1885); and Weaver v. State, 22 Ala. App. 469, 116 So. 893 (1928).
26. "The Color of Negro Babies," *Medical World* 12 (1860): 460.
27. W. E. B. Du Bois, "Opinion: Rhinelander," *The Crisis* 31, no. 3 (Jan. 1926): 112–13.
28. For example, Adolf H. Shultz, "Relation of the External Nose to the Bony Nose and Nasal Cartilages in Whites and Negroes," *American Journal of Physical Anthropology* 1, no. 3 (1918): 329–38. In this study funded by the Carnegie Institution of Washington, Shultz examined twenty Negro fetuses and children ages two to five to explain the growth and greater breadth of the Negro nose. The nose, like skin, was considered of anthropological importance in proving racial difference. See Bird Thomas Baldwin, *The Physical Growth of Children from Birth to Maturity*, vol. 1, iss. 1 (Iowa City: University of Iowa, 1921); and "The Color of the Iris During Infancy," *Journal of the American Medical Association* 73 (Nov. 1919): 1444–45.
29. Robert B. Morrison, "Notes on the Formation of Pigment in the Negro," *Medical News* 54–55 (Jan.–June 1889): 396.
30. Lynn M. Morgan, "Materializing the Fetal Body, or, What Are Those Corpses Doing in Biology's Basement?" in *Fetal Subjects, Feminist Positions*, ed. Lynn M. Morgan and Meredith Wilson Michaels (Philadelphia: University of Pennsylvania Press, 1999), 44, 48–50, 55–56.
31. Morgan, "Materializing the Fetal Body," 44, 48–50, 55–56.
32. Thomas, "Note on the Skin and Scalp of the Negro Foetus," 282.
33. William Allen Pusey, *The Principles and Practice of Dermatology* (New York: D. Appleton, 1907), 19–21.
34. "The Color of Negro Children When Born," *Pediatrics* 6 (1898): 40.
35. "*The Lancet* and the Color of Newly Born Negro Children," *Medical News* 73 (July–Dec. 1898): 766.
36. "Negro Children Not Born White," *Phrenological Journal and Science of Health* 109–110 (1900): 35.
37. "Correspondence—the Color of New-Born Negro Infants," *Pediatrics* 6 (July 1–Dec. 15, 1898): 430.
38. "Correspondence," 430.
39. Morton, "The Color of Newly-Born Negro Children," 1605.

40. "The Color of Negro Babies," *Medical News* 73 (1898): 844–45.
41. H. C. Riley, "Color of New-Born Negroes," *Medical Brief* 28, no. 1 (1900): 537.
42. "The Colour of Negro Babies," *Medical Press and Circular* 118 (Feb. 15, 1899): 174.
43. "The Color of Negro Babies," *Medical News* 73 (July–Dec. 1898): 845.
44. "*The Lancet* and the Color of Newly Born Negro Children," 766.
45. "The Color of Negro Babies," *The Lancet* 1, no. 1 (Jan. 28, 1899): 276.
46. For a full history of this discussion among physicians and anthropologists during the late nineteenth and early twentieth century, see Joseph Brennemann, "The Sacral or So-Called 'Mongolian' Pigment Spots of Earliest Infancy and Childhood, with Especial Reference to Their Occurrence in the American Negro," *Archives of Pediatrics* 24 (Jan.–Dec. 1907): 426–44.
47. Albert E. Vipond, "Observations Upon the Colored Children of Jamaica, with Especial Reference to Rickets and to Mongolian Spots," *Archives of Pediatrics* 25 (Jan.–Dec. 1908): 511–12. See also A. S. Ashmean, "The Mulberry-Colored Spots on the Skin of the Lower Spine of Japanese and Other Dark Races: A Sign of Negro Descent," *Journal of Cutaneous Diseases* 23 (May 1905): 203–14; Frederick Starr, "Sacral Spots of Mayo Indians," *Science* 27 (1903): 422–23; and Newell H. Wardle, "Evanescent Congenital Pigmentation in the Sacro-lumbar Region," *American Anthropologist* 4 (1902): 412–20.
48. Vipond, "Observations Upon the Colored Children of Jamaica," 512.
49. Brennemann, "The Sacral or So Called 'Mongolian' Pigment Spots," 440.
50. Henry Holt, "Atha Sorrells v. A. T. Shields, Clerk, Petition for Mandamus (Nov. 14, 1924)," *Encyclopedia Virginia*, Dec. 7, 2020, accessed Feb. 15, 2025.
51. See, for example, Linda Janet Holmes, *Listen to Me Good: The Life Story of an Alabama Midwife* (Columbus: Ohio State University Press, 1996); Susan L. Smith, *Sick and Tired of Being Sick and Tired: Black Women's Health Activism in America, 1890–1950* (Philadelphia: University of Pennsylvania Press, 1995); Gertrude Jacinta Fraser, *African American Midwifery in the South: Dialogues of Birth, Race, and Memory* (Cambridge, MA: Harvard University Press, 1998); Valerie Lee, *Granny Midwives and Black Women Writers: Double-Dutched Readings* (New York: Routledge, 1996); Debra Anne Susie, *In the Way of Our Grandmothers: A Cultural View of Twentieth-Century Midwifery in Florida* (Athens: University of Georgia Press, 1988); and Molly Ladd-Taylor, "'Grannies' and 'Spinsters': Midwife Education Under the Sheppard-Towner Act," *Journal of Social History* 22 (Winter 1988): 260.

CHAPTER 9: "GO 'LONG, WHITE MAN, I AIN'T NO 'SEPTEMBER MORN'!"

1. Anna Louise Bates, *Weeder in the Garden of the Lord: Anthony Comstock's Life and Career* (Lanham, MD: University Press of America, 1995).
2. For more on the life of Anthony Comstock and his anti-vice campaigns, see Amy Werbel, *Lust on Trial: Censorship and the Rise of American Obscenity in the Age of Anthony Comstock* (New York: Columbia University Press, 2018); Nicola Kay Beisel, *Imperiled Innocents: Anthony Comstock and Family Reproduction in Victorian America* (Princeton, NJ: Princeton University Press, 1998); Heywood Broun and Margaret Leech, *Anthony Comstock: Roundsman of the Lord* (New York: Boni & Liveright, 1927); Amy Sohn, *The Man Who Hated Women: Sex, Censorship, and Civil Liberties in the Gilded Age* (New York: Farrar, Straus and Giroux, 2021); Charles Gallaudet Trumbull, *Anthony Comstock, Fighter: Some Impressions of a Lifetime Adventure in Conflict with the Powers of Evil*, 2nd ed. (New York: Fleming H. Revell, 1913); Kimberly A. Hamlin et al., "The History and Legacy of Anthony Comstock and the Comstock Laws," *Journal of the Gilded Age and Progressive Era* 23, no. 4 (2025): 431–37; and Robert Corn-Revere, *The Mind of the Censor and the Eye of the Beholder: The First Amendment and the Censor's Dilemma* (Cambridge: Cambridge University Press, 2021), 14–54.
3. There is much debate among scholars about the origins of pornography and what constitutes it, as well as its impact on sexual behavior. Walter Kendrick writes in *The Secret Museum* that the term "pornography" comes from the Greek "pornographos, writing about prostitutes." Walter M. Kendrick, *The Secret Museum: Pornography in Modern Culture* (Berkeley: University of California Press, 1987), 1. By the mid-nineteenth century, the word "pornographer" meant someone who produced obscene representations. He also argues that the increased output of sexual literature in the second half of the nineteenth century reflects larger social, economic, demographic, and technological developments. During Comstock's era, pornography included medical texts, pseudo-scientific works, books, songs, poems, drawings, postcards—any written or visual representations that depicted sex. As Kendrick and other scholars have noted, Comstock freely interpreted what was obscene, lewd, lascivious, or indecent. Comstock and others in power constructed these definitions and were concerned with how sexual images and ideas shaped thoughts and behaviors of certain groups that needed to be controlled. Although he believed that the primary purpose of obscene literature and pictures was to cause arousal, he also believed that arousal was not merely a private sensation but a catalyst for behaviors—masturbation, prostitution, abortion—that threatened Protestant moral order. It is important

to note that the definition of pornography and its function is subjective and continues to change over time. It can also be masked by and traffic in humor, as the cards in this chapter do. Although these sexual depictions of Black children may not cause arousal in viewers, that does not disqualify them as pornographic, lewd, obscene, lascivious, and indecent, even by Comstock's definitions.

4. Harry L. Reichenbach, *Phantom Fame: The Anatomy of Ballyhoo* (New York: Simon & Schuster, 1931); see also Mark Borkowski, "Media: Nice Stunt—Never Mind the Story," *London Independent*, June 27, 2000.
5. See Kendrick, *The Secret Museum*. Kendrick reports that shortly before Congress passed the "Comstock Act," the Committee on Appropriations earmarked $3,425 for the use of a "special agent" with a promise from the Postmaster General that Comstock would receive the appointment and authority to enforce the law restricting the sale and circulation of "obscene" material through the mails. Though Comstock was given a badge to signal his official status, he was not on a payroll, had no superior, and was free to interpret and apply the law as he saw fit. Kendrick also reports that Comstock had no restrictions on the means by which he could catch criminals. Comstock's appointment as special agent to the United States Post Office Department also allowed him to police obscenity at the national level.
6. For more on Comstock's views about art and obscenity, see Anthony Comstock, *Traps for the Young*, ed. Robert Bremer (1883; repr. Cambridge, MA: Harvard University Press, 1967), 9; Anthony Comstock, *Frauds Exposed; or How the People Are Deceived and Robbed, and Youth Corrupted* (New York: J. Howard Brown, 1880); Anthony Comstock, "The Suppression of Vice," *North American Review* 135 (1882): 285; and Anthony Comstock, *Morals Versus Art* (New York: J. S. Ogilive, 1887). See also Charles G. Trumbull, *Anthony Comstock, Fighter* (New York: Revell, 1913); and Broun and Leech, *Anthony Comstock*.
7. "Picture of September Morn on His Chest May Bar Him from the Navy," *San Jose Mercury News*, published as *Evening News*, Oct. 16, 1913; "September Morn Is Draped with Skirts," *Bellingham (WA) Herald*, Oct. 9, 1913; "With 'September Morn' Tattooed on His Back, Man Cannot Join Navy," *Duluth (MN) News-Tribune*, Sept. 22, 1913.
8. "Artists Object to Removal of Picture Showing Nude Girl," *Grand Forks (ND) Daily Herald*, Mar. 7, 1913; "Police 'Art Critic' Seizes Prints of Famous Painting," *Duluth News-Tribune*, Mar. 19, 1913; *Sunday (WA) Olympian*, Mar. 22, 1913; "Art Dealer Held for Showing Nude Picture in Window but Jury Declares Vice Commissioner's Judgment Bad and Frees Him," *Idaho Daily Statesman*, Mar. 22, 1913; "When Is Art Art? When Wicked?" *Chicago Daily Tribune*, Mar. 14, 1913; "September

Morn Pits Her Beauty Against Censors," *Chicago Daily Tribune*, Mar. 21, 1913; "Nude Held Not Lewd; Art Dealer May Continue to Show Painting," *Morning Oregonian*, Mar. 22, 1913; "September Morn Wins Case," *Chicago Daily Tribune*, Mar. 22, 1913; "Picture Returns to Show Window—Chicago Jury Finds Everything Proper in Display After Witnesses Disagree," *Duluth News-Tribune*, Mar. 22, 1913; "Art Triumphs in Chicago; Jury Decides Paul Chabas' 'September Morn' Isn't Too Immodest," *New York Times*, Mar. 22, 1913; "September Morn Caused Jam—Traffic Blocked Half Hour in Milwaukee When Picture Was Shown," *Kansas City Star*, Apr. 24, 1913; "September Morn Not Guilty a Milwaukee Judge Says the Painting Sure Is a Work of Art," *Kansas City Star*, Apr. 27, 1913; "Pictures as Evidence; Judge Approves It," *Duluth News-Tribune*, Apr. 30, 1913; "Police Put Ban on Art, 'Miss September Morn' and Other Paintings Are Barred," *Fort Worth Star-Telegram*, May 4, 1913; "September Morn Her Pose, $50 Her Fine; Mayor of Harrisburg Punishes Woman Who Gives Exhibition," *Philadelphia Inquirer*, Sept. 17, 1913; "City Must Pay to Keep Man in County Jail—Frank Sulten Modern Adam Poses as 'September Morn,'" *Belleville (IL) News Democrat*, Aug. 14, 1913.

9. James Kincaid, *Child-Loving: The Erotic Child and Victorian Culture* (London: Routledge, 1992); James R. Kincaid, *Erotic Innocence: The Culture of Child Molesting* (Durham, NC: Duke University Press, 1998); Anne Higonnet, *Pictures of Innocence: The History and Crisis of Ideal Childhood* (London: Thames and Hudson, 1998).
10. Anthony Comstock, New York Society for the Suppression of Vice, *Sixth Annual Report* (1880), 11–12; Comstock, *Frauds Exposed*, 391; Anthony Comstock, New York Society for the Suppression of Vice, *First Annual Report* (1875), 10–11; Nicola Beisel, *Imperiled Innocents: Anthony Comstock and Family Reproduction in Victorian America* (Princeton, NJ: Princeton University Press, 1997).
11. Grace Elizabeth Hale, *Making Whiteness: The Culture of Segregation in the South, 1890–1940* (New York: Vintage, 1998), 15.
12. Lynn Hunt, ed., *The Invention of Pornography, 1500–1800: Obscenity and the Origins of Modernity* (Cambridge, MA: MIT Press, 1993).
13. Larry Wolff, "Childhood and the Enlightenment: The Complications of Innocence," in *The Routledge History of Childhood in the Western World*, ed. Paula S. Fass (New York: Routledge, 2013), 78–100.
14. Jane M. Ford, *Patriarchy and Incest from Shakespeare to Joyce* (Gainesville: University Press of Florida, 1998), 147.
15. Quoted in Ford, *Patriarchy and Incest from Shakespeare to Joyce*, 19.
16. Brian Connolly, *Domestic Intimacies: Incest and the Liberal Subject in Nineteenth-Century America* (Philadelphia: University of Pennsylvania Press, 2014), 168.

17. "A Black Brute Lynched," *Times-Picayune* (New Orleans), May 10, 1893; US Senate, *Congressional Record*, vol. 151, pt. 9, "Apologizing to Lynching Victims and Their Descendants" (Washington, DC: US Government Publishing Office, 2005), 12262–87.
18. "Colored Boy, 19, Describes How Lynchers Hanged Him," *New York Daily News*, Feb. 27, 1933; "Youth Saved as Mob Begins to Hang Him from Bayou Bridge," *Louisiana Weekly*, Oct. 21, 1933.
19. "Negro Hanged on Bridge," *Assumption Pioneer* (Napoleonville, LA), Oct. 14, 1933; *Louisiana Weekly* (New Orleans), Oct. 14, 1933; "Negro Is Lynched by Louisiana Mob," *Atlanta Journal-Constitution*, Sept. 13, 1935; "Negroes Kept from the Vicinity of Jail Night of Lynching," *Louisiana Weekly*, Apr. 11, 1933; "Louisiana Mob Lynches Negro," *Montgomery (AL) Advertiser*, Oct. 13, 1933; "White Mobs Get Help from Jailors in Savage Orgies," *Chicago Defender*, Oct. 25, 1933.
20. *Assumption Pioneer*, Nov. 4, 1933.
21. Adam Fairclough, *Better Day Coming: Blacks and Equality, 1890–2000* (New York: Viking, 2001), 26.
22. "Make $2,400 Settlement in Labadieville Lynch Case," *Louisiana Weekly*, Aug. 17, 1940; "Sheriff Forced to Pay $2,500 for Lynching," *Chicago Defender*, May 30, 1936; "Sues Sheriff Who Turned Boy Over to La. Mob," *Chicago Defender*, May 5, 1934; "Parents of Lynched Youth Awarded $2,500," *Atlanta Daily World*, May 23, 1936; "Lynching Award Heartens South," *New York Amsterdam News*, May 30, 1936; "Lynched Negro's Parents Win $2,500 in Suit Against Sheriff," *Washington Post*, May 22, 1936; "White Jury Gives $2,500 to Kin of Lynched Negro," Associated Press, May 22, 1936.
23. US District Court, Eastern District of Louisiana, Louis Moore et al. v. Lezin H. Himel, Sheriff of the Parish of Assumption, et al. Case No. 412 (1934–1937), and related filings.
24. "A Lie, the Sheriff Says," *New York Times*, Dec. 27, 1933.
25. See DuRocher, *Raising Racists*, 153–56.
26. DuRocher, *Raising Racists*, 152–53.

CHAPTER 10: "WE WANT TO KILL THEM ALL IF WE CAN"

1. "Negroes and Oklahoma," *Chicago Herald*, Jan. 22, 1890. For a fuller discussion of the emergence of Jim Crow in Oklahoma, see Murray R. Wickett, "The Fear of 'Negro Domination': The Rise of Segregation and Disenfranchisement in Oklahoma," *Chronicles of Oklahoma* 78 (2000): 44–66.
2. "Negroes and Oklahoma," *Chicago Herald*.
3. Treaty Between the United States of America and the Creek Nation of Indians, proclaimed Aug. 11, 1866.

4. Various scholarly works have examined the post–Civil War and Reconstruction periods in Indian Territory, the results of the 1866 treaties signed by the Five Civilized Tribes with the US government, the impact those treaties had on the tribes and ex-slaves, and how some tribes accepted the integration of the freedmen into their nations while others rejected them. See Thomas Andrews, "Freedmen in Indian Territory: A Post–Civil War Dilemma," *Journal of the West* 4 (1965): 367–76; Denise A. Joseph, "African Americans, Native Americans, and the Treaties of 1866: The Impact of Federal Policy Towards Slave-Owning Native American Nations" (thesis, Howard University, 1996); and Barbara Krauthamer, "Blacks on the Borders: African Americans' Transitions from Slavery to Freedom in Texas and the Indian Territory, 1836–1907" (PhD diss., Princeton University, 2000). For discussions on all-Black towns and Black migrations to Oklahoma, see Daniel F. Littlefield and Lonnie E. Underhill, "Black Dreams and 'Free Homes': The Oklahoma Territory, 1891–1894," *Phylon* 34 (1973): 342–57; Norman L. Crockett, *The Black Towns* (Lawrence: Regents Press of Kansas, 1979); Scott Ellsworth, *Death in a Promised Land: The Tulsa Race Riot of 1921* (Baton Rouge: Louisiana State University Press, 1982); Jimmie Lewis Franklin, *Journey Toward Hope: A History of Blacks in Oklahoma* (Norman: University of Oklahoma Press, 1982); and Murray R. Wickett, *Contested Territory: Native Americans and African Americans in Oklahoma, 1865–1907* (Baton Rouge: Louisiana State University Press, 2000).
5. "Creek 'Freedman,'" *Dallas Morning News*, Jan. 1, 1905.
6. Gary Zellar, *African Creeks: Estelvste and the Creek Nation, Race and Culture in the American West* (Norman: University of Oklahoma Press, 2007), 22–23.
7. Zellar, *African Creeks*, 78, 84–85, 113.
8. See Donald A. Grinde Jr. and Quintard Taylor, "Red vs. Black: Conflict and Accommodation in the Post Civil War Indian Territory, 1865–1907," *American Indian Quarterly* 8, no. 3 (Summer 1984): 211–29. The authors argue that prior to the Civil War, Blacks and Natives had lived in relative harmony. Emancipation, which liberated seven thousand slaves living in Indian Territory, severely altered the status of Blacks there. The federal government subsequently allowed the five nations to decide how to integrate the former slaves as citizens with full civil and political rights. Grinde and Taylor reveal that attitudes toward freedpeople varied among the nations, with Seminoles and Creeks being the most liberal, the Cherokees moderate, and the Choctaws and Chickasaws generally taking the most restrictive and at times violent positions. Even so, in the immediate postwar years many freedmen remained in Indian Territory and, in comparison to conditions in the Deep South, were often able to

reside and work there without the systematic campaigns of racial terror that characterized Reconstruction-era white Southern regimes.

9. For an explanation of the issues surrounding the allotment policy and how the Dawes Commission records were created and used to determine who was eligible to receive a share of land in Indian Territory, see Ken Carter, *The Dawes Commission and the Allotment of the Five Civilized Tribes, 1893–1914* (Orem, UT: Ancestry, 1999). For a discussion of the tensions between Indians and freedmen resulting from the distribution of land allotments, see also F. G. Speck, "Observations in Oklahoma and Indian Territory," *Southern Workman* 36, no. 1 (1907): 23–27.
10. See Senate Report Document No. 439, 63rd Congress, Second Session, Creek Equalization Fund by R. C. Allen, National Attorney for the Creek Nation, Mar. 3, 1914, Washington, DC.
11. Prior to statehood, Jim Crow education statutes were enacted in the Territory. One statute enacted in 1890 mandated a vote every three years to determine if the Territory should provide separate schools for white and Black children. An 1897 statute required a separate district to be established for Black children wherever there were at least eight Black children attending a school. The statute also made it unlawful for any white child to attend a school for Black children or vice versa. Between 1907 and 1957, Oklahoma passed sixteen Jim Crow laws.
12. Elliott West, "Reconstructing Race," *Western Historical Quarterly* (Spring 2003): 22–23.
13. This number includes Blacks lynched from 1889 to 1913, one year before Du Bois's call for the establishment of a Children's Department in the NAACP. This compiled data is from the NAACP report *Thirty Years of Lynching* (New York: NAACP, 1919).
14. *The Crisis* 8, no. 6 (Oct. 1914): 292.
15. Thomas Piketty and Emmanuel Saez, "Income Inequality in the U.S., 1913–1998," *Quarterly Journal of Economics* 118, no. 1 (Feb. 2003): 8.
16. *The Crisis* 8, no. 5 (Sept. 1914): 229–30; *The Crisis* 10, no. 5 (Sept. 1915): 279; *The Crisis* 8, no. 6 (Oct. 1914): 292; *The Crisis* 7, no. 4 (Feb. 1914): 175; *The Crisis* 20, no. 1 (May 1920): 53.
17. *The Crisis* 7, no. 4 (Feb. 1914): 175.
18. *The Crisis* 7, no. 4 (Feb. 1914): 175.
19. *The Crisis* 7, no. 4 (Feb. 1914): 175.
20. William M. Irvin v. State of Oklahoma, State of Oklahoma Criminal Court of Appeals, No. A-1776, Feb. 6, 1911.
21. *Irvin v. State of Oklahoma*, 38.
22. "Home Blown Up with Dynamite," *Muskogee (OK) Times-Democrat*, Mar. 23, 1911; "House Blown Up; Children Killed," *Daily Oklahoman*, Mar. 24, 1911.

23. Testimony of Jim Whitaker in William M. Irvin v. State of Oklahoma, No. A-1776, State of Oklahoma Criminal Court of Appeals, Feb. 24, 1915, 303.
24. "Plot to Murder Zeb Mackey or Conspiracy to Get Children Out of Way Is Theory of Officers," *Muskogee Times-Democrat*, Mar. 24, 1911.
25. "Threaten Only White Man—Negroes of Taft Say They Will Kill Dr. Rodgers If He Doesn't Get Out," *New York Times*, Sept. 19, 1908.
26. "Threaten Only White Man," *New York Times*.
27. "Plot to Murder Zeb Mackey," *Muskogee Times-Democrat*; "Negro Children Owned Fortunes, the Victims of Dynamite at Taft Had Property in Glen Pool," *Daily Oklahoman*, Mar. 24, 1911.
28. Gertrude Bonnin, Charles H. Fabens, and Matthew K. Sniffen, *Oklahoma's Poor Rich Indians: An Orgy of Graft and Exploitation of the Five Civilized Tribes—Legalized Robbery* (Philadelphia: Office of the Indian Rights, 1925), 21.
29. "Two Held After Double Killing; White Man Accused of Dynamiting Home of Wealthy Black Children," *Daily Oklahoman*, Apr. 4, 1911; "Dynamiters Play for High Stakes, Sells Children Believed to Have Been Murdered for Their Property," *Daily Oklahoman*, Apr. 9, 1911.
30. "Dynamiters Play for High Stakes," *Daily Oklahoman*.
31. Original indictment, Oklahoma State Archives.
32. "Grand Jury Names Five—Dynamiting Probe Results in Accusation of Former Mayor's Brother," *Oklahoman*, Apr. 18, 1911; "Martin—Brother of Ex-Mayor Arrested Under Indictment for Murder," *Muskogee Times-Democrat*, Apr. 18, 1911; "Two Have Made Their Bonds," *Muskogee Times-Democrat*, Apr. 19, 1911.
33. "Biggest Murder Case Coming Up," *Muskogee Times-Democrat*, Sept. 12, 1911.
34. "Startling Charges Made in Taft Case," *Muskogee Times-Democrat*, Dec. 14, 1911.
35. "Doc Allen Makes Confession," *Muskogee Times-Democrat*, Dec. 16, 1911; "Taft Dynamiter Has Confessed," *Tulsa World*, Dec. 17, 1911.
36. "Irvin Guilty; Life Sentence," *Muskogee Times-Democrat*, Dec. 22, 1911.
37. "Buoyant Bill Irvin Has Lost Nerve Since Friday," *Muskogee Times-Democrat*, Dec. 23, 1911; "D. R. Allen Guilty; Life Term," *Muskogee Times-Democrat*, Dec. 26, 1911.
38. "Judge Allen to Try F. L. Martin," *Muskogee Times-Democrat*, Dec. 28, 1911; "A Jury Is Selected to Try F. L. Martin," *Muskogee Times-Democrat*, Dec. 30, 1911; "Evidence Closed in Martin Case," *Muskogee Times-Democrat*, Jan. 1, 1912; "Close Arguments in Martin Case," *Muskogee Times-Democrat*, Jan. 3, 1912; "F. L. Martin Not

Guilty; Sam Lowe on Trial," Jan. 4, 1912; "Sam Lowe Soon to Learn His Fate," *Muskogee Times-Democrat*, Jan. 5, 1912.

39. "Negro Boy Gets $190 a Day but What Are Riches to 10-Year-Old Dan Tucker?" *Kansas City Star*, May 3, 1914.
40. "Negro Lad Made Rich from Oil Royalties: His Income Now Amounts to About $300 a Day," *Dallas Morning News*, May 31, 1914.
41. "Creek 'Freedmen,'" *Dallas Morning News*, Jan. 1, 1905; "Much Grafting in Creek Nation. Government Unable to Protect Its Wards from the Wiles of the Unscrupulous," *Fort Worth Star-Telegram*, May 14, 1904.
42. "Negro Lad Made Rich," *Dallas Morning News*.
43. "Negro Boy Gets $190 a Day," *Kansas City Star*.
44. "Millions to a Negro Girl—Sarah Rector, 10-Year-Old, Has Income of $300 a Day from Oil," *Kansas City Star*, Sept. 6, 1913; "Oil Well Produces Neat Income—Negro Girl's $112,000 a Year," *Savannah (GA) Tribune*, Sept. 20, 1913. See also "Negro Girl's Big Income," *Oregonian*, Feb. 8, 1914; "A True Fairy Tale," *Duluth News-Tribune*, Feb. 20, 1914; and "Ten-Year-Old Girl Richest in Oklahoma," *Salt Lake Telegram*, Feb. 21, 1914.
45. "Oil Made Pickaninny Rich—Oklahoma Girl with $15,000 a Month Gets Many Proposals," *Kansas City Star*, Jan. 15, 1914.
46. Marie Dillie, "Women Who Lead the Way," *Oregonian*, Aug. 31, 1915.
47. Dillie, "Women Who Lead the Way."
48. Cited in Suzanne J. Crawford and Lynn R. Musslewhite, "Kate Barnard, Progressivism and the West," in *Oklahoma I Had Never Seen Before: Alternative View of Oklahoma History*, ed. Davis D. Joyce (Norman: University of Oklahoma Press, 1998), 62.
49. See Angie Debo, *And Still the Waters Run: The Betrayal of the Five Civilized Tribes* (Princeton, NJ: Princeton University Press, 1940), 185.
50. W. E. B. Du Bois, *The Crisis* 7, no. 4 (Feb. 1914): 40.
51. *The Crisis* 10, no. 6 (Oct. 1915).
52. State ex rel. Dale et al., State Bar Com'rs v. Curd, Oklahoma Supreme Court, May 27, 1919.
53. Telephone interview with Bruce Reed, Oct. 30, 2009.
54. *The Crisis* 13, no. 1 (Nov. 1916); Clark v. DeGraffenreid, Oklahoma Supreme Court, July 10, 1917; Peterson v. Brook, Oklahoma Supreme Court, Nov. 18, 1919; and Indian Appropriation Bill: Hearings Before the Committee on Indian Affairs, US Senate, 64th Congress, Second Session on H. R. 18453 (Washington, DC: Government Printing Office, 1916).
55. Kate Barnard, *Annual Report of the Commissioner of Charities and Corrections* (Oklahoma City: Press of Oklahoma Engraving and Printing Co., 1912), 162.

56. Tanis C. Thorne, *The World's Richest Indian: The Scandal Over Jackson Barnett's Oil Fortune* (New York: Oxford University Press, 2003), 44; Bonnin, Fabens, and Sniffen, *Oklahoma's Poor Rich Indians*, 14.
57. "$180,000 Oil and Gas Bonus," *Dallas Morning News*, May 27, 1916.
58. *The Crisis* 16, no. 2 (June 1918).
59. Petition for Appointment of Guardian, *In re Estate of [Full Name of Durant]*, Muskogee County Court, Aug. 31, 1917, Guardianship Records, Muskogee County Courthouse, Muskogee, OK.
60. Order Appointing Guardian and Bond Approval, *In re Estate of Edith Durant*, Sept. 7, 1917, Guardianship File, Muskogee County Court Records, Muskogee County Courthouse, Muskogee, OK; Order Vacating Appointment of Guardian, *In re Estate of Edith Durant*, Jan. 21, 1918, Guardianship File, Muskogee County Court Records, Muskogee County Courthouse, Muskogee, OK.
61. "Guardian for Heiress Asked—Negro Girl of Indian Blood Has 1/2 Million Dollar Oil Estate," *Kansas City Star*, Feb. 4, 1922.
62. "Riches Fail to Dazzle Girl—Negro Girl to Manage Her Own Business," *Savannah Tribune*, Mar. 30, 1922; *The Crisis* 24, no. 2 (June 1922).

EPILOGUE: THE COLD CASE OF JUSTICE

1. W. E. B. Du Bois, *Darkwater: Voices from Within the Veil* (New York: Harcourt, Brace and Howe, 1920), 164.

INDEX

NOTE TO READER: Names with numbers in parentheses indicate lynching victims and their ages.